Tobacco in Russian History and Culture

Routledge Studies in Cultural History

1. The Politics of Information in Early Modern Europe
Edited by Brendan Dooley and Sabrina Baron

2. The Insanity of Place/The Place of Insanity
Essays on the History of Psychiatry
Andrew Scull

3. Film, History, and Cultural Citizenship
Sites of Production
Edited by Tina Mai Chen and David S. Churchill

4. Genre and Cinema
Ireland and Transnationalism
Edited by Brian McIlroy

5. Histories of Postmodernism
Edited by Mark Bevir, Jill Hargis, and Sara Rushing

6. Africa after Modernism
Transitions in Literature, Media, and Philosophy
Michael Janis

7. Rethinking Race, Politics, and Poetics
C.L.R. James' Critique of Modernity
Brett St Louis

8. Making British Culture
English Readers and the Scottish Enlightenment, 1740–1830
David Allan

9. Empires and Boundaries
Rethinking Race, Class, and Gender in Colonial Settings
Edited by Harald Fischer-Tiné and Susanne Gehrmann

10. Tobacco in Russian History and Culture
From the Seventeenth Century to the Present
Edited by Matthew P. Romaniello and Tricia Starks

Tobacco in Russian History and Culture

From the Seventeenth Century to the Present

**Edited by
Matthew P. Romaniello
and Tricia Starks**

Routledge
Taylor & Francis Group
New York London

First published 2009
by Routledge
711 Third Avenue, New York, NY 10017

Simultaneously published in the UK
by Routledge
2 Park Square, Milton Park, Abingdon, Oxon, OX14 4RN

Routledge is an imprint of the Taylor & Francis Group, an informa business

First issued in paperback 2011

Typeset in Sabon by IBT Global.

Library of Congress Cataloging-in-Publication Data

Tobacco in Russian history and culture : from the seventeenth century to the present / edited by Matthew P. Romaniello and Tricia Starks.
p. cm. — (Routledge studies in cultural history ; 10)
Includes bibliographical references and index.
1. Tobacco--Social aspects—Russia (Federation) 2. Tobacco—Russia (Federation)—History. 3. Russians—Tobacco use. 4. Russia (Federation)—Social life and customs. I. Romaniello, Matthew P. II. Starks, Tricia, 1969–
GT3021.R8T63 2009
362.29'60947—dc22
2008054212

ISBN10: 0-415-99655-4 (hbk)
ISBN10: 0-415-89597-9 (pbk)
ISBN10: 0-203-87573-7 (ebk)

ISBN13: 978-0-415-99655-6 (hbk)
ISBN13: 978-0-415-89597-2 (pbk)
ISBN13: 978-0-203-87573-5 (ebk)

Contents

Figures

Acknowledgments

The two of us had been colleagues for years, so when we each found out the other had been gathering material for a project on tobacco, it was an easy decision to combine forces. As we realized how little had been written on the subject, we gathered others working on aspects of tobacco's influence in Russian history and culture to fill in some of the enormous gaps in the literature while pointing to areas warranting further research. This resulting volume represents far more than we hoped to achieve and is far richer for the insightful contributions of our fellow scholars.

In preparing the volume, we have accrued many debts, which might never be fully repaid. To each, we can only offer our thanks. Rex Wade and Wendy Walker of the American Association for the Advancement of Slavic Studies must be acknowledged for accommodating three panels on tobacco at the annual meeting in New Orleans in November 2007. The conference allowed the contributors an opportunity to share and discuss each other's work, greatly enriching the final product. The enthusiasm for the project of Harley Balzer, Carol Benedict, and Cynthia Buckley reinforced our decision to broaden the scope and pursue publishing this large volume of essays, which was a choice our kind publisher shared. Finally, our colleagues at the University of Arkansas, George Mason University, and the University of Hawai'i must be acknowledged for long-term support.

Financial and other support from several organizations created opportunities for the editors to conduct their own research on tobacco. The Kennan Institute of the Woodrow Wilson Center and the University of Illinois' Russian and East European Center provided short-term grants for research opportunities. Tricia Starks received a National Council for Eurasian and East European Research Collaborative Research Fellowship in 2005 that supported both her research and the work of Iurii Bokarev that is published in this volume. The librarians of the Russian State Library in Moscow, the Library of Congress' European Reading Room, the National Institute of Medicine in Washington, DC, the University of Arkansas, and George Mason University aided in research. In the final stages of the process, Pat Polansky of the University of Hawai'i provided assistance with double-checking the citations of the older materials cited throughout the volume.

Finally, the illustrations that appear throughout the volume would not have been possible without the kind permission of the following institutions. The Russian State Archive of Ancient Acts in Moscow gave permission for the manuscript page in Chapter 3, and the Gregoriou Monastery of Mount Athos in Greece kindly supported the republication of the smoking monk in that chapter. The Hillwood Estate, Museum, and Gardens in Washington, DC, granted permission for the snuffbox that appears in Chapter 6. Figures 2, 3, and 4 in Chapter 12 were reproduced from the collection of the Hoover Archives of Stanford University. Every effort has been made to locate the original copyright owner but in most cases, the artist is deceased and the copyright ownership is unclear. The Russian State Library's poster collection provided Figures 7.1, 7.6, 12.1, 12.5, 12.6, and 12.7; the Russian National Library provided figure 11.1. When necessary, permission has been granted for these reproductions. Leonid Sinelnikov provided us the photograph of himself included in Chapter 13. We thank him for his permission to reproduce it here. Finally, Figure 15.1 and 15.3 were originally published in A. Gilmore and M. McKee, "Exploring the Impact of Foreign Direct Investment on Tobacco Consumption in the Former Soviet Union," *Tobacco Control*, 14 (2005): 13–21, and Figure 15.6 was published in A. Gilmore et. al. "Prevalence of Smoking in Eight Countries of the Former Soviet Union: Results from the Living Conditions, Lifestyles and Health Study," *American Journal of Public Health*, 94 (2004): 2177–84. We thank the publishers for their permission to reprint those tables here.

1 *Tabak*

An Introduction

Matthew P. Romaniello and Tricia Starks

During his 1698–1699 tenure as the Hapsburg secretary to Peter the Great's court, Johann Georg Korb detailed the outrageous activities of the Russian court. In a highly sensationalistic account, he claimed to be privy to one of the tsar's infamous, carnivalesque, religious ceremonies. Dedicated to Bacchus instead of the Christian God, the ceremony began with a procession of vice rather than virtue. Korb rapturously detailed the spectacle of servants parading forward with:

> . . . great bowls full of wine, others mead, others again beer and brandy, that last joy of heated Bacchus. . . . they carried great dishes of dried tobacco leaves, with which, when ignited, they went to the remotest corners of the palace, exhaling those most delectable odors and most pleasant incense to Bacchus from their smutty jaws. Two of those pipes through which some people are pleased to puff smoke—a most empty fancy—being set crosswise, served the scenic bishop to confirm the rites of consecration.[1]

Peter's ceremony turned the conventional Russian Orthodox service on its head. Instead of the sacrificial host and sanctified wine, Peter ended his bacchanal with the use of tobacco smoke to consecrate the unholy rite. The smoke—like the ceremony it enhanced—was an attack upon the past and religious tradition. In the church, the smoke of incense wafted prayer up to the heavens on its wisps; in Petrine parody, tobacco smoke sinuously embraced the onlookers, penetrated them, and made them party to the sin and blasphemy of the host. Peter forced all those who came in contact with his smoke to experience for themselves a little taste of his grand, and aggressive, cultural mission.

Tobacco was far more than a simple accompaniment to Peter the Great's amusements. With the embrace of tobacco, he toppled a ban that had been in place from tobacco's first appearance inside Russia's borders early in the seventeenth century. The Russian prohibition lasted almost the entire seventeenth century, staying in place for seventy years, longer than anywhere else in the world. Under the ban Muscovite authorities called for arguably the most severe penalties of any society, with increasingly harsh punishments—from beatings with the knout, to slitting of the nostrils, and even, most severely, the death penalty—for tobacco trade or use.[2]

Russia's reaction to tobacco was unique. While most countries banned tobacco upon its arrival, they legalized it shortly thereafter, generally less than ten years after the initial prohibition. For example, the English East India Company began curing tobacco in its Indian factories in 1612, which inspired Emperor Jahangir to ban smoking in 1617. Profits from potential taxes, however, led the emperor to reverse the ban by the early 1620s, as the Indians adopted local tobacco production to reap the rewards of this new commodity.[3] As detailed in Chapter 2, the Indian response was hardly unusual, which makes Russia's seventy-year-long ban surprising. Cultural anxieties explain this difference in part. Tobacco, symbolizing both Russia's newly-expanding presence in the emerging early modern global economy and the increasing foreign presence in Muscovy, was not a welcome guest. Muscovite Russia held a conflicted view of foreigners and their customs. When tobacco came to Russia, it only confirmed authorities' worst suspicions rather than allaying them. Public disorder ensued, including the 1609 burning of a house in Iaroslavl' from smoking.[4] Reports soon reached Moscow of pervasive tobacco use in Siberia, resulting in large debts among the tsar's military servitors. State authorities put forward their ban in 1627.[5]

Russia's early opposition to tobacco was more than a worry over societal disorder. When Peter the Great overturned this longstanding ban, used tobacco in his private ceremonies, and strode through town puffing upon tobacco, spreading his rancor at the Church in the acrid clouds that followed him, he triumphed over the very things that had made others in Russian society wary. Peter saw in tobacco use the modern and the Western, but in his ceremonies it became something even more hazardous. Tobacco symbolized the transgressive and dangerous. By the 1640s, the Orthodox faithful reported visions of the Mother of God including warnings against the temptations and corruption of smoking.[6] By the 1680s, the Russian Orthodox Church preached sermons against the evil intoxication produced by tobacco consumption.[7] By the eighteenth century, Old Believers, who claimed to hew more closely to the Church's traditions, depicted tobacco as an attack on Russian morals from outside forces. According to their legends, tobacco came from sin, an evil plant that had sprung up from the unhallowed ground of the grave of Jezebel's daughter. They alleged that the Greeks then sent the weed to pervert the true Church.[8] Russian Orthodoxy, the religion of state, did not hold a similar origin story for tobacco, though many of its officials criticized the Petrine regime's embrace of Western culture, including the prominent role of tobacco.[9]

Peter used tobacco in his mocking ceremonies to offend Church ritual and taint onlookers, and while it is tempting to paint Peter the Great as a maverick and cultural crusader, he removed the ban with other interests in mind than a cultural campaign. Economic incentives figured heavily in both the longstanding prohibition of tobacco in Russia and also Peter's overturning of the ban. During the seventeenth century, when Russia shunned tobacco, even though there was much resistance from the Church and society towards the weed, the action itself was largely for economic reasons. Tobacco was not performing well as a commodity. When Peter began allowing the tobacco trade in 1697, he did so in pursuit of profit, even though he certainly must have enjoyed the addition of tobacco to his revelries. By opening up the Russian tobacco market, Peter, and many others, held high hopes for massive earnings even as they took on a culture filled with opprobium for tobacco use.[10]

Peter the Great's ceremony, its meanings, and its origins, highlight the major issues for tobacco in Russia not just in his time, but for the centuries to come. Tensions between economic and cultural missions continued to weave through the later history of tobacco in Russia. Tobacco use rose slowly through the eighteenth century and nineteenth centuries, with a precipitous increase in the late nineteenth century as a new form of tobacco delivery emerged with the *papirosa*—a Russian variation of the cigarette. Just as tobacco use developed, so too did the cultural opposition to tobacco. Religious opponents of tobacco were joined by new bourgeois authorities and anti-tobacco activists who brought medical, gendered, social, generational, and nationalist agendas to their arsenals in the cultural fight against tobacco. Over the course of the nineteenth, and then twentieth, centuries the economic boon of tobacco became more evident, but cultural, especially medical, critiques became more developed and sophisticated as well.

The essays in this volume follow the course of these multiple, conflicting agendas from the introduction of tobacco to the present day. The first four essays investigate the circumstances surrounding Russia's singular, seventy-year-long prohibition of tobacco. The ban on tobacco importation emerged from the state's realization that tobacco created only debt and no profit for anyone inside Russia's borders. Cultural opposition played into the case against tobacco, as xenophobia, traditionalism, and distrust of foreign merchants energized the ban as well. As Matthew Romaniello argues, the tremendous reversal of Russia's treatment of the tobacco trade under Peter the Great was a result of a transformation of Russia's economic policies, not a decision about tobacco itself as a product or its moral danger. This transformation becomes only more noticeable when comparing the treatment of tobacco to that of another new, foreign commodity in the seventeenth century—rhubarb. Erika Monahan reveals, by contrasting the treatment of the two medicinally suspect and potentially profitable products, how truly exceptional the long-lasting prohibition against tobacco was.

Economic reasons for the tobacco taboo are reinforced with an examination of religious and medicinal materials from the period. In his essay, Nikolaos Chrissidis argues that even though Orthodox authorities outside of the country had already called for a condemnation of the product on moral grounds, the Russian Orthodox Church did not become actively involved in the debate over tobacco until the late seventeenth century. Chrissidis's work suggests that as long as the state's economic decision remained in force, the Church itself did not need to become involved. When the economic decision was reversed, so was the position of the Church. This transformation of the Church's activities is paralleled in the medicinal issues raised by Eve Levin. Though tobacco began its life in Russia as a concern of the economic chancelleries, once it was officially adopted as a legal product, it became an anxiety for medical authorities. While there was no official consensus about tobacco in Russia, the debate over tobacco's medicinal properties parallels this issue worldwide, even if occurring more than a century later than it began elsewhere. With each of these cases, cultural issues were merely ancillary to the economic decision of the state, even though the public was more likely aware of the moral and medicinal fears than the tsar's economic concerns.

As Peter the Great's ceremony makes clear, the morality of tobacco use—as well as its Western associations—were already in play by the late seventeenth and early eighteenth centuries. As the next set of essays reveals, the cultural and political associations of tobacco were becoming more articulated and were now joined by inferences regarding class, order, and societal problems. Konstantin Klioutchkine examines Russian literature and the attitudes therein towards tobacco, social rank, and the transformation of society during the era of Alexander II (1855–1881) and his Great Reforms. Snuff symbolized the "old" social elites; cigarettes reflected changing attitudes of the new "modern" society. The more tobacco became associated with change, the more the traditionalists in Russia condemned its use. Roy R. Robson argues that the Russian Orthodox Old Believers focused on tobacco as a symbol of pollution and corruption, which both continued a religious debate more than two centuries old, and provided new reasons for supporting a fundamental rejection of modern society. Others embraced tobacco as an element of the modern. Playing with the concept of a social divide created by tobacco use, Sally West shows that tobacco manufacturers and advertisers exploited the association of tobacco and modern society to encourage sales to late imperial society. Advertisements end up revealing as much about Russian social values and class distinctions as they do about marketing. While in Robson's essay rejection of tobacco serves to mark inclusion in a closed community, in both Klioutchkine and West's essays, tobacco consumption serves as a marker of gender and status. Some eschewed tobacco, but many more would use tobacco consumption to show their inclusion in an even greater community—the modern, the forward-thinking, the revolutionary, and the young.

Against the background of rising consumption and a booming market for tobacco products, more and more important for both the state and business interests, Tricia Starks details both the rise, and the ineffectiveness, of anti-smoking initiatives at the turn of the twentieth century.

The joint opinions of religious and medical authorities made few inroads against consumers, producers, and advertisers, and were not effective in convincing the state to work against its short-term economic interests. With the Bolshevik takeover, tobacco's dangers received serious attention, but their proposed, national tobacco initiative, so neatly in accordance with Soviet concerns about the health of the new Soviet citizen, was resoundingly rejected by the economic authorities of the Soviet Union. Even a Communist economy was not free from market pressures. As Robson, West, and Starks uncover the persistence of cultural and medical concerns, Iurii Bokarev's statistical study examines a transitioning economy struggling to meet Russia's soaring demands. Bokarev details the increasing centralization of tobacco production to satisfy the growing demands of a modern, industrial society. Nearly three centuries after tobacco's arrival, these essays demonstrate that no one had yet presented an argument that could settle the debate as to whether tobacco represented a drain or a boon to the state.

If even a Communist state hostile to tobacco could not overcome its lure, it is not surprising to see widespread smoking among all members of Soviet society, including its children. As Catriona Kelly uncovers in her essay on childhood smoking, Soviet authorities primarily looked the other way while society encouraged smoking by boys as an essential aspect of their maturation into full-fledged members of society. It was obviously a long way from the century-long prohibition of the seventeenth century. While anti-smoking advocates had difficulty, Karen F.A. Fox shows that such efforts did continue throughout the Soviet period. These further campaigns, however, were largely limited and never assessed for success or reception. Examination of the major waves of propaganda from the early 1920s and 1930s, and later in the 1970s, reveals a public health campaign that used consistent imagery to educate Russians on the dangers of tobacco, yet these were health marketing campaigns that never succumbed to innovation or even research on effectiveness.

The tension between halfhearted tobacco prohibitions and increasing consumption reflects the long, uneven history of tobacco's place in Soviet society. In fact, much of the twentieth century was defined by a Soviet and a post-Soviet scramble to keep society amply supplied for its tobacco habits. Elizaveta Gorchakova relates the view of Soviet-era tobacco producers through the experiences of the head of Russia's largest tobacco firm, Iava. His experience reveals the tremendous political and cultural pressures for tobacco production to be increased rather than a push against tobacco consumption. Even as the rest of the world turned against smoking, the director of Iava struggled to meet larger and larger state quotas. Soviet anti-smoking efforts were weak in comparison to the all-out push for increased yield that the state demanded of tobacco producers. These pressures on tobacco companies to perform continued well after the state began counter-initiatives against its own products by flirting with warning labels in the late 1970s.

As Mary Neuburger reveals, international research and warning labels did little to staunch demand, and supplies would continually be a problem. During the Cold War, Eastern European ally Bulgaria supplied the Russian tobacco market with products produced with Western technology and following international tastes. This Western influence occurred with the tacit approval of Soviet authorities. Tobacco consumption, apparently, trumped Cold War tensions.

In the post-Soviet era the overwhelming presence of foreign tobacco producers and Western-style marketing, has complicated the scene, as has the increasing evidence of a demographic crisis in Russia. Anna Gilmore looks at one of the major suppliers of tobacco in post-Soviet Russia, the British American Tobacco Company. While it has been increasingly common for public health officials in Russia to blame the current incidence of smoking on foreign advertisers, the history of tobacco clearly demonstrates that this is not a new problem, regardless of the companies involved. Gilmore's data clearly demonstrates tobacco consumption was and is on a continuous rise in Russia.

Today, Russia has become the third highest per capita smoking country in the world and tobacco use is a deadly claimant to Russia's current demographic crisis.[11] According to the World Health Organization, approximately 70% of men and 30% of women in Russia smoke, and the WHO estimated that at the close of the twentieth century 280,000 Russians died every year from smoking-related illnesses—a rate over three times higher than the global average.[12] When Michael Bloomberg and Bill Gates announced their joint initiative "to combat [the] global tobacco epidemic" on July 23, 2008, Russia was singled out alongside of India, China, Indonesia, and Bangladesh as a targeted country for new tobacco control efforts.[13] In the final essay for the volume, Judyth Twygg assays the increasingly dire health situation, the escalating demographic crisis in Russia, and the potential consequences for the future.

While the primary purpose of this volume is to illuminate the history of tobacco use in Russia, there is little doubt that this narrative is distinctive in comparison to experiences in other countries.[14] To go from the country that prohibited tobacco for the greatest length of time, to one of its foremost consumers, is a striking evolution. This turnaround is all the more amazing given the fact that Russian society attempted to stamp out the habit as culturally, morally, and medically reprehensible many times over the centuries. But throughout the history of tobacco in Russia, these other issues have taken a back seat as economic imperatives determined the state's actions. The seventeenth-century ban, followed by Petrine acceptance, was a sign of the transformation of Russia's economic system, not a symbol of "Westernization," even if religious authorities tended to conflate the issues. Later, Soviet health authorities sacrificed worker health for the vigor of the economy in their pursuit of a profitable commodity. This pattern continues in post-Soviet society—taxes created by tobacco sales are far too valuable to the state's interest to allow any weight to medical concerns about tobacco's dangers or any teeth to the multiple anti-advertiser laws that have been proposed since the 1980s. While contemporary authorities in Russia struggle to place the blame for tobacco's ills on a foreign doorstep, there can be little doubt that this is a crisis of their own making.

NOTES

1. F. L. Glaser, ed., *Scenes from the Court of Peter the Great: Based on the Latin Diary of John G. Korb*, (New York: N. L. Brown, 1921), 126–7. For a critique of this episode, see Ernest A. Zitser, *The Transfigured Kingdom: Sacred Parody and Charismatic Authority at the Court of Peter the Great*, (Ithaca, NY: Cornell University Press, 2004), 1–7.
2. Richard Hellie, trans. and ed., *The Muscovite Law Code (*Ulozhenie*) of 1649: Part 1, Text and Translation*, (Irvine, CA: Charles Schlacks, 1988), chap. 25, article 11, 228.
3. B. G. Gokhale, "Tobacco in Seventeenth-Century India," *Asian Agri-History*, 2:2 (1998): 87–96.
4. Isaac Massa, *A Short History of the Beginnings and Origins of these Present Wars in Moscow under the Reign of Various Sovereigns down to the Year 1610*, trans. and ed. G. Edward Orchard, (Toronto: University of Toronto Press, 1982), 190.
5. See Monahan, this volume.
6. See Levin, this volume.
7. See Chrissidis, this volume.
8. Roy R. Robson, "A Legend on the Appearance of Tobacco," in *The Human Tradition in Modern Russia*, ed. William B. Husband, (Wilmington, DE: Scholarly Resources, 2000), 19–30.
9. For a discussion of the Church's relationship with Peter and his reforms, see Lindsey Hughes, *Russia in the Age of Peter the Great*, (New Haven, CT: Yale University Press, 1998), esp. chaps. 8 and 10.
10. Matthew P. Romaniello, "Through the Filter of Tobacco: The Limits of Global Trade in the Early Modern World," *Comparative Studies in Society and History*, 49 (2007): esp. 927–37.
11. William C. Cockerham, "The Social Determinants of the Decline of Life Expectancy in Russia and Eastern Europe: A Lifestyle Explanation," *Journal of Health and Social Behavior,* 38 (June 1997): 117–30. Murray Feshbach, *Ecological Disaster: Cleaning up the Hidden Legacy of the Soviet Regime,* (New York: Twentieth Century Fund Press, 1995).
12. Lawrence Holland, "The East: Marlboro Man Rides High as Smoking, Death Rates Soar," *Radio Free Europe: Radio Liberty,* June 26, 1997. The problem is the focus of A. K. Demin, ed., *Kurenie ili zdorov'e v Rossii,* (Moscow: Zdorov'e i okruzhaiushchaia sreda, 1996).
13. The press release from the announcement is available at <http://tobaccofreecenter.org/files/pdfs/en/Bloomberg-GatesReleaseFinal.pdf>, accessed on August 30, 2008.
14. For comparison to tobacco's history in Russia, see Sander L. Gilman and Xhou Zun, eds., *Smoke: A Cultural History of Smoking Around the World,* (London: Reaktion books, 2004), or John Goodman, *Tobacco in History: The Cultures of Dependence,* (New York: Routledge, 1994). Anti-tobacco work has been presented in some forums though nothing has focused on

Russia or the Soviet Union. See, Robert N. Proctor, *The Nazi War on Cancer*, (Princeton, NJ: Princeton University Press, 1999); Richard Kluger, *Ashes to Ashes: America's Hundred-Year Cigarette War, the Public Health, and the Unabashed Triumph of Philip Morris*, (New York: Vintage, 1997); or Cassandra Tate, *Cigarette Wars: The Triumph of the "Little White Slaver,"* (New York: Oxford University Press, 1999).

2 Muscovy's Extraordinary Ban on Tobacco

Matthew P. Romaniello

By the beginning of the seventeenth century, tobacco had become a global commodity. Emerging from the New World in the sixteenth century, first Spain, Portugal, and then England cultivated this productive cash crop in their colonies and sold it throughout Europe. Following tobacco's introduction to the Middle East, South Asia, and East Asia, initial resistance to the new product quickly gave way to domestic cultivation and the potential of new taxes and trade. No country in the seventeenth century was resistant to the lure of tobacco profits, with one notable exception—Muscovite Russia.[1]

Tobacco's arrival in the seventeenth century was ill-timed, as Muscovy recently had begun a series of reforms to develop trade and domestic production, as well as to control the foreign influence over Muscovy's economy. The culmination of these reforms was the New Commercial Code (*Novotorgovyi ustav*) of 1667, which regulated all foreign trade.[2] Tobacco, as a foreign commodity, was subject to Muscovite official control regardless of its success as a profit-maker in other European and Asian countries.

Tsar Mikhail Fedorovich first prohibited tobacco in March 1627, when he instructed the governor of Tobol'sk to prevent all future imports and sales of tobacco in Siberia.[3] Historical explanations for this ban have varied but include some combination of pressure from the Russian Orthodox Church against foreign influences, increasing and debilitating debts among military servitors in Siberia, who spent money on tobacco rather than necessary equipment, and a series of domestic accidents. One of the earliest appearances of tobacco in Muscovy was in 1609, when the smoking of an English envoy posted in Iaroslavl' started "a great conflagration that caused much damage," according to one eyewitness.[4] The result of the ban was that no tobacco product could be legally imported into Muscovy until seventy years later, when Peter the Great reversed the policy in 1697 following discussions with King William III of England.[5] No other country in the world maintained a legal prohibition on tobacco for more than fifteen years, making Muscovy's resistance to the new commodity a singular event in the early-modern world.

The official state resistance to tobacco was not a policy that appealed to all the tsar's subjects or foreign merchants. The latter were tantalized with the thoughts of limitless profits from the possibility of an exclusive monopoly to sell tobacco to an untapped market. English merchants would later refer to the potential tobacco market in Muscovy as "better to us than Mines of Silver."[6] The market certainly existed. Domestic consumers purchased leaf smuggled by English, Dutch, and Swedish merchants to feed a growing habit throughout the seventeenth century. The limited state control of the borders created ample opportunity for an illicit trade, calling into question the practicality of the state's official ban. However, no trade or lobbying by foreign merchants altered the official determination to ban tobacco.

While most countries rejected tobacco upon its initial arrival, acceptance of tobacco as a new commodity generally occurred in less than ten years. Opponents of tobacco relied upon arguments based on the morally corrupting influence of foreign or new commodities, and others on the negative health impact.[7] However, the economic benefits, either through sales or taxes, ultimately trumped cultural or medicinal fears; not so in Russia. Muscovy lacked both a climate to sustain domestic tobacco production and the possibility of selling tobacco to a neighbor, as all of its neighbors began either trading or producing tobacco earlier than the Russians. As a result, no argument could ever hope to demonstrate a potential economic benefit, as legalized tobacco sales would inevitably require importation and the resultant loss of specie to foreign powers. With no economic benefit for the state, both medicinal and cultural fears of tobacco were given greater weight in the public discourse, ultimately reinforcing the state's decision to enforce an extraordinary seventy-year ban on tobacco.[8]

THE EMERGENCE OF A GLOBAL ECONOMY

The global market for commodities expanded steadily in the sixteenth and seventeenth centuries, driven by new technologies and entrepreneurial ideas. The Portuguese and Spanish commercial empires moved raw materials and new products from Africa, Asia, and the Americas to serve the new demands of European consumers, creating and expanding new markets. Other European countries strove to compete, with the English, French, and Dutch carving out new enclaves with their own merchant navies. In some regions, this European movement displaced traditional economic exchanges, but in others European traders merely attempted to find space within developed economies.

No country declined to regulate its new trade or failed to enact policies to regulate these exchanges. National economic interest meant state regulation for its own "profit," later described as mercantilism. It centered on one primary goal—to accumulate specie through a favorable balance of trade achieved through an export economy or at least domestic autarky. Historical discussions over the nuances of the mercantilist economy are exhaustive; there is general agreement that early-modern countries strove to achieve a protectionist economy, using some variation of taxes on imports, regulation through trade monopolies, tariffs on sales, and expansion into new markets, either through subsidies, trade penetration, or outright colonization.[9]

National interest, as defined by states in this mercantilist era, dictated how new trade was received, especially if a new commodity came from a foreign power. Tobacco followed a typical pattern upon its first arrival in any country.[10] Initial skepticism from state authorities, if not an outright ban, was followed quickly with legalization, as the local government discovered the revenue to be made regulating the import, production, or export of leaf or finished tobacco products. With most countries in Europe, Asia, and the Americas implementing frankly discriminatory tariff and subsidy policies designed to raise revenue from the global economy, tobacco found a role as another profitable commodity. Of course, in countries with a suitable climate for production, or at least with suitable colonies, the transformation of tobacco from suspicious foreign product to a domestic good was easiest. Spain and Portugal, for example, developed tobacco plantations in their American colonies as a potential cash crop that was easy to produce, which in turn led to large profits. Spain experimented first in its Latin American colonies with tremendous success.[11] Portuguese success was similar, with the early emergence of Bahia in Brazil as one of the major centers of tobacco export from the New World.[12]

So much success, in fact, that England encouraged its own tobacco plantations in the Chesapeake Bay in order to stop the drain of specie to Spain for tobacco exports from the New World. Pamphleteers such as Edward Bennett, in his *Treatise touching the Importation of Tobacco out of Spaine*, argued that it would be in the kingdom's best interest to develop tobacco plantations in Virginia to avoid a dependence upon imported tobacco. England's own colonies afforded an excellent opportunity to defend the crown's exchequer, perfectly expressing the early-modern economic orthodoxy.[13] Other London merchants interested in England's balance of trade echoed Bennett's assessment. Thomas Mun, in his *England's Treasure by Forraign Trade*, instructed his fellow merchants that England must "prevent the importations of Hemp, Flax, Cordage, Tobacco, and divers other things which now we fetch from strangers to our great impoverishing."[14] As the Virginian plantations became commercially viable by the 1620s, merchants in England and Scotland invested heavily to expand production and reap the financial benefits.[15] The mercantile support for tobacco production emerged in spite of the strong condemnation of tobacco throughout England. King James I, with his famous *Counterblaste to Tobacco*, was the most notable, but he was powerless to defy the wishes of a mercantile Parliament. Even Oliver Cromwell failed to halt its sales.[16] English trading interests could argue that as long as the money was kept within the empire, no revenue was lost. Furthermore, potential exports would in fact create revenue, enriching England's colonial and mercantile interests.

Even countries without the ability to support domestic production at home or in their colonies accepted tobacco as a consumer product. Both the Dutch and the French experimented with tobacco production at home and abroad, but with middling success. France's American colonies eventually produced sufficient leaf to meet domestic demand, but France never became a volume exporter.[17] For the Dutch, the problem was greater. Not a colonial power on a large scale, or at least with suitable tobacco-producing land, the Dutch followed their established economic model: that of the middlemen of Europe. Dutch merchants purchased tobacco from England, Spain, and smaller producers like the French, mixed the leaf, and re-marketed it as high-quality English leaf.[18] The Baltic market, in fact, was dominated by Dutch-sold leaf, much to the indignation of English traders, who saw it as another Dutch tactic to undermine English economic strength.[19]

State entrepreneurship could produce sufficient tariffs to entice other reluctant tobacco countries. Sweden, for example, undoubtedly lacked a tobacco climate. However, by purchasing Dutch tobacco and then reselling the product to interior countries, Muscovy included, Swedish merchants generated revenue for the state through customs duties without any exertion on the part of Swedish merchants. A condition of the Treaty of Stolbovo (1617) stipulated that Russian merchants deal only with Swedish agents. This gave Swedish trade an exclusive position in the Russian-Baltic trade, inserting Swedish middlemen into all port cities where the Russians could purchase Baltic goods, such as Narva and Riga.[20]

The producer and middleman models may be applied nearly universally. Among the Muslim empires, the Ottomans, Safavids, and Mughals all produced and sold tobacco soon after its introduction in the early seventeenth century. In each case, Muslim religious authorities protested tobacco's arrival as a moral danger, which temporarily halted its consumption, much to the dismay of English and Dutch merchants.[21] However, the export potential of domestically produced leaf rendered religious prohibitions against importation and consumption moot. In each country, tobacco had been prohibited upon its initial entry, but each government reversed its decision shortly thereafter.

In India, the English East India Company (EIC) began curing tobacco in its India factories as early as 1612. In response to tobacco's arrival, Emperor Jahangir forbade smoking by decree in 1617, but revenue from Mughal taxes on tobacco was too great to ignore. By the 1620s, the Mughals allowed commercial tobacco production inside their borders, creating new opportunities for the EIC as an exporter of tobacco throughout Asia.[22] The EIC charted a similar course in Iran, where Shah 'Abbas prohibited tobacco early in the 1600s, followed by another ban in 1621, but conceded legalization while heavily taxing consumption. The taxes became a valuable source of state revenue, and tobacco remained legal; the EIC began selling tobacco by 1628–1629.[23] The Ottoman Sultan Murad IV (1623–1640) attempted to ban tobacco a decade after its introduction into Turkey, but this failed to dissuade Ottoman subjects from adopting the habit. A fatwa issued shortly after Murad's death declared tobacco smoking permissible.[24] In each country, profits from the trade overrode prohibitions. The Muslim empires quickly became tobacco exporters, not only to each other but also to the Caucasus and Central Asia, including the trade entrepôt of Bukhara.

In late Ming China, as in Europe and Muslim Asia, officials found tobacco too valuable to ban. Extensive regions in China were very suitable to tobacco cultivation, supporting tobacco cultivation as early as the sixteenth century. By the beginning of the seventeenth century, domestic production of tobacco was allowed to flourish, producing enormous amounts of leaf that prevented any interest in foreign tobacco imports. After the Qing dynasty rose to power in the middle of the seventeenth century, China became an active exporter of tobacco, selling to the Mongols and the indigenous populations of Siberia.[25]

Thus, by the early decades of the seventeenth century, tobacco merchants encircled Muscovy looking for new markets for export. The English and the Dutch had established direct contact with the Russians at their shared port of Arkhangel'sk, and each also sold tobacco to the Swedish merchants in the Baltic ports, who resold it to Russian merchants. The Ottoman empire supported a trade route north through Moldova, introducing tobacco to Polish Ukraine, where its consumption and production were legal. Ukrainian farmers had established tobacco production in those regions that would become part of Muscovy after the union with left-bank Ukraine following the Thirteen Years' War (ending in 1667). By the middle of the seventeenth century, both the Mughals and Safavids arrived in the Muscovite port of Astrakhan on the Caspian Sea with cargoes of Asian tobacco. Bukharan merchants resold tobacco throughout Central Asia, which left Moscow's customs agents a puzzling treaty problem, as Moscow had granted the Bukharans special caravan privileges within Muscovy's borders.[26] Finally, Chinese merchants traded tobacco inside Muscovy's borders by selling the crop in Siberia.

Without question, tobacco had arrived in Muscovy no later than 1609. However, Muscovite religious and government officials emphasized that it was a foreign product, whether Protestant, Muslim, or Chinese. Furthermore, Muscovy could not produce it, or adapt the Dutch or Swedish model easily, as it could neither be grown in Muscovite territory nor be easily resold to the ring of producers surrounding Muscovy. The profits from the regulation of the tobacco trade that flowed to other state treasuries could not be tapped so easily when Muscovy could expect to be a consuming state, not a producer or middleman. Future tobacco merchants, as well as potential customers, faced the state's almost categorical refusal to accept the drain of precious specie for a product with no investment value and no revenue potential. There was no financial community large enough in Muscovy to support tobacco's arrival against the entrenched resistance of state authorities. With no valid argument being offered to counteract the ban, the struggle to import tobacco to Russia was over as soon as it began.

MERCANTILIST MUSCOVY

Muscovy's economic policies were no different than any other early-modern state—accumulate specie and develop the economy in order to maintain a favorable balance of trade, in other words, the classic mercantilist goals.[27] However, Muscovy had a fundamental weakness from its lack of domestic sources of precious metals. Though development of domestic mining, achieved with the assistance of foreign specialists, became a driving goal for the state, the situation was not easily rectified in the seventeenth century. The lack of metal also created difficulties from the lack of ability to produce munitions, creating serious expenses incurred from Muscovy's wars.[28]

In a weak position, Muscovy was almost entirely dependent on foreign trade to generate specie. This fact, however, should not imply that the Muscovite authorities allowed great freedoms to foreign merchants. Rather, the Muscovite response was to regulate foreigners' actions in the country strictly so as to be able to control their sales and potential exports. In June 1628, for example, Tsar Mikhail Fedorovich signed a new agreement with the English Muscovy Company for its operations in his kingdom. The English agreed to buy no other good in the country except those things produced by the Russians, and to have their own goods inspected closely upon arrival in Arkhangel'sk.[29] These privileges provided the customs officials in Arkhangel'sk tremendous authority to enforce Muscovite interests, and prevent export of specie through the port. These were necessary steps, as the lack of a merchant navy in a country that conducted 80% of its foreign trade through the seas positioned Muscovy in a dependent role in almost any negotiation with its neighbors.[30]

With its structural weaknesses, the Muscovite government enacted an increasingly restrictive set of controls over all aspects of the economy. Tariffs on imports became essential both for its ability to generate revenue for the state and also for its additional control mechanisms on foreign trade. From this perspective, tobacco potentially created an opportunity for a weak economy. A new commodity could create a new market, which in turn could produce needed revenue. However, the drain of specie created by Russian consumers could not be overcome. Though the state might benefit directly from taxes on imports, the drain of revenue from the population was too dangerous. In the 1620s, the tsar received explicit warnings of the danger of tobacco's cost. In February 1627, the governor of Tobol'sk petitioned Tsar Mikhail Fedorovich with a request for the tsar to resolve the problem of the accumulating debts of military servitors in Siberia, incurred from their tobacco habits. The tsar's resolution to this problem was a comprehensive blockade against tobacco's presence. He decreed that no one would be allowed inside a Russian or Siberian city with tobacco, and that no merchant could be allowed to sell tobacco to a military servitor anywhere. Furthermore, any merchant caught with tobacco should be "exiled" from Russian lands, physically removing the tobacco and any potential of it being purchased within Muscovy's borders.[31] The damage resulting from specie lost to foreign merchants and an inherent weakening of the military preparedness in the region could hardly be offset by the possibility of tariff revenue.

The formal prohibition against tobacco was only the opening salvo in a long campaign to curtail tobacco sales and use. By 1633–1634, the tsar extended his ban on tobacco to all cities in his kingdom, "on pain of the death penalty."[32] While there are no official accounts of the death penalty being enforced, accounts of public torture of Russian tobacco merchants do exist. Adam Olearius, a secretary in the embassy of the Duke of Holstein, observed eight men and one woman being beaten with a knout as punishment for selling tobacco and vodka on September 24, 1634.[33] In a largely illiterate society, the exhibition of the state's penalties imposed on tobacco was more effective than just the written word. It is hard to imagine that anyone in Muscovy was unaware of the serious consequences for selling tobacco.

Certainly foreign merchants in Muscovy did comprehend the seriousness of the state's prohibition. The tsar received repeated complaints from English merchants throughout the 1630s about illegal searches for tobacco in Arkhangel'sk and Vologda. By 1639, the complaints had become so numerous that the tsar questioned officials in Vologda about their invasive searches, warning them to halt their actions for fear of limiting foreign trade.[34] While it is not certain how much tobacco was arriving inside the borders, the tsar certainly was convinced that his officials had been consistently enforcing his prohibition. Of course, this instruction was not a command to stop forcing merchants to declare all of their trade goods upon entry into any Muscovite city for tax purposes, just to be more judicious in their tobacco accusations.

In light of the economic weakness and the potentially serious consequences for Muscovite military success, maintaining and enforcing the tobacco ban was essential for the state. As a result, the *Ulozhenie* (Law Code) of 1649 contained yet more restrictions on tobacco sales. It included eleven articles concerning tobacco, beginning with upholding the earlier death penalty for Russians and foreigners (*inozemtsy*) trading or possessing tobacco.[35] Tobacco consumers would not be executed, but: "If musketeers, and wanderers, and various people are brought in for arraignment with tobacco twice, or thrice: torture those people many times, beat them with a knout on the rack. . . . For many arraignments slit the nostrils and cut off the noses of such people."[36] As most Russian tobacco consumers used snuff, the slit nostrils became their scarlet letter, publicly marking their crime. News of these punishments could only spread, as the tobacco criminals were exiled "after the torturings and punishment . . . so that others will learn not to do that."[37]

Furthermore, there was an attempt to resolve the continuing problem of tobacco smuggled into Muscovy. The most likely suspects were "Lithuanians," who could have sold tobacco to anyone traveling from the Baltic coast. However, if the tobacco had been purchased "from Russians, or from foreigners, those who are serving the sovereign," they should also be arrested, interrogated, and forced into an "eye-to-eye confrontation" to uncover the truth. Torture could be used as necessary.[38]

The tsar continued to sign further restrictions and penalties for tobacco use, which suggests the seriousness of the state's commitment but also its limited success in permanently curtailing tobacco, particularly on the periphery of the empire. By 1648, the Swedish envoy in Moscow gained responsibility for reporting on tobacco usage in the country as the tobacco trade through Sweden's Baltic ports had become so profitable.[39] Similarly, Siberia remained a concern for its continuing tobacco habits, despite any number of specific prohibitions. This continued into 1664, when Tsar Aleksei Mikhailovich added another restriction for Siberia: any dealer, Russian or foreign, in tobacco would be whipped publicly and imprisoned for one week. Furthermore, all confiscated tobacco would be burned "to discourage the people."[40] Previously, both merchant and tobacco would be expelled from Russia, but there had not been punitive damages enacted. The increased penalties were a sign of the state's commitment to the tobacco prohibition, and likely an indication of the continuing presence of tobacco throughout the kingdom.

Adding greater weight to the consistent ban on tobacco was the state's increasing interest in regulating all aspects of the economy, particularly foreign merchants and goods. The first attempt to provide a comprehensive restructuring of foreign trade arrived in the form of the Commercial Code of 1553, which instituted a higher tax rate on all foreign goods than Russian merchants paid, in a perfect example of mercantilist principles. Foreign merchants protested the new fines loudly, but this only confirmed the state's decision. With the New Commercial Code of 1667, not only did the punitive tariffs remain on foreign merchants but also they were physically restricted inside the kingdom. Foreign merchants could conduct business only in Arkhangel'sk, Novgorod, Pskov, Smolensk, Putivl', and Astrakhan, severely curtailing their presence in the Muscovite market.[41] Complaints against the injustice were frequent, but did nothing to dissuade the state's decision.[42]

With tobacco having become a focus of the state's economic restrictions on foreigners, Muscovite subjects drew upon tobacco as an example of foreigners as social and moral dangers. In a remarkable complaint from the northern city of Kholmogory in December 1663 the local townsmen (*posadniki*) protested the scandalous actions of the Dutch merchant Michael Meier. Whenever he received other foreigners traveling from Arkhangel'sk, "they drank and smoked tobacco, and played many games." During Lent, Meier consumed enough "tobacco, meat, and fermented milk" that "a great stench" emanated from his house strong enough to be smelled in church.[43] Considering the great number of legal restrictions on tobacco, it seems improbable that a foreign merchant would flaunt his smoking publicly. However, such an accusation would be an effective way of having any undesirable member of the community removed. In this sense, the tobacco ban had gained acceptance with the Muscovite public, even if their rejection of tobacco itself could not be assured.

The persistence of the state's prohibition and support from Russians inside the country created an opportunity for the Russian Orthodox Church to join the chorus of discontent. The Church had rejected foreign customs as a matter of doctrine since the promulgation of the *Stoglav* in 1551. It ruled that the "evil customs" of other countries and faiths defiled Russia with their "lawlessness."[44] Furthermore, though tobacco was not mentioned explicitly in the Bible, the general condemnation of everything that issued from a man's body for its uncleanliness included tobacco smoke.[45] While the smuggling of tobacco products that continued in the seventeenth century indicates the Church's objections did not prevent Muscovite acceptance of a foreign custom, the Church's rejection of tobacco offered reinforcement to the state's ban.

By the 1660s, the decades of the tobacco prohibition, regulation of foreign merchants, and a growing public awareness of tobacco's illegality created a formidable barrier to tobacco. No Muscovite authority supported tobacco's legalization. Rather than recognizing Muscovy's mercantilist regulations, foreigners seemed even more inspired to force the Muscovite market open. In particular, the pressure from the English in Moscow remained a persistent thorn in the side of Muscovite authorities. In England, the potential of the Muscovite tobacco market became something of a *cause célèbre* among free-trade advocates. With a decades-long ban, an untapped market loomed large in their vision of Muscovy. Josiah Child, writing in the 1660s, called for an immediate expansion of trade to Muscovy, necessary to break the growing English dependence on Dutch exports from Muscovy. In particular, he worried that currently nine-tenths of the English timber supply was purchased from Dutch middlemen; an English return to preeminence in Moscow would correct this situation.[46] Similarly, John Pollexfen decried the diminishing returns from the Muscovy Company's trade, which resulted in further lost revenues to the Dutch, in addition to the ongoing supply problems with limited access to timber, tar, pitch, and hemp.[47]

In addition to the continuing interest of the English to sell tobacco to Muscovy, the global tobacco economy had transformed over the course of the seventeenth century. By the 1690s, an over-production of tobacco in North and South America had produced excessive supplies in both the Chesapeake for the English and in Bahia for the Portuguese.[48] There is no single explanation for the overproduction. Certainly, such a large amount of land was now dedicated to tobacco production that in the Chesapeake, for example, colonial authorities took steps to force other commodities into production, as even basic staples such as wheat were not being grown in sufficient quantities in the region to keep the population fed.[49] In addition, environmental conditions improved globally with the end of the "little ice age" of the seventeenth century, producing increasing harvests worldwide.[50] Even the French, not the most productive tobacco growers, suffered from oversupply by the end of the century. French attempts to control the imports of foreign tobacco through tariffs only mitigated the economic consequences, but did not produce any domestic sales increase.[51] Globally, the excess supply also created a sharp decline in tobacco prices, which only made persuading any country of its potential value from trade revenue more difficult.

Even if tobacco consumption had continued to increase steadily, the increased tobacco supply still outpaced the slow growth of consumption in tobacco countries. As tobacco had been in common usage throughout the Americas, Europe, and Asia for decades, there was no large supply of new consumers to absorb the new leaf. Therefore, the one country that had successfully resisted legalized importation of tobacco for the entire century—Muscovy—became even more of a concern to tobacco exporters. The English, the bearers of the brunt of the overproduction, unsurprisingly became the most persistent voices to open Muscovite markets; on their side were decades of experience with tobacco sales. From a mercantilist perspective, this was an ideal model for economic exchange for England, though it was implicitly based on a rejection of any idea of Muscovy's ability to regulate its own economy. While the English understood their own gains from tobacco sales, they failed to offer any argument that could persuade the tsar's government to alter its policies.[52] Foreigners remained under constant suspicion as tobacco smugglers, even in light of the draconian Muscovite restrictions.[53] Regulation and control were the watchwords for economic development in Muscovy; open markets and lost specie were not.

OVERTURNING THE BAN

Considering the decades invested in prohibiting tobacco and punishing merchants and consumers, the legalization of tobacco sales in Muscovy was abrupt. In order to raise revenue for the Grand Embassy, Peter the Great granted Martyn Bogdanov a contract to sell tobacco in Muscovy for one year beginning on December 1, 1696. The contract required Bogdanov to pay the government directly the taxes for his sales, though the mechanism for him to acquire tobacco to sell was left to his own devising. In Peter's explanation of the contract, the benefits to the state outweighed the losses. Direct involvement in the tobacco trade would curtail smuggling, and more control over tobacco equaled more tax revenue for the government.[54] Therefore, tobacco's legalization was a rethinking of Muscovite economic policy to achieve its long-term objective in controlling specie, rather than a decision influenced by outside forces or interests. There was no movement toward decentralizing economic control.

The reevaluation of tobacco's role in the economy created other opportunities for negotiating with foreign merchants. In the same year as Bogdanov's contract, Peter changed tobacco policies in Astrakhan, one of the designated cities in the New Commercial Code for foreign merchants to conduct business. In Peter's instruction to the governor of Astrakhan, tobacco would be confiscated from foreign merchants upon their arrival in Astrakhan, but returned to them upon their departure; individual merchants could carry approximately eighteen pounds for their personal use into the city.[55] This was a concession that did not produce immediate financial results, but it was intended as a palliative to the new economic restrictions and controls placed on merchants arriving in Astrakhan. Peter required more invasive searches of foreign merchants who gained the privilege of trading in a limited region outside of Astrakhan, but these merchants were "rewarded" with the right to keep a portion of their tobacco. Once again, more control of the economy was the primary goal for the state, but easing tobacco restrictions became the solution.

Peter the Great's formal embrace of the tobacco trade followed shortly after these decisions. In 1698, following discussions in Utretcht with King William III of England, Peter signed a formal contract for a group of English merchants to import tobacco to Moscow.[56] The signed tobacco contract allowed a newly-formed "company" to import 3,000 hogsheads of tobacco (about one-and-a-half million pounds) in the first year (1699), and 5,000 hogsheads in the second. After the second year, the contract was renewable annually for another 5,000 hogsheads. Under the terms of the contract, tobacco could be sold anywhere in the kingdom, and the tsar agreed to ban all other tobacco imports, which was hardly a concession as no other supply of tobacco was legally allowed into Muscovy. The tsar agreed that domestic Ukrainian tobacco could only be sold in Ukraine to prevent it from cutting into English sales. With the money received from tobacco sales, English merchants had the right to buy and export any Muscovite product, keeping Muscovite specie in the country. If all the tobacco was not sold at the end of the second year of the contract, its clauses remained in effect until all the imported tobacco was sold. For this exclusive privilege, the English tobacco contractors paid £12,000 in advance for their customs duties.[57]

Peter's advantages with the contract far outweighed the English's. The customs duties were the most obvious since Peter profited regardless of the success or failure of tobacco sales. Furthermore, the contract itself was granted to a group of specific Englishmen, as Peter used an economic privilege to pay off debts accrued on the Grand Embassy.[58] In other words, legalized tobacco sales were the result of pressing economic concerns on Peter's government, not a serious reversal of the economic policies of the past century.

Of course, there was a genuine transformation toward tobacco sales occurring. Mercantilist reforms, which had been gaining traction in the government throughout the seventeenth century, had been largely accomplished by the beginning of the eighteenth century. Therefore, regulating the economy was somewhat easier, and the possibility of controlling tobacco through sales rather than prohibitions became enticing. With the earlier legalization under Martyn Bogdanov, Peter's rationale suggested that public sales of tobacco could prevent the ongoing drain of specie through smuggling.

Considering tobacco's history in Muscovy, it should not have been unexpected that tobacco sales were difficult for the English. Tobacco carried decades of suspicion with it—it had been inside the borders of the kingdom, but as a smuggled, illicit product. Though the English merchants complained to Muscovite officials that tobacco sales failed to meet their expectations, these complaints fell on deaf ears, as the Muscovite goals had already been achieved. Most of the documents generated by the Petrine government insisted on the imposition of their own privileges at the expense of English interests. For example, in April 1699, the tsar wrote to King William III with a clarification to the contract, forbidding the tobacco contractors from importing any other commodity into Muscovy and from purchasing any commodity for which other merchants held export contracts. Peter argued that allowing the contractors to export products would limit future "free trade with the usual goods."[59] The English believed this to be a violation of the contract, which had promised the right to purchase any good in Moscow. In order to resolve this situation, the contractors dispatched a new negotiator to Moscow, though the subsequent negotiations failed to alter the Petrine position.

In light of the longstanding prohibition of tobacco, the first official tobacco contract was a mixed success. Only 5,500 hogsheads were imported in the two years of the contract, though the contract called for imports of 8,000. Even at a lesser volume, the contractors failed to sell all of their tobacco. The English blamed Russian merchants for smuggling less expensive Ukrainian tobacco into Moscow as undercutting their sales, and the English travel in the country remained proscribed, preventing their access to the potential Siberian market.[60]

Apparently unknown to the English were the Petrine government's attempts to fulfill the contract's terms. Peter's obduracy did not doom the contract; in fact he attempted to facilitate the trade. When the English complained of domestic (Ukrainian) tobacco devaluing their imported stock, Peter instructed his own government officials to stop purchasing tobacco from any source other than the English. In 1701, Peter wrote to Andrei Vinius, a Russian official of Dutch descent, directing that tobacco imported through Siberia could no longer be purchased in Moscow because of the English contract. If the English tobacco trade diminished or produced financial losses, Peter warned that Vinius "would be questioned."[61] Peter also never wavered in his commitment to the importation of tobacco from Western Europe. In 1706 after the failure of the English attempt, he discussed the possible importation of tobacco with Aleksei Kurbatov, future governor of Akhangel'sk, though with the Dutch or the Swedish as the importers.[62] Furthermore, it remained illegal to sell Ukrainian tobacco in

Muscovy's central provinces until 1727.[63] Certainly, long after the failure of the English tobacco monopoly, Peter maintained incentives to encourage trade in imported tobacco. The economic climate of Russia had been transformed, and the idea that tobacco was a valuable commodity that could produce financial benefits had been expected.

In the end, the history of the tobacco ban in Muscovy reveals more about the state's implementation of mercantilist reforms than it does about Russian attitudes toward tobacco as a new commodity. Upon tobacco's first introduction in Muscovy, suspicion of the new product and an early ban was the typical response of almost every country in the seventeenth century. However, the lack of an immediate economic benefit from its importation created a climate that sustained the tobacco prohibition far longer than in any other country. Once the mercantilist reforms succeeded in reorganizing the Muscovite economic structure, particularly in terms of greater regulation over foreign trade, the state did find a way to reap some reward from tobacco imports. Therefore, the English tobacco contract, the first agreement for large-scale tobacco importation into Muscovy, was not a victory for the foreign merchants opening the Muscovite markets to a new commodity as much as it was a victory for the tsar's government profiting from its successfully implemented economic reforms. While the Muscovites did not become large-scale producers of tobacco or even middlemen in the tobacco trade, the state found profit in the potential sales of a commodity that in fact no one seemed particularly interested in buying.

NOTES

1. For a general introduction to tobacco, see Sarah Augusta Dickson, *Panacea or Precious Bane: Tobacco in Sixteenth Century Literature*, (New York: New York Public Library, 1954); Grace G. Stewart, "A History of the Medicinal Use of Tobacco, 1492–1860," *Medical History*, 11 (1967): 228–268; Jordan Goodman, *Tobacco in History: The Cultures of Dependence*, (London: Routledge, 2000).
2. For an introduction to the Muscovite economy, see Joseph T. Fuhrmann, *The Origins of Capitalism in Russia: Industry and Progress in the Sixteenth and Seventeenth Centuries*, (Chicago: University of Chicago Press, 1972); and J. T. Kotilaine, *Russia's Foreign Trade and Economic Expansion in the Seventeenth Century: Windows on the World*, (Leiden: Brill, 2005).
3. The instruction mentions this law as a reiteration of an earlier ban in 1618, which has not been recorded elsewhere. Audrey Burton, *The Bukharans: A Dynastic, Diplomatic and Commercial History, 1550–1702*, (New York: St. Martin's Press, 1997), 508–9.
4. Isaac Massa, *A Short History of the Beginnings and Origins of these Present Wars in Moscow under the Reign of Various Sovereigns down to the Year 1610*, trans. and ed. G. Edward Orchard, (Toronto: University of Toronto Press, 1982), 190. For further discussions of the introduction of tobacco in Russia, see Jacob M. Price, "The Tobacco Adventure to Russia: Enterprise, Politics, and Diplomacy in the Quest for a Northern Market for English Colonial Tobacco, 1676–1722," *Transactions of the American Philosophical*

Society, New Series, 51:1 (1961): 1–120; Igor' Bogdanov, *Dym otechestva, ili kratkaia istoriia tabakokureniia*, (Moscow: Novoe literaturnoe obozrenie, 2007).

5. *Pis'ma i bumagi imperatora Petra Velikago*, (St. Petersburg: Gos. Tip., 1887), vol. 1, no. 234, 234–9.
6. Goldsmiths'-Kress Library of Economic Literature, no. 3675.8, "Some considerations relating to the englarging the Russia trade, and the contract for importing tobacco into that countrey," (n.p., 1700).
7. For the positive side of these arguments leading toward tobacco consumption, see Woodruff D. Smith, *Consumption and the Making of Respectability, 1600–1800*, (New York: Routledge, 2002), 161–9.
8. See Chrissidis and Levin, this volume.
9. J. N. Ball, *Merchants and Merchandise: The Expansion of Trade in Europe 1500–1630*, (London: St. Martin's Press, 1977); and Philip D. Curtin, *Cross-Cultural Trade in World History*, (Cambridge: Cambridge University Press, 1984).
10. Jacob M. Price, "Tobacco Use and Tobacco Taxation: A Battle of Interests in Early Modern Europe," in *Consuming Habits: Drugs in History and Anthropology*, ed. Jordan Goodman et al., (New York: Routledge, 1995), 165–85.
11. Rafael Torres Sánchez, "The Failure of the Spanish Crown's Tobacco Tax Monopoly in Catalonia during the XVIII Century," *The Journal of European Economic History*, 34 (2005), 721–60.
12. Catherine Lugar, "The Portuguese Tobacco Trade and Tobacco Growers of Bahia in the Late Colonial Period," in *Essays Concerning the Socioeconomic History of Brazil and Portuguese India*, ed. Dauril Alden and Warren Dean, (Gainesville, FL: University of Florida Press, 1977), 26–70; and Carl A. Hanson, "Monopoly and Contraband in the Portuguese Tobacco Trade, 1624–1702," *Luso-Brazilian Review*, 19 (1982), 149–68.
13. Edward Bennett, *A Treatise Touching the Importation of Tobacco from Spaine*, (n.p., 1620; reprint Amsterdam: De Capo Press, 1977).
14. Mun's study was first published in 1664. Goldsmiths'-Kress Library of Economic Literature, no. 5034, Thomas Mun, *England's Treasure by Forraign Trade* (London, 1713), 15–6.
15. Jacob M. Price, "The Beginnings of Tobacco Manufacture in Virginia," *The Virginia Magazine of History and Biography*, 64 (1956): 3–29; Neville Williams, "England's Tobacco Trade in the Reign of Charles I," *The Virginia Magazine of History and Biography*, 65 (1957): 403–49.
16. Rudi Matthee, "Exotic Substances: The Introduction and Global Spread of Tobacco, Coffee, Cocoa, Tea, and Distilled Liquor, Sixteenth to Eighteenth Centuries," in *Drugs and Narcotics in History*, Roy Porter and Mikulas Teich, ed., (Cambridge: Cambridge University Press, 1995), 33.
17. Jacob M. Price, *France and the Chesapeake: A History of the French Tobacco Monopoly, 1674–1791, and of Its Relationship to the British and American Tobacco Trades*, 2 vols., (Ann Arbor: University of Michigan Press, 1973); and Marc Vigié and Muriel Vigié, *L'herbe à Nicot: Amateurs de tabac, fermiers généraux et contrebandiers sous l'Ancien Régime*, (Paris: Fayard, 1989)
18. For an introduction to the Dutch middlemen in the Atlantic, see Pieter Emmer, "The West India Company, 1621–1791: Dutch or Atlantic?" in *The Dutch in the Atlantic Economy, 1580–1800: Trade, Slavery, and Emancipation*, (Brookfield, VT: Ashgate, 1998), 65–89; and Victor Enthoven, "Early Dutch Expansion in the Atlantic Region, 1585–1621," in *Riches from Atlantic Commerce: Dutch Transatlantic Trade and Shipping, 1585–1817*, ed. Johannes Postina and Victor Enthoven, (Leiden: Brill, 2003), 17–47.

19. The early Baltic smuggling is discussed in Price, *The Tobacco Adventure*, 5–17.
20. Maria Bogucka, "The Role of Baltic Trade in European Development from the XVIth to the XVIIIth Centuries," *The Journal of European Economic History*, 9 (1980): 5–20; I. P. Saskolskij, "New Phenomena in the Baltic Trade of Russia in the Seventeenth Century," *Scandinavian Economic History Review*, 34 (1986): 41–53.
21. Aziz A. Batran, *Tobacco Smoking under Islamic Law*, (Beltsville, MD: Amana, 2003).
22. B. G. Gokhale, "Tobacco in Seventeenth-Century India," *Asian Agri-History*, 2:2 (1998): 87–96.
23. Rudi Matthee, *The Pursuit of Pleasure: Drugs and Stimulants in Iranian History, 1500–1900*, (Princeton, NJ: Princeton University Press, 2005), 117–43.
24. Kātib Chelebi, *The Balance of Truth*, trans. G. L. Lewis, (London: Allen and Unwin, 1957), 50–9; James Grehan, "Smoking and 'Early Modern' Sociability: The Great Tobacco Debate in the Ottoman Middle East (Seventeenth to Eighteenth Centuries)," *The American Historical Review*, 111 (2006): 1352–77.
25. Timothy Brook, "Smoking in Imperial China," in *Smoke: A Global History of Smoking*, ed. Sander L. Gilman and Zhou Xun, (London: Reaktion, 2004), 84–99.
26. R. D. McChesney, *Central Asia: Foundations of Change*, (Princeton, NJ: Darwin Press, 1996), 42–3; Burton, *The Bukharans*, passim.
27. J. T. Kotilaine, "Competing Claims: Russian Foreign Trade via Arkhangel'sk and the Eastern Baltic Ports in the 17th Century," *Kritika*, 4 (2003): 279–312; and Jarmo T. Kotilaine, "Mercantilism in Pre-Petrine Russia," in *Modernizing Muscovy: Reform and Social Change in Seventeenth-Century Russia*, (London: RoutledgeCurzon, 2004), 143–73.
28. For an extended study of mining and metallurgy in Russia, see Fuhrmann, *Origins of Capitalism*.
29. The National Archives, Kew, England (NA), State Papers (SP) 91/2, ff. 139 r–145 r., "Emperor Michael–grant of privileges to the Muscovy co.," June 13, 1628.
30. Kotilaine, "Competing Claims," 289.
31. *Russkaia istoricheskaia biblioteka*, vol. 8, (St. Petersburg: Kommissiia, 1884), No. 27, no earlier than April 27, 1627, 451–2.
32. Richard Hellie, trans. and ed., *The Muscovite Law Code (Ulozhenie) of 1649: Part 1, Text and Translation*, (Irvine, CA: Charles Schlacks, 1988), chap. 25, article 11, 228.
33. See for example, Adam Olearius, *The Travels of Olearius in Seventeenth–Century Russia*, trans. and ed. Samuel H. Baron, (Stanford, CA: Stanford University Press, 1967), 230–1.
34. *Akty iuridicheskie, ili sobranie form starinnago dieloproidvodstva*, (St. Petersburg: Tip. II-go otdieleniia Sobstvennoi E.I.V. Kantseliarii, 1838), no. 344, October 18, 1639, 368–70.
35. Hellie, *Ulozhenie*, chap. 25, article 11, 228.
36. Hellie, *Ulozhenie*, article 16, 229.
37. Ibid.
38. Hellie, *Ulozhenie*, articles 12 and 13, 228–9.
39. For example, K. Iakubov, "Rossiia i Shvetsiia v pervoi polovine XVII vv., VI: 1647–1650 gg. "Doneseniia koroleve Khristine i pis'ma k korolevskomu sekretariu shvedskogo rezidenta v Moskve Karla Pommereninga," *Chteniia v imperatorskom obshchestve istorii i drevnostei rossiskikh pri Moskovskom universitete*, 1 (1898): 426, September 19, 1648.

40. V. A. Gorokhov and P. M. Golovachev, *Tomsk v XVII v.*, (St. Petersburg: Russkaia skoropechatka, 1900s), 155.
41. E. V. Chistiakova, "Novotorgovnyi ustav 1667 goda," *Arkheograficheskii ezhegodnik za 1957 god*, (Moscow, 1958): 102–26; and Kotilaine, *Russia's Foreign Trade*, 220–5.
42. For example, the English attempted to both pressure the tsar through the Muscovy Company and with direct appeals from the king to the tsar. NA, SP 91/3, Part 2, ff. 210r–212v, "Instructions from the Right Woell. the Governor and fellowship of English Merchants for Discovery of New Trades, Usually called the Muscovia Company, unto John Hebdon Esq., London," September 16, 1676; and SP 91/3, Part 2, ff. 217r/v, letter from Charles II to Feodor Aleksevich, September 16, 1676.
43. Meier is identified as Mikhail Ivanov in the document; the Meiers used Ivanov as their last name in Russia. S. P. Orlenko, *Vykhodtsy iz zapadnoi Evropy v Rossii XVII veka*, (Moscow: Drevlekhranilishche, 2004), no. 6, December 1663, 292–3.
44. This resolution is published in chap. 39 of the *Stoglav*, the canons of the 1551 council: E. B. Emchenko, ed., *Stolgav: issledovaniie i tekst*, (Moscow: Indrik, 2000), 302.
45. For the Biblical restrictions, see Leviticus, 15:2–3.
46. In his preface, Child placed the importance of trading in Muscovy as the first priority of English trade. Goldsmiths'-Kress Library of Economic Literature, no. 2804, Sir Josiah Child, *A New Discourse of Trade* (London, 1693), preface and p. 105.
47. Goldsmiths'-Kress Library of Economic Literature, no. 3665, John Pollexfen, *A Discourse of Trade, Coyn and Paper Credit* (London, reprint 1700), 90–1.
48. L. C. Gray, "The Market Surplus Problems of Colonial Tobacco," *William and Mary College Quarterly Historical Magazine*, 7 (1927): 231–45.
49. Philip Alexander Bruce, *Economic History of Virginia in the Seventeenth Century*, vol. 1, (New York: Peter Smith, 1935): 424–86; Stephen Adams, *The Best and Worst Country in the World: Perspectives on the Early Virginia Landscape*, (Charlottesville, VA: University of Virginia Press, 2001), 211–31.
50. Brian Fagan, *The Little Ice Age: How Climate Made History, 1300–1850*, (New York: Basic Books, 2000).
51. Vigié and Vigié, *L'herbe à Nicot*, 217–52.
52. For examples of the English failure to open Muscovy to tobacco in the second half of the seventeenth century, see my "Through the Filter of Tobacco: The Limits of Global Trade in the Early Modern World," *Comparative Studies of Society and History*, 49:4 (2007): 914–37.
53. See for example, the instructions from the governor of Astrakhan to his customs officials. K. A. Antonova and N. M. Gol'berg, eds., *Russko-Indiiskie otnosheniia v XVII v.: Sbornik dokumentov*, (Moscow: Izdatel'stvo Vostochnoi literatury, 1958), no. 98, July 28, 1672, 174–9.
54. *Polnoe sobranie zakonov* (henceforth PSZ), 37 vols., (St. Petersburg: lzd. arkheograficheskoi kommissii, 1862–1928), vol. 3, 329; and Burton, *Bukharans*, 525–7.
55. PSZ, vol. 3, 313–18.
56. A. V. Demkin, *Britanskoe kupechestvo v Rossii XVIII veka*, (Moscow: Institut rossiiskoi istorii RAN, 1998), 107–14.
57. See Note 5.
58. W. F. Ryan, "Peter the Great's English Yacht: Admiral Lord Carmarthen and the Russian Tobacco Monopoly," *Mariner's Mirror*, 69 (1983): 65–87; Bogdanov, *Dym otechestva*, 35–42.

59. Contemporary translation of letter from Peter Aleksevich to William III, April 10, 1699, NA, SP 104/120, fos. 17r–18r. King William's reply was to reopen trade negotiations, letter from William III to Peter Aleksevich, September 12, 1699, NA, SP 104/120, fos. 16r–17v.
60. These points are explicitly made in Letter from William III to Peter Aleksevich, May 29, 1701, SP 104/120, fos. 31r–32r; letter from Anne to Peter Aleksevich, January 20, 1702, SP 104/120, fos. 35r–36r; and also in Simon Dixon, ed., *Britain and Russia in the Age of Peter the Great*, (London: School of Slavonic and East European Studies, 1998), no. 44, petition from the British Merchants to Peter I, February 1703, 39–40.
61. *Pis'ma i bumagi*, I, no.369, 443.
62. *Pis'ma i bumagi*, IV, no. 1142, p. 147; and IV, no.1189, 201–202.
63. PSZ, VII, no. 5164, September 26, 1727, 865–8.

3 Sex, Drink, and Drugs

Tobacco in Seventeenth-Century Russia[1]

Nikolaos A. Chrissidis

The year 1652 was a trying one for the St. Sabbas Monastery in Zvenigorod, an institution that had enjoyed the tsar's diligent patronage. Members of the monastic brotherhood had incurred the wrath of Tsar Aleksei Mikhailovich and a governmental investigating team was scrutinizing the community. The trouble had started when the monk Nikita expelled a group of musketeers stationed at the monastery, an act that cost him his rank as steward. He responded defiantly by spreading (unspecified) rumors about the tsar. In his report to the tsar, court official (*stol'nik,* lit. "table attendant") A. B. Musin-Pushkin, relayed that during his investigation into Nikita's insubordinate conduct, two monastics, the priest Aleksei and the elder (*starets*) Vassian, were caught smoking (lit. "drinking") tobacco. They were immediately arrested and interrogated by Musin-Pushkin. The priest Aleksei acknowledged smoking tobacco and confirmed that Vassian did the same. Vassian, in turn, denied doing so and claimed that he only held the "paper with the tobacco," thus helping Aleksei "drink it."[2] Musin-Pushkin further interrogated the musketeers, who confirmed that both arrestees were smoking. He also reported that Vassian bought the tobacco from a market policeman, but that he did not know what his name was, nor would he be able to recognize him if he saw him. Finally, Musin-Pushkin informed the tsar that he kept the two in chains under guard until further instructions from the monarch.[3] The tsar did order that the two smokers be sent to Moscow in chains, and commanded that monastic officials go to the capital to deal with the Nikita issue. In this letter, the tsar disapprovingly emphasized that the monastic brotherhood drank both wine and tobacco.[4]

Tobacco smoking was not the center of the investigation in this case, nor does it feature prominently in the archival file. After all, this case mainly concerned Nikita's unbecoming behavior towards Tsar Aleksei, who had been a fervent patron and protector of the monastery. But it is illustrative of the seriousness with which the Muscovite prohibition of tobacco smoking (as reflected most recently in the Law Code of 1649) was taken.[5] For the authorities, tobacco was a part of the general disorder that characterized the life of the monks in the St. Sabbas Monastery, and that was a concern to the tsar, although not as important as the rumors spread against his person by Nikita. Indeed, in this case tobacco smoking was a legal infraction, uncovered in the course of another investigation. Although tobacco contributed to the overall lawlessness of the monastic community, nowhere in the archival file was it castigated as a sin, or an infraction of Church rules. Instead, one has the sense that it was breaking the tsar's law that was at issue. Smoking was a legal affront to state, not Church law.

But what were the Church regulations regarding smoking, or as they said back then "drinking" tobacco, in the seventeenth century? What was the official, if any, Church policy on this matter? This chapter is an attempt to chart the attitudes of the official Russian Orthodox Church towards tobacco in the seventeenth century. Specifically, it has the following two main aims: (a) to ascertain whether tobacco use was considered a sin; and (b) to investigate whether and how the Church formulated a consistent public position on tobacco use. The main sources for the study are seventeenth-century sermons written and/or pronounced by Russian clerics.[6]

I argue that the Russian Orthodox Church came to regard tobacco as a sin or as a habit leading to sin only late in the seventeenth century. Until then, by all indications, it exhibited a guardedly negative attitude towards it, but it did not develop a consistent, public teaching on tobacco.[7] Rather, the Church seems to have left it to the Muscovite state to formulate official policy on this matter. Despite the reported condemnation of tobacco by Patriarch Filaret (1619–1633),[8] Russian patriarchs and bishops do not appear to have been very concerned with it, if sermons are any indication. It was only in the last quarter of the seventeenth century that Patriarchs Ioakim (1676–1690) and Adrian (1690–1700) and other clerics openly and forcefully condemned tobacco use. They did so by connecting it to drunkenness, foreign habits, and fornication (*blud*).[9] Both increased contact with the West and the growing acquisition of foreign habits, at least among the elite, as well as the impact of a developed Ruthenian Orthodox tradition of condemnation contributed to the appearance of a more activist struggle against the weed on the part of the Russian Orthodox hierarchy. The newfangled message of condemnation was echoed by provincial clerics. By then, however, it was too late: once more, it was the state, in the person of Peter the Great, that decided to allow the use and trade of tobacco once and for all, over the objections of the Church. In this sense, the Church lost the smoking battle, as it did many other ones in the Petrine era.

TOBACCO IN SERMONS

Tobacco is mentioned in a well-known Russian collection of sermons, entitled *Statir* and dated 1683–1687. Compiled by an anonymous priest in the town of Orel in the Urals, *Statir* consciously imitated many of the themes that had appeared in court sermons in the previous decade. Although the famous sermonizers of the court in the 1670s (such as Simeon Polotskii) do not appear to have been concerned with tobacco,[10] the compiler of the *Statir* was. In one of the last sermons of this enormous collection, entitled "On Sundays," tobacco figures in connection to idleness, drunkenness, avoidance of going to church, and improper behavior while in church.[11] It therefore is associated with a general sense of lawlessness, disobedience, and misbehavior on the part of parishioners.

The author (or compiler) of the sermon starts with the story of Christ's expulsion of the traders from the Temple in Jerusalem. He immediately concludes that those who do not exhibit proper behavior in church should not be allowed in. Instead of devoting the seventh day of the week to God, as commanded, they prefer to visit satanic taverns and drinking establishments. During banquets and all-night drinking bouts immoderate imbibing leads to the excitement of the flesh and to fornication. People transform Sundays into occasions for sinful behavior that leads to perdition. Specifically, the sermonizer castigates those who turn to "the stinking (*smradnyi*) tobacco that aggravates the brain and darkens [or "clouds"] the mind."[12] He brands them lawless (*bezzakoniki*) and thunders:

> Their end will be eternal perdition and their glory will be shame. Their place of rest will be eternal fire; their abode will be in the lowest Hades with their father Satan.[13]

Although the warning is not unusually threatening when compared with other such clerical thunderings, the message was clear: tobacco was forbidden because it contributed to lawlessness. But the sermon did not stop there: it went on to lament the fact that many people appeared to confuse the church with a barber shop or a perfume store. Women came to church highly bejeweled and tempted people (this is a favorite theme of the compiler in other sermons as well). In addition, believers talked about all kinds of different things in church, instead of paying attention to the service. They did not behave respectfully, but rather they screamed and laughed. Some of them argued that they did not hear, nor understand what was said. But the sermonizer argued back that they should pay attention: the church was after all a place of edification, education, and salvation.[14]

Overall, then, the *Statir*'s objections to tobacco were that it is an intoxicant, it aggravates the brain and clouds the mind, and it is an accessory to the lawlessness and disorder that idleness and excessive drinking cause. Ultimately, this kind of behavior of course leads to other more serious offenses such as carnal passions and fornication. Hence, tobacco is to be avoided because it leads to a multitude of sins and transgressions.

If the connection to lawlessness and sexual transgression is evident in the *Statir* sermon, Patriarch Ioakim chose to emphasize another unseemly attribute of tobacco, its foreign provenance. Although he did connect it to drunkenness (a running theme among all Church commentators on tobacco, as we shall see),[15] Ioakim underscored its foreign origin. This kind of criticism appears at its most potent in a Lenten sermon that he delivered to the Russian army probably in 1689. Entitled "Without Faith, It is Impossible to Please God," the sermon was a blistering attack on those who questioned faith and Church teachings, avoided fasts and other religious obligations, and adopted foreign habits in everyday life.[16] It was in Ioakim's arguments against association with foreigners that tobacco figures more prominently.

The sermon begins with an affirmation of the need for faith, and immediately asserts that the traditions of the Church Fathers are complete, and therefore need no additions or emendations. Fear of God is the first prerequisite of faith: that is why the heretics are condemned to perdition, because they have no fear of God. Ioakim brings up the example of Metropolitan of Rus' Aleksei who indeed exhibited such faith. Aleksei kept both his body and his soul clean. Among his actions was that he did not direct his flock towards foreign habits.[17] But nowadays, Ioakim continues, many ignore the fasts, even the Great Lent. Men, women, and children and even clergymen are always drunk "both with wine and with tobacco" and with all other kinds of drink. And they end up getting involved in brawls and beat one another. Rather, Ioakim admonishes, they should strive to do everything with a certain kind of moderation. Therefore, not only tobacco (which is *vrednyi* [harmful] and *skarednnyi* [unclean]) but also wine is bad and harms people. Drunkards, after all, are condemned all over the world. And in any case, the drunk will not inherit the kingdom of God. [18]

Another contemporary habit that Ioakim targets is what he perceives to be a widespread questioning of major tenets and practices of the Church by many common believers. He laments the fact that they dare to question faith and the Church's customs, although they are not clergymen and they know not the proper Church practices, nor do they care to ask. Instead, Ioakim argues, "They behave like fools because of the tobacco pipes and of the calumnies of the Lutherans and the Calvinists and of the remaining heretics."[19] These doubters, Ioakim implies, behave like drunks: they are influenced by heretical, foreign practices and ideas, and hence they end up asking questions about matters that they should not. Instead, Ioakim admonishes, they should obey. After all, even the Turks and the Persians condemn such behavior. There is a proper behavior for everyone and that is why faith and obedience to Church teachings is needed.[20]

Ioakim's argument is that in essence tobacco is a foreign habit, which, in addition to other ones, leads one away from religious truth and makes believers question the main tenets of the faith and their clergy. His main attack therefore is on disobedience and his chief enemy is the foreign customs that breed it. Although tobacco is not explicitly referred to as a sin *per se*, given that it leads to the sin of drunkenness, it opens the way to sin. One is tempted to see in Ioakim's remarks on measured wine-drinking some kind of potential acceptance of tobacco, if drunk in moderation.[21] Most possibly, that would be overreading Ioakim's actual message: after all tobacco is clearly identified as harmful. It therefore is always bad, if one is to accept that wine is good in some occasions, but not in others (that is, when drunk immoderately). In the remainder of the sermon, Ioakim openly asks his flock to avoid contact with foreigners, fast properly, and follow the Church's dietary rules. In addition, he exhorts them to imitate the example of the saints who followed the correct path and did not shave nor drink tobacco but remained sober. The opposite of these practices are foreign habits, Ioakim seems to imply, and are best avoided. (This connection between sobriety, avoidance of tobacco, and not shaving one's beard of course became a staple of Old Believer teachings later on.)[22] Finally, at the end of the sermon, after an enumeration of the fruits of a Christian life, Ioakim emphasizes that drunkenness, uncleanliness, anger, and other such sins are to be avoided.[23]

Ioakim's sermon provides another reason for the condemnation of tobacco in seventeenth-century Russia: its connection to a way of life that was considered foreign (as least by the more culturally conservative elements among the Russian elite) and therefore leads away from Orthodoxy. Despite associating it with drunkenness, the patriarch chooses to underscore that it is a foreign invention that causes true believers to question or lose faith, and to doubt Church practices. It thus foments sinful behavior and heresy and results in ultimate perdition.[24]

Patriarch Ioakim's condemnation of tobacco as a foreign habit was echoed in the well-known encyclical of Patriarch Adrian, entitled "Two Authorities."[25] Soon after ascending the patriarchal throne in 1690, Adrian issued a letter to his flock in which he expounded on the relation between the secular and religious authorities and asserted the prerogatives of the latter because of its divine origins. There followed twenty-four exhortations to all classes of Russian society, both lay and clerical people, with specific instructions geared towards each. In one of these exhortations (without specifying social group, it should be noted), he singled out drunkenness for particular excoriation. Arguing that wine was itself innocent, he emphasized that drunkenness was not. Even pagan people punished wine and tobacco drinkers, hence it befit Orthodox Christians to express even stronger condemnation. Using similar language to that of Ioakim, he called the consumption of tobacco "abominably unclean" and a "stinking evil." However, he went further than Ioakim in underscoring that drunkenness of either kind led to fornication and to all kinds of lawlessness. After condemning taverns and drinking establishments for directing believers to perdition, Adrian ended this particular exhortation by threatening that those who get drunk "on the day of judgment will drink from the cup of God's wrath."[26]

Patriarchs Ioakim and Adrian as well as the anonymous author/compiler of the *Statir* mark a chronological watershed in the Russian Church's official attitude towards tobacco use. Using the traditional condemnation of drunkenness as a springboard, both high-ranking clerics and provincial priests proclaimed a fairly consistent message. According to this message, tobacco was associated with all the evils that drunkenness usually involved. It generated lawlessness, fomented disobedience, encouraged misbehavior,

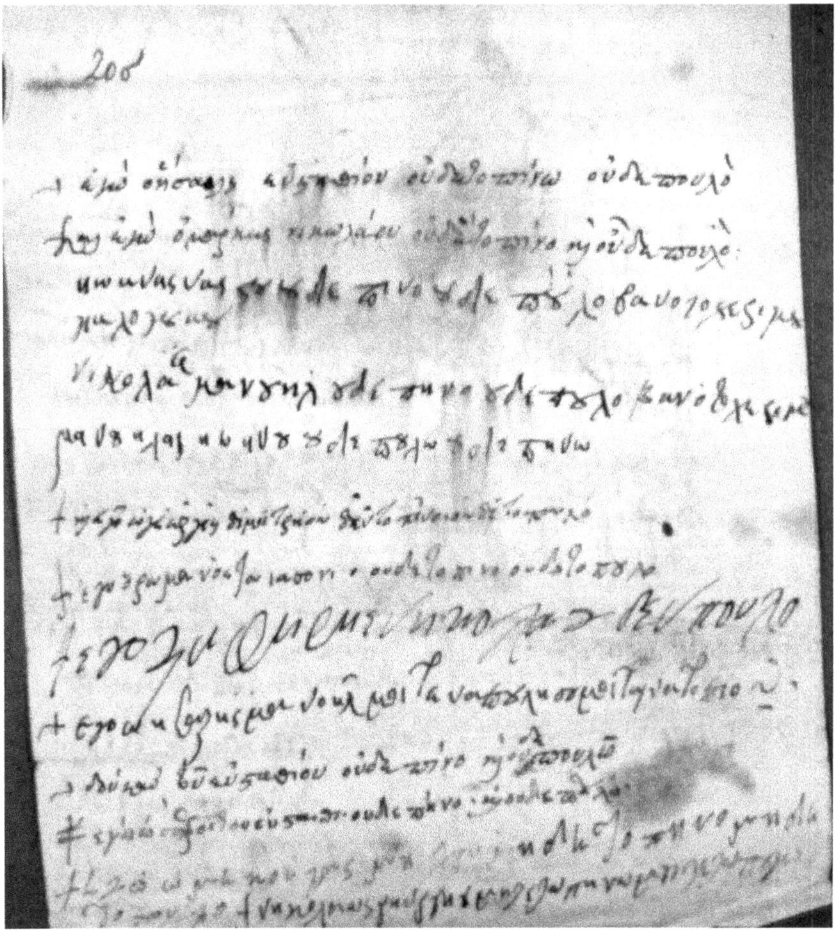

Figure 3.1 Greek merchants' signatures: "I [so and so] neither drink tobacco, nor sell it." Source: Russian State Archives of Ancient Acts, Moscow, f. 52, op. 1, d. 22 (1661), reprinted with permission.

and, last but not least, incited carnal passions. Ultimately, therefore, it led people away from the Church, contributed to sinful behavior, even stirred up heresy, and certainly resulted in one's ultimate perdition.

If the last two decades of the seventeenth century were indeed a watershed in the Church's attitudes to tobacco, why did the Russian Church decide to finally come out and officially condemn tobacco use at the time? Here I would like to suggest several factors that appear relevant. First, despite the persistent prohibition of tobacco trade in state legislation, its use, by all indications, did not wane.[27] Secondly, the latter half of the seventeenth century was a tumultuous time for the Russian Orthodox Church. The schism of the Old Belief had weakened it with regard to state authority and had undermined its prestige and role as the arbiter of morality and provider of spiritual guidance. After Patriarch Nikon's formal deposition in 1666–1667, it was only under Ioakim that the Church tried to reassert its status vis-à-vis the state.[28] But it was a formidable task. Culturally, the Russian elite was acquiring new, Western habits (in education, in music, in learning foreign languages, in home decoration, and to a certain extent in dress) that were viewed suspiciously by several hierarchs. Opposition to these innovations was not necessarily widespread but when expressed, it could be biting.[29] Himself rather conservative culturally, Ioakim was dismayed at the creeping Western habits in court. Thus, in his last will and testament, he thundered against the employment of foreign officers in Russian regiments. Intent upon reasserting hierarchy within the Church and in solidifying the Church's role as the authority on morality and proper behavior, Ioakim sponsored a series of measures that sought to elevate the status of the priest in society and to suppress any challenges to the Church's authority as the arbiter of social habits and moral norms. For example, he sought to abolish rowdy popular festivities on Church holidays and insisted upon obedience to the official pronouncements of the Church. Himself not highly educated, he nevertheless supported educational initiatives but was all too aware that the intricacies of theological belief could not be the theme of discussion for the many, nor should they be. Therefore, the main concerns of his patriarchate were enhancing the Church's authority and ensuring that the believers exhibited unquestioning adherence to its pronouncements. It was in this context that he connected tobacco and its resultant drunkenness to dissolute behavior inspired by foreign customs. His successor Adrian followed his lead but he had to face a more formidable opponent in the case of Peter the Great.[30]

A third and significant factor was the influence of Ruthenian theological and didactic literature on the Russian Church after mid-century. Trained in the Jesuit-style curriculum, Ukrainian and Belarusian immigrant monks served as a conduit through which Roman Catholic-influenced theological and pious trends found their way into Russia.[31] By at least the 1660s and 1670s, the Orthodox Church in the Ukraine had already formulated a view of tobacco as a sin.[32] Specifically, the voluminous treatise on sin that Innokentii Gizel' (ca. 1600–1683) published under the title *Mir s Bogom Cheloveku* (two editions, Kiev 1669 and 1671) appears to have been used as a source of guidance by priests in the Russian provinces starting in the late seventeenth century and all the way through the beginning of the eighteenth.[33] Gizel''s remarks on tobacco use were quite short but rather poignant. In the part of his treatise discussing the seven most important mortal sins, Gizel' devoted a section to the five senses. In this section, he placed a chapter entitled "On Uncleanliness." His remarks on tobacco come at the end of his discussion on unclean and foul smells. It is there that Gizel' makes the claim that tobacco use "clouds the brain." After vaguely referring to "other harms it causes to both body and soul," he adds that it also leads to excitement of carnal passions and to fornication. He therefore concludes that it is a “not small, abominable to God, sin.”[34] Given Gizel’’s sustained attempts to ingratiate himself with the Russian court elite and his Russophilia, his work must have enjoyed welcome reception among Russian clerics. In any case, given the similarity in argumentation, it is quite conceivable that his remarks on tobacco influenced the views of the Russian ruling ecclesiastical elite. The comments certainly did find their way into collections of sermons for the use of Russian provincial priests.[35]

CONCLUSION

Censure of tobacco use may have found its way into sermons by the 1680s, but until then clerical attitudes to it were mixed at best. For example, Metropolitan Makarii of Novgorod in the 1650s admonished his flock to avoid the weed. During the same period, the monk Andreian, protégé of Patriarch Nikon, in his capacity as cellarer of the Kornil’ev Monastery in Vologda, enriched himself by selling tobacco to peasants.[36] Nor was opposition to it confined to clerical circles. Thus, by the 1640s a miracle cult had developed at the Church of the Savior at Krasnyi Bor, a small village by the Northern Dvina in the region of Velikii Ustiug. As scholars have noted, the cult’s censure of tobacco use was central to the message: the miracle stories presented tobacco smoking as an unforgivable sin for both clergy and laity and enumerated a series of strict punishments.[37]

Figure 3.2 A monk smoking his pipe from a wall in the Gregoriou Monastery. Mt. Athos, Greece, from 1739. Reprinted with permission.

The Krasnyi Bor case proves that condemnation of tobacco was beginning to surface in religious literature already by the 1640s. However, it does not appear to have registered itself among the primary concerns of the Russian Church elite until very late in the century. Indeed, neither in the *Kirillova Kniga* (Moscow, 1644), nor in the published sermons of Simeon Polotskii, nor in the *Sobornik iz 71 slov* (a collection of sermons by Church Fathers which obviously could not have treated tobacco use), nor even in sermons published for newly-appointed priests (1670 and 1696 editions), nor, finally, among seventeenth-century lists of sins found in questionnaires (*voprosniki*)[38] and in published service books (*trebniki*)[39] does tobacco figure as a sin, or a habit that could lead to sin.[40] The most plausible explanation for this absence is the impact of Muscovite state legislation. Given the legal prohibitions imposed on the use and trade of tobacco by the 1640s, the Church does not appear to have felt the need to enter the battle against it. Neither the Bible, nor the Church Fathers, nor the Greek Orthodox Churches had any ammunition to offer against it.[41] Instead, the Russian Church took a wait-and-see stance until other considerations induced it to tackle the issue head on. Despite the sporadic voices of censure, it was only in the late seventeenth century that tobacco became firmly connected to drunkenness, intoxication, and lawlessness, and hence, to sin in the pronouncements of the Russian Church elite. Leading clerics publicly thundered against it as an intoxicant that led to improper behavior and, given its foreign associations, to heresy. It was therefore condemned. A similar denunciation was echoed in the provinces as evidenced by the *Statir* and other examples.[42]

Comparatively speaking, where does the seventeenth-century Russian Church fit in the condemnation of tobacco? How does its attitude (as reflected in the sermons just discussed) relate to contemporary discourses on tobacco in other geographic and political contexts? Both Roman Catholic and Protestant as well as Muslim commentators engaged in a lively debate on the medical, moral, and economic aspects of tobacco use and trade. Opinions ranged from outright condemnation to mild disapproval to enthusiastic recommendation for medical reasons. Thus tobacco was variably censured for its pagan connections, blamed for its intoxicating effects and its sinful associations, and endorsed for its beneficial medical qualities during the early modern period throughout Europe[43] and the Middle East.[44] In seventeenth-century Russia, commentators pointed out tobacco's foreignness, intoxicating qualities, and connection to immorality. These attributes share many similarities with the ones highlighted in both the Western European and the Middle Eastern contexts. But there seems to be an important difference. Unlike the Ottoman Empire or European states, Russia does not appear to have developed a sustained medicalized discourse on tobacco at least in the seventeenth century.[45] During the same century, the Russian Orthodox Church ceded the floor to the mercantilist state. It was only when the Church realized that legal prohibitions had little effect that it marshaled an array of moral arguments against tobacco use and sought to combat it by emphasizing its foreign provenance and its intoxicating effects. These arguments carried little weight in the face of tobacco's popularity. When the Russian state's economic interests led to legalization, the Church was unable to stem the tide. Eventually, economic considerations trampled the moral ones.

NOTES

1. I am deeply grateful to Dr. Cathy Potter for generously sharing her research materials. I also wish to thank a number of individuals and institutions without whose help this work could not have been written: Eve Levin, Matthew Romaniello, Erika Monahan, Paul Bushkovitch, and Michael Pesenson. Nikos Bonovas of the Museum of Byzantine Civilization in Thessaloniki (Greece) gave me helpful pointers to tobacco imagery. I am particularly thankful to Evgenii Evgen'evich Rychalovskii (of the Rossiiskii gosudarstvennyi arkhiv drevnikh aktov [henceforth in notes RGADA]) and to Archimandrite Georgios, Hegumen of the Gregoriou Monastery (Mt. Athos, Greece) for giving me permission to reproduce materials from their collections. I also wish to acknowledge the assistance of the staff of the Museum of the Book in the Rossiiskaia gosudarstvennaia biblioteka (henceforth in notes RGB). Finally, I thank the reading group of the History Department at Southern Connecticut State University for penetrating critiques. All remaining errors are mine alone.
2. RGADA, f. 27, d. 77, ll. 9–16. Vassian's denial in the original reads "a skazyvaet tolko Gosudar' on Vasian Alekseiu popu derzhal bumashku s tabakom kak on Aleksei pil." (l. 10).
3. Ibid., l. 10. On the reign of Aleksei Mikhailovich, see Philip Longworth, *Alexis Tsar of All the Russias*, (New York: Franklin Watts, 1984), and esp. 72–3 on Aleksei's dealing with the Nikita affair; also, Igor' Andreev, *Aleksei Mikhailovich*, (Moscow: Molodaia Gvardiia, 2006).
4. RGADA, f. 27, d. 77, l. 19.
5. See *Sobornoe Ulozhenie 1649 goda. Tekst, Kommentarii*, ed. by A.G. Man'kov (Leningrad: Nauka, 1987), chapter 25, articles 11–21, and pp. 397–400 for commentary. On Muscovite and Imperial Russian tobacco legislation, see M. Chulkov, "Istoriia zakonodatel'stva o tabachnoi promyshlennosti v Rossii do Ekateriny II," in *Iuridicheskii sbornik izdannyi Dm. Meierom*, (Kazan': n.p., 1855), 495–538; see also Matthew P. Romaniello, "Through the Filter of Tobacco: The Limits of Global Trade in the Early Modern World," *Comparative Studies in Society and History*, 49:4 (2007): 914–37, esp. 920–924.
6. On the history of tobacco in Russia, see Igor' Bogdanov, *Dym otechestva, ili kratkaia istoriia tabakokureniia*, (Moscow: Novoe Literaturnoe Obozrenie, 2007), a largely impressionistic but witty account which focuses mostly on the modern period; on Siberia, see Monahan's contribution, this volume, and Andrei Valer'evich Shapovalov, *Ocherki istorii i kul'tury potrebleniia tabaka v Sibiri XVII–pervaia polovina XX veka*, (Novosibirsk: Izdatel'skii Tsentr "Progress-Servis," 2002), esp. 17–36 for the early modern period. On sermons, see among others, Bishop Iakov (I. P. Domskii), *Istoricheskii ocherk russkogo propovednichestva*, (St. Petersburg: Tip. F. G. Eleonskogo i Ko, 1878); P. Zavedeev, *Istoriia russkogo propovednichestva ot XVII veka do nastoiashego vremeni*, (Tula: Tip. N. I. Sokolova, 1879); Paul Bushkovitch,

Religion and Society in Russia: The Sixteenth and Seventeenth Centuries, (New York: Oxford University Press, 1992), esp. chap. 7.

7. Orthodoxy in general views sin as disobedience to God's law that can occur in both deed and in thought. Orthodox lists of sins fluctuated over time (especially under Roman Catholic and Protestant influence) but, overall, Orthodoxy has avoided a strictly legalistic approach to sin and allows the confessor a lot of leeway in assigning penance. See in general *Thrēskeutikē kai Ēthikē Enkyklopaideia*, v. 8, s.v. "Metanoia;" I. K. Angelopoulos, *Hē Metanoia kata tēn Orthodoxon Katholikēn Ekklēsian*, (Athens: n.p., 1998); Chrēstos Androutsos, *Dogmatikē tēs Orthodoxou Anatolikēs Ekklēsias*, 2nd ed., (Athens: "Astēr," 1956), 376–89.
8. This condemnation is often mentioned in the literature, but to date I have found no firm evidence that it ever occurred: see A.V. Artsikhovskii, ed., *Ocherki russkoi kul'tury XVII veka*, 2 vols., (Moscow: Izd-vo Moskovskogo universiteta, 1979), 2:13, where it is reported that Filaret condemned tobacco as a "God-hated act" (*bogomerzkoe deianie*) similar to playing cards and participating in minstrel games or fornication. But no proof is offered for this statement. In the English-language literature, Filaret's condemnation appears to have entered the discussion through the work of Jacob M. Price, "The Tobacco Adventure to Russia: Enterprise, Politics, and Diplomacy in the Quest for a Northern Market for English Colonial Tobacco, 1676–1722," *Transactions of the American Philosophical Society*, New Series, 51, Part 1 (1961): esp. 17–18. Price asserts that the Russian Church "forebade the taking of tobacco as an 'abomination to God' on the 'Biblical grounds that it is not that which entereth into a man that defileth him, but that which proceedeth from him'." But the only contemporary evidence he cites is Adam Olearius, who visited Moscow in the 1630s and who reported that in 1634 Tsar Michael forbade the sale and use of tobacco for three reasons: the danger of fire, the economic impact it had on the poor, and the irreverence it entailed in front of icons (ibid., 17–18). Olearius's original text regarding this last reason reads: ". . . and before the ikons, which were supposed to be honored during church services with reverence and pleasant-scented things, the worshippers emitted an evil odor. Therefore, in 1634, at the suggestion of the Patriarch, the Grand Prince banned the sale and use of tobacco along with the sale by private taverns of vodka and beer." See *The Travels of Olearius in Seventeenth-Century Russia*, trans. and ed. by Samuel H. Baron (Stanford: Stanford University Press, 1967), 146. It should be noted that Patriarch Filaret died in 1633, and therefore his impact on the 1634 decree is open to question. On Filaret's policies, see among others, John Keep, "The Regime of Filaret (1619–1633)," *Slavonic and East European Review,* 38 (1960): 334–60; Paul Bushkovitch, "The Court of Tsar Michael in Swedish Sources 1619–1634," in *Russische und Ukrainische Geschichte vom 16.–18. Jahrhundert*, ed. Robert O. Crummey et al., *Forschungen zur osteuropäischen Geschichte* 58 (2001): 235–42. It should also be noted that in a letter to the *stroitel'* of the Pavlov-Obnorskii Monastery dated 1636, Tsar Michael censured the monks for their indulgence in tobacco and drink and their participation in peasant celebrations: see S. M. Solov'ev, *Sochineniia v. vosemnadtsati knigakh,* 18 vols., (Moscow: Mysl', 1988–), kn. 5, 206–07. In any case, it is important to note that the condemnation of tobacco use and sale were not simply religiously motivated. Indeed, Olearius's description makes it clear that Russians greatly loved tobacco and that economic reasons as well as concerns about fire safety played an equally, if not more, important role in the prohibition. Other travelers, especially in the second half of the seventeenth century, also reported

the Russians' love of tobacco, but generally did not attribute the prohibitions to religious reasoning. Indeed, several travelers commented on Russians' avid tobacco smoking but few related any religious opposition to it. Thus, Olearius's observation regarding icons is repeated in Guy Miège, *A Relation of Three Embassies from His Sacred Majestie Charles II to the great Duke of Muscovie . . . performed by the Right Hoble. the Earle of Carlisle in the years 1663 & 1664*, (London, 1669; reprinted, London 1926), 29. On the other hand, Jacob Reutenfels remarks that Tsar Aleksei prohibits tobacco smoking for fear of fires, but that the Russians nevertheless greatly engage in this pastime: see Iakov Reitenfels, "Skazaniia gertsogu Toskanskomu o Moskovii," in *Utverzhdenie dinastii*, ed. A. Liberman, (Moscow: Fond Sergeia Dubova, Rita-Print, 1997), <http://www.vostlit.info/Texts/rus9/Reutenfels/text4.phtml>, accessed December 26, 2007. Furthermore, Paul of Aleppo, who visited Moscow in the escort of Patriarch of Antioch Makarios in the mid-seventeenth century, claimed that foreigners caught smoking were put to death or imprisoned. But he did not refer to any ecclesiastical prohibition against it: see Paul of Aleppo, *Puteshestvie Antiokhiiskogo patriarkha Makariia v Rossiiu v polovine XVII veka opisannoe ego synom, arkhidiakonom Pavlom Aleppskim*, ed. G. Murkos, 5 vols., (Moscow: Universitetskaia Tipografiia, 1896–1900) <http://www.vostlit.info/Texts/rus6/Makarij/text2.phtml> and <http://www.vostlit.info/Texts/rus6/Makarij/text3.html>, accessed December 26, 2007. Adolphus Lyseck, secretary of an embassy to Aleksei Mikhailovich, indicated that tobacco use was a crime against state laws, without making any connection to religious condemnation: see Adol'f Lizek, *Skazanie Adol'fa Lizeka o posol'stve ot imperatora rimskogo Leopol'da k velikomu Tsariu Moskovskomu Alekseiu Mikhailovichu, v 1675 godu* (first published in Latin, Salzburg, 1676), <http://www.vostlit.info/Texts/rus10/Lizek/text.phtml> in Russian, accessed December 26, 2007. Finally, Johann Georg Korb who visited Moscow in the late 1690s reported that the Russian clergy were vehemently opposed to tobacco as a devilish act. But that was the time of Patriarch Adrian and he was no match for Peter the Great: see *Rozhdenie imperii*, ed. A. Liberman, (Moscow: Fond Sergeia Dubova, Rita-Print, 1997), <http://www.vostlit.info/Texts/rus13/Korb/text6.phtml>, accessed December 26, 2007.

9. On the concept of *blud*, see Eve Levin, *Sex and Society in the World of the Orthodox Slavs, 900–1700*, (Ithaca, NY: Cornell University Press, 1989).
10. For example, his sermons *Pouchenie ot iereov sushchim pod nimi v pastve ikh*, written in 1670 and printed in Moscow in 1674 together with his *Pouchenie o blagogoveinom stoianii v khrame* (written in 1671), do not mention tobacco. Nor does yet another undated and anonymous sermon on proper behavior in church, which was probably printed in 1675: for a discussion of these three sermons, see Cathy Potter, "The Russian Church and the Politics of Reform in the Second Half of the Seventeenth Century," 2 vols., (Ph.D. Diss., Yale University, 1993), 2: 357–69.
11. The complete title is *Na den' nedel'nyi. Pouchenie na lenivyia v tserkov' prikhoditi i na prikhodiashchiia bez strakha, izbrano ot besed zlatoustovykh: izhe na poslaniia Pavla apostola. i chast' ot inykh pisanii.* The sermon appears at the very end of the manuscript after the table of contents of the second part and following the verses thanking God: see RGB, *Sobranie Rumiantseva*, n. 411, ll. 808–811ob. It lacks original pagination, but the script is the same as in the rest of the manuscript, therefore it must have been written by the manuscript's original compiler. (It should be noted that the table of contents does not include this sermon.) It has some similarities with the sermon entitled "Pouchenie na poseshcheniie tserkvi novosozdannoi," by Kirill Trankvillion

(Stavrovetskii), published in his *Evangelie Uchitel'noe* (Unev, 1696; first published in 1619, republished 1668). But Trankvillion's work does not mention tobacco. In any case, the *Statir*'s compiler did mention that he was influenced by Trankvillion's work. On the *Statir*, see P. T. Alekseev, "Statir. (Opisanie anonimnoi rukopisi XVII veka)," *Arkheograficheskii ezhegodnik za 1964 god*, (Moscow, 1965), 101; on its presumed author/compiler, see *Slovar' knizhnikov i knizhnosti drevnei Rusi, XVII v.*, (St. Petersburg: Dmitrii Bulanin, 1998), chast' 3, s.v. "Potap Prokof'ev Igol'nishnikov;" Potter, "The Russian Church and the Politics of Reform," II: 369–72.

12. "na smradnuiu tabaku: izhe otiagchaet mozga i um pomrachaet:" RGB, *Sobranie Rumiantseva,* n. 411, ll. 808–809, quote l. 809.
13. Ibid., quote, l. 809–809ob.
14. Ibid., ll. 809ob–811.
15. Tobacco's intoxicating effects, its association with frequenting taverns, and last, but not least, the linguistic usage "to drink tobacco," common all over Europe at the time, must have contributed to the connection to drinking.
16. *Bez very ne vozmozhno ugodit' bogu*: Gosudarstvennyi Istoricheskii Muzei (henceforth GIM), Sinodal'noe Sobranie, no. 261/221, ll. 206–225ob. See A.V. Gorskii–K.I. Nevostruev, *Opisanie slavianskikh rukopisei Moskovskoi Sinodal'noi Biblioteki,* (Moscow: Sinodal'naia Tip., 1855–1917), Part 2, vol. 3: 252–66. Copied for Patriarch Adrian, the manuscript includes the lives of Metropolitans Aleksei, Petr, Iona, Filipp, as well as a number of other sermons, at least two of which are specifically directed to the army. It is a collection of Lenten sermons. On Ioakim, see Potter, "The Russian Church and the Politics of Reform," esp. vol. 2; and Bushkovitch, *Religion and Society*, 172–75.
17. GIM, Sinodal'noe Sobranie, no. 261/221, ll. 206–211ob.
18. Ibid., ll. 212ob–213ob.
19. "No ot pipok tabatskikh, i zloglagolstv liutorskikh, kalvinskikh, i prochikh eretikov, obiurodesha"; ibid., l. 214.
20. Ibid., ll. 214ob–217.
21. The relevant text reads: "v zhitel'stve ubo chilovekov, obshchaia poslovitsa nositsia: vse to liudem izian, ot chego kto pian. Mera vo vsem cheloveka v dobroe delo budit, bezmerno zhe ne tokmo vrednyi i skarednyi tabak, no i renskoe vino gubit"; ibid., l. 213.
22. In essence, then, here the Old Believers and their implacable foe, Ioakim, agreed. On the Old Believers, see the contributions of Levin and Robson, this volume.
23. GIM, Sinodal'noe Sobranie, no. 261/221, ll. 214–225ob, references to drunkenness and uncleanliness on l. 222.
24. Interestingly, despite his thundering condemnation of the ills that tobacco can contribute to, Ioakim fails to mention fornication.
25. *Dva nachalstva*: see G. V. Esipov, *Raskolnich'i dela XVII stoletiia,* 2 vols., (St. Petersburg: Izd. D. E. Kozhanchikova, 1861–1863), vol. 2, appendix, 76–96. On Adrian, see Grigorii A. Skvortsov, *Patriarkh Adrian. Ego zhizn' i trudy v sviazi s sostoianiem russkoi tserkvi v poslednee desiatiletie XVII veka,* (Kazan': Tsentr. Tip., 1913).
26. Esipov, *Raskolnich'i dela,* II, appendix, 90–91.
27. As an indication, the Greek files at RGADA mention several cases of tobacco contraband in the second half of the seventeenth century. For example, in 1661 the Foreign Office called in all the Greek merchants then in Moscow and interrogated them on rumors that the Greeks were selling tobacco secretly. Part of the process included an oath in front of the icon of Christ that the Greek merchants were neither to hold tobacco for personal use, nor

sell it. All merchants duly took the oath and each signed his name next to a variant of the following declaration: "I [so and so] neither drink tobacco, nor sell it." See RGADA, f. 52, op. 1, d. 22 (1661); for the list of signatures see l. 2ob and Figure 3.1. Several foreigners also commented on the Russian love for tobacco: see Note 8. See also the case of Archbishop Afanasii of Kholmogory cited in Note 42 and also Monahan, this volume, which traces the state's mixed enforcement of prohibition.

28. On Nikon, see most recently S. V. Lobachev, *Patriarkh Nikon,* (St. Petersburg: Isskustvo-SPb, 2003).
29. On the issue of Westernization, see among others: Nikolaos Chrissidis, "Creating the New Educated Elite: Learning and Faith in Moscow's Slavo-Greco-Latin Academy, 1685–1694," (Ph.D. Diss., Yale University, 2000); Lindsey Hughes, *Sophia Regent of Russia 1657–1704*, (New Haven, CT: Yale University Press, 1990); Hughes, *Russia in the Age of Peter the Great*, (New Haven, CT: Yale University Press, 1998; A.S. Lavrov, *Koldovstvo i religiia v Rossii 1700–1740gg.*, (Moscow: Drevlekhranilishche, 2000); Bushkovitch, *Religion and Society*; Potter, "The Russian Church and the Politics of Reform"; P. V. Sedov, *Zakat moskovskogo tsarstva. Tsarskii dvor kontsa XVII veka,* (St. Petersburg: "Dmitrii Bulanin," 2006), esp. 491–550.
30. For more details, see Potter, "The Russian Church and the Politics of Reform," 2: esp. 512–13 on the testament. Ioakim's criticism that tobacco was foreign was technically correct: tobacco was not indigenous to Russia. But that it was Lutheran and Calvinist is, strictly speaking, incorrect given that tobacco came to Russia also from China and Persia.
31. Bushkovitch, *Religion and Society*, chap. 3; Potter, "The Russian Church and the Politics of Reform," 1, chaps. 3–4.
32. Interestingly, by the mid-eighteenth-century manuals of penance also mentioned tobacco. See M. V. Korogodina, *Ispoved' v Rossii v XIV–XIX vv.*, (St. Petersburg: "Dmitrii Bulanin," 2006), 295 and 497–98 for the text of an eighteenth-century questionnaire for confession of priests from the Ukraine. The question requires the priest to answer whether he has been in taverns where he was a spectator of or participant in dances and games; whether he has taken snuff or smoked pipe tobacco; and whether he has castigated similar behaviors among his parishioners. The question includes justification for the prohibition against tobacco: "because with our lips we accept the Body and Blood of our Lord Jesus Christ" (p. 498). Such questions are absent from Russian questionnaires if one is to judge by the texts included in Korogodina's book. However, the iconographic record of the Last Judgment provides evidence that it was not just priests who were condemned for tobacco use in Ukraine. As John-Paul Himka has noted, eighteenth-century Ukrainian icons of the Last Judgment placed smokers (together with gamblers and other tavern goers) squarely in hell: see his "'Social' Elements in Ukrainian Icons of the Last Judgment through the Eighteenth Century," in *Letters from Heaven: Popular Religion in Russia and Ukraine*, ed. John-Paul Himka et al., (Toronto: University of Toronto Press, 2006): 235–50, esp. 239.
33. See for example, RGB, f. 178, Muzeinoe Sobranie, n. 3345: this is an early eighteenth-century miscellany containing excerpts from the *Kormchaia*, the *Paterik,* and the *Prolog*, as well as from sermons by Church Fathers and from lives of saints. Its provenance is from Nizhnyi Novgorod and it appears to be compilation of sources for priestly use. On l. 606, it includes references to the 1649 Law Code's prohibition of tobacco as well as excerpts from Gizel's work cited in Note 34 following. Interestingly, Old Believers also copied Gizel's argument verbatim: see for example, RGB, f. 178, Muzeinoe Sobranie, n. 4143: an early eighteenth-century Old Believer miscellany, which mirrors n.

3345 in its selection of references to tobacco. Specifically, it cites excerpts from the 1649 Law Code and from Gizel's book: see ll. 91–92 and 92–92ob respectively.

34. Gizel', *Mir so Bogom Cheloveku*, 252–3. It should be noted that the next section is a discussion of taste, in which drunkenness is castigated as also leading to fornication. On Gizel' see *Slovar' knizhnikov i knizhnosti drevnei Rusi, XVII v.*, (St. Petersburg: Dmitrii Bulanin, 1993), chast' 2, s.v. "Innokentii Gizel'". Gizel''s work was dedicated to Aleksei Mikhailovich. Tobacco also made an appearance in at least one seventeenth-century *Zertsalo Dukhovnoe* (Spiritual Mirror), a sort of encyclopedia of edificatory definitions of sins and virtues attributed to Arsenii Satanovskii, a Kiev-educated hieromonk who worked in Moscow as a translator and corrector of liturgical and foreign books: see GIM, Sinodal'noe Sobranie, n. 329/760, ll. 325ob–326ob. Entitled "Tobacco: which is the devil's seed" (*Tabaka: si est' semia besovskoe*), this small article excoriates the enjoyment and drunkenness that tobacco causes as "the mother of all evils," while making an attempt to prove its condemnation with references to Biblical and patristic sources that condemned drunkenness and indulgence. On the manuscript, see Gorskii–Nevostruev, *Opisanie*, Part 2, vol. 3: 714–29. On Satanovskii, see *Slovar' knizhnikov i knizhnosti drevnei Rusi, XVII v.*, (St. Petersburg: Dmitrii Bulanin, 1992) chast' 1, s.v. "Arsenii Satanovskii."
35. See Note 33.
36. See Georg Michels, "Opportunists, Idealists, and Functionaries: The Men Who Ruled the Russian Church Under Nikon (1652–66)," in *Russische und Ukrainische Geschichte vom 16.–18. Jahrhundert*, ed. Crummey et al., 199–206, esp. 201 and 203.
37. See Levin, this volume. The miracle stories and Ioakim's sermon underscore proper behavior in Church and obedience to divine commands. In that sense, as one commentator has remarked, in both cases the moral code emphasized is the same: Buskovitch, *Religion and Society*, 116. However, there is an important difference: unlike the miracle stories, Ioakim, speaking to a different audience and clearly aware that the Church Fathers did not condemn tobacco, did not mention any such prohibition emanating from them. Instead, he took another track and castigated tobacco as a foreign habit. Although both the miracles and the sermon strongly disapproved of tobacco use because of its associations with drunkenness, their condemnations squarely reflected the different cultural milieux in which they were composed.
38. Recently studied in Korogodina, *Ispoved' v Rossii*; see also Korogodina, "Penitential Texts and the Changing Political Culture of Muscovy," *Russian Review*, 66 (2007): 377–90.
39. I have checked the following Moscow editions: 1680, 1688, 1697.
40. The only appearance is in the *Kniga o vere* (Moscow, 1648), a collection of sermons and theological treatises, in which tobacco was condemned for causing drunkenness. Thanks to Eve Levin for pointing it out. That collection reflected the Catholic-influenced Ukrainian-Belarusian tradition: see T. A. Oparina, *Ivan Nasedka i polemicheskoe bogoslovie kievskoi mitropolii*, (Novosibirsk: Nauka, 1998), chap. 8.
41. It was only in 1722 that Nikolaos Mavrokordatos (1670–1730), Prince of Moldavia and Prince of Wallachia (on two different periods of time) as well as scion of one of the most influential Phanariot families in Istanbul, authored an anonymous treatise against tobacco entitled "Censure of Nicotine" (*Psogos Nikotianēs*) as well as an epistle and dialog on the topic. However, in the

dialog his arguments were overwhelmingly based on medical, physiological, and environmental concerns, whereas the epistle and the dialog were highly polemical and personal attacks against Mētrophanēs Gregoras (born 1630), a monk and corrector in Bucharest's printing house who had allegedly authored a praise of tobacco: for critical editions of all three texts, see Monique Trudelle, "Nicolas Mavrocordatos. Discours contre le tabac. Edition critique, traduction et commentaires," (M.A. Thesis, Université de Monréal, 1992). Indeed, to my knowledge, the very first time in which tobacco use was condemned in writing by a cleric in the Greek Orthodox Church was at the very beginning of the nineteenth century. Specifically, Nikodēmos the Hagiorite (1749–1809), an Athonite monk, wrote about tobacco use in two of his works, *The Spiritual Exercises (Pneumatika Gymnasmata),* 7th ed., (Venice: Para N. Gykei, 1800; Thessaloniki: Ekdotikos Oikos Vas. Rēgopoulou', 1991) and *The Handbook of Counsel (Symvouleutikon Engheiridion,* (Vienna: n.p., 1801; revised edition by Monk Sophronios, Athens: Ekdoseis "Ho Hagios Nikodēmos," n.d.). In the former, tobacco comes up for censure because it betrays absence of good morals (1800 ed., 132–33); in the latter work, the discussion is more extensive and focuses on the prohibition of tobacco use by clergymen. In particular, clergy are urged to avoid tobacco for three reasons: (1) it is a sign of immorality; (2) it is not befitting the high status of clergy; (3) it is a detriment to both body and soul (pp. 72–76 of the 1801 edition). However, Nikodēmos allows for the moderate use of tobacco as a medicine, provided its use is not public (ibid., 76). For a discussion of Nikodēmos' views (as well as a partial English translation of the relevant passages) see Constantine Cavarnos, *Smoking and the Orthodox Christian*, trans. Bishop Chrysostomos of Etna, (Etna, CA: Center for Traditionalist Orthodox Studies, 1992). It should be noted that Cavarnos does not present the complete text of Nikodēmos' original in the case of *The Handbook of Counsel*; he leaves out Nikodēmos' allowance of moderate use for medical reasons, most likely because he uses a later edition of Nikodēmos' work that had been revised by the Monk Sophronios. Neither does Cavarnos indicate the largely compilatory character of both of Nikodēmos's works, which were based on Western, Catholic prototypes. On this issue, see Gerhard Podskalsky, *Griechische Theologie in der Zeit der Türkenherrschaft, 1453–1821*, (München: C.H. Beck, 1988), esp. 377–82. Overall, then, condemnation of tobacco use among the Greeks was medicalized in nature, or was expressed in monastic circles. In the latter case, it reflected a monastic take on morality and was addressed primarily, though not exclusively, to clergymen, both inside and outside monastic circles. Indicative in this regard is a wall painting in the cemetery chapel of the Gregoriou Monastery, Mt. Athos, dated 1739 (see Figure 3.2). It depicts a monk smoking a long-stemmed pipe surrounded by demons. The inscription reads: "If a monk smokes, the demons are his servants." Other paintings on the same wall portray still other conduct unbecoming a monk: see unpaginated appendix, plate no. 235, in Thomas Provatakēs, *Ho diavolos eis tēn Vyzantinēn technēn: symvolē eis tēn ereunan tēs orthodoxou zographikēs kai glyptikēs,* (Thessalonike: n.p, 1980). On the Gregoriou Monastery, see *V. Angelakos, Hē en Hagiō Orei Hiera Monē tou Hagiou Grēgoriou 1300–1921*, (Thessaloniki: Typ. N. Christomanou, 1921). Tobacco condemnation, however, does not make an appearance in scenes of the Last Judgment in Greek churches, at least if one is to judge by the study of Miltiadis Garidis, *Etudes sur le Jugement dernier post-byzantin du XVe à la fin du XIXe siècle: iconographie, esthétique*, (Thessalonikē: Hetaireia Makedonikōn Spoudōn, 1985). By the above indications, therefore, whatever disapprobation there was among the Greeks, it was not always religiously motivated. When it was, it was addressed primarily to the clergy, both secular and monastic, and appeared only in the eighteenth century.

42. The case of Archbishop Afanasii of Kholmogory (1682–1702) is instructive in this regard. As part of his effort to "clean up" his diocese, Afanasii sent a version of Adrian's *Dva Nachalstva* circular to the parishes. He paid particular attention to the lawlessness that he witnessed in the various monasteries of his diocese, notably Solovki, in which the monks indulged and traded in drink and tobacco: see Georg Michels, "The Monastic Reforms of Archbishop Afanasii of Kholmogory (1682–1702)," in *Die Geschichte Russlands im 16. und 17. Jahrhundert aus der Perspektive seiner Regionen*, ed. Andreas Kappeler, *Forschungen zur osteuropäischen Geschichte,* 63 (2004): 220–35, esp. 223.
43. On Western European attitudes to tobacco in the early modern period see Count Corti, *A History of Smoking*, trans. Paul England (London: Bracken Books, 1996), esp. chaps. 4–7; Iain Gately, *La Diva Nicotina: The Story of How Tobacco Seduced the World*, (London: Simon & Schuster, 2001), esp. chaps. 2–5; Tanya Polard, "The Pleasures and Perils of Smoking in Early Modern England," in *Smoke: A Global History*, ed. Sander L. Gilman and Zhou Xun, (London: Reaktion, 2004), 38–45; Eric Burns, *The Smoke of the Gods: A Social History of Tobacco,* (Philadelphia: Temple University Press, 2007), esp. chaps. 1–3; Peter C. Mancall, "Tales Tobacco Told in Sixteenth-Century Europe," *Environmental History*, 9:4 (2004): 648–78; Simon Schama, *The Embarrassment of Riches: An Interpretation of Dutch Culture in the Golden Age*, (New York: Knopf, 1988), esp. 188–220; David Harley, "The Moral Symbolism of Tobacco in Dutch Genre Painting," in *Ashes to Ashes: The History of Smoking and Health*, ed. Stephen Lock et al., (Amsterdam: Rodopi, 1998), 78–86; Georg A. Brogers, *Nicotiana Tabacum: The History of Tobacco and Tobacco Smoking in the Netherlands*, (Amsterdam: H. J. W Becht's Uitgeversmaatschappij N.V., 1964); Benjamin B. Roberts, "The 'Marlboro Men' of the Early Seventeenth Century: Masculine Role Models for Dutch Youths in the Golden Age?" *Men and Masculinities*, 9:1 (2006): 76–94; Joel Best, "Economic Interests and the Vindication of Deviance: Tobacco in Seventeenth Century Europe," *The Sociological Quarterly*, 20:2 (1979): 171–82; David Harley, "The Beginning of the Tobacco Controversy: Puritanism, James I, and the Royal Physicians," *Bulletin of the History of Medicine*, 67:1 (1993): 28–50. On the spread of tobacco, coffee, tea, and chocolate, see Annerose Menninger, *Genuss im kulturellen Wandel. Tabak, Kaffee, Tee und Schokolade in Europa (16.–19. Jahrhundert)*, (Stuttgart: Franz Steiner Verlag, 2004). For a comparative overview of the dissemination of tobacco, coffee, tea, cocoa, and distilled liquor, see Rudi Matthee, "Exotic Substances: The Introduction and Global Spread of Tobacco, Coffee, Cocoa, Tea and Distilled Liquor, Sixteenth to Eighteenth Centuries," in *Drugs and Narcotics in History,* ed. Roy Porter and Mikuláš Teich, (Cambridge: Cambridge University Press, 1995): 24–51.
44. James Grehan, "Smoking and 'Early Modern' Sociability: The Great Tobacco Debate in the Ottoman Middle East (Seventeenth to Eighteenth Centuries)," *The American Historical Review*, 111 (2006): 1352–77; see also Ayşe Saraçgil, "Generi voluttuari e ragion di stato: politiche repressive del consume di vino, caffè e tabbaco nell' impero ottomano nei secc. XVI e XVII," *Turcica*, 28 (1996): 163–94; for Persia, see Rudi Matthee, *The Pursuit of Pleasure: Drugs and Stimulants in Iranian History, 1500–1900,* (Princeton: Princeton University Press, 2005), esp. chaps. 5 and 6.
45. See Levin, this volume. As she shows, there was medical discussion of tobacco starting in early eighteenth century. This discussion picked up speed during

the late nineteenth and early twentieth centuries when Russian clerical commentators on tobacco tended to emphasize its bad effects on health and the air in the context of a medicalized religious discourse. See for example, Hieromonk Mikhail, *Neskol'ko slov o tabake s tochek zreniia: istoricheskoi, meditsinskoi i nravstvennoi*, 2nd ed., revised and augmented, (Kazan': Tip. Kokovinoi, 1878); Priest S. N. Slepian, *O tabake: beseda*, 3rd ed., (St. Petersburg: Tip. P. P. Soikina, 1897); Priest Vvedenskii, *O kurenii tabaku*, (Moscow: Izdanie otd. rasprostraneniia dukhovno-nravstvennykh knig pri Mosk. Obshch. Liubit. dukhovn. prosveshcheniia, 1900).

4 Tobacco and Health in Early Modern Russia[1]

Eve Levin

In early modern Europe, when the discovery of the link between tobacco and cancer, stroke, and heart and respiratory disease still lay in the future, the consequences for health of tobacco use already engendered serious discussion. Proponents of tobacco lauded its benefits to body and spirit. They appreciated its virtues as a mild stimulant in recreational use, and exalted it as the long-sought "panacea"—a medicine that could cure all diseases. Meanwhile, tobacco's opponents warned that it destroyed physical and mental well-being. Recreational use could enfeeble the body and the brain, while legitimate medicinal uses of tobacco were few to none. The medical issue took on a religious and a political cast as well. King James I of England, for example, opposed tobacco use and regarded it as a threat to users' moral fiber as well as to their physical health. Tobacco, he argued, caused laziness, which was sinful as well as detrimental to the interests of King and realm. No good could be expected of a product and custom that had originated amongst Native Americans, whom he characterized as devil-worshippers.[2]

Russia, too, experienced the debates about the morality and health of tobacco use. As in the West, Russians used tobacco recreationally and medicinally, and expressed concern about its deleterious effects on body and soul. As in the West, religious and political issues became intertwined with medical ones. As scholars have already noted, for Muscovites tobacco was a Western European product, emblematic of Russia's relationship with the West. Social conservatives objected to the corrupting effects of a foreign custom that originated among the Catholic and Protestant "heretics," and that was perpetuated within the already suspiciously hedonistic culture of the tavern.[3] Governmental authorities worried equally about the economic implications; if foreign merchants had their way, Muscovy could expend huge amounts of money on a product that provided no benefit to the state.[4] Consequently, the Muscovite state of the seventeenth century took the extreme step of forbidding the sale, use, and possession of tobacco. Ultimately, however, Peter the Great cut through both objections. He promoted tobacco use as a manifestation of the Western style of social interaction that he preferred, and he negotiated favorable terms for its sale. But while the spiritual and political aspects of the tobacco issue in early modern Russia have received scholarly attention, the medical aspects have not.

In Russia, unlike in Western Europe, the medical debate about tobacco was complicated by a deep-seated suspicion of physical medicine and particularly of herbal remedies. Muscovy remained steeped in a religious culture that attributed illness to the interference of supernatural spirits, rather than to natural causes. Sinful behavior led to physical ailments, of course, although the presence of demons in a fallen world guaranteed that even the innocent would be at risk of disease. Because disease resulted from supernatural causes, its treatment, too, involved spiritual healing. Prayer and pilgrimage were common therapies, and the cults of miracle-working relics and shrines proliferated in the seventeenth century.[5] In monasteries and at shrines, clerics provided palliative care to patients, but Russian Orthodox healing emphasized spiritual rather than medicinal treatments.

Unlike its Western European counterparts, seventeenth-century Muscovy had no indigenous tradition of learned physical medicine. Only a few scraps of the Hippocratic and Galenic texts came to Russia with its Byzantine inheritance, and so the humoral theory of health gained little circulation in premodern Russia. It and other Western conceptual innovations, such as that of the "miasma" (a cloud of putrid, disease-bearing air) and Paracelsian "chemical" medicine, filtered in piecemeal in the form of popularized therapies. Rather than studying abstract medicine, as Western physicians-to-be did at universities, Russians healers were amateurs who learned through experience and informally-conveyed knowledge. Healers often combined medicinal treatments with spiritual ones, using charms that freely integrated Christian and non-Christian elements, much to consternation of ecclesiastical officials. Numerous ecclesiastical texts warned believers against consulting "physicians" (*vrachi*) or "sorcerers" (*volkhvy* or *kolduny*) and consuming herbal medicines (*travy*) or "potions" (*zeliia*), thus equating physical medicine with witchcraft.[6] The Muscovite state gave the religious imperative the force of law. Folk practitioners were constantly vulnerable to allegations of witchcraft, whether they proffered physical treatments or magical ones.

Because the Muscovite government shared the Russian Orthodox Church's suspicion of indigenous folk healers, it turned to foreigners for physical medicinal treatment. By the early seventeenth century, the Muscovite government had an established office, called the "Pharmacy Chancellery" (*Aptekarskii prikaz*), to provide necessary medical care to the imperial family, the court, and the army. The chancellery hired foreigners as the primary practitioners of the chancellery; Russians could be "students" or "medics" (*lekari*), but could not rise to the rank of *dokhtur*. As the name suggests, a significant aspect of the chancellery's role involved provision of pharmaceuticals. Working from the assumption that any substance that could heal could also cause harm, the Muscovite state closely controlled the collection, dissemination, and possession of herbs. Unauthorized possession of herbs could be enough to convict a person of witchcraft.[7]

Although all medicinal substances fell under suspicion, the Muscovite authorities singled out two—tobacco and vodka—for specific regulation. (Vodka infused with herbs formed a common medicine.[8]) Unlike most ordinary herbs or elixirs, tobacco and vodka enjoyed widespread recreational use. The prohibitions on tobacco and vodka were not intended to forestall medicinal use, but rather to control raucous behavior, particularly at drinking establishments. The anti-tobacco legislation included in the *Ulozhenie* of 1649 comes in Chapter 25, "Edict on Taverns," which outlawed the possession and sale of tobacco. The law particularly focused on identifying vendors of tobacco, specifying that they could be either Russians or foreigners, and on users, who were identified by their "drunken" demeanor.[9] Didactic texts of the period similarly warned against the complex of taverns, drinking, and tobacco use. The 1648 printed *Kniga o vere* (*Book on the Faith*) railed against the proliferation of sinful behavior, "as it also was in the days of Noah": "For all together are inclined towards benighted drunkenness, and that is the greatest amusement and pleasure, and along with it, demonic tobacco is arising. It is the most harmful to people, and they do not want to be aware of it." Significantly, these admonitions appear in the context of disputations against Roman Catholicism; tobacco and taverns are yet another manifestation of the menace of the West.[10]

Yet even the clergy, whose spokesmen objected so vociferously to the sins of intoxication and carousing, partook of the allure of tobacco. When clerical use became a public scandal, the government had to step in to control it. For example, in 1636 Tsar Mikhail issued a warning to the administrator and monks at the Pavlov monastery:

> It has become known to us, that at the Pavlov monastery there is much disorder and drunkenness and willfulness. Intoxicating drink and tobacco are kept at the monastery, and nearby the monastery taverns and bathhouses operate, and drink is sold. And the monks [visit] the bathhouses and the taverns and the peasants in the villages, and they constantly go to feasts and fraternal gatherings for beer, and they get tipsy and unruly, and create all sorts of disorder and many things that did not occur before. . . . And as soon as you [i.e., the administrator] receive our letter, you must, according to our decree, investigate this and prohibit it strongly, so that the monks and servants do not get drunk and unruly; and that there is no intoxicating drink anywhere in the monastery; and the monks do not go anywhere outside the monastery without your permission and do not get drunk; and they do not go to [monastery] estates for feasts and drink intoxicating drink; and that baths and taverns shall not be built near the monastery, and you shall

> order that [the ones there] be torn down immediately, or be moved to a more distant place . . .[11]

In this case, indulgence in tobacco numbered among numerous other sins, particularly drinking and secular entertainment, and the focus was on the latter, rather than on the sin of smoking. The tsar's order, significantly, focused on the elimination of the source of temptation to the monks, namely taverns and bathhouses in close proximity, and the opportunity to attend parties with lay people. The order did not specify that tobacco be banned from the monastery, although the prohibition on "intoxicating drinking" doubtless was intended to preclude tobacco as well. In common parlance in seventeenth-century Muscovy, users consumed tobacco by "drinking" (*piti*), although descriptions (see later) of actual use describe smoking leaves or taking snuff rather than imbibing a liquid.[12]

Tobacco led to misconduct outside of the tavern setting as well. In 1632, a woman Mar'itsa Semenova *doch'* Shadrikova petitioned the tsar to complain about a group of rowdy men who forced tobacco on her. Mar'itsa complained that she had been sick, suffering from the "black illness," when "that Grigorei,"—the doorman at her house—"seeing me, Mar'itsa, in that poor state, poured tobacco into my, Mar'itsa's, nose, and dishonored and shamed me, Mar'itsa, and abused my sinful body." When the intruders left, they took Mar'itsa's jewelry and many pieces of valuable clothing and household items. While it is possible that Grigorei and his friends forced snuff on Mar'itsa in an attempt to treat her for her illness, the physical abuse—Mar'itsa strongly implies rape—and the theft of her property suggests instead less altruistic motives. If tobacco was thought to cause intoxication, Grigorei and his friends may have been intending to get her drunk so as to take advantage of her.[13]

Frequently, admonitions against tobacco formed only part of a larger set of warnings against common sins of behavior. A woman, Fekla Spiridonova *doch'* Nekhorosheva Klimytieva *zhena*, enunciated such a set of reprimands to the community of Krasnyi Bor while attending the festivities connected with the holiday of the Dormition in August 1641. She claimed to have experienced a series of visions of the Savior and the Mother of God, who appeared to her in the form in which they were depicted on the icons in the village's famous church. According to Fekla's first person testimony, they told her:

> Peasants (*krest'iane*) and all ranks of people should pray to the Lord and to the Most Pure Mother of God constantly, with tears. They should not drink that cursed drink, tobacco. Unfaithful people should not enter the church. In church, they should stand in fear and trembling of God, and pray constantly, and not talk with each other. They should not think ill of each other. They should not curse with mother swears. They should live according to the law of the holy fathers lest from their unlawful doings the whole earth should quake.[14]

In this version of Fekla's vision, tobacco appears among misbehaviors other than drunkenness: not paying attention in church, gossiping, and cursing. In another version of Fekla's experience, included in the miracle book from the church at Krasnyi Bor, the list of sinful behaviors is more extensive (including coming drunk to church and getting into drunken brawls), and tobacco use is singled out as especially heinous:

> And they are not permitted in any way to keep or drink the herb called tobacco. For it is a temptation from the Devil, for the destruction of human souls. It is loathsome to God and damned by the holy fathers.[15]

According to the shrine's miracle book, a second visitor to Krasnyi Bor, Akilina Stefanova *doch'* Bakhmakovykh, reported a vision in which the Mother of God gave similar instruction in regard to tobacco.[16] Fekla, Akilina, and the other ordinary individuals who claimed to speak on behalf of the Savior and the Mother of God of Krasnyi Bor warned of divine retribution against the community if its members did not give up sinful ways. Fekla warned of earthquakes, Boris Lukianov *syn* Smetannykh of "famine and plague and invasion by foreigners."[17]

Admonitions that God's anger will be manifested in the form of natural disasters have formed a staple of Christian discourse since Biblical times. However, the texts of the Krasnyi Bor cult preached not only misfortune for the community as the wages of sin in general, but singled out tobacco use, which alone caused users immediate consequences in the form of physical illness and death. This message is explicit in the entry in the Vologda chronicle concerning the Krasnyi Bor icon, which also highlights the anti-tobacco message as the cult's primary focus:

> There were awesome miracles from that icon [relating to] transgressing and evil people, whoever drank accursed and God-forsaken tobacco. It exhibited over those people various punishments and they were afflicted with various illnesses—severe diseases of the face and eyes, arms and legs turned around and distorted every which way; and whatever person drank that accursed and God-forsaken tobacco and approached the holy icon, at that time he suffered worse and worse. And whoever among them came to the icon of the Savior with a contrite heart and a humble soul and with tears, asking help and healing of illness, Lord God, who loves humankind (correcting and teaching me, Lord), did not give death, but rather will give health and healing to those who come with faith in his most pure and most holy icon.[18]

The chronicle passage highlights both the centrality of the anti-tobacco message of the cult, and also the dire and direct consequences for persons who transgressed the divine commandment. While didactic literature frequently depicts holy figures taking revenge on scoffers by inflicting illness on them, the punishment of tobacco users is exceptionally rapid and virulent.[19]

The shrine's miracle book contains two instances in which petitioners approached the Krasnyi Bor icon after using tobacco. Both incidents occurred within days of Fekla's vision and its concomitant instructions from divine authorities. The deacon Vasilei Molokov from Solvychegodsk:

> . . . did not believe the teachings of the Savior not to drink the herb called tobacco. He took that accursed herb and began to drink it, and at that moment he covered his face with his hands and cried out in a loud voice: "Forgive me, Lord, a sinner, who greatly sinned in transgressing your instruction." And at that moment, everything went dark and he was unable to see with his eyes. And he went to the village called Krasnyi Bor, and repented his transgression in the Church of the All-Merciful Savior. He wept bitterly, but he did not accomplish anything at all. And he returned to his home weeping and bitterly distraught about his illness and his transgression.[20]

In Vasilei's original testimony which "he himself told," the story line is the same, but extra details are present. Vasilei consumed tobacco in the form of snuff ("*v nos*") and his eyes "swam with foam" (*zap"lyv puskom*").[21] It is particularly notable that in both versions of the account, the deacon did not receive healing. This outcome contrasts with the chronicle account's promise that repentent sinners could and did find relief. Moreover, miracle tales rarely recount failures; the purpose of the miracle tale as a genre is to testify to the power of the saint to redeem and heal. Even those sinners who become ill because of their own fault—drinking and scoffing are the most common transgressions—usually receive healing when they repent and visit the shrine of the miracle-worker.[22] Instead, despite his genuine remorse, Deacon Vasilei remained ill. In that way, tobacco use was depicted as literally an unforgivable sin.

The same lesson is driven home in the subsequent miracle account. Trofim is described as "accursed" (*okaiannyi*), because he dared to violate the Savior's prohibition on consuming tobacco. So "an unseen force picked him up and threw him on the ground and he was dead." Because he had died in sin, his household buried him without Christian rites (*ne otpevana*).[23]

Such hostility towards tobacco is usually associated with Old Believers. They made rejection of tobacco as emblematic of their rejection of the corruption from the heretical Latin West and the Russian state that had, they believed, undermined the sanctity of the Orthodox Church.[24] Old Believers became fervent propagandists against tobacco use, and they eagerly mined the corpus of earlier Russian Christian writings to find texts that propounded their views. So, for example, an Old Believer miscellany of the late seventeenth century reproduced the homily against drunkenness and tobacco from the 1648 *Kniga o vere* published by the Moscow Patriarchate.[25] Similarly, the lessons recorded in the texts of the Krasnyi Bor cycle accorded with their views. However, the cult surrounding the Krasnyi Bor icon of the Savior was not exclusive to Old Believers. The manuscript of the shrine's miracle book carefully uses the official Church's Nikonian spelling of the name "Jesus"—something that was literally anathema to Old Believers.[26] However, the cult did come under suspicion, particularly in 1723, after Peter the Great's social and ecclesiastical reforms were instituted. To judge from the materials gathered for the investigation, the cult's hostility toward tobacco constituted one of its most disquieting elements. Investigators culled from documents connected with the cult not only the reports of visions condemning tobacco use (among numerous other sins), which had continued into their day, but also the accounts of the miraculous non-healing of Deacon Vasilei and Trofim. Ultimately, though, ecclesiastical authorities decided that the shrine could remain open; although they warned the clergy against continuing to foment "superstition," they did not regard them as schismatic.[27]

The "Legend about the Origin of Tobacco" enunciated a similar message to that of the Krasnyi Bor icon.[28] (Possibly the text has a direct connection to the Krasnyi Bor cult, because a "maiden Fekla" appears in it as the recipient of a vision from the Mother of God very similar to that attributed to the woman of the same name in the miracle cycle.[29]) In keeping with many religious didactic texts, the Legend presents spiritual renewal as the pathway to true healing, and disparages physical medicine and its practitioners. This text is often associated with Old Believers because of its anti-tobacco message, and, indeed, it circulated widely among them.

The Legend recounts how tobacco originated from the body of a prostitute daughter of Jezebel. She was cast down by an angel of God for her many sins of the flesh, including, significantly, the peddling of an "accursed potion" (*merzskoe zelie*).[30] The tobacco plants that grew up from her rotting grave attracted the attention of a pagan Greek (*ellin*) physician (*vrach*) named Tremikur, who was gathering medicinal herbs. Tremikur cut some tobacco, inserted it into his nose—using it, that is, as snuff—and became "cheerful" (*vesel*) from it, "as though drunk." He then planted the tobacco in his garden, and began to sell it "to whomever had silver," so that many people began to grow tobacco in their yards. The people not only snuffed tobacco, but also smoked it, with deadly results: "Some are dying; some are dead; and every person is transformed, sometimes pale, like the dead; sometimes dizzy with shaking; some are reeling, as though drunk."[31] The king of that country, dismayed by the destruction wrought on his realm, sought advice that ultimately led him to accept Christianity with its condemnation of tobacco. So while the neighboring peoples who had also received "that potion" from the pagan Greeks—"Germans, Turks, Tatars, and Circassians"—continued to experience earthly suffering and eternal damnation, the Christians heeded divine instruction and rooted tobacco out from their gardens.[32]

While the primary message of the Legend is intended to be a moral one, the graphic depiction of the instantaneous physical disability from tobacco use is notable. Although certainly marked by hyperbole for the purpose of driving home the spiritual message, the descriptions of physical illness brought about by tobacco use in the Legend and in the accounts in the Krasnyi Bor cycle coincide quite closely with those contained in the memoirs of Western travelers to Russia. Certainly these foreigners were familiar with tobacco from their homelands and they did not share the harsh anti-tobacco inclination or the religious perspective of the Muscovite authors. Yet they, too, reported witnessing the same sorts of reactions to tobacco as the Russian spiritual authors.

Guy Miege, a diplomat who published his account in 1669, noted Russians' great propensity toward intoxication by tobacco and alcohol both, the severe prohibitions by the state and the Church notwithstanding. Muscovites, he wrote, "take [tobacco] so brutishly that I was almost frighted to see such of them as waited on the Ambassador." Fashioning a cow's horn into a sort of waterpipe, Muscovites:

> . . . suck the smoak thorough the horn with such greediness, that they make not above two sucks of a pipe; and when they whiffe it out of their mouths, they raise such a cloud that it hides all their face; and immediately after they fall drunk upon the ground . . . and for half a quarter of an hour they will ly in this pickle as insensible as if they had the falling sickness. But as soon as they begin to revive, and the smoak of the tobacco hath had its operation, they leap up in an instant one after another more brisk and lively than they were before, pronouncing it a most admirable invention for purging the head.[33]

A few decades later, a Dutch physician, Engelbert Kaempfer, witnessed a similar scene in Kazan':

> . . . [they] emptied in a few pulls of a horn of a beef perforated and full of leaves with coals placed above them. This results in their falling down like epileptics, exhaling mucus and foam. Although the leaves are poisonous, the smoke becomes familiar to man by custom, so that it not only does not harm by its evil quality, but, by the operation of a more beneficial sal, draws the moisture from the recesses of the head and fills the brain with joyousness.[34]

The Dutchman Evert Ysbrant Ides, employed by Peter the Great to travel overland to China, found the Ostiaks in Siberia similarly affected by tobacco, which they smoked from a large kettle:

> . . . they swallow the Smoak, after which they fall down and lye insensible, like dead Men with distorted Eyes, both Hands and Feet trembling

> for about half an Hour. They foam at the Mouth, so that they fall into a sort of Epilepsie: and we could not observe where the Smoak vented it self, and in this manner several of them are lost. . . . some weaker Constitutions are sometimes suffocated even thus with the Smoak which they let into their Bodies.[35]

In all three of these accounts, we see the same picture as in the Krasnyi Bor texts and the Legend: tobacco users intoxicated as though from alcohol, and experiencing immediate symptoms of extreme illness: loss of equilibrium, blindness, foaming, convulsions, unconsciousness, and even death. Western observers explain the observed phenomena differently from Russians. Instead of attributing the physical effects to divine punishment, they see the operation of a salutatory health regime. Tobacco can aid the rebalancing of the humors through purging, and thus contribute to physical and mental well-being. However, because tobacco can have a strong effect on the organism, it should be used with caution.[36]

With so many accounts of independent origin attesting to the narcotic, convulsive, even fatal effects of tobacco, we cannot dismiss the descriptions as mere hyperbole. Western Europeans did not, for the most part, experience the same extreme physical symptoms from tobacco use, and health-related objections to it lay more in its unclean vapors and fears of long-term effects. Yet occasional Western authors warned of more violent reactions from excessive use, such as vomiting, cramps, and convulsions.[37] Dr. Thomas Willis classified tobacco as a "Narcotik" and an "Opiate" that could cause "very great disturbances in their Brain and Nerves." An inexperienced user:

> . . . is immediately taken with a swimming and a cloudiness in his Brains, which is often attended with vomitting and purging; their feet fail them, their hands tremble, and their tongue stammers, or talks idly. Many times also a cold sweat and terrible fainting fits ensue thereupon . . .[38]

Such reactions to tobacco seem to have been the exception, rather than the rule, both in Western Europe and in America, where tobacco originated. Native Americans were well aware of the mind-altering potential of tobacco, and early European visitors remarked upon the religious use indigenous peoples made of it, valuing the visions that it inspired. For the most part, Native Americans employed tobacco for a wide range of medicinal and social purposes, regarding it as mild and beneficial, and Europeans copied them. Despite dissenting voices, both Europeans and Native Americans were more likely to regard tobacco as healthful than potentially deathly, as it appears in the Russian context.[39]

If the accounts reflect reality, how could tobacco in Russia have caused such unusually severe physical consequences? First, the modern domesticated plant contains less nicotine, an alkaloid that can be poisonous in large doses, than the wild varieties.[40] It is possible, then, that seventeenth-century varieties could have been richer in nicotine, and so could have triggered stronger reactions. But in addition, it is quite possible that tobacco was sometimes confused with other plants of the same family (Solanaceae = nightshade), such as henbane. Tobacco was, in fact, sometimes identified as a variety of henbane.[41] Two different genuses of plants are known commonly as henbane: *Datura,* an American native; and *Hyoscyamus*, an Old World native known from ancient times. Both varieties, when ingested, can cause hallucinations, delirium, coma, and death. Both superficially resemble tobacco in the shapes of the leaves and in the appearance of the flowers.[42] In addition to accidental confusion, the illegal status and inflated price of smuggled tobacco in Muscovy[43] created favorable conditions for the adulteration of the product. The substance sold as tobacco in Muscovy (and perhaps elsewhere in the world also) could, sometimes, have been a different plant than the one that now bears that name.

Like its cousin henbane, tobacco could be used medicinally. Indeed, among Native Americans, medicinal use was more prominent than recreational.[44] Europeans also soon employed tobacco to treat a wide variety of conditions, including relieving pain, healing wounds, cleansing toxins, alleviating coughs, and fumigating against the plague. While challenges to the medicinal qualities of tobacco arose early, physicians continued to promote its curative value until modern times.[45] Given that Western European medical practitioners generally regarded tobacco as a legitimate therapeutic substance, it is not surprising that it should make an appearance among the medicines used in the Pharmacy Chancellery, whose foreign apothecaries determined which items should be acquired.

Despite the legal prohibition on the possession and sale of tobacco, the Muscovite government authorized the Pharmacy Chancellery to stock it. In September 1661, an edict from Tsar Aleksei ordered Boris Ermolaevich Begichev, the *voevoda* (military governor) of Kadom, to ship to Moscow to the Pharmacy Chancellery "three puds [over 115 pounds] of good tobacco leaves and half an *osmina* of fresh tobacco seeds." The leaves and seeds, the edict specified, must be "taken from the field this year." Begichev was supposed to obtain the tobacco locally; he was authorized to draw upon "all ranks of people" to collect it. For purposes of security for the tobacco, as with all medicinal herbs, the *voevoda* was to include a document enumerating the contents of the shipment.[46] The specification that "fresh seeds" be included suggests that the Chancellery intended to propagate tobacco. It had its own gardens, founded in 1657, and through the 1660s and 1670s, new plantings were periodically brought from the hinterlands to be placed there.[47]

The Chancellery also purchased tobacco abroad. Dr. Arthur Dee was involved in the tobacco trade while he was in Russia in the 1620s and 1630s. Working with English merchants, he facilitated the shipment of tobacco through the border towns of Smolensk and Mozhaisk on to Moscow. Although the amount of tobacco, measured in "hodyheads" (barrels) and valued at hundreds of rubles, suggests that it could have been intended for recreational rather than medicinal use, Dee was not smuggling. On the contrary, Dee's partners deliberately sent the tobacco to locations where the tsar and his armies were encamped.[48] Even after the legal prohibition on tobacco use became well-established in Muscovy, the Pharmacy Chancellery continued to import it. The list of some 126 medical items the Dutch merchant van Horn purchased in Hamburg in 1668 includes four pounds of *opium tebaikum*.[49] Similarly, medical supplies purchased in 1654 in Mogilev—then disputed territory between Muscovy and Poland-Lithuania—included a pound of *opium-teobaikum*.[50]

The purchases in Mogilev corresponded to a list issued seven weeks earlier; it specified "opium," but did not designate a specific type.[51] The categorization of tobacco as an opiate, as Dr. Willis's tract makes clear, was not unusual. Medical books dating back to the classical period discuss a substance called "thebaic opium." "Thebaic" in ancient texts did not refer to the American tobacco, of course, but rather to the city of Thebes, from whence the tincture originated, according to legend. The actual composition of thebaic opium remains uncertain. One premodern source describes it as "the juice or germ of a black poppy . . . from India,"—that is, the substance commonly associated with the word "opium."[52] Other sources suggest the thebaic tincture could be composed of deer musk or larch tree resin.[53] Thus, the term thebaic cannot be unequivocally identified with tobacco, although the linguistic similarity, particularly in Russian, allows such a reading.

Although the Pharmacy Chancellery kept a supply of tobacco for medicinal use, it does not seem to have been prescribed very often. One list of medicines dispensed for the treatment of soldiers on campaign in 1633 includes one grain of *opiem tabaikom*, but dozens of similar lists do not.[54] Given the likelihood that medicinal tobacco would be purloined or converted to recreational use, the government's reluctance to dispense it is understandable. Dr. Samuel Collins prescribed a medication for Boyar Ilia Danilovich Miloslavskii that included "tobacco salts" and "tobacco ash," among other ingredients.[55] Similarly, Dr. Laurentius Blumentrost's prescription for an unnamed patient contained "Opii thebaic."[56] The incongruity of a government office holding a forbidden product cannot have gone entirely overlooked, because one version of the oath Chancellery guards took required them to swear not to sell its stores of vodka—also used in the formation of medicines—or tobacco.[57]

The use of tobacco as a medicine does not appear commonly outside of the circle of the Pharmacy Chancellery, with its foreign staff. However, the "Legend about the Origin of Tobacco" hints that its authors knew of the medical use, because the tale attributes the appearance of tobacco to a "physician," who had come across it while gathering herbs to use to treat disease.[58] Even so, folk healers do not seem to have used tobacco to treat their patients, and healing books rarely list it among their treatments. An exception is a mid-seventeenth century manuscript book that contains an extensive list of treatments, including both medicines and incantations. As one of a number of remedies for coughs, it recommends either the herb "*poleshnina*" (wild ginger?) and tobacco, which, it advises, can be found "in Moscow in the vegetable market and in the chandlery." To prepare the medicine, the two herbs are shredded together, and then steamed in pot.[59] The instructions on where to obtain tobacco suggest that it was not a familiar product, at least to readers of popular herbal manuals. But if tobacco could be purchased at the vegetable market, then we must doubt the strict enforcement of government regulations restricting possession of tobacco and herbs that could be used in witchcraft.

The legalization of tobacco for recreational use under Peter the Great made it more readily available.[60] By using tobacco, as Peter did himself, Russians could demonstrate that they did not share the recalcitrant Old Believers' hostility to his regime. The official Russian Orthodox Church muted its opposition to tobacco, as it did to many other Western customs, including the practice of physical medicine. At the same time the discourse in Russia on the health effects of tobacco shifted into the patterns of Western European debates: was the recreational use of tobacco beneficial or harmful in the long term to the human organism? The conceptions of the sources of disease and health similarly drew from Western concepts rooted in the Galenic humoral system, rather than in traditional Russian ideas.

An essay entitled "On Tobacco," from a handwritten compendium of medical advice from the early eighteenth century reveals how Russian thinking was evolving.[61] The author explains his attention to tobacco, or "the French powder, as it is called in Spanish," by its widespread contemporary use, and the differing opinions that European experts have offered about it. Some European writers—Cesar de Rochefort ("Rokherfort") is specifically named—"ascribe wonderous action to the strength of tobacco," tracing its use first to the Indians of America, and to the Europeans who copied them. Specifically, tobacco cleansed the nose and drained moisture from the brain, and so could be beneficial to health.[62] Taking an opposing view, the Danish physician Simon Paulli ("Simon Pavl") argues that tobacco powder should be taken only with great care, because it dries up first the inside of the head, and then the other internal organs, and it could deprive users of eyesight. Smoking is not better, because the smoke can destroy the brain. Autopsies of the bodies of English soldiers have revealed drying of the body and blackening of the skull.[63]

As a counterpoint to these two opposing views, the Russian author presents the opinion of the Polish "economist" (*ekonom*) Jakub Kazimierz Haur ("Iakov Kazimer Gavr"). Haur observed the wide usage of tobacco among all ranks of people, including women. He, too, noted how snuff could eliminate moisture from the head. But by drying up the humidity in the body, tobacco could destroy the seed, and therefore young men were advised to abstain from it, except in order to "preserve purity," as clergy are required to.[64]

Here we see a Russian author adopting Western discourse concerning tobacco. Implicitly invoking a humoral model of the body, the author presents opinions about whether the effects of tobacco on the human organism can be positive or negative. In this system derived ultimately from classical Galenic precepts, lifestyle is the primary determinant of health, and the substances individuals ingest interact with other elements that influence their bodies. Thus readers are not ultimately told whether tobacco use is, or is not, good for them; they can make their own decision based on their own situation. The effects of tobacco that are healthful for some individuals may be detrimental to others. However, readers do learn unequivocally that many people enjoy tobacco; recreational use is socially acceptable. And although this essay is found within a compendium of medical advice, no treatment within the volume contains tobacco as a element. The strictly medicinal use of tobacco as a drug, then, had disappeared.

Thus, in the Petrine era, Russians attuned to the Westernization espoused by their leaders copied Western discourse about the merits of tobacco. While tobacco might or might not be good for one's health, it was morally neutral; it had no direct effect on the state of one's soul. But because opposition to tobacco had arisen out of an anti-Western religious discourse in seventeenth-century Muscovy, it remained marked by a moralizing and politicized agenda. The rejection of tobacco became a mark of old-fashioned piety, as well as dissent from the state's agenda of Westernization and modernization. In the nineteenth century, it was not only Old Believers who expressed their critique of the religion and society of their day through the vehicle of tobacco, but also the eminent novelist Leo Tolstoy, for whom the casual use of tobacco became emblematic of the moral decline of his age.[65]

Many of Tolstoy's arguing points replicated seventeenth-century Muscovite polemics against tobacco: anxieties about spiritual danger coupled with concerns about health; worries about financial drain coupled with suspicion of modern influences. Yet condemnations formed only part of seventeenth-century Russians' response to tobacco. At the same time that some Russians portrayed tobacco as innately evil, destructive of bodies and souls, others authorized its use as controlled substance to treat illness. Ironically, the promotion of tobacco as a recreational product, which Peter intended as part of an effort to Westernize Russia, undermined its status as a therapy within a system of medicine imported from the West. If tobacco was mild enough to be enjoyed freely without deleterious effects, then it could not also be powerful enough to cure illness. Thus, the medical context of tobacco illustrates the complexity of Russia's reception of Western culture. Between implacable hostility and wholesale imitation lay a middle ground of selective engagement.

NOTES

1. I would like to thank Tricia Starks, Matthew Romaniello, Nikolaos Chrissidis, Nathaniel Wood, Maria Carlson, and Jon Giullian for their valuable assistance in researching this chapter, and the International Research and Exchanges Board and the Hall Center for the Humanities at the University of

Kansas for financial support for research in Russia. None of them is responsible for the opinions expressed herein.

2. David Harley, "The Beginnings of the Tobacco Controversy: Puritanism, James I, and the Royal Physicians," *Bulletin of the History of Medicine*, 67 (1993): 28–50; Grace G. Stewart, "A History of the Medicinal Use of Tobacco, 1492–1860," *Medical History,* 11:3 (1967): 233–6; 262–3; Katherine T. Kell, "Tobacco in Folk Cures in Western Society," *Journal of American Folklore*, 78 (1965): 99–105.
3. See Chrissidis, this volume.
4. On the commercial implications of the tobacco market, see Matthew P. Romaniello, "Through the Filter of Tobacco: The Limits of Global Trade in the Early Modern World," *Comparative Studies in Society and History*, 49:4 (2007): 914–37; O. J. Frederiksen, "Virginia Tobacco in Russia Under Peter the Great," *Slavonic and East European Review*, American Series, 2 (1942–1943): 40–56.
5. For more information on healing cults, see Eve Levin, "Eastern Orthodoxy: Traditional Healing and Modern Medicine," *Modern Greek Studies Yearbook*, 18/19 (2002–2003): 15–33.
6. See, for example, the penitential questions: "Ne khodil li esi k vrachiu, ili po vlokhom, ili k sebe privodil esi?" ("Did you not go to a physician, or amongst sorcerers, or bring them to yourself?"—for monks); and "Ili kogo zeliem portil esi i travoiu dokhodil esi si zheny" ("Or did you hex someone with a potion or with an herb, or did you go to such women?"—for laymen). A. Almazov, *Tainaia ispoved' v pravoslavnoi vostochnoi tserkvi*, vol. 3, (Odessa: Tipo-litografiia Shtaba Odesskago Voennago Okruga, 1894), 176, 155. For an example of a text that attributes an enormous range of sins and failings to the consumption of a fictional herb "shikh," see "Stikh o zloi trave shikhe," *Chteniia v imperatorsom obshchestve istorii i drevnostei rossiiskikh pri Moskovskom universitete*, 1894, book 4, 4–12.
7. On the practice of medicine in Muscovy, see Eve Levin, "The Administration of Western Medicine in Seventeenth-Century Russia," *Modernizing Muscovy: Reform and Social Change in Seventeenth-Century Russia*, ed. Jarmo Kotelaine and Marshall Poe, (London: RoutledgeCurzon, 2004), 363–89; Levin, "State Pharmacy Practice in Seventeenth-Century Russia," NCEEER Working Paper, 2001; Levin, "Witches and Healers," forthcoming in the memorial volume for Aron Gurevich, ed. Yelena Matusevich and Alexandra Korros, (Leiden: Brill, 2008). Reliable works on the history of medicine in premodern Russia that nonetheless present a much more positive picture of the status of physical medicine than I have adopted here are N.P. Zagoskin, *Vrachi i vrachebnoe delo v starinnoi Rossii*, (Kazan', 1891); N. Novombergskii, *Vrachebnoe stroenie v do-Petrovskoi Rusi*, (Tomsk, 1907); N. A. Bogoiavlenskii, *Drevnerusskoe vrachevanie v XI–XVII vv.*, (Moscow: Medgiz, 1960); M. B. Mirskii, *Ocherki istorii meditsiny v Rossii XVI–XVIIIvv.*, (Vladikavkaz: Reklamno-izdatel'skoe agenstvo Ministerstva pechati i informatsii, 1995).
8. See, for example, the recipes in the "Register of Doctors' Science" by Archbishop Afanasii of Kholmogory from the late seventeenth century, in T. B. Panich, *Literaturnoe tvorchestvo Afanasiia Kholmogorskogo*, (Novosibirsk: Sibirskii khronograf, 1996), 192–6.
9. *Sobornoe Ulozhenie 1649 goda*, (Leningrad: Nauka, 1987), 134–5; 394–400.
10. *Kniga o vere*, (Moscow, 1648), f. 128. This book is described in the catalog by A. S. Zernova, *Knigi kirillovskoi pechati izdannye v Moskve v XVI–XVII vekakh,* (Moscow: Biblioteka im. Lenina, 1958) as item 209.

11. "Gramota tsaria Mikhaila Feodorovicha stroiteliu Pavlovskago monastyria Feoktista Koledinskomu . . ." (June 23, 1636), in *Sbornik Kniazia Khilkova*, (St. Petersburg: Tipografiia brat. Panteleevykh, 1879), 194.
12. Western Europeans also originally spoke of "drinking" tobacco; it is likely that Russians adopted this usage from them. See Peter C. Mancall, "Tales Tobacco Told in Sixteenth-Century Europe," *Environmental History*, 9:4 (2004): 648–78.
13. *Akty Kholmogorskoi i Ustiuzhskoi eparkhii*, part 1, Russkaia istoricheskaia biblioteka, vol. 12, (St. Petersburg, 1890), cols., 115–17.
14. Rossiiskaia natsional'naia biblioteka, (henceforth in notes RNB), f. 351, Biblioteka Kirillo-Belozerskogo monastyria, no. 116/1193, "Sbornik patristisheskii i bogozluahebnyi," (17th c.), ff. 269–269v.
15. RNB, Solovetskoe sobranie, No. 661/719, "Tale of the Icon of the Savior Not Made By Hands in Krasnoborsk" (17th c.), ff. 36v–37.
16. Akilina's testimony is found both in the miracle cycle book, RNB, Solovetskoe sobranie No. 661/719, ff. 16v.–17, and in a first-person testimony included in a different list of early miracles from the shrine. See A. I. Nikol'skii, "Pamiatnik i obrazets narodnago iazyka i slovesnosti severo-Dvinskoi oblasti," *Izvestiia otdeleniia russkago iazyka i slovesnosti Imperatorskoi Akademii nauk*, 17:1 (1912): 97–8.
17. RNB, Solovetskoe sobranie No. 661/719, f. 45. In the original record of Boris's testimony, he warned of different punishments: snow and frosts into the summer, and hot stones raining down on the earth; see RNB, Biblioteka Kirillo-Belozerskogo monastyria, No. 116/1193, ff. 272v–273v.
18. *Polnoe sobranie russkikh letopisei*, vol. 37: *Ustiuzhskie i vologodskie letopisi XVI–XVIII vv.*, (Leningrad: Nauka, 1982), 175–6. The passage is found under the year 1627, even though the miracle cycle and the original reports state that the miracles began only in 1641. It appears to be a later interpolation. The church itself was founded in 1617; See RNB, Solovetskoe sobranie No. 661/719, f. 5v; RNB Biblioteka Kirillo-Belozerskogo monastyria No. 116/1193, f. 261.
19. For more on the phenomenon of heavenly figures punishing scoffers and sinners, see Michael P. Carroll, *Madonnas that Maim: Popular Catholicism in Italy since the Fifteenth Century*, (Baltimore, MD: Johns Hopkins University Press, 1992), 69–82.
20. RNB, Solovetskoe sobranie No. 661/719, ff. 38–39v. The version of Vasilei's testimony recorded in one of the lists of miracles.
21. Nikol'skii, 104.
22. For examples of healed sinners, see Eve Levin, *Dvoeverie i narodnaia religiia v istorii Rossii*, (Moscow: Indrik, 2004), 110–21; Levin, "Innocent and Demon-Possessed," forthcoming.
23. RNB, Solovetskoe sobranie No. 661/719, ff. 40–1. The version of the testimony to miracles published by Nikol'skii, 104, is substantially the same.
24. Roy R. Robson, "Old Believers in Imperial Russia: A Legend on the Appearance of Tobacco," in *The Human Tradition in Modern Russia*, ed. William B. Husband, (Wilmington, DE: SR Books, 2000), 19–29.
25. This miscellany (MS C38) is held in the Spencer Research Library of the University of Kansas. For a description, see Eve Levin, "A Kansas Apocalypse: A Russian Manuscript of the Seventeenth Century and Its Vision of the Last Days," forthcoming. The text in question is found on ff. 228–39.
26. RNB, Solovetskoe sobranie No. 661/719, for example f. 1v.
27. Rossiiskii gosudarstvennyi istoricheskii arkhiv, St. Petersburg, (henceforth RGIA), f. 796, Kantselarii Sinoda, op. 5, no. 375, "Miracles from an icon of the Savior (1724–1725)." For further discussion of this investigation, see

Eve Levin, "False Miracles and Unattested Dead Bodies: Investigations into Popular Cults in Early Modern Russia," in *Religion and the Early Modern State: Views from China, Russia, and the West*, ed. James D. Tracy and Marguerite Ragnow, (Cambridge: Cambridge University Press, 2004), 267–8.

28. "Legenda o proiskhozhdenii tabaka," in *Pamiatniki starinnoi russkoi literatury, vyp.* 1, ed. N. Kostomarov, (St. Petersburg: P.A. Kulish, 1860), 427–35. For a discussion and partial translation of a later, but quite similar, version of this text, see Robson.
29. "Legenda o proiskhozhdenii tabaka," 434.
30. "Legenda o proiskhozhdeniii tabaka," 428.
31. "Legenda o proiskhozhdenii tabaka," 430.
32. "Legenda o proiskhozhdenii tabaka," 433.
33. Guy Miege, *A Relation of Three Embassies From his Sacred Majestie Charles II to the Great Duke of Muscovie, The King of Sweden, and The King of Denmark*, (London: John Starkey, 1669), 101–02. Much of Miege's explication of Muscovite attitudes towards tobacco replicates closely the text of his predecessor, Adam Olearius. See *The Travels of Olearius in Seventeenth-Century Russia*, ed. and trans., Samuel H. Baron, (Stanford, CA: Stanford University Press, 1967), 146. However, Olearius does not provide any description of physical reactions among tobacco users.
34. From Engelbert Kaempfer, *Amoenitatum Exoticarum . . .* (1712), quoted in George Arents, *Tobacco: Its History Illustrated by the Books, Manuscripts and Engravings in the Library of George Arents, Jr., Together with an Introductory Essay, a Glossary and Bibliographic Notes by Jerome E. Brooks*, vol. 3, (New York: Rosenback Co., 1941), 75–6.
35. Evert Ysbrant Ides, *Three years travels from Moscow over-land to China, thro' Great Ustiga, Siriania, Permia, Sibiria, Daour, Great Tartary, &c. to Peking . . .*, (London: W. Freeman, 1706), 22–3.
36. See Stewart, "History," 236–7, 241–2; R. B. Walker, "Medical Aspects of Tobacco Smoking and the Anti-Tobacco Movement in Britain in the Nineteenth Century," *Medical History*, 24:4 (1980): 391–3; Mancall, "Tales."
37. Harley, "Beginnings," 36–41; Jeffrey Knapp, "Elizabethan Tobacco," *Representations*, 21 (Winter 1988): 30–2.
38. Thomas Willis, *Opera Omnia*, quoted in Arents, vol. 2, (New York: Rosenbach Co., 1938), 456.
39. Stewart, "History," 228–68; Robbie F. Ethridge, "Tobacco among the Cherokees," *Journal of Cherokee Studies*, 3:2 (1978), 77–86; Kell, "Tobacco in Folk Cures," 99–114.
40. Stewart, "History," 229.
41. Ibid., 233, 235–6; Harley, "Beginnings," 29.
42. Deni Brown, *New Encyclopedia of Herbs and Their Uses,* (New York: DK, 2001), 190–1, 239–40; *Botanica: The Illustrated A–Z of over 10,000 Garden Plants,* (n.p.: Random House Australia, 1999), 291; 604; 961; Frantisek Stary, *The Natural Guide to Medicinal Herbs and Plants*, (New York: Barnes & Noble, 1994), 92–3.
43. See Romaniello, "Filter," 920–3.
44. Mancall, "Tales Tobacco"; Kell, "Tobacco in Folk Cures," 100–1.
45. Stewart, "History," 239–47; Walker, "Medical Aspects," 391–402.
46. *Mater'ialy dlia istorii meditsiny v Rossii*, vyp. 2, (St. Petersburg: Tip. B. G. Ianpol'skago, 1883), 738.
47. *Mater'ialy dlia istorii meditsiny*, vyp. 3 (St. Petersburg: Tip. B. G. Ianpol'skago, 1884), 667, 722; vyp. 2, 205–7; vyp. 4, (St. Petersburg: Tip. B. G. Ianpol'skago, 1885), 902–4.

48. Arthur Dee and his business partners got into a protracted legal dispute concerning the Moscow trade, in which some of the partners accused Dee of embezzling the proceeds from the sale of the tobacco—a charge he denied. See John H. Appleby, "Dr Arthur Dee: Merchant and Litigant," *Slavonic and East European Review*, 57:1, (1979), 51–2.
49. *Mater'ialy*, vyp. 2, 335.
50. Ibid., 156.
51. Ibid., 152–3.
52. Michael McVaugh and Lola Ferre, "The 'Tabula Antidotarii': Of Armengaud Blaise and Its Hebrew Translation," *Transactions of the American Philosophical Society*, 90 (2000): 142.
53. <http://wiki.hmssurprise.org/index.php/Lexicon:Thebaic_tincture>, accessed on February 25, 2008; <http://www.vitanaturalis.com/camfor.shtml>, accessed on February 25, 2008.
54. *Mater'ialy*, vyp. 1, (St. Petersburg: M. M. Stasiulevicha, 1881), 31–2; compare with lists in this vypusk and the subsequent volumes.
55. *Mater'ialy*, vyp. 2, 299.
56. Wilhelm Michael von Richter, *Geschichte der Medicin in Russland*, vol. 2, (Moscow: N.S. Wsewolojsky, 1815), 90.
57. *Mater'ialy*, vyp. 3, 730.
58. "Legenda o proiskhozhdenii tabaka," 429–30.
59. M. Iu. Lakhtin, *Starinnye Pamiatniki meditsinskoi pis'mennosti*, Zapiski Moskovskago Arkheologicheskago Instituta, (1911): 40.
60. On the legalization of tobacco in Russia, see Romaniello, "Filter," 927–8; Frederiksen, "Virginia Tobacco," 41.
61. "Lechebnik," RGADA, f. 181 Ministerstvo inostrannykh del, no. 1029/1612, ff. 55v–57. The manuscript contains a variety of texts on diagnosing illness through astrology and uroscopy, treatment with herbal medicines and bloodletting, and plague control.
62. Rochefort (b. 1605) is best known for his works of the natural history of the Caribbean; see his *History of Barbados, St Christophers, Mevis, St Vincents, Antego, Martinico, Monserrat, and the rest of the Caribby-Islands, in all XXVIII*, (London: John Starkey, 1666); tobacco is discussed on 55–6.
63. Simon Paulli (1603–1680) wrote a number of treatises against tobacco, coffee, tea, and chocolate. In his *Commendarius de Abusu Tabaci*, he wrote "as Tobacco is of a narcotic Quality, and its Fumes penetrate intimately into the Brain, so, of course, Smoaking must be more prejudicial than Snuffing," quoted in Arents, vol. 2, 380.
64. Haur was the author of both a guide to household management and a manual of household medicine; see *Polski Slownik Biograficzny*, vol. 9, part 2, (Wroclaw: Zaklad narodowy imienia ossolinskich wydawnictwo Polskiej Akademii nauk, 1961), 311–2; Marcin Lyskanowski, *Medycyna i lekarze dawnej Warszawy,* (Panstwowy Instystut Wydawniczy, 1976), 37, 121. In his *Oekonomika ziemianska generalna* (Warsaw, 1744), Haur recommends the use of a mixture of tobacco together with wormwood and blood from a young rabbit to drive rabbits from their warrens for easy hunting; see p. 96. I appreciate Nathan Wood's assistance in locating and reading the Polish texts.
65. Leo Tolstoy, "The Ethics of Wine-Drinking and Tobacco-Smoking," *Contemporary Review*, 59 (1891): 170–87.

5 Regulating Virtue and Vice

Controlling Commodities in Early Modern Siberia[1]

Erika Monahan

In 1756, towards the end of his career, the German academic Gerhard Friedrich Müller wrote an account of Siberian trade. In it, he noted that the Russian government restricted the trade of both tobacco and rhubarb, two coveted Eastern products that made their way from China through Siberia to Russia.[2] While Russians would drink to each other's health with chunks of dried rhubarb in the bottom of a glass of vodka (the rhubarb added for salubrious measure), tobacco, the fruits of the daughter of Jezebel's grave, occupied a sinister role in the folk imagination.[3] In other words, one was a virtue, one was a vice, even though, for Müller, they both belonged in the same category of things that came from China. This chapter injects a comparative perspective into this multi-faceted examination of tobacco's place in Russian history and culture by examining the history of how two important plants—tobacco and rhubarb—were regulated by the Muscovite state and how those regulations were enforced in Siberia in the seventeenth century. A focused look at the history of tobacco alongside the history of other controlled substances in early modern Russia lays bare the pragmatic, mercantilist economic strategies that informed and anchored Muscovite tobacco policy, while also highlighting the particularly charged cultural baggage that tobacco carried with it. Cultural anxieties about tobacco conflicted with the state's mercantilist aims and made for inconsistent state decrees and administrative practices. Illustrative of the pragmatism that guided so much of Muscovite politics and policies, Russia tinkered with its policies on both tobacco and rhubarb throughout the seventeenth and eighteenth centuries. While the state did not waiver in its commitment to enriching the treasury through the trade of these plants, it did alternate its tactics, sometimes selling tax-farms to Russians and/or foreigners, and sometimes taking direct control of the tobacco and rhubarb markets with its own administrators managing sale, distribution, and tax collections.

This chapter focuses on Siberia, where tobacco was initially restricted, yet never wholly eliminated, from circulation or use in the local economy. Siberia was a bridge between East and West, two regions whose commercial relationships and cultural constructions were evolving during this period. It was also a region distinct from Russia.[4] Siberian conquest began as an experiment, with a charter to the entrepreneurial Stroganov family. Once deemed worth appropriating, it was referred to as the tsar's own estate (*votchina*). Throughout the Muscovite period, lowly porters and high-ranking officials spoke of leaving Rus' for "Sibir," and vice versa, indicating distinct territorial categories in Muscovite minds. Property rights, servitude, monasticism, trade laws, tax regimes, and myriad institutions that constituted the fabric of Russian life developed and were applied idiosyncratically in Siberia. This vast colony remained administratively distinct, with its affairs handled by a dedicated department, the Siberian Office.[5] The reforms of Michael Speransky in the 1820s did much to bring Siberia more onto administrative par with European Russia, but the twentieth-century projects of Akademgorodok and Magnitogorsk reveal that in influential Russian minds Siberia remained a blank slate, a land in which and with which to experiment.[6] Such grandiose experimentation had precedent in earlier practices, for Muscovite tsars experimented with policies—such as those for tobacco and rhubarb in Siberia in previous centuries.

RHUBARB, TOBACCO, AND THE MARKET FORTUNES OF BIOLOGICAL EXCHANGE

Rhubarb was an important and costly commodity to the early modern world. Marco Polo noted that rhubarb grew in "great abundance" in the province of Sukchur and that "thither merchants come to buy it, and carry it thence all over the world."[7] It is well-known that Columbus's New World adventures brought pineapple, tomatoes, and tobacco to the Old World, but the journal entry and letters exclaiming his discovery of rhubarb have gotten far less attention.[8] Rhubarb was a major premodern medicine and remained widely used into the nineteenth century, but few people are aware that in 1839 in the lead-up to the Opium Wars (1839–1842), the Chinese state threatened that the constipated of Europe would suffer without relief if China cut off the west-bound rhubarb trade.[9]

It was not leaf or stalk but the rhubarb root that merchants carried from the highlands of China to pharmacists in Western Europe and lands between. The Chinese had known since ancient times what increased contact between East and West made known to Europe: that rhubarb root was precious for its purgative effects.[10] As a laxative, rhubarb root was famous for catalyzing a catharsis that followed constipation. This astringent property along with its mildness relative to other purgatives made it especially desirable. Some turned to rhubarb root to treat jaundice, various skin complaints, and fight fevers. *The Universal Dictionary on Trade and Commerce* lauded rhubarb root as a particularly useful drug because it:

> . . . possesses the double virtue of a cathartic and astringent; it readily evacuates particularly the bilious humors, and afterwards gently

> astringes and strengthens the stomach and intestines. It is given with great success in all obstructions of the liver, in the jaundice, in diarrhoeas, and in the fluor albus and gonorrhoeas; it is also an excellent remedy against worms. It is sometimes given as a purgative, sometimes as only an alterant; and which way ever it is taken it is an excellent medicine, agreeing with almost all ages and constitutions.[11]

Rhubarb had been brought to the medieval markets of the Near East and Mediterranean from at least medieval times. As medicine became an industry and medicinal knowledge spread, so too did the popularity of rhubarb root in Western Europe. The publication of herbal and pharmaceutical guides, such as Jean de Renou's *Dispensatorium medicum* (1615) and Johann Bobart's *Catalogus horti botanici Oxoniensis* (1648) reflected myriad modernizing developments in early modern European society. Concretely, such publications helped to spread knowledge about rhubarb's useful effects, and thereby increased demand. More broadly, the development of medicinal knowledge, scientific study of the natural world, popularization of printing presses, and the increasing contact Europeans had with Eastern products are all manifest in the early modern history of the rhubarb trade.[12]

Thus, the precious root would be dug up in the rugged highland territory of western China and dried to prepare for transport. The Scotsman John Bell in 1720 reported that Mongols would string rhubarb root across their yurts or from the horns of their sheep for drying. A Polish Jesuit missionary in China (1643–1659) and the *Universal Dictionary of Trade and Commerce* described a shorter and less exotic drying process, in which roots were dug up in winter and dried on shaded tables (the sun was believed to sap their potency), then in the wind.[13] Once the curing process was complete,[14] the root would be transported via numerous routes—by sea, from the Indian Ocean to ports of Amsterdam and London; across Persia and Turkey to Aleppo, or on camelback across Eurasia to Arkhangel'sk and beyond—until it ended up as powder in an apothecary's mortar in London, Amsterdam, Paris, Venice, or elsewhere.

In contrast to salubrious rhubarb stood deleterious tobacco. If one digs in the early modern world, he or she may be able to find people who championed the health benefits of tobacco. For example, in Siberia tobacco was mixed with sal ammoniac (ammonium chloride, also known as "Bukharan salt") and used to treat malignant anthrax in livestock.[15] But in the main, Muscovites roundly regarded tobacco as a vice—dangerous, intoxicating, and foreign.[16] When the central government in Moscow wrote to its provincial administrators in Siberia, it was usually insisting that state officials enforce tobacco prohibitions, the motivations for which were largely economic. But it is telling of the cultural anxiety associated with tobacco that in these instructions references to tobacco are regularly packaged alongside dice, cards, and wine—tools of ungodly endeavors.

Cultural anxieties surrounding tobacco were primarily grounded in its foreign and unholy associations, as other articles in this volume describe. The resistance that tobacco use faced in Russia and the slowness—in spite of its addictive properties—with which it took hold there speaks to Muscovite distrust of the habit.[17] Tobacco ultimately came to be heavily cultivated in Siberia, and, in modern times, avidly embraced by Russian subjects and Soviets, yet never entirely shook the vice wrap. Of course, Muscovy was not especially unique in its adverse reaction to tobacco. As a rule, the introduction of tobacco created tremendous anxiety, as James I's *Counterblaste to Tobacco* and Ottoman prohibitions clearly illustrate.[18] In Muscovy, under the particularly conservative Tsar Mikhail Fedorovich, it comes as no surprise that Church and state moved to shield his flock from the scourge of tobacco. Rhubarb was also foreign and remained so, despite the administration's efforts to make it otherwise by sourcing rhubarb domestically.[19] Yet, it never made it into the pantheon of suspicious foreign plants, such as potatoes and tobacco.[20]

This chapter pauses at a moment in which rhubarb and tobacco were arguably commodities of similar market importance. Yet since any suggestion that they might be so in the twenty-first century is absurd, the dramatically changed market fortunes of these commodities requires an explanation. The obsolescence of rhubarb and the rise of tobacco were as much a result of plant etymology as economic pressures. In other words, it was the plant's fault.[21] Rhubarb has a wily disposition: the plant tends towards bastardization; several varieties exist and the same seeds manifest variably in different climates; it took botanists who traveled to distant Chinese highlands to find the root quite some time to appreciate that the plant reproduces closer to the likeness of the parent from sprigs rather than seeds.[22] Consequently, neither Muscovy nor other European countries successfully cultivated medicinal rhubarb root in the early modern period. Moreover, these particularities complicated large-scale commercial propagation, making rhubarb a less appealing investment.

In contrast, tobacco's regularity and reproductive predictability made it highly conducive to plantation production, explaining why tobacco production so quickly found itself accelerating forward with the engines of organized capital behind it. From the 1620s onward, Europeans successfully farmed tobacco in the Virginia colonies, and it was this product for which so many English investors were motivated to find lucrative market outlets.[23] Moreover, the first plantation crops of Virginia tobacco were coming online just as Dutch merchants were working hard to supplant the English as the economic imperialist on the ground in Muscovy.[24] Muscovy captured the attention of organized, committed businessmen highly motivated to find markets for tobacco (and survive in the face of competition). These trading companies—juggernauts of economic imperialism—may be more critical than tobacco's stimulant properties in explaining tobacco's infiltration into Russia. That the English pushed so hard to secure Russian consumers for their tobacco product but faced such resistance from the general population, Church hierarchy, and the Muscovite state underscores the complicated history of tobacco in Russia.[25]

MUSCOVITE POLICY IN THE AGE OF MERCANTILISM

Through this virtue and this vice—one first arriving in English vessels, the other on Bukharan caravans—the Muscovite state sought profit. Although the dynamics of these trades were fundamentally different, both commodities were soon channeled into the abiding economic logic of the day, becoming objects of state policies that shared the common mercantilist goal of enriching the state. Further, the state deployed similar means in its attempts to shape the industries surrounding these commodities. Prohibition, regulation, private and state monopolies, tax-farming, and domestic procurement were all brought to bear, in varying formulas, to generate profit from these plants. This section highlights some of the similar and disparate ways in which the Muscovite state regulated rhubarb and tobacco.

The original motivations behind the regulation of these commodities and how these plants got the administration's attention differed. In Siberia, the state first worried that tobacco was a problem for soldiers that could lead to a more vulnerable army. Next came concerns that natives would use furs to purchase tobacco rather than submit furs to the state. Only later did the possibility that tobacco itself would generate revenue through domestic sales begin to be considered. Rhubarb had a more positive and international valence from the start: the state saw potential profit in rhubarb sales to foreigners. Thus, they held opposite revenue potential. As Romaniello explained, the state recognized that tobacco was an end product in Russia, with potential to deplete the national wealth. The state therefore wanted to control the tobacco market to stem the flow of specie from Russia. Rhubarb, on the other hand, was a transit product, to which Russia would "add value" as the product made its way from east to west across Russian domains. The state wanted to control the rhubarb market to generate specie flow into Russia. As Russian economic strategies became more sophisticated in the eighteenth century, Russia instituted a quality control system that added value to this root as it moved across Eurasia bound for apothecaries in Amsterdam or London. Rhubarb was inspected at the Chinese-Russian border and then again in St. Petersburg before being exported to Western Europe. Substandard and rotting rhubarb was burned publicly. These measures account for the fact that during the eighteenth century "Russian rhubarb" commanded higher prices and enjoyed a better reputation than Turkish or Chinese rhubarb.[26]

These regulatory histories share similar chronological bounds and are necessarily considered in the context of mercantilism. During the seventeenth century, the new Romanov dynasty—ambitious, ascendant, and faced with the challenge of financing increasingly modern armies on several fronts—sought to build its wealth and position through an activist role in the economy. As the state sought to both consolidate and expand its realm, it maneuvered actively to take increasing control.[27] Their moves are typical of early modern states persuaded that the acquisition of specie via state-regulated commerce was the means to wealth, stability, and power. Like its Western contemporaries, Muscovy embraced the aspirations and promises of such economic strategies later dubbed mercantilism.[28] Additionally, the chronology of the evolution of tobacco and rhubarb policies reflects Muscovy's relations with the regimes from whence these commodities arrived.

One commonality in the histories of these commodities is that it is not entirely clear when precisely the state restricted trade. However, it is known that, although tobacco entered the Russian scene much later, it was regulated decades before rhubarb. This fact is linked to their geographical provenance and the forces those places exerted on the new Romanov dynasty. Tobacco first entered Muscovy in the late sixteenth or early seventeenth century from the West, brought by aggressive merchants. If the first tobacco to enter Muscovy was for the Englishmen's own use, English merchants quickly looked to cultivate a tobacco market in Russia. The successful exportation of plantation crops from Virginia increased their incentive to develop "free trade" with Muscovy. While the Muscovy Company and the English throne used the term "free trade," unrestricted trade was not their goal.[29] They meant to secure exclusive, enforceable access to the markets they desired. As English tobacco merchants commented in 1695, "As a farther Consequence of the Russes having no Shipping, they will thereby be rendered uncapable of Entring into a Sea-War; and so we shall have the greater likelyhood of always enjoying a free and open Trade with them [sic]. . ."[30] For early modern Muscovy, the concept of "free trade" in the modern sense was not operative either. Rather, the assumption was that the state regulated exchange. Where, when, between whom, at what prices, goods were exchanged, as well as revenue generation by the state from both taxation and direct participation in commerce were squarely within the purview of the state from its emergence. The eighteenth-century program to "add value" to rhubarb through systematic quality inspections epitomizes this proactive stance.

In any case, it is no accident that Moscow began to regulate tobacco in the wake of English solicitations to secure trade rights.[31] Muscovy's establishment of a strict regulatory regime over tobacco was inherently reactive and defensive—intended to stem specie flow instigated by aggressive foreign competitors. Englishmen did not introduce the notion of state trade monopolies to the Russian state—the Muscovite state monopoly on alcohol predated English presence—but English aggressiveness in finding a friendly market in Russia was unsettling for many among Moscow's policy makers. Thus, English products pushed by aggressive English merchants faced regulations before lucrative Eastern products whose pliers sent no lobbies to the Muscovite court.[32] Incidentally, English ambitions saw Muscovy as both an end market and a gateway to Asia. Just as Russia regulated tobacco in response to English pressure, so too did English interest in the East, manifested in appeals for passage through Muscovy en route to Persia and Asia, pique Russian interest in Asian trade, a circumstance which further reifies the chronology discussed here.

Rhubarb came from China, whose merchants rarely if ever ventured to Muscovy. Substantial, direct Russo-Chinese trade got underway much later, and when it did Russians were the more proactive market-seekers.[33] While Bukharan merchants had brought rhubarb to Novgorod in the late fourteenth century, and one could find certain Chinese goods in Moscow in the 1500s, trade with China attained a credible volume only in the late seventeenth and eighteenth centuries.

The shared foreignness of these important commodities illustrates Muscovy's increasing contacts with East and West. When tobacco first entered Muscovy, it was a decidedly Western product brought by the English. The Law Code of 1649 makes particular mention of tobacco entering Russia from the Baltic region to the west.[34] But for many, tobacco, along with rhubarb, was considered Eastern. Take for example the comments from the eighteenth-century German academic that began this essay. From Müller's highly educated, Siberiocentric perspective, tobacco was an Eastern product.

If Europeans were the catalysts for the introduction of tobacco into the Eurasian world, they were probably not solely or directly responsible for its appearance in Siberia because, although tobacco emerged from the Americas, it was soon cultivated across the globe. Although without 100% success, the first Romanov tsars consistently endeavored to keep Englishmen west of the Urals, but by the seventeenth century tobacco could reach Siberia from many different quarters. In Ukrainian lands, tobacco was an increasingly lucrative cash crop. Indeed, imported Circassian tobacco may in large part account for English failures to realize the profits they envisioned. The Ottoman world embraced tobacco, too.[35] By the 1690s Chinese tobacco was reaching Siberia from the East.[36] *Shar'*, the word used for Chinese tobacco, actually appeared in Siberian records as early as 1640, when it was confiscated from a Cossack in Tobol'sk.[37] Gradually, the adjectives "Chinese" or "Turkish" regularly accompanied mentions of tobacco.[38]

Amidst English pressure to gain a monopoly, Eastern merchants were also moving tobacco into Russia. The Dutchmen Nicolaas Witsen smoked tobacco when visiting the quarters of a Persian merchant in Moscow in 1665.[39] A 1676 memo from the Foreign Office reported that Persians and Tajiks sold much tobacco in Moscow.[40] Along the southern border Chinese, Indian, and Persian merchants gained reputations in Astrakhan for smuggling tobacco into Russia during Sophia's regency; a 1693 report to Moscow declared that great losses to the treasury had resulted from their illicit tobacco trade.[41] By the eighteenth century, "Chinese tobacco" was one of the products frequently associated with incoming Bukharan merchants. The historical dynamics of tobacco's production and distribution—that tobacco went from being a Western product to being an Eastern one—indicate change in a world and economy that were far from moribund or stagnant. In a mere century, in a remote kingdom whose connections to the rest of the world were deeply challenged by distance and geography, the conventional wisdom of the provenance of the tobacco plant shifted from West to East. Change was not glacial.[42]

TOBACCO AND RHUBARB IN SIBERIA

Any of the several trade depots across Siberia would severely disappoint the observer who measured commercial vitality against the busy ports of Amsterdam, London, or Venice in the seventeenth century. Nonetheless, a steady and sizeable volume of goods crossed the Eurasian steppe, with some goods finding final buyers among the growing populace of Siberia and others continuing on to centers farther east and west. Fabrics spanning from English wool to Persian linens and Chinese silks were recorded as often as furs at Siberian customs posts. These are sprinkled with the buying and selling of goods that sustained the population living there. A regular trade in cows, goats, and horses existed. For new Russian householders and natives, boots, locks, mirrors, fry pans, axes, spoons, eyeglasses, needles, knit socks, salted pork fat, beef fat, and fish were staple wares. Salt, pepper, nuts, raisins, and occasionally other spices enlivened the Siberian diet. Wax and paper kept administrative offices running. Gunpowder and sugar were rarities, as was rhubarb. Tobacco does not appear in the customs records—understandably given its prohibited status—but other evidence reveals that it was circulating.

Demographically, Siberia differed dramatically from European Russia. Since military outposts were the front guard of this expanding frontier, soldiers represented a significant portion of the Siberian population. Since tobacco has historically been particularly prevalent among soldiers, the contention that tobacco use was more popular in Siberia than in European Russia may be a consequence of the disproportionate military presence.[43] Conversely, there was a deficit of women, although we also find them involved with tobacco. Finally, Siberian natives resided in Siberia in far greater numbers than in European Russia. The native population was quite important to the tobacco trade, and indeed much of the attention that the state paid to tobacco in Siberia was directly related to native access.

As mentioned above, Siberia was one of the earliest theaters in which the state restricted tobacco trade and use. The Law Code of 1649 articulates a series of prohibitions against tobacco, citing a 1633/4 decree by Tsar Mikhail Fedorovich forbidding Russians and foreigners in Russia to possess, imbibe, or trade tobacco.[44] In fact, the prohibitions were even older than that. Surviving decrees show that the state had already curtailed tobacco circulation by the 1620s (1627 and 1629).[45] The first time the state imposed restrictions on tobacco in Siberia, the concern seems to have been practical—soldiers' excessive use of tobacco was undermining the army's functionality. In 1627 the governor of the Siberian capital of Tobol'sk wrote to Moscow asking what to do about the tobacco problem: soldiers were spending their salaries on tobacco and drinking through their money.[46] Moscow responded by outlawing the possession of tobacco in towns in Siberia, and in Russia (Muscovy) as well. While soldiers were the primary focus, the instruction also expressed concern that fur trappers, artisans, and others would get caught up in tobacco and neglect their trades.[47] The report explained, "Serving men and other people buy tobacco at an expensive price; a pud of tobacco for 100 rubles or more and they smoke that tobacco and drink wine and become drunk more than from wine alone. From this many become impoverished and fall into debt."[48] This tale of addiction and poverty echoed familiar writings. Olearius used the same formulaic phrase in his description of Muscovites, writing, "The poor man gave his kopek as readily for tobacco as for bread. . . . Servants and slaves lost much time from their work . . ."[49] Rather than a response to widespread nicotine-induced truancy in Muscovy, the remarks likely reflect deep cultural anxieties about the use of tobacco.

Fretting about soldiers' welfare masked more specific economic concerns. Soldiers in Siberia did double duty as military and economic units. Early-modern Russia's reach consistently exceeded its grasp when it came to provisioning the army, especially in Siberia, because the state was land rich but human resources poor. The state's inability to adequately supply its army's needs created a long tradition of soldiers fending for themselves.[50] By plying wares on the side, and carrying some goods with them to sell or barter, soldiers supplemented their meager state incomes. At the same time, however, the state worried that this arrangement created a loophole through which they could lose significant revenue, not only due to soldiers' becoming petty merchants, but, even worse, by acting as middlemen for other merchants who sought to avoid taxes. Such worries were well founded; soldiers regularly transacted business at Siberian customs posts. In the case of tobacco, soldiers escorting exiles from Moscow to Siberia would take tobacco from merchants in Moscow on credit to sell in Siberia as well as to the exiles in their charge.[51] Records from the micro-credit operations of the elite Moscow merchant Gavril Romanov Nikitin reveal soldiers as a substantial portion of his client base, illustrating their involvement in Siberian commerce, and suggesting their established relationships with merchants.[52] Loath as it was to sacrifice profit, the state recognized that soldiers' ability to feed and outfit themselves by their own means alleviated the burden on the state to do so. That is, if the instructions to Siberian towns early in the century insisted that soldiers were not to engage in trade at all, the state soon acquiesced in allowing them to transact business on their own behalf at Siberian customs posts. In time the practice of allowing soldiers to trade up to fifty rubles worth of goods tax-free became official policy.[53]

Another major concern for the state was natives. Although natives of the Americas introduced tobacco to Europeans, it is likely that Europeans introduced tobacco to Eurasian natives. Natives quickly embraced tobacco, but the state did not advocate selling to them. The historian Chulkov paternalistically argued that the state wisely recognized the native proclivity to become addicted to tobacco, and therefore took measures to protect them from it.[54] Although the first articulated fear about tobacco in Siberia concerned soldiers' welfare, the chief concern was that tobacco use among the natives would reduce its fur tributes.[55] Even in the Mikhail Fedorovich's reign, a decline in fur tribute that may have been attributable to tobacco consumption by natives was seen. From the 1640s onward instructions from Moscow regularly ordered administrators to vigilantly ensure that tobacco not be taken into native settlements.[56]

Among native populations that did not submit fur tribute to the tsar, the Muscovite government saw tobacco as a tool in Eurasian steppe politics and used it as a diplomatic gift. In 1657 when Moscow dispatched envoys to trade with China, the Main Treasury in Moscow supplied the envoys with several pounds of tobacco to gift Kalmyk leaders when they passed through their territory.[57]

Towards the end of the century, the state became less opposed to even its own natives using tobacco. In fact, tobacco became an incentive to promote fur tribute payments. The way that state policy shifted over the burning of tobacco further illustrates the ambivalence of the state towards this product.[58] The 1694 instructions to Iakutsk order the provincial administration to punish servitors found with wine, tobacco, or excess wares of their own to trade. The provincial administration should use the confiscated wares towards local needs, give the confiscated wine to natives who pay their fur tribute, and burn the tobacco publicly on the market square.[59] In instructions issued to Nerchinsk in 1696, however, the state insisted that confiscated dice and cards—moral affronts—be burned publicly on the market square, but tobacco and wine were to be kept and given to natives who came and paid their fur tribute.[60] Instructions to Tobol'sk in 1697, however, again instructed officials to burn confiscated tobacco on the market square so that "nobody anywhere would have tobacco."[61]

At the level of enforcement, the illicit leaves of tobacco received more attention and elicited more punishment from Russian law enforcers than did the rhubarb root, whose uses remain unclear but were generally salubrious or domestic (dyeing).[62] For example, a sample of 158 cases in the Siberian town of Tobol'sk during the years 1639–1642 contains a dozen cases of individuals being punished for tobacco possession and/or trade, but none for rhubarb. The beatings meted out evoke the images that Adam Olearius penned of eight men and women in Moscow being beaten for selling tobacco and vodka in 1634.[63]

Most typically, people got the attention of authorities for engaging in trading tobacco, but in five of the twelve cases, possession and/or smoking is the crime listed. Soldiers in the military service were most heavily represented among the punished. Given the worries of the 1620s that tobacco was driving soldiers into debt, this is not surprising. Curiously, Siberian natives and non-Russian locals such as Tatars and Bukharans were not among those punished for tobacco use or trade. This absence is especially curious since Bukharans were particularly active in all trade, and were subject to state justice: the sample of cases includes only five involving Bukharans. While we do not see natives being punished by the Russian justice system for tobacco, Russians from all ranks—townsmen, clerks, soldiers, retired soldiers, Cossacks, merchants, women, peasants, vagrants, an exile (whose fine was waived for his impecuniousness), and provincial nobility—were all among those fined and/or beaten publicly for tobacco offenses from 1639 to 1641. During this time, rhubarb was probably not yet subject to special restrictions, for significant quantities were declared at Siberian customs posts, but later community legal records (as opposed to trade records) do not show people being punished for rhubarb infractions as they were for tobacco trade and use.[64]

What is striking in this small sample of records is how many women are among the punished. In a region where women were in such deficit that the state had hundreds of maidens and widows shipped to Siberia and bachelors sometimes resorted to kidnapping native women for wives, the regular appearance of women among those punished for tobacco crimes seems oddly disproportionate.[65] Whether women were disproportionately involved with tobacco smuggling, or disproportionately monitored remains unclear. Five women were caught and beaten for trading tobacco. In July 1639 Ofimka Sidorova and a Cossack's wife named Ulianka were fined for buying and selling tobacco.[66] On that same day six more individuals, including five men and one woman, were also fined and placed on surety bonds for smoking and selling tobacco.[67] Over a year later, Daritsa Filateva, the widow of a fur man, along with four serving men, were beaten with the knout on the market square for smoking and selling tobacco.[68] Eight months later in July 1641 a similar scenario played out on the same market square when Liubavka, the wife of a Cossack, was beaten along with seven men—this time a mix of servitors and petty merchants, as well as the "men" (slaves or servants) of the governor and a state secretary.[69] In 1706, after tobacco use had been somewhat liberalized but was once again a state-administered monopoly, Iakov Ikonnikov, a townsman in Verkhotur'e, a gateway between Siberia and European Russia, was arrested for stealing tobacco from the peasant woman, Fedota Tomilova.[70]

These 1639–1642 cases point to another constant battle in the state's struggle to regulate the trade of tobacco and prohibited goods: its own servitors were among the most conspicuous violators. For example, in the 1639 case involving the peasant woman Ofimka Sidorova, the four servitors were beaten for taking a bribe of four rubles from Ofimka and releasing her before the party reached the Tobol'sk governor's house.[71] Instructions sent to Tobol'sk, Verkhotur'e, and Nerchinsk are typical in expressing the state's suspicion of its highest servitors.[72] Moscow recognized (in harsh language) that the self-serving schemes of its highest provincial administrators undermined its imperial aims, that those at its disposal to enforce the law were often systematic violators of it. The central government knew that provincial officials let forbidden trade pass unscathed in exchange for bribes, channeled profit to themselves by means that ranged from tinkering with valuations, weights, and reporting, to outright theft and embezzlement, from covert cooperation with merchants to intimidation and bullying of them, but it did not know how to eliminate the inside undermining of its laws.[73]

For all this enforcement, punishment was never as severe as the death penalty promised in the 1633/4 decree. Subsequent orders backpedaled and promised beatings, confiscation, and imprisonment.[74] Reading instructions to Siberian towns closely, one finds that in the event of infractions, governors were instructed to immediately confiscate the contraband and fine, beat, and jail the perpetrators. Next, governors should write to Moscow for further instructions in the case and *then* have the town crier cry out to the public for many days a warning that execution was the punishment.[75] Moreover, that subsequent law codes specify punishments for violations of the tobacco or rhubarb laws further suggests that execution was not employed. The orders sent to Siberian towns do not instruct law enforcers to execute anyone for possession, use, or trade of tobacco or rhubarb. In the case of rhubarb, there was temporary confiscation, forced sale to the state treasury, and a warning, but not one case has been found of rhubarb possessors being beaten or imprisoned. Therefore, it is doubtful that anyone was executed under rhubarb or tobacco laws.

Rather, the state made allowances for ignorance. Instructions to the governor of Tobol'sk about tobacco prohibitions instruct that if people claim they do not know about the restrictions, then take their tobacco, but do not punish them further; rather, inform them so that "in the future they will know."[76] Similar provisions exist in edicts regarding rhubarb: the 1657 edict that threatens the death penalty for rhubarb smuggling also instructs that foreign traders who claim ignorance of the law should have their rhubarb temporarily impounded, to be returned to them when exiting Russia.[77] Russian and Bukharan merchants both took advantage of this ignorance loophole on the Russian frontier. In 1656 a Moscow merchant returning to Russia escaped punishment when he explained that he had been living the year and a half in Kalmyk lands and knew nothing of the new rules.[78] When a party of Bukharans arrived to Tobol'sk to sell rhubarb in the winter of 1655 only to find the state had authorized only a single buyer they were not contrite and petitioned the state to buy their product and cease this hassle.[79] As the Russian proverb states, "The severity of Russian law is meliorated only by the flexibility in its enforcement."[80] That said, we can still appreciate the sustained effort to keep communities clear of tobacco by having the town crier regularly warn the community against its use.

However contradictory, the state backpedaled on its policy of tobacco prohibition.[81] In 1646, the state authorized a merchant to sell over 14,440 pounds of tobacco in Siberia. The authorization, peculiarly, came in the same document that admitted a high-ranking merchant, Kirill Bosov, to the elite merchant corporation. The tobacco was to be officially issued to him, but would be taken to Siberia and sold by his cousin, the merchant Ivan Eremeev and Eremeev's colleagues.[82] In January 1647 Ivan Eremeev, along with a townsman, Ivan Tret'iakov, left Moscow for Siberia with 4,694 pounds of tobacco to sell on the state's behalf.[83] Other evidence reveals that state mechanisms were in place to distribute tobacco. The successful merchant Aleksei Grudtsyn was appointed in 1647 to head Siberian customs collections for salt, tobacco, and wine.[84] The administration in Verkhotur'e was instructed to choose some "sworn men" to help in the project.[85] Later that same year two different merchants were dispatched to Iakutsk to sell tobacco and collect salt taxes.[86] Thus, amidst its own prohibitions, the state authorized individuals to sell tobacco on its behalf and institutionalized oversight of the trade. That the final articles of the Law Code of 1649 address specifically people involved in state authorized tobacco tax-farms and tobacco taverns further demonstrates that a state-sponsored framework existed for the distribution of tobacco throughout Russia.[87] These state administrators, incidentally, were subject to beating, fines, loss of position, but not the death penalty for tobacco infractions.[88]

According to historian Paul Miliukov, the creation of this state monopoly, on a substance considered ungodly and accursed, amounted to fuel for the riots that ignited in Moscow in 1648.[89] Indeed, the cursory description of a drunken incident in June 1642 hints at existing tensions at the perceived inconsistency and unfairness of state regulatory policy. It was just a few days after the summer solstice when the Tobol'sk foot Cossack Kondratii Redozubov got loose-lipped after drinking at the house of the widow Malka Kalinikh. He railed against how it was prohibited to drink homebrewed beer, but other people associated with the state taverns and tobacco houses could trade it. In other words, tobacco and homebrew, theoretically banned substances, were sold in state taverns and tobacco taverns, a hypocrisy not lost on the populace. Later, Kondratii confessed to the remarks although he insisted that he did not remember any of it, since he had been intoxicated at the time. He received a public beating nonetheless.[90]

A prevailing interpretation in Russian history has been that of the patriarchal state—in which the tsar conceived of his domains as his property, a state in which the public and private purse of the ruler were not separate. Siberia, unmarred and unconstrained by the history and negotiations that mediated the tsar's relationship with the neighboring kingdoms that Muscovy gradually incorporated, was to an even greater extent conceived of as the tsar's estate or property. Such an understanding may help explain such inconsistent policy.

In 1664 Tsar Aleksei Mikhailovich called for stepped up consequences for tobacco offenders, but the Siberian tobacco punishments during the remainder of the seventeenth century are fewer and farther between than those under Tsar Mikhail Fedorovich. Enforcement was not abandoned—a provincial noble in Tomsk was caught trading tobacco in 1666;[91] a woman in Tiumen' was punished for smoking in 1686[92]—but it may have been less of a priority, and perhaps less severe. For example, a townsman in Verkhotur'e was fined for selling tobacco in 1648, but it is not clear that he was beaten for it.[93] Rather, where tobacco does surface in criminal records, it is often for theft, such as the case of a Russian stealing tobacco in 1648 or the reported loss from a Bukharan merchant in 1688.[94] Near the turn of the century when Eniseisk provincial gentryman Vasilii Chemesov accused a state investigator of abuses including severe unjustified beating and stealing his things from his house, he included his pipes in the list of items stolen.[95] That Siberian officials took action to prosecute people who stole tobacco implies it respected tobacco as personal property, which acknowledges both the herb's presence in Siberia and the state's acceptance of it. In its actions the state tacitly accepted tobacco's prevalence in ways that peripatetic edicts prohibiting its use could not counteract. Bogoslovskii noted that by Peter's reign Russians had acquired a taste for the "harmless, but impious leaf."[96] Crull, an Englishman in Moscow, wrote that Muscovites were highly keen for the herb.[97] By 1700 non-contract tobacco was sold openly in streets of Pskov and Novgorod.[98] Most tellingly, perhaps, the "rhubarb"[99] that ensued with the Stroganovs when the cash-strapped Russian state issued a tobacco contract to Martyn Bogdanov in 1696 provides further evidence that tobacco was a product for which institutions of distribution, procurement, and consumption, albeit tacit, predated Peter's legalization of tobacco and smoking.[100]

Outsourcing in the form of tax-farms had a long history in Muscovy. The practice resonated with the even older practices of "feeding" (*kormlenie*) that constituted Muscovy's early method for mobilizing men and institutions to channel resources to the state. More often, tax-farms were linked to a particular product, such as grain, alcohol, and eventually tobacco and rhubarb.[101] In some cases, the state tax-farmed out customs collections altogether, such as in the Belosludtskoi borough, a community outside of Verkhotur'e, in 1684.[102] Towards the end of the seventeenth century, the tremendous need for cash to finance a new model army in multiple military conflicts spurred Russia to close deals on tax-farms with specie-rich foreigners.

Rhubarb was a state-administered monopoly from 1657 until probably the late 1670s. There may have been some liberalization during the reign of Tsar Fedor Alekseevich, as state documents speak of monitoring traffic, rather than merely eliminating it. In 1681 the state awarded an exclusive export contract on rhubarb to the Dutch merchant A. A. Gutman. In 1691 the Russian merchant Ivan Isaev secured a domestic tax-farm contract. In 1695, however, the tax-farm was transferred to a merchant from Hamburg, Matvei Poppe.[103] In 1704 the state again took over the rhubarb trade.[104] In 1738 the state made a four-year exclusive supply contract with a Bukharan merchant, Murat Bachim.[105] There were some brief periods of liberalization, but for the most part, a state monopoly remained into the reign of Catherine II.[106]

In the case of tobacco, it appears that in the middle of the century, the state maintained a theoretical monopoly, such as was the case when Ivan Eremeev was issued tobacco through his uncle, the elite merchant Kirill Bosov.[107] As with rhubarb, near the turn of the century, instead of smaller tax-farms to regional merchants and administrators, one finds "national" tobacco tax-farms sold to foreigners such as Martyn Bogdanov (1696) and Lord Carmarthen (1698).[108] In 1705 the state reasserted its control over the tobacco trade, only to have tobacco again given over to tax-farm contracts in the last decade of Peter's reign (1716–1727).[109] While tobacco enjoyed some regime liberalization in other years and places, it remained a tax-farm item in Tiumen' up until the late eighteenth century.[110]

In Siberia, the lines between outsourced tax-farm and centralized, state market-control blurred. For example, since foreigners were prohibited from traveling to Siberia themselves, those who secured tax-farm contracts had to rely on Russian agents east of the Urals to do their bidding. It was not Martyn Bogdanov, but his agent, the Russian Peter Semenov, and others, sometimes even local officials, who were in Siberia selling tobacco on Bogdanov's behalf in 1699.[111] The need to subcontract tobacco duties to Andrei Vinius, the head of the Siberian Office, caused great consternation among the English tobacco contractors.[112]

CONCLUSION

According to the Russian historian P. Smirnov, the "radicalism, breadth, and volume" of the economic policies of the first two Romanovs (Mikhail Fedorovich and Aleksei Mikhailovich) "certainly got the full attention of the observer of social life in the first half of the seventeenth century and forced [him/her] to think that all the country in the period was being mobilized for trade and commerce."[113] This examination of tobacco and rhubarb indeed illustrates how the state's economic aspirations touched the lives of simple men and women in Siberia. Though in different proportions, the state applied similar recipes that included tax-farms, state-administered monopolies, and outright prohibition punctuated by epidodes of liberalized trade. In true mercantilist spirit, it attempted domestic procurement and tried to control the sourcing. The quality-control program established for rhubarb was an innovative measure to "add value" to this transit product.

All of these points demonstrate a dynamic, working state continually modifying its strategies to optimize resource outlays relative to profits garnered. Further, this pragmatism and experimentation in early modern Siberia in some ways anticipates "modern" Russian state policies in which the bottom line trumped other considerations. The dynamism in Russian policy reflects not only the state's internal experimental and activist stance towards the economy but also its responsiveness to its broader international context. Tobacco policy in Moscow began as a reaction to English pressure, and rhubarb laws developed in recognition of Russia's unique position as a bridge between east and west.

But tobacco, with its sinister associations, was a culturally loaded plant in ways that rhubarb was not. The paternalistic language of numerous edicts to the Siberian provinces that repeatedly group tobacco and wine with smuggled trade wares, as well as with such ungodly vices as dice and cards, speak to the state's motives, which were both economic and paternalistic. State policy towards tobacco was steeped in ambivalence. The Muscovite state did conceive of itself as shaping a good, God-fearing society, yet the economic agenda often trumped moral and religious imperatives. In Siberia, the state garnered profit even as it prohibited use. The state desired to keep the "God-hated herb" out of natives' hands until it found tobacco to be a useful incentive in promoting fur tributes. These contradictory policies towards the commodity need not undermine an economic interpretation, but they do reveal more about the cultural role that tobacco played. With rhubarb as well as with tobacco, the strident pronouncements were not matched by severity of action.

This examination of these commodities of vice and virtue in Siberia helps us to appreciate some of the dynamism in early modern world economies. That the state took notice to regulate these commodities was a function of the increasing interconnectedness of the world. That it could add value to rhubarb as it transited from east to west reveals an activist state engaged with the opportunities presented in its broader context. Finally, that over the course of the seventeenth century tobacco went from being a nasty foreign product that Englishmen brought to a plant that highly educated men such as the academician Müller understood came from China, speaks to the consequential investment-driven changes in the early modern economies in which Russia participated.

The shifts of tobacco went beyond geographic provenance and Russia's regulatory regime. As so much of this volume demonstrates, the meanings and implications of tobacco were changing profoundly in Russia. Peter the Great embraced tobacco as part of a Westernization program, and for all its distance eighteenth-century Siberia was increasingly within the orbit of the deliberately European St. Petersburg. And yet, since tobacco reached Tobol'sk from the east in Peter's reign, one wonders with which hemisphere—with which cultural package—the Siberian men and women beaten for tobacco possession there associated their smoke or snuff.

NOTES

1. I would like to express my gratitude to Nancy Kollmann for bringing several relevant tobacco references to my attention, and to the editors, Tricia Starks and Matthew Romaniello, for their inspiring leadership at each stage of this project.
2. G. F. Müller, *Opisanie o torgakh' Sibirskikh*, (St. Petersburg: pri Imperatorskoi Akademii Nauk, 1756), 135.
3. B. G. Kurts, *Sochinenie Kil'burgera o russkoi torgovlie v tsarstvovanie Alekseia Mikhailovicha*, (Kiev: Tip. I. I. Chokolova, 1915), 288.
4. The debate about continental ideology literally elevated the squatty Ural mounains to the status of continental divide in the writings of the historian Tatishchev in the 1730s.
5. For example, the Siberian tax regime did not hew exactly to that of European Russia. The 1653 tax reform, part of a centralization effort that streamlined taxation to a 5% per ruble sales tax, was not enforced in Siberia. The 1663 and 1667 tax reforms were not immediately and/or uniformly enforced in Siberia. In 1680 customs and distillery revenues were transferred to the jurisdiction of the Main Treasury Department for all of Russia except Siberia. For more, see A. Merzon, *Tamozhennye knigi i uchebnoe posobie po istochnikovedenii istorii SSSR*, (Moscow: Krasnyi voin, 1957), chap. 1, esp. 16.
6. Marc Raeff, *Michael Speransky: Statesman of Imperial Russia, 1772–1839*, (The Hague: M. Nijhoff, 1957); Stephen Kotkin, *Magnetic Mountain: Stalinism as Civilization*, (Berkeley, CA: University of California Press, 1995); Evgenii Vodichev, *Siberia's Academic Complex: The History of an Experiment*, (Washington, DC: Woodrow Wilson Center, Kennan Institute for Advanced Russian Studies, 1995).
7. Marco Polo, Henry Yule, Henri Cordier, Amy Frances Yule, *The Book of Ser Marco Polo, the Venetian*, (New York: Scribner's, 1903), 217.
8. See Adolph Caso, *To America and Around the World: The Logs of Christopher Columbus and Ferdinand Magellan*, (Boston: Branden, 2001), 202–03; Christopher Columbus, "Letter to Lord Raphael Sanchez," March 14, 1493, <http://www.wise.virginia.edu/history/wciv1/civ1ref/colum.htm>, accessed July 2, 2008.
9. Lin Zixu Lin Tse-Hsü (1839 CE), "Letter of Advice to Queen Victoria," <http://acc6.its.brooklyn.cuny.edu/~phalsall/texts/com-lin.html>, accessed June 5, 2007.
10. For the notion that the Chinese used rhubarb for incense, veterinary purposes, or fuel, but did not use rhubarb medicinally on humans, see Audrey Burton, *The Bukharans: A Dynastic, Diplomatic, and Commercial History, 1550–1702*, (Surrey, England: Curzon, 1997), 459.
11. Malachy Postlethwayt, *The Universal Dictionary of Trade and Commerce*, 4th ed., 2 vols., (1774; repr., New York: Augustus M. Kelley Publishers, 1971), 2: n.p.
12. Denis Leigh, "Medicine, the City and China," *Medical History*, 18 (1974): 54; Clifford M. Foust, *Rhubarb: The Wondrous Drug*, (Princeton, NJ: Princeton University Press, 1992), 21, 34.
13. Postlethwayt, *Universal Dictionary of Trade and Commerce*, 2: n.p.; Foust, *Rhubarb*, 23, 25.
14. For a description of transport methods by Bukharan merchants in 1653, see former Leningradskoe otdelenie institut istorii, St. Petersburg (henceforth LOII-SPB), f. 187, op. 1, d. 126, l. 1.
15. Burton, *Bukharans*, 457.
16. See Levin and Chrissidis, this volume.

17. Romaniello, this volume.
18. Matthew P. Romaniello, "Through the Filter of Tobacco: The Limits of Global Trade in the Early Modern World," *Comparative Studies in Society and History*, 49 (2007): 915.
19. Erika Monahan, "Russian Rhubarb Reconnaissance: Digging up a Forgotten Episode in Russian History," lecture given at Cherepnin Conference, (Moscow, Russia), November 30, 2005.
20. Redcliffe Salaman, J.G. Hawkes, William Glynn Burton, *The History and Social Influence of the Potato*, (Cambridge: Cambridge University Press, 1985), 113–16, 136.
21. My thinking here owes much to Michael Pollan's recent popularization of the concept of evolutionary success, in Michael Pollan, *The Botany of Desire: A Plant's-Eye View of the World*, (New York: Random House, 2001). See also Michael Pollan, *The Omnivore's Dilemma: A Natural History of Four Meals*, (New York: Penguin Books, 2006), 15–117, 290.
22. The protracted efforts of botanists and the medical establishment to understand rhubarb is admirably examined in Foust, *Rhubarb*.
23. Romaniello, this volume; Jacob M. Price, "The Tobacco Adventure to Russia: Enterprise, Politics, and Diplomacy in the Quest for a Northern Market for English Colonial Tobacco, 1676–1722," *Transactions of the American Philosophical Society*, New Series, 51:1, (1961): 20.
24. S. F. Platonov, *Moskva i zapad*, (Berlin: Obelisk, 1926), 100–05. Price, *Tobacco Adventure*, 7; Romaniello, this volume.
25. Romaniello, this volume.
26. Foust, *Rhubarb*, chap. 3. Most of this rhubarb came from China; the names signify the route the root traveled.
27. P. P. Smirnov, "Ekonomicheskaia politika Moskovskago gosudarstva v XVII veke," in *Russkaia istoriia v ocherkakh i statiakh*, ed. M. V. Dovnar-Zapol'skii, (Kiev: Izd. Knizhnogo magazina N. Ia. Ogloblin, 1912), 402–04.
28. Jarmo Kotilaine, "Mercantilism in Pre-Petrine Russia," in *Modernizing Muscovy: Reform and Social Change in Seventeenth-Century Russia*, ed. Jarmo Kotilaine and Marshall Poe, (New York: RoutledgeCurzon, 2004), 143–74; Romaniello, this volume.
29. Guy Miege, *A Relation of Three Embassies from His Sacred Majestie Charles II to the Great Duke of Muscovie, the King of Sweden, and the King of Denmark*, (London: n.p., 1669), 62.
30. "Reasons for Enlarging and Regulating the Trade To Russia and the Narve," quoted in Jarmo Kotilaine, *Russia's Foreign Trade and Economic Expansion in the Seventeenth Century: Windows on the World*, (Boston: Brill, 2005), 119.
31. Consider, for example, the histories of Anthony Jenkinson and John Merrick of Muscovy. E. Delmar Morgan and C. H. Coote, eds., *Voyages and Travels to Russia and Persia by Anthony Jenkinson and other Englishmen*, vol. 1, (London: The Hakluyt Society, 1886), 108–13; S. M. Solov'ev, "Moskovskie kuptsy v XVII v.," in *Sochineniie v. 18 kn.*, Bk. 20, *Dopolnitel'naia raboty raznykh let*, ed. I. D. Koval'chenko, (Moscow: Mysl', 1996), 504–16.
32. Charles Whitworth, sent to Russia as ambassador and to lobby for English tobacco rights, was kept so busy with tobacco problems that he had little time to respond to the Royal Society of London's questions about rhubarb. See O. J. Frederikson, "Virginia Tobacco in Russia Under Peter the Great," *Slavonic and Eastern European Review*, American Series, 2:1 (March 1943), 48; Foust, *Rhubarb*, 53.
33. L. A. Derbov, "Nachalo diplomaticheskikh i torgovykh otnoshenii Rossii s Kitaem," *Uchenye zapiski*, 68, (Izd. Saratovskogo universiteta, 1959),

103–09; N.F. Demidova and V. S. Miasnikov, *Pervye Russkie diplomaty v Kitae: "Rospis'" I. Petlina i stateinyi spisok F. I. Baikova*, (Moscow: ANSSSR, 1966).
34. *Polnoe sobranie zakonov*, vol. 1 in 40 vols. with 5 additional vols. of indices, (St. Petersburg: n.p., 1830), chap. 25, art. 12, 160, hereafter cited as PSZ 1.
35. Burton, *Bukharans*, 534; Clifford M. Foust, *Muscovite and Mandarin: Russia's Trade With China and Its Setting*, (Chapel Hill: University of North Carolina Press, 1969), 105; James Grehan, "Smoking and 'Early Modern' Sociability: The Great Tobacco Debate in the Ottoman Middle East (Seventeenth to Eighteenth Centuries)," *American Historical Review*, 111:5 (2006): 1353–5.
36. M. Chulkov, *Istoriia zakonodatel'stva tabachnoi promyshlennosti v Rossii do Ekateriny II*, (Kazan': Izd. Knigoprodavtsa Ivana Dubrovina, 1855), 15.
37. *Chteniia v imperatorskom obshchestve istorii i drevnostei rossiiskikh pri Moskovskom universitete*, Bk. 1 (1883), I.11, 37.
38. Bogdanov, *Dym otechestva*, 21.
39. A. N. Kirpichnikov, *Rossii v XVII v. v risunakh i opisanniiakh Gollandskogo puteshestvennika Nikolaasa Vitsena*, (St. Petersburg: Slavia, 1995), 187.
40. Surendra Gopal, *Indians in Russia in the Seventeenth and Eighteenth Centuries*, (Calcutta: Naya Prakash, 1988), 97.
41. Gopal, *Indians*, no. 249, 129–30.
42. For a comment on the rate of economic change in the premodern world, see Jan De Vries, "Economic Growth Before and After the Industrial Revolution: A Modest Proposal," in *Early Modern Capitalism: Economic and Social Change in Europe, 1400–1800*, ed. Maarten Prak, (New York: Routledge, 2001), 177–93.
43. Chulkov, *Istoriia zakonodatel'stva*, 20.
44. PSZ 1, chap. 25, art. 11; M.M. Bogoslovskii, *Petr I: materialy dlia biografii*, vol. 2, ed. V.I. Lebedeva, (Moscow: Ogiz, 1914), 286.
45. Burton writes that Tsar Mikhail Fedorovich prohibited sale of tobacco in Siberia in 1618, although this decree does not survive. Burton, *Bukharans*, 508.
46. Inhaling tobacco was referred to as "drinking" tobacco in seventeenth-century Russia. The term applies to soldiers drinking through their salaries by spending on both tobacco and alcohol.
47. RGADA, f. 214, stb. 16, ll. 410a–415.
48. Chulkov, *Istoriia zakonodatel'stva*, 11; Foust, *Rhubarb*, 47. 1 pud = 36.11 lbs. = 16.4 kg
49. Adam Olearius, *The Travels of Olearius in Seventeenth-Century Russia*, trans. and ed., Samuel H. Baron, (Stanford, CA: Stanford University Press, 1967), 146.
50. See for example Carol Belkin Stevens, *Soldiers on the Steppe: Army Reform and Social Change in Early Modern Russia*, (DeKalb, IL: Northern Illinois University Press, 1995). Army deficits continue into the present: Simon Saradzhyan, "Army Tells Soldiers to Forage for Food," *Moscow Times*, August 15, 1998.
51. RGADA, f. 214, stb. 16, ll. 410a–15.
52. RGADA, f. 214, d. 1128.
53. In 1671 the state decreed that soldiers would be taxed on any goods above fifty rubles, O.N. Vilkov, *Gorod Surgut*, (Novosibirsk: RAN-OLSOII, 1997), 58. The fifty-ruble tax-free exemption was reiterated in 1693, PSZ 3, no. 1474, 160–7.

54. Chulkov, *Istoriia zakonodatel'stva*, 12.
55. For an introduction to this topic see Yuri Slezkine, *Arctic Mirrors: Russia and the Small Peoples of the North*, (Ithaca, NY: Cornell University Press, 1994).
56. RGADA, f. 214, stb. 16, ll. 410–15; PSZ 3, no. 1670, 574 (Instructions to Tara, 1633); PSZ 3, no. 1542, 239 (Instructions to Nerchinsk, 1696); PSZ 3, no. 1590; PSZ 3, no. 1670, 558 (Instructions to Tiumen', 1699).
57. N. F. Demidova and V. S. Miasnikov, comp. *Russko-kitaiskie otnosheniia v XVII veke,* vol. 1, *1608–1683,* ed. S. L. Tikhvinskii, (Moscow: Nauka, 1969), no. 87, 219.
58. Burning rhubarb was also a strategy of state control. For rhubarb, however, the intention was to control supply and quality so as to keep prices high and maximize profit. Beginning in 1737, incoming rhubarb was inspected on the frontier and substandard stock was publicly burned. See Foust, *Rhubarb,* 60.
59. *Akty istoricheskie, sobrannye, izdannye,* (St. Petersburg: Izd. arkheograficheskoi kommissii, 1842), vol. 1, no. 240, 439–40 (Instructions to Iakutsk, 1694).
60. PSZ 3, no. 1542, 247 (Instructions to Nerchinsk. February 18, 1696)
61. PSZ 3, no. 1594, 348. (Instructions to Tobol'sk, September 1, 1697)
62. Kh. Trusevich, *Posol'skie i torgovye snosheniia Rossii s Kitaem*, (Moscow: Tip. T. Malinskogo Moroseika, 1882), 109.
63. Olearius, *Travels of Olearius*, 230–1.
64. O. N. Vilkov, "Bukhartsy i ikh torgovlia," in *Torgovlia gorodov Sibiri kontsa XVI-nachala XX v.*, (Novosibirsk: ANSSSR, 1987), 186.
65. A. Khitrov, *K istorii Irbitskoe iarmarki,* (n.p., 1872), 2.
66. *Chteniia,* I.4, 17.
67. Ibid.
68. Ibid., I.41, 24.
69. Ibid., I.61, 27.
70. RGADA, Description of the Archive Collection of Verkhoturskaia Prikaznaia Izba, f. 1111, op. 2, d. 868, ll. 1–3; G. I. Ivantsova, E. I. Dolgushina, E. A. Perminov, *Tiumenskaia tamozhnia: proshloe i nastoiashchee*, (Tiumen': GATO, 1998), 49.
71. *Chteniia,* I.5, 18.
72. See for example, PSZ 3, nos. 1594, 1595, 1670, esp. no. 1594, 359.
73. For a small sample of such infractions see: RGADA, f. 1111, op. 2, d. 301, ll. 88–105; d. 347, ll. 72–8; d. 416, l. 82; LOII-SPB, f. 28, op. 1, d. 1234 (1666).
74. See Instructions to Tara, 1633: PSZ 3, no. 1670, 574; Instructions to Iakutsk, 1644: *Dopolneniia k akhtam istoricheskim,* 12 vols, (St. Petersburg: Izd. arkheograficheskoi Kommissii, 1846–1872), 2, no. 100, 274, qtd. in Chulkov, 4; Law Code, 1649: PSZ, chap. 25, art. 11–21; Instructions to Iakutsk, 1670: *Akty istoricheskie* 4, no. 209, 451, qtd. in Chulkov, 8; Instructions to Iakutsk, 1694: *Akty istoricheskie* 1, no. 240, 429–42; Instructions to Nerchinsk, 1696: PSZ 3, no. 1542, 247; Instructions to Tobol'sk, 1697: PSZ 3, no. 1594; Instructions to Tiumen', 1699: PSZ 3, no. 1670, 558.
75. PSZ 3, no. 1594, 1697 Instructions to Tobol'sk. The state also instructed the Tobol'sk governor to have the town crier announce prohibitions against rhubarb trading in 1652. See RGADA, f. 214, stb. 414, ll. 1–4.
76. RGADA, f. 214, stb. 16, l. 413.
77. PSZ 1, no. 215, 412–3 (1657); RGADA, f. 214, stb. 414, l. 6 (1658). Although the rhubarb restriction first appears in the Russian law code in 1657, possession, trade, and procurement were prohibited in Siberia from at least 1652. See Monahan, "Russian Rhubarb Reconnaissance."
78. RGADA, f. 214, stb. 499, ll. 210–17.
79. RGADA, f. 214, stb. 462, l. 133.

80. My thanks to Evgenii Victorovich Anisimov at the Institute of History in St. Petersburg, Russia for sharing this Russian proverb.
81. Some historians have noted this, but the matter has yet to be explicitly taken up. Bogoslovskii, *Petr I*, 2: 286–7; Frederikson, "Virginia Tobacco," 40, follows Bogoslovskii's account; Price, *Tobacco Adventure*, 18. Price assumes that the Siberian monopoly was abolished after the 1648 revolts and restored under Tsar Aleksei Mikhailovich.
82. T. B. Solov'eva and T. A. Lapteva, *Privilegirovannoe kupechestvo Rossii vo vtoroi polovine XVI-pervoi chetverti XVIII v. Sbornik dokumentov*, (Moscow: Rosspen, 2004), no. 39, 171.
83. Semenov, *Istoriia predprinimatel'stvo,* 110; RGADA, f. 1111, op. 1, chap. 3, stb. 64/3, ll. 52–4, 60–6.
84. *Akty istoricheskie,* vol. 4, no. 19.
85. RGADA, Description to the Archival Collection of the Verkhoturskaia Prikaznaia Izba, see f. 1111, op. 1, pt. 3, stb. 64, ll. 52–4, 60–6.
86. DAI, vol. 3, (Moscow, 1848), 98–9.
87. PSZ 1, chap. 25, art. 16, 17, 21. The tobacco "sworn man" on the books in the town of Ustiug in 1648, when tobacco was already technically illegal in central Russia, shows that this was not a Siberia-specific occurrence. See S. A. Iazykov, "'Vybori' posadskikh obshchin Sibiri XVII-nachala XVIII v. kak istoricheskii istochnik," in *Istochniki po istorii obshchestvennogo soznanaiia i literatury perioda feodalizma*, ed. N.N. Pokrovskii, (Novosibirsk: Nauka Sib. Otd., 1991), 167.
88. PSZ 1, chap. 5, art. 16–21.
89. Paul Miliukov, *History of Russia,* vol. 1: *From the Beginnings to the Empire of Peter the Great*, (New York: Funk & Wagnalls, 1968), 151.
90. *Chteniia,* I.102, 33.
91. *Russko-Mongol'skie otnosheniia, 1654–85*, no. 71.
92. LOII-SPB, Description of the Archive Collection of the Tiumenskaia voevodskaia kantseliariia. See, f. 187, op. 1, dd. 796–823.
93. LOII-SPB, f. 28, d. 438, l. 2.
94. RGADA, f. 214, stb. 134, l. 77v.; Burton, *Bukharans*, 381.
95. RGADA, f. 1111, op. 2, d. 599, l. 7.
96. Bogoslovskii, *Petr I*, vol. 2, 286.
97. Price, *Tobacco Adventure*, 19.
98. Frederiksen, "Virginia Tobacco," 45. NB: Frederiksen and Price overstate Aleksei's conservatism. For an account that appreciates his relative liberality, see Philip Longworth, *Alexis: Tsar of All the Russias,* (London: Secker & Warburg, 1984).
99. One tertiary definition for rhubarb is "argument or quarrel."
100. PSZ 3, no. 1622.
101. R. I. Kozintseva, "Uchastie kazny vo vneshnei torgovle Rossii," *Istoricheskie zapiski*, 91 (1973), 267–337.
102. Merzon, *Tamozhennye knigi,* 20. See LOII, f. 28, op. 1, karton 8, l. 2.
103. Foust, *Rhubarb,* 48–50.
104. Ibid., 51, cites PSZ 4, no. 1967.
105. Ibid., 62.
106. Kozintseva, "Uchastie kazny vo vneshnei torgovle Rossii," 320; Foust, *Rhubarb,* 50–60, 76.
107. Solov'eva and Lapteva, *Privilegirovannoe kupechestvo Rossii,* 171.
108. PSZ 3, nos. 1580, 1607, 1628. Prior to the Bogdanov tax-farm, in 1695, Peter seems to have issued smaller local rights to sell tobacco to the foreigners Patrick Gordon, (James) Jacob Bruce, Thomas Fadenbracht (van de Bracht). See Price, *Tobacco Adventure*, 20.

109. Ivantsova et al., *Tiumenskaia tamozhnia*, 49.
110. Ibid.
111. RGADA, f. 1111, op. 2, d. 611, l. 43; see also RGADA, Description of Archival Collection for Verkhoturskaia Prikaznaia Izba, f. 1111, op. 1, pt. 3, stb. 196, ll. 297–9.
112. Price, *Tobacco Adventure*, 52.
113. Smirnov, "Ekonomicheskaia politika XVII v.," 404.

6 "I Smoke, Therefore I Think"

Tobacco as Liberation in Russian Nineteenth-Century Literature and Culture

Konstantine Klioutchkine

During much of the nineteenth century, the consumption of tobacco in Russia was associated with the educated people of the upper and middle classes who adopted the habits and mores characteristic of Western-style secular society. The distinctive aspect of the history of Russian smoking was the relatively slow pace of tobacco's penetration beyond the educated elites, metropolitan areas, and major trade routes. An expensive and primarily imported product in an expansive country whose communication infrastructure unavoidably lagged behind those of its Western counterparts, tobacco took a relatively long time to permeate rural areas. Moreover, the Russian Orthodox Church and, to a lesser but significant extent, the government saw smoking as seditious with regard to religious and social norms of native life.

Associated with a violation of—or liberation from—traditional social conventions, smoking came to serve as an index of a person's participation in the modernizing secular society, in which individual life was a matter of personal choice rather than religious prescription, state regulation, social origin, or professional affiliation. The distinction between modernity and tradition was particularly apparent in the attitudes towards smoking from the institution of medicine as opposed to that of the Church. Whereas the Church viewed smoking as sinful, many in medicine regarded it as beneficial if pursued in moderation, prescribing tobacco for a variety of infirmities, such as headaches, toothaches, anxiety, and constipation.[1] Doctors appearing in nineteenth-century fiction tended to smoke, reflecting the attitudes of their own institution as well as those of literature.[2] Concerned with expressing and describing non-conformist individuality and, like smoking, finding itself under pressure from conservative social forces, literature had a special interest in exploring the manifestations of modernity in the representative habits of quotidian life.

The institutional conflict of interest inherent in literary representations of smoking contributes to, rather than detracts from, their value in providing material for understanding the cultural attitudes to tobacco in nineteenth-century Russia. Although in the course of the century smoking became an increasingly important aspect in the country's social, economic, and political life, our knowledge of tobacco consumption during that period is only fragmentary. Falling under the formerly neglected category of everyday life, this topic is only now beginning to receive sustained attention from historians.[3] The limited nature of documentary information about tobacco has made this topic difficult to address within the perspectives of social, economic, or political history. By contrast, cultural history, relying on an extensive and coherent corpus of references to smoking in canonical literature can shed significant light on the prevalent trends in the use of tobacco, and, more pertinently, on the meanings Russian culture associated with this increasingly pervasive commodity.

Moreover, the value of literature for the study of nineteenth-century smoking derives from its formative cultural role. From the opening decades of the century until the 1880s, literature was the primary medium for representing, creating, and disseminating cultural trends among educated Russians. At the turn of that decade, literature began to yield its formative role to mass newspapers, popular illustrated magazines, self-help publications, as well as to various forms of advertising.[4] Considering the change in the status of literature, the discussion of Russian attitudes to smoking after the turn of the 1880s belongs in a separate study and is addressed in this volume in the essay by Tricia Starks. By the time literature yielded some of its power to shape opinion, however, most of the nineteenth-century Russian literary canon, with the exception of Chekhov's oeuvre, had been completed. The representations of smoking in canonical texts, which are the focus of the present study, have had a lasting influence on Russian cultural perceptions and continue to exert this influence on readers to the present day.

Although nineteenth-century Russia differed from the West in that its vast territories and strong traditions hindered the proliferation of tobacco, the country was in step with European trends pertaining to the relative popularity of the distinct methods of its use. The taking of snuff, prominent in the eighteenth century, quickly went out of fashion thereafter. Pipes, the main tool of tobacco consumption since its introduction to the country in the seventeenth century, continued to be prevalent in the nineteenth, but gradually lost their popularity to cigars and especially cigarettes. Cigars became fashionable in the 1820s and reached the height of their appeal in the 1840s and 1850s. Cigarettes appeared in the 1830s and steadily gained ground on the rest of tobacco products to become the leading form of smoking in the early 1900s.

In developing the core meanings associated with these four methods of tobacco consumption, Russia also conformed to the European trends. In literary presentations, snuff and chewing tobacco were increasingly seen as anachronistic and became relegated to the lower classes. Cigars, the most expensive tobacco product, consistently signified worldly success and high social status, strongly tinged with connotations of profligate opulence. Cigarettes came to be associated with youthful energy when they rose to prominence during the Crimean War of 1853–1856. Pipes, as the dominant and the most varied form of tobacco consumption, encompassed the widest range of meanings, including those associated with cigars and cigarettes. Pipe smoking, the prevalent method of tobacco consumption during the Romantic age, inspired paradigmatic associations between all forms of smoking and individual freedom.

From the foundation of these shared attitudes, Russian literary culture came to ascribe to smoking a range of particularly intense meanings, whose development is the focus of this chapter. Smoking, and especially the smoking of cigarettes, symbolized the emancipation of personality from traditional social norms and political constraints. Furthermore, from the middle of the century onward, literature increasingly encouraged readers to select particular tobacco products and to develop special smoking habits in order to display their progressive ideology and politics.

SNUFF

Increasingly antiquated, the taking of snuff served as a benchmark against which other forms of smoking would come to develop their own distinct meanings in the course of the nineteenth century. Following European trends, snuff became fashionable in Russia during the reign of the empresses Elizabeth (1741–1762) and Catherine (1762–1796), who were avid snuff-takers themselves.[5] By contrast, the century's male emperors, Peter the Great and Paul I, preferred pipes, and the reign of the latter brought the popularity of snuff to a close at the turn of the 1800s. During the subsequent decades, snuff became associated with the ancien-régime culture of the previous century (for example, figure 6.1). Accordingly, literature portrayed snuff-taking as a quaint habit of older women. Alexander Pushkin's story *The Queen of Spades* (1834) established the paradigmatic example by featuring an elderly countess who faithfully maintains the habits she developed during her youth in the 1770s.[6] Her snuffbox serves as a symbol of an antiquated world based on a rigid social hierarchy and firmly regimented behavior. Fedor Dostoevsky drew on Pushkin's example in his novel *The Insulted and the Injured* (1861) in his portrayal of the elderly Countess K., whose snuffbox and lapdog double as markers of her anachronism. In the same novel, Dostoevsky ascribes snuff-taking to the deceased grandfather of the novel's female protagonist. In a dream, she imagines that her function with respect to her ancestor involves collecting alms in order to sustain him with tobacco.[7]

Figure 6.1 Snuffbox with a portrait of Field Marshal Zakhar Chernyshev, 1773 (St. Petersburg, Russia). Georg Kuntzendorf (attr.); Alexander Roslin (after); gold, silver, enamel, four-color gold; miniature (on copper?); h. 1–7/16 in., w. 3–1/4 in., d. 2–1/2 in. Hillwood Estate, Museum and Gardens; bequest of Marjorie Merriweather Post, 1973; (acc. no. 11.33). Photo by E. Owen, reprinted with permission.

The meaning of snuff as a sign of the past available to contemporaries only in fantasies and dreams formed the core premise of Vladimir Odoevskii's tale *A Town in A Snuff-Box* (1834). This tale describes the descent of a boy into a diminutive town located in his father's musical snuffbox. Fascinated by an image enameled on its lid, the boy falls into reverie and finds himself in a world whose participants are governed by their functions in a musical mechanism. The dream ends as the boy inadvertently interferes with the mechanism's operation, marking his own transition from the order of an imaginary community to the chaos of real-life individuation. The reference to snuff creates the aura of patriarchal coherence bound to dissolve in a changing world.

The association between snuff and the regimented premodern society was reinforced by the imperial tradition of bestowing snuffboxes on subjects who earned distinction in the eyes of the tsar.[8] Such snuffboxes, adorned with portraits of celebrated military or government figures, had the power to insert their otherwise socially inferior owners into an ostensibly coherent world of the Russian state. This cultural mechanism provided the material for Nikolai Gogol's portrayal of the absurdity of bureaucratic existence in his story *The Overcoat* (1842). A snuffbox figures as a possession of the tailor Petrovich, who, evoking Peter the Great as a creator of Russian bureaucracy, supplies an overcoat and, therefore, an identity to the petty clerk Akakii Akakievich. Petrovich's snuffbox used to feature a picture of a general, but this symbol of social organization became obliterated through use.[9] This detail highlights the story's overall import as a narrative of Akakii's abandonment in a regimented impersonal world that is no longer able to invest the life of its subjects with meaning. Gogol's Petersburg stories consistently use the theme of snuff-taking in order to convey social inferiority by ascribing it to those who rely on obsolescent cultural practices, such as a military officer, an alcoholic barber, and a petty newspaper clerk in *The Nose* (1836) as well as German cobbler and blacksmith in *Nevsky Prospect* (1835).

Evoking rigid hierarchies of the past, snuff-taking was associated with those who found themselves on the margins of society, including elderly women and men, members of the lower urban classes, and petty government officials. Snuff-taking marked their futile attempts to gain the meaning of individual existence by way of inscribing themselves into a bygone traditional world. In contrast to the consumption of snuff, smoking came to signify overcoming traditional conventions, manifesting individuality, and, in the extreme, expressing commitment to progress toward a society in which everyone can be free.

PIPE SMOKING IN THE ROMANTIC AGE

After yielding ground to snuff-taking during the eighteenth century, pipe smoking regained cultural prominence at the beginning of the nineteenth. Increasingly fashionable during the Romantic era, pipe smoking evoked contemporary associations with the liberation of the individual. In Russia, the meanings of tobacco consumption evolved in the context of particularly strong taboos on smoking in traditional social spheres. Prohibited by the Church, banned from military institutions, and forbidden in public spaces, smoking was also impermissible in polite society, the company of ladies, and the family circle. These prohibitions helped to define smoking as expressive of the freedom a person experienced once he, and increasingly she, escaped traditional conventions and became an independent and individual agent in his or her own life. The association between smoking and the emancipation of personality flourished during the age when the Romantic emphasis on the individual combined with the growing social freedoms of the gentry, as well as with the development of commerce, monetary economy, and the culture of consumption. The lasting impact of the Romantic association between smoking and individuality should be attributed to the growing development of literature and the press, which codified the meanings of social practices and continued to broadcast them throughout the century and beyond.

Nineteenth-century attitudes to smoking took shape when the pipe became a characteristic emblem of Romantic culture and a distinctive attribute of a Romantic hero. Smoking evoked intellectual independence, which distinguished an individual from the rest of society. This core meaning found expression in a central text of Romantic philosophical fiction, Vladimir Odoevskii's *Russian Nights* (1843), which notes that in order to understand why humans smoke one needs to recognize that animals do not.[10] This comment finds an explanation in another formative Romantic text, Alexander Bestuzhev-Marlinskii's tale *The Test* (1830):

> Plato believes that man is a two-legged animal without feathers. The physiologists think that he is unique because he can drink or love whenever he wants [. . .] In our smoky age, I would define man in a far more distinctive way by saying that he is "an animal who smokes, *animal fumens*" [. . .] I will not stop with this, as I have a passion for philosophy [. . .] "I think, therefore I am," says Descartes. "I smoke, therefore I think," say I.[11]

Within the Romantic worldview, smoking signified the ability for independent intellection, which endowed man with individuality and made him distinct not so much from animals, as the above comments ironically suggest, but rather from the majority in a traditional society, seen as incapable of and uninterested in independent thought.

Independence of mind related to other aspects of Romantic personality, which, in connection with smoking, received an extensive description in Nikolai Pavlov's tale *Masquerade* (1839):

> I once observed Levin [the hero of the tale] in a moment of extreme excitement. Looking at him today, you would not believe that he was capable of inspiration provoked by mathematical conclusions of the mind or by hopes for the future [. . .] I used to visit him daily, and he greeted me in the same dry and indifferent manner characteristic of old friendship based on regular meetings. Half asleep in his armchair, he would quietly turn his head and extend his arm, saying: "Oh, hello! Please sit down! Would you like a pipe or a cigar?" Such was the beginning of our every conversation. He exuded an air of terrifying grandeur and sadness, beyond my ability to divert.[12]

The characteristically Romantic traits of Pavlov's hero include his ability for independent thought and strong feeling, penchant for solitary contemplation, and disappointment in social life.

In the context of the Romantic hero's avoidance of convention, smoking became emblematic of alternative and primarily non-pragmatic modes of life. At its logical extreme, this attitude became associated with aesthetically inflected fantasies, often associated with smoking, as in the following passage from Pavlov's tale *The Auction* (1835):

> "Hand me a pipe, light up the logs in the fireplace, and take away the lamp!" said T. [to his valet] [. . .] After taking off his jacket, T. turned over the embers while his pipe emitted a thick wave of smoke. Magical rays traversed the darkness in the room, illuminating the paintings and engravings on the walls. Phantoms of imagination [. . .] suddenly began to appear and disappear.[13]

As a symbol of aesthetically-charged contemplation, smoking became a stock device that framed storytelling in Romantic prose, which commonly relied on tales exchanged in a company of friends. The lighting of a pipe by a narrator or a listener indicated the beginning of a new tale, emphasized its important points, and, finally, marked its conclusion.[14] Beyond the narrative itself, references to smoking invited readers to disengage from routine social concerns and to join with other individuals, or with a book, in an alternative space of genuine intellectual and emotional communion.

Whereas in prose, references to smoking framed storytelling, in poetry they figured as a regular feature in a friendly epistle, one of the more informal genres of the time, and were frequent, for instance, in Pushkin's verse.[15] In his *Epistle to Delvig* (1827) the reference to smoking comes to symbolize the unconventional personality of the addressee, who is portrayed with a pipe and in the clouds of tobacco smoke.[16] The epistle's Delvig jettisons military service and career aspirations in favor of the arts, sciences, and philosophy, confirming his reputation in the Pushkin circle as a person who preferred Romantic contemplation over traditional noble occupations.

The most intense manifestation of Romantic rebellion against convention was associated with demonism. A representative demonic figure of Romantic prose is the protagonist of Pushkin's story *The Shot* (1830). Silvio stands in symbolic opposition to the institution of marriage as he plots to avenge an offence only after his offender marries. Pushkin's description of Silvio uses the theme of smoking in order to emphasize his demonic resolve: "Gloomy pallor, sparkling eyes, and thick smoke emanating from his mouth made him appear as a genuine devil."[17]

Evoking modes of existence that were at odds with convention, Romantic smoking developed its meanings in the shadow of one of the most regimented institutions of the time, the army. Gentry men responsible for establishing attitudes to smoking were expected to serve, and the army functioned as a crucible of male identity. Forbidden during the performance of military duties, smoking became emblematic of substantive rather than formal aspects of a nobleman's existence. It evoked the spirit of friendship that was deeper than the one defined purely by military association. In the epigraph to Bestuzhev-Marlinskii's aforementioned tale *The Test*, smoking signals the friendly community of gentlemen-officers by referring to the author's own poem *The Toast* (1829). In this hymn to male friendship, "the fragrant pipe smoke" figures as a symbol of "the family of dear brothers, a constellation of friends."[18] Besides evoking genuine human bonds, military smoking was emblematic of individual excellence in battle. Exemplifying this aspect of smoking, Denis Davydov, a famous guerrilla of the Napoleonic War and later a champion of noble independence from the state, was commonly portrayed with a pipe (Figure 6.2). The most influential military smoker as well as a notable model of

Figure 6.2 Portrait of Denis Davydov. From *Istoricheskii vestnik*, no. 7, 1890.

noble masculinity, Davydov was also a poet, and two of his representative poems about hussar life open with references to pipes.[19]

In the context of conventional social regimes, Romantic smoking became associated with noble independence of spirit, the passion for intellectual activity, and the cult of friendship. Beginning in the 1830s, the pipe became a prominent feature of diverse philosophical circles and literary salons, such as the ones surrounding Nikolai Stankevich, Vladimir Odoevskii, and even the Maikov family, whose meetings transpired in an atmosphere of thick tobacco smoke.[20] In such contexts, smoking became a marker of the Russian version of what Jürgen Habermas described as a nascent public sphere distinct from traditional social institutions and state supervision, a sphere in which self-actualizing individuals came together for cultural, aesthetic, philosophical, and increasingly political discussions.[21]

THE PIPE, CIGAR, AND CIGARETTE AT MID-CENTURY

If during the Romantic era smoking was more common among the upper metropolitan strata, by the 1840s it had extended to all walks of city life, all ranks of the army, most provincial cities, and many country estates.[22] The pipe, formerly the exclusive mode of smoking, had been joined by the cigar and cigarette. For the representation of smoking in Russian culture, another development was no less important: literature, which had privileged aesthetically appealing aspects of gentry life, now expanded its focus to the ordinary existence of all social classes. In a concurrent development, smoking acquired a new meaning as one of the more democratic habits available to all males except those in the more traditional walks of life, namely, the peasants and the clergy. Initially, this new meaning came to be associated with the pipe as the most broadly available form of tobacco consumption. Seen now as democratically commonplace, the pipe ceded the distinctive meanings it had acquired during the Romantic era for further development by the cigar and the cigarette.

From the 1840s onward, the democratic nature of pipe smoking associated it with the lives of professional men of the middle and lower classes, such as lower-rank army officers and bureaucrats, as well as merchants, artisans, traders, and even servants. Pipe smoking was seen as a positive attribute of a modest professional man, signifying his ability to perform his work in an unhurried and effective manner. A modest captain Maksim Maksimovich from Mikhail Lermontov's *A Hero of Our Time* (1841) is an exemplary representative of this type as a highly professional, good-natured, but rather narrow-minded man. Captain Godnev in Aleksei Pisemskii's novel *A Thousand Souls* (1858) inherits from Lermontov's hero not only his passion for the pipe but also his good nature and strong moral fiber, combined with an unsophisticated outlook on life. Similarly, Captain Tushin in Leo Tolstoy's *War and Peace* (1860s) displays both a penchant for the pipe and the distinctions of a modest and effective military professional.[23]

Descending the social scale, the pipe was yielding its space at the top of the hierarchy to the cigar. Since its appearance at the turn of the 1830s, the cigar has been the most expensive form of smoking in contrast to the pipe and the cigarette whose price and refinement depended on the quality of tobacco and paraphernalia. Accordingly, cigar smoking was limited to the more affluent segments of society. Borrowing from the pipe its association with noble individualism and aesthetic refinement, the cigar came to signify upper-class elegance and worldly success. The process of transition from the pipe to the cigar is evident in Lermontov's *A Hero of Our Time*. The novel's protagonist, the exemplary dandy Pechorin, smokes both pipes and cigars. However, the author's main description of the hero, emphasizing his elegance and high social status, features him receiving a box of cigars from his valet.[24]

Although the cigar primarily implied worldly success, it could retain the pipe's Romantic associations with freedom and non-conformist socialization. One of the most influential memoirs of the century, Alexander Herzen's *My Past and Thoughts*, describes cigars as common among the upper classes as early as the turn of 1830s and uses them as markers of his worldview as a young man. Herzen remembers that as a teenager he repeatedly evaded adult supervision in order to share a cigarillo with his close friend poet Nikolai Ogarev.[25] In such moments, the cigar symbolized the cult of Romantic friendship as well as an escape from the constraints of traditional society. Highlighting these implications, Herzen writes that during his brief incarceration in the Moscow University's Detention Center in 1832 his friends brought him cigars and wine so as to relieve him from the tedium of his ordeal as well as to celebrate their values.[26] Developing the implications of smoking in the political arena, Herzen's cigar signifies the spirit of human dignity and individual freedom in a text that proved formative for many readers committed to intellectual, political, and human emancipation. In addition to these political associations, however, the reference to the cigar contributed to the image of Herzen as a wealthy and self-indulgent nobleman. This implication became particularly relevant to the next generation of progressive men and women who related cigars, as opposed to cigarettes, to morally questionable self-indulgence.[27]

The meaning of the cigar as a sign of upper-class elegance received representative treatment from Ivan Panaev, an author whose journalism and fiction were influential in establishing fashion trends during the 1840s and 1850s. His *Essay on Dandies* (1854–1857) portrayed the cigar as a permanent attribute of wealthy and elegant men. Contrasting the habits among the wealthy to those among the nascent aesthetic elite, Panaev's *Essay* indicated that the association the Romantic pipe had had with artistic activity failed to extend to the cigar. Portraying the meetings at the art salon of the aforementioned Maikov family, Panaev referred to pipes and cigarettes instead of the fashionable cigars.[28]

From the turn of the 1860s onward, the association with wealth and noble elegance extended from cigars to expensive cigarettes. Addressing this trend, Ivan Turgenev's novel *Smoke* (1864) described Russian aristocratic men and women as smoking cigarettes while at the resort of Baden-Baden, revealing their vain desire to appear current with the latest trends in European fashion.[29] This psychological detail is related to smoke as the organizing metaphor of the novel as a whole: the text suggested that the pursuit of European trends both in fashion and in intellectual life clouded the judgment of Russian educated classes.

On a moral rather than analytical note, Leo Tolstoy ascribed both cigar and cigarette smoking to Stiva Oblonsky as well as to other noble characters in *Anna Karenina*. A director of a government office, Oblonsky indicates his fashionable commitment to liberal values by displaying a pack of cigarettes in front of his subordinates and then proceeding to step out of the building for a smoke. While noting the liberal implications of Oblonsky's gesture, the novel focuses on the theme of moral corruption its author associates with tobacco.[30] The negative attitude to smoking in *Anna Karenina* foreshadowed Tolstoy's unequivocal disparagement of the habit in his last novel *Resurrection* (1899) as well as in his late didactic texts. His *Christian Teaching* (1895) and *Life Path* (1910) draw on the traditional religious view of smoking as sinful and treat it as representative of any kind of intoxication, including those by alcohol and opium, all of which obscure man's moral judgment.[31]

Whereas in his later works Tolstoy disparaged smoking, his early masterpiece *Sebastopol Stories* (1856) focused on classifying pipes, cigarettes, and cigars by the moral and social type of smoker. Pipes emerged as a habit of common soldiers and lower-rank officers, reflecting the growing link between this form of smoking and the lower classes.[32] Cigarettes became an attribute of frontline officers of gentry background whose psychology and heroism were the foci of Tolstoy's stories.[33] This form of smoking symbolized youthful vigor and noble bearing in the face of danger. Finally, cigars were characteristic of staff and high-ranking officers and indicated their self-indulgent turpitude even in the context of a national tragedy.[34]

The proliferation of tobacco in the middle of the nineteenth century brought about the development of new meanings of smoking. However, the Romantic associations between smoking and individual distinctions remained influential. Pipes now tended to imply effectiveness in the performance of middle and lower-class professional tasks, cigars indicated elevated social status, and cigarettes signified youthful vigor, progressive views, or aesthetic inclinations.

The increasing variety in the forms of tobacco consumption requires a discussion of the terms used to refer to cigarettes and cigars. Unlike the consistently expensive cigars, cigarettes varied greatly in kind, quality, and price, causing the Russian language to develop a range of words for this commodity. The standard term for a cigarette in the second half of the century was *papirosa*, which referred both to cigarettes one rolled oneself and to those one purchased pre-rolled. *Papirosa* tended to refer to those rolled in various kinds of paper. For those rolled in tobacco leaf and similar to a small cigar, known in Europe as *cigarillo*, Russian also reserved the term *sigarka*. By contrast, the substandard *tsigarka* was used by the lower classes to refer to any kind of cigarette. Finally, the words *pakhitoska* and *papil'etka* designated thinly rolled elegant cigarettes smoked exclusively by women. The French word *cigarette* did not enter common Russian usage until the twentieth century.

THE CIGARETTE AND PROGRESSIVE LIBERATION

From mid-century onward, the main trend in cultural implications of smoking involved the rising prominence of the cigarette. Signifying youthful vigor, energy, independence, as well as a measure of elegance and artistic inclination, the cigarette was available to consumers of diverse economic means and social classes. Across Europe, the cigarette's rise to prominence began during the Crimean War (1853–1856), which occasioned a shift in male fashion toward the scruffy look inspired by the appearance of military officers in the field of war. The first major war to be recorded in photographs, the Crimean campaign had a particularly spirited influence on European public imagination. In Russia, the effect of the war was especially strong as it immediately preceded the era of Great Reforms of Alexander II. The overwhelming desire for liberation from the constraining patriarchal regime of Nicholas I precipitated the emancipation of the serfs, the relaxation of censorship, court reform, economic liberalization, as well as the rise of the non-noble classes and the proliferation of radical ideology among the educated youth. Whereas across Europe the cigarette signified vigor and youthfulness, in Russia it also evoked wholesale social modernization.

Expressive of the desire for change, smoking became an important aspect in the self-fashioning of progressive men and women. When in the spirit of liberal reforms the government lifted the ban on smoking in the streets in 1865, this deregulation engaged the longstanding association between smoking and individual freedom. Nikolai Nekrasov quipped, "In my old age, I found happiness: I smoked in the street and wrote without censorship."[35] In everyday life, the authorization to smoke related to the abolition of university uniforms as well as to the permission for students, government officials, and military officers to grow facial hair. Progressive young men grew beards and shoulder-length hair, wore broad-brimmed hats and long cloaks, and carried crude walking sticks. Women turned to masculine articles of dress, cut their hair short, wore glasses, and intentionally neglected to clean their nails. For both men and women, the smoking of *papirosy*, punctuated by purposeful slovenliness in disposing of tobacco and cigarette butts, became part of the stylistic vocabulary that emphasized egalitarian coarseness of behavior and appearance.[36] This everyday aspect of radical life was registered in the painting *A Party* (1875) by Konstantin Makovskii, portraying people of diverse social backgrounds engaged in a political discussion. Nearly half of the dozen assembled characters smoke, and the floor depicted in the foreground is conspicuously bestrewn with cigarette butts.

Starting at the turn of the 1860s, representations of progressive men and women consistently mentioned smoking. Turgenev, characteristically sensitive to the ways in which details of human behavior expressed cultural and social change, captured the role of smoking as a symbol of radical ideology in his influential novel *Fathers and Sons* (1861). Bazarov, the prototypical "new man" of the novel, is an inveterate smoker of cheap cigarillos or a pipe. His noble friend Arkadii Kirsanov fails to adopt democratic habits and prefers cigars. Kukshina, to display her commitment to radical values, rolls her own cigarettes. In keeping with radical style, Kukshina is unkempt and slovenly dressed, her fingers are brown from constant smoking, and her room is littered with cigarette butts as well as with reading materials of radical persuasion. Kukshina's male double Sitnikov claims that his sybaritic penchant for cigars and champagne, reminiscent of Herzen's *My Past and Thoughts*, does not prevent him from maintaining progressive views.[37] Whereas Turgenev's *Fathers and Sons* portrays a measure of variation in the smoking habits at an early stage in the formation of new behavioral norms, his novel *Virgin Soil*, describing the standards that have become well-defined by the time of its publication in 1877, is unequivocal in ascribing only cigarettes to the truly progressive intelligentsia heroes.[38]

Seen as a requisite attribute of a progressive man, cigarette smoking figures as a representative feature of such characters as Kalinovich in Pisemskii's *A Thousand Souls*, Razumikhin in Dostoevsky's *Crime and Punishment* (1866), as well as an entire range of radical figures in Nikolai Leskov's *Nowhere* (1864). A remarkable deviation from this overarching trend occurs in Nikolai Chernyshevsky's novel *What is to Be Done* (1863), which became an enormously influential blueprint for the everyday life of new men and women. Chernyshevsky's protagonists are committed smokers, but they smoke cigars rather than egalitarian cigarettes. This aberration is representative of a tension in Chernyshevsky's novel and, more broadly, in his view of the nature of radical activity. On the one hand, Chernyshevsky advocated self-effacing effort on behalf of the oppressed, but on the other he believed that the engine of social progress was powered by individual self-interest. As a person of non-gentry origin, Chernyshevsky associated self-interest with the pleasures that had already been available to the nobility, whose elegant habits stimulated his middle-class imagination.[39]

While following his blueprints for social commitment, Chernyshevsky's radical followers rejected his vision of self-indulgence. In the progressive worldview, a penchant for cigars, as an index of ideologically inappropriate desire for upper-class pleasures, became indicative of deviation from radical principles. Observing this attitude in the culture of the 1870s, Turgenev used it to organize the narrative of *Virgin Soil*.[40] The novel tests the commitment of its radical heroes by tempting them with aristocratic cigars. Whereas the strong hero Nadezhdin resists the temptation, the weaker Paklin yields to it, revealing the plan for radical insurrection to government authorities.[41] Trying to determine what caused him to betray his friends, Paklin realizes that he had done it "for a good cigar."[42] As government authorities disperse the radical community, the only progressive hero who remains functional in the novel's world subscribes to the gradualist view. This hero, Solomin, does not believe in rebellion and instead pursues "small deeds" for the benefit of the downtrodden. In everyday life, Solomin's gradualist vision allows him to indulge in upper-class habits. As a sign of such indulgence, Solomin accepts the gift of expensive cigars, without, however, yielding his independence.[43] Turgenev's view of the progressive intelligentsia in *Virgin Soil* became a focus of intense critical polemic, which questioned the ideological and moral implications of Solomin's position, symbolized in the novel by his smoking of both cigars and cigarettes.[44]

Literary representations of smoking during the 1860s and 1870s articulated the new ideological implications inherent in the choices between distinct forms of tobacco consumption. Yet literature also focused on the ambivalence involved in the day-to-day practices adopted by smokers. Although progressive stylistic vocabulary prescribed slovenly cigarette smoking and discouraged cigars, the members of the democratic intelligentsia often found cigars exceedingly appealing and, moreover, could associate the smoking of cigars with ideological flexibility. Ambivalence of a different kind characterized smoking choices among the nobility. Although cigars tended to signify worldly success and elegance as well as support for the established social regime, the nobles could turn to cigarettes in order to signify their democratic sympathies or in order to pursue trends in European fashion. A similar dynamic distinguishing the straightforward ideological implications and the ambivalent meanings of social practices emerged in the portrayal of smoking among women.

SMOKING AND WOMEN

A striking aspect in the literary portrayals of the "new people" of the 1860s and 1870s was that women smoked as much, if not more, than men. In keeping with the overarching association between smoking and emancipation, smoking by women expressed their independence from the expectation that they perform traditional roles of wives and mothers. From the perspective of conventional morality, however, the emancipation of women was associated with moral corruption and, more specifically, with sexual promiscuity.

With regard to the consumption of tobacco, this association dated back to the eighteenth-century tradition of snuff-taking. As mentioned above, snuff-taking in Russia was made especially popular by the empresses Elizabeth and Catherine the Great. As a murderer of her husband Peter III and a subject of widespread sexually-themed gossip, Catherine fashioned an influential example of how a moral shadow could be cast on a figure of a powerful and independent woman, one of whose representative habits was the love of tobacco. Popularized by the empresses, snuff-taking became a ritual element of imperial court as well as noble courtship. Although going out of fashion in the first decades of the nineteenth century, snuff-taking persevered for some time as an erotically charged gesture available to unmarried noblewomen. In 1814, Pushkin's poem "To a snuff-taking beauty" described this habit as still seductive and already anachronistic.[45]

Whereas snuff-taking among noblewomen had been common, smoking was slow in becoming fashionable. In the absence of influential women smokers, the association between tobacco and promiscuity established a strong taboo on female smoking both in Europe and in Russia.[46] This association found reflection in Panaev's short story *The Cigarette* (1848), which relied on a commonplace narrative device in European fiction that treated traces of tobacco in a woman's life as indicative of her unfaithfulness to her husband. Panaev's story describes a gentleman who suspects his wife of infidelity when he detects an aroma of tobacco on her person. Determined to discover the truth, he surprises her in her bedroom, thinking she must be entertaining a lover. Instead, he discovers that cigarettes have been prescribed to her by a doctor as a common treatment for toothache.[47]

A revolution in the European attitudes to female smoking took place in the 1830s and 1840s and was associated with George Sand, a famous advocate of women's emancipation, who adopted pipe smoking in order to symbolize her own liberation from the constraints of the patriarchal social regime. Attacked by the guardians of traditional morality both in Europe and in Russia, Sand was portrayed as notorious not only on account of her views, fiction, and lifestyle but also on account of her pipe smoking habit.[48] By contrast, progressive men and especially women saw Sand's smoking as a symbol of emancipation from the strictures of traditional society. Although in Russia Sand's fame reached its height during the 1840s, her example as a smoker became particularly influential at the time of the Great Reforms when educated young women adopted smoking in order to express their progressive views.

A remarkable development in the history of women's smoking, however, was not so much its broad popularity among the progressives but rather its acceptability among educated women who subscribed to no particular ideology. A representative example of this trend occurs in Leskov's aforementioned novel *Nowhere*, which portrays cigarette smoking as widely characteristic of young people regardless of gender. Although Leskov was seen as resistant to the modernizing trends in the society of his time, his novel offers a positive and even endearing view of young female smokers. The opening pages portray two young and highly attractive women returning from a Moscow institute for noble girls to their familial country estates. These women have not yet developed an articulate worldview, but they instinctively see themselves as independent from traditional expectations. Arriving to their ancestral province, they repeatedly manifest their independence by avoiding conventional social rituals, such as going to mass, in order to share a cigarette.[49] Leskov's characters face the challenge of discovering their roles in a society in which the established paths to noble wifehood and motherhood are no longer influential. Strikingly, their parents do not prevent them either from smoking or from choosing their own paths in life.

During the 1870s, the role of smoking as an index of women's independence received representative treatment in Tolstoy's *Anna Karenina*. Reflecting his increasingly conservative views, the novel ascribes smoking to Princess Bettsy Tverskaia, Sappho Shtolz, as well as to Anna, in order to emphasize their moral infirmity. Bettsy and Sappho take advantage of their independence as single women, deriving pleasure from the company of men, and Anna takes up cigarettes after she leaves her husband.[50] By contrast, tobacco is inconceivable for Kitty and Dolly Oblonsky in their conventional roles as wives and mothers. Sappho is particularly emphatic about her smoking: whereas Bettsy and Anna prefer the effeminate thinly-rolled *pakhitoski*, Sappho chooses the masculine thicker *papirosy* in the style more characteristic of radical women than of upper-class ladies such as herself. The masculinity of Sappho's smoking foregrounds the phallic implication inherent in the symbolism of the cigarette. The novel describes Sappho as representing a "new, completely new style," which involves behaving with masculine vigor as she moves more energetically than other women and delivers firm handshakes.[51] The novel also indicates a likely attitude of men to noble women-smokers. Despite sharing Tolstoy's moral instincts, the protagonist Konstantin Levin perceives Anna's smoking not so much as a marker of her moral degradation but rather as an index of her status as a powerful and independent noble lady.[52] Ultimately, the novel's treatment of smoking indicates that cigarettes expressed female independence and power in ways that became increasingly acceptable in the society of the time.

* * *

As literature presented it, the history of Russian smoking from the beginning of the nineteenth century until the turn of the 1880s gained shape as a narrative about the smoker's emancipation from traditional conventions and his self-realization as an independent agent in a modernizing society. In the opening decades of the century, this narrative received its impetus from the Romantic focus on the individual. In poetry and prose, gentry authors, many of whom were military officers, celebrated pipe smoking as symbolizing the independence of spirit, the passion for intellectual activity, and the cult of friendship. During the 1830s and 1840s, smoking became a feature of philosophical and literary circles, in which self-actualizing individuals came together in a public sphere independent from traditional models of socialization. Beginning in the middle of the century, the proliferation of tobacco consumption and the increasing variation in the methods of tobacco use allowed smokers to manifest a broad range of individual distinctions. Most prominently, pipes symbolized professional effectiveness, cigars conveyed high social status, and cigarettes expressed youthful vigor. Beginning with the Great Reforms at the turn of the 1860s, progressive young people used cigarettes to express not only their own independence but also their commitment to liberating all members of society. At that time, smoking became increasingly common among women. Despite the associations between female smoking and promiscuity, growing numbers of women smoked, expressing their freedom from social convention and, often, their commitment to progressive values.

Although literary representations of tobacco consumption were predominantly positive, concerns about the moral implications of smoking began to arise in the second half the century. In particular, cigar smoking could be seen as indicative of gratuitous self-indulgence. The most notable critic of smoking was Leo Tolstoy who increasingly associated this habit with moral corruption. During the seventies, members of the progressive intelligentsia also began to suspect that an excessive pursuit of the habit could undermine their ideological commitment.

During the 1880s, both the Russian media environment and tobacco production underwent significant changes. Mass newspapers, popular magazines, self-help brochures, as well as advertising overtook literature in representing, creating, and codifying the meanings of smoking, just as tobacco was becoming increasingly available to consumers owing to the invention of cigarette-making machines. Despite yielding its formative role, nineteenth-century literature has continued to influence Russian culture by providing it with the meanings of smoking developed and disseminated by its canonical texts.

NOTES

1. For positive views on the medicinal properties of tobacco in Russia, see Igor' Bogdanov, *Dym otechestva, ili kratkaia istoriia tabakokureniia*, (Moscow: Novoe literaturnoe obozrenie, 2007), 52–3, 60–1, 70–1. For a summary of similar views in Europe, see W. A. Penn, *The Soverane Herbe: A History of Tobacco*, (London: Grant Richards, 1901), 296–320. For a history of medical debates about tobacco in Europe, see Jordan Goodman, *Tobacco in History: The Cultures of Dependence*, (London: Routledge, 1993), 115–21.
2. A. N. Neminushchii and E. P. Borodkina, "Iantar v ustakh ego dymitsia. . .: K semiotike motiva kureniia v russkoi literature XIX veka," *Zvezda*, no. 4, 2007, 195–6.

3. In addition to the aforementioned sources, see A. V. Shapovalov, *Ocherki istorii i kultury potrebleniia tabaka v Sibiri: XVII—pervaia polovina XX vv.*, (Novosibirsk: Progress-servis, 2002) and A. N. Zubritskii, *Tabak i tabakokurenie: osnovnoi bibliograficheskii ukazatel' otechestvennoi i zarubezhnoi literatury*, (Moscow, 2005).
4. Jeffrey Brooks, *When Russia Learned to Read: Literacy and Popular Literature,* (Princeton, NJ: Princeton University Press, 1985), 109–41. Robert L. Belknap, "Survey of Russian Journals, 1840–1880," in *Literary Journals in Imperial Russia*, ed. Deborah A. Martinsen, (Cambridge: Cambridge University Press, 1997), 91–116.
5. R. M. Kirsanova, *Russkii kostium i byt XVIII—XIX vekov*, (Moscow: Slovo, 2002), 59–64, 81; Bogdanov, *Dym otechestva*, 81–94.
6. A. S. Pushkin, *Polnoe sobranie sochinenii v desiati tomakh*, 2nd ed., (Moscow: Akademiia nauk SSSR, 1956–1958), vol. 6:325.
7. F. M. Dostoevsky, *Unizhennye i oskorblennye*, (Moscow: Khudozhestvennaia literatura, 1964), 117, 189.
8. Bogdanov, *Dym otechestva*, 88–9.
9. N. V. Gogol, *Sobranie khudozhestvennykh proizvedenii v piati tomakh*, (Moscow: Akademiia nauk SSSR, 1951–52), vol. 3:183–8.
10. Vladimir Odoevskii, *Sochineniia v dvukh tomakh*, (Moscow: Khudozhestvennaia literatura, 1981), vol. 1:38.
11. A. Bestuzhev-Marlinskii, *Polnoe sobranie sochinenii*, 3rd ed., 12 vols., (St. Petersburg, 1838–1839), vol. 1:17–8. For other examples of this attitude in the works of Pushkin, Gogol, Goncharov, and Iazykov, see Neminushchii and Borodkina, "Iantar v ustakh," 196–8.
12. N. F. Pavlov, *Sochineniia*, (Moscow: Sovetskaia Rossiia, 1985), 104.
13. Ibid., 30.
14. Lermontov widely used this device in *A Hero of Our Time*. See Neminushchii and Borodkina, "Iantar v ustakh," 197.
15. See, e.g., Pushkin, "K Pushchinu" (1815), vol. 1:127; "Vospominanie: K Pushchinu" (1815), vol. 1:139; "Poslanie k Galichu" (1815), vol. 1:144.
16. Pushkin, "Poslanie Delvigu," vol. 3:26. For other examples of this theme, see Neminushchii and Borodkina, "Iantar v ustakh," 196.
17. Pushkin, vol. 6:90.
18. A. A. Bestuzhev-Marlinskii, *Sobranie stikhotvorenii,* (Moscow: Sovetskii pisatel, 1948), 29.
19. "Gusarskii pir" (1804) and "Pesnia starogo gusara" (1817); see Neminushchii and Borodkina, "Iantar v ustakh," 195–6.
20. On the Stankevich circle, see John Randolph, *The House in the Garden: the Bakunin Family and the Romance of Russian Idealism*, (Ithaca, NY: Cornell University Press, 2007); on the Odoevskii circle, see D.V. Grigorovich, "Literaturnye vospominaniia," in *Polnoe sobranie sochinenii*, 3rd ed., 12 vols., (St. Petersburg: Niva, 1896), vol. 12:291; on the Maikov family, see Ivan Panaev, "Opyt o klyshchakh," *Izbrannaia proza,* (Moscow: Pravda, 1988), 240, 475.
21. Jürgen Habermas, *The Structural Transformation of the Public Sphere: An Inquiry into a Category of Bourgeois Society,* (Cambridge, MA: MIT Press, 1989).
22. Bogdanov, *Dym otechestva*, 52.
23. See Neminushchii and Borodkina, "Iantar v ustakh," 199–200.
24. M. Iu. Lermontov, *Sobranie sochinenii v chetyrekh tomakh*, (Moscow: Akademiia nauk SSSR, 1958–1959), vol. 4:331.
25. Alexander Herzen, *Sobranie sochinenii v tridtsati tomakh*, (Moscow: Akademiia nauk SSSR, 1954–1965), vol. 8:84–5.

26. Ibid., 121–2.
27. For a discussion of ambivalent implications of the cigar in the image of a progressive person, see my article "Sacrifice or Indulgence? Nikolai Nekrasov as a Model for the Intelligentsia," *Slavic Review*, 66 (2007): 45–63.
28. Panaev, "Opyt o klyshchakh," 240, 245, 271, 282, 475. See also I. A. Goncharov, "Gospodin Podzhabrin," in *Polnoe sobranie sochinenii i pisem v dvadtsati tomakh,* (St. Petersburg: Nauka, 1997–), vol. 1:103.
29. I. S. Turgenev, *Polnoe sobranie sochinenii i pisem v dvadtsati vosmi tomakh*, (Moscow: Nauka, 1960–1968), vol. 9:240–8. For smoking among progressively-minded émigrés, see ibid., 156, 164.
30. Leo Tolstoy, *Anna Karenina*, (Moscow: Nauka, 1970), 11, 14, 19, 23.
31. For a discussion of smoking in *Resurrection*, see Neminushchii and Borodkina, "Iantar v ustakh," 200. For discussions of the sin of smoking, see *Khristianskoe uchenie,* in Leo Tolstoy, *Polnoe sobranie sochinenii*, 90 vols., (Moscow: Khudozhestvennaia literatura, 1928–1958), vol. 39:140–3, 171–3; and *Put' zhizni* in ibid., vol. 45:111–3.
32. Leo Tolstoy, *Povesti i rasskazy*, (Moscow: Moskovskii rabochii, 1956), 44, 52–53, 68, 79.
33. Ibid., 52, 55, 69, 81.
34. Ibid., 108, 137.
35. N. A. Nekrasov, *Polnoe sobranie sochinenii i pisem v piatnadtsati tomakh*, (Leningrad: Nauka, 1981–2000), vol. 2:218. For similar reactions, see Bogdanov, *Dym otechestva*, 57.
36. For a general discussion of the changes in fashion at the turn of the 1860s, see Kirsanova, *Russkii kostium*, 183–206.
37. Turgenev, *Polnoe sobranie sochinenii*, vol. 8:200, 206–7, 257–60, 311.
38. Turgenev, *Polnoe sobranie sochinenii*, vol. 12:6–10, 54.
39. For a discussion of the tensions in Chernyshevsky's view of the progressive self see my "Between Ideology and Desire: The Rhetoric of the Self in the Works of Nikolai Chernyshevsky and Nikolai Dobroliubov," forthcoming in *Slavic Review*.
40. Turgenev's treatment of smoking in *Virgin Soil* bears extensive resemblance to the representation of this habit in a representative radical novel of the decade, Konstantin Staniukovich's *Without Escape* (*Bez iskhoda,* 1873).
41. Turgenev, *Polnoe sobranie sochinenii*, vol. 12:53–4.
42. Ibid., 265, 255–64.
43. Ibid., 181.
44. Ibid., 532–43.
45. Pushkin, *Polnoe sobranie sochinenii*, vol. 1:50–1.
46. In European culture, the most influential texts establishing the links between female smoking and promiscuity were Prosper Mérimée's *Carmen* (1845) and George Bizet's opera of the same name (1875), based on Mérimée's novella. See Richard Klein, *Cigarettes are Sublime*, (Durham, NC: Duke University Press, 1993), 105–34.
47. Ivan Panaev, "Papiroska: Istinnoe proisshestvie," in *Sovremennik* (1848), vol. 7, part 2, sect. 4, 1–22.
48. Richard Stites, *The Women's Liberation Movement in Russia: Feminism, Nihilism, and Bolshevism, 1860–1930*, (Princeton, NJ: Princeton University Press, 1978), 20.
49. N. S. Leskov, *Sobranie sochinenii v odinnadtsati tomakh*, (Moscow: Khudozhestvennaia literatura, 1956–1958), vol. 2:32, 39–40, 165–6.
50. Tolstoy, *Anna Karenina*, 254, 257, 583.
51. Ibid., 253, 255, 257.
52. Ibid., 583.

7 Smokescreens

Tobacco Manufacturers' Projections of Class and Gender in Late Imperial Russian Advertising

Sally West

Tobacco was a booming industry in late imperial Russia, with 272 factories throughout the Russian Empire in 1897 producing 126 million pounds of loose tobacco, over 181 million cigars, and more than 6 billion large, Russian-style cigarettes (*papirosy*), as well as other tobacco products such as snuff, altogether worth over thirty-one million rubles.[1] By 1908, although the number of factories had decreased to 241, the number of cigarettes manufactured had risen to 10.4 billion and the total worth of production had almost doubled to fifty-eight million rubles.[2] Clearly, many Russians smoked, and the market was expanding.

With so many factories offering essentially similar goods across the social spectrum, marketing success demanded the targeting of brands to particular audiences. Tobacco advertising provides rich material for analysis of manufacturers' attitudes towards their consumers precisely because products were often aimed differently to men and women, and to lower and upper classes.

By virtue of their role in the expanding market, manufacturers found themselves joining a confluence of social and cultural changes, appealing to an increasingly mobile and urban population, in which class and gender hierarchies were shifting. Manufacturers were part of the industrialization and modernization of trade that was transforming Russia's economy and society.[3] They actively promoted Russia's emergent consumer culture, with its new identity of consumer encouraging individual (if mass-produced) aspirations and needs that could be satisfied only through the goods of a modern rather than traditional economy.[4] In order to reach their potential customers, they sponsored advertising in the mass-circulation press that had risen out of the late nineteenth-century era of reforms.[5] These new media spanned the socioeconomic spectrum, not only encouraging literacy and public engagement but also fostering yellow journalism's love of scandal and sensation.

Tobacco advertisers—the manufacturers, tradesmen, and their hireling writers and artists—were thus implicit supporters of the changes sweeping Russia in the late tsarist period, but their social attitudes did not necessarily keep pace with the forces they helped unleash. Ambitious as they were to create consumers in all social groups, they were also personally invested in a culture that they did not want to change too much, lest the shifting terrain threaten their own piece of turf. Far more than reflecting the society to which they appealed, tobacco manufacturers' advertising unwittingly revealed their own anxieties as they attempted to limit the implications of the transformations they themselves were promoting. Tobacco advertisements offer insight into identity formation in late imperial Russia—not so much of consumers as of a business community unwilling to change as fast as the modernizing society around them. That the manufacturers' own attitudes are discernable in their advertising is due to the fact that the advertising industry was in its formative stages during the early twentieth century, and the writing and illustrating of advertisements remained largely an in-house procedure. In both Russia and the West until well into the 1910s, professional advertising agencies existed almost exclusively as intermediaries to arrange the placement of advertisements rather than as the market researchers, creative designers, and copywriters they would later become. Merchants and manufacturers in Russia were left to their own devices as far as advertising content was concerned. Many companies hired the skills of independent writers and artists to compose their more creative attempts at publicity, but evidence suggests an ongoing and high level of control over the results. It is thus accurate to see manufacturers as advertisers of their own products.

* * *

One of the most obvious tensions tobacco manufacturers faced in expanding their market was appealing to women. As both Konstantine Klioutchkine and Tricia Starks' chapters in this volume make clear, female smoking was not uncommon but was fraught with cultural taboos. Even for men, as Catriona Kelly shows here, full acceptance of smoking arrived only by the late nineteenth century. For women, the habit was seen as an act of rebellion and boyishness; thus advertisers from at least the 1890s took pains to counteract this image by creating brands deliberately marketed as feminine and refined. In 1892, for instance, the owner of the Ottoman Company advertised its *Vizitnyia* (Visiting) cigarettes as "a pleasant and useful novelty for ladies who smoke or are beginning to smoke. I have put out these thin cigarettes made from ten-ruble tobacco especially for the ladies. It is entirely possible to substitute them for candies, to give the ladies a surprise."[6] This advertisement was consciously venturing into unfamiliar territory, as far as the gender of its intended consumers. In spite of the fact that *Vizitnyia* cigarettes were expressly for women, the advertiser could not help but address men as the intermediaries between the tobacco market and female consumers. A decade later tobacco advertisements for women, in the rare cases they appeared at all, were still clearly establishing a tentative foothold in the market. In 1903, a St. Petersburg tobacco warehouse announced a new brand called *Pioner* (Pioneer) for "elegant ladies."[7] The choice of name was hardly coincidental, and the advertisement made a great point of the product's lack of dust and odor—elegant ladies need not fear soiling their feminine appearance with this tobacco. Neither of the above advertisements actually depicted a woman smoking.

Figure 7.1 Advertisement for *Mechta* (Dream). From the Russian State Library, Poster Collection, December 1905.

As the new century progressed, more advertisers began to show women holding cigarettes, although in Bogdanov's poster for *Mechta* (Dream) brand, the lady in question is decidedly refined and upper class, even though enjoying one of the cheaper brands (Figure 7.1). The association

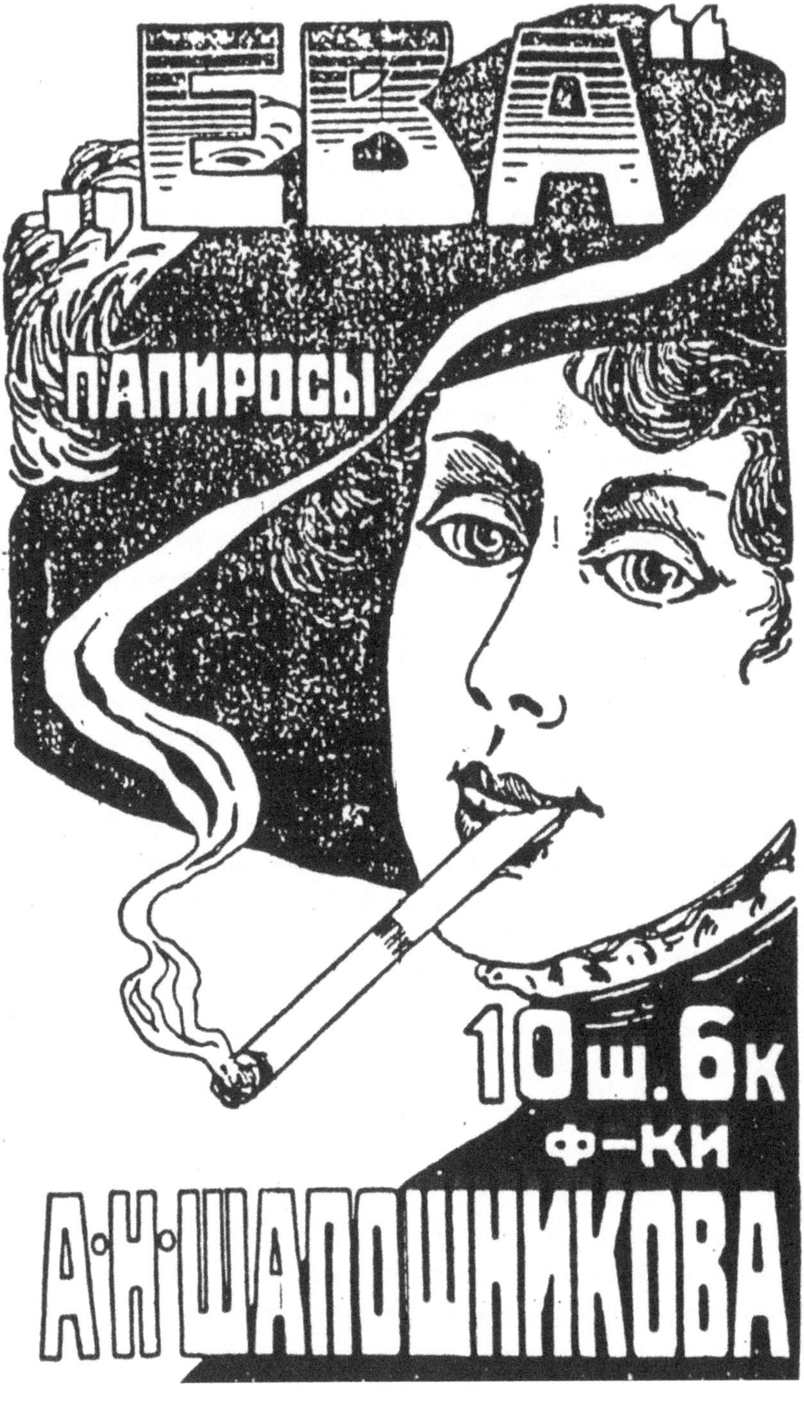

Figure 7.2 Advertisement for *Eva* cigarettes. From *Russkoe slovo*, November 28, 1910.

of femininity with the women's brands, it seems, was only realizable through an upper-class image. By the 1910s, some advertisers began to embrace the rebellious nature of female smoking. In the mass-circulation press, however, such images remained extremely rare, and tobacco advertisements were so predominantly male that what may have been the first newspaper advertisement featuring a woman with a cigarette actually in her mouth still retains a jarring quality for the present-day peruser of Russia's prerevolutionary dailies. For about two years, the Shaposhnikov Company had been picturing a weathered, bohemian man smoking *Krem* (Cream) cigarettes; at the end of 1910, they suddenly substituted genders, using a female version of the same picture for their *Eva* brand (Figure 7.2).[8] Her open enjoyment of the smoke seems almost brazen in the cultural context; she stares straight ahead with no hint of apology. The daring aspect of this advertisement is evident only in light of the almost total absence of such images in the press up to that point. As Erving Goffman noted in his study of gender and advertising in the 1970s, the engrained nature of gender roles is most apparent when we are brought up short by an exception to a rule we did not consciously know existed.[9] Role reversal shocks the audience by transgressing an invisible yet entrenched boundary between the sexes.

Given that tobacco was an accepted male activity across society by the turn of the century, it might seem that advertising cigarettes to men would be unproblematic. In the broader context, however, promoting consumption in general among men held its own, more subtle challenges. Contemporaries associated consumer culture with women; the desire to consume carried connotations of essentialized female nature: vanity, passion, and whims uncontrolled by reason. As Rita Felski discusses in her study of gender and modernity, to tempt men into the sphere of consumption carried the implied threat of emasculating them by encouraging female characteristics.[10] Tobacco advertisements, however, could overcome this threat by emphasizing the already existing associations of smoking and masculinity, assuring the continuity of gender identity within consumer culture.

One of the most common methods of showing the manliness of tobacco was to connect sexual pleasure and prowess with smoking. Tobacco was among the industries most apt to link its products with a fantasy world of young female beauties, images through which smokers consumed sexually available women as much as cigarettes. Variations of the exotically clad woman appeared in advertisements for many brands, from a seductively statuesque beauty dreamily lifting her hair to mix with the emerging smoke of an eastern hookah in Shaposhnikov's advertisement for *Albanskii* (Albanian) tobacco (touted for its "genuine eastern taste and aroma"), to Laferm's Godiva-like beauty, long hair covering bare breasts on the *Chudo-Tsvet* (Miraculous Bloom) cigarette package, or Laferm's bare-footed, smoking *Duchess* dressed like a ancient courtesan and lying supine in an inviting pose. All promised sensual delight for the male smoker through orientalist images of odalisque-type fantasy.[11]

In contrast to the commodification of women, one particularly striking theme in tobacco advertising directed to men involved the marginalization or even denigration of women. In such advertisements, women were seen as distractions or detractors from manliness. Consumer goods in these messages proved far worthier of male devotion than the fairer sex. Exclaimed a jingle for Shapshal's *Deia* cigarettes:

> I am angry! Furious! I'm trembling all over!!!
> Vengeance! Death to the villain!!!
> He's stolen my dress coat, lured away my wife
> And smoked up all my *Deia*!!!
> The wife and the coat . . . that's neither here nor there,
> But . . . to be without *Deia*—now that's disaster!![12]

Such attitudes about wives reflected a dismissive attitude towards women that was a common theme of Russian male culture—and late imperial urban society was disproportionately male due to the influx of peasant migrant laborers into the working class.[13] The patriarchal social structure relegated women to the lowest rungs of the family hierarchy—even lower, if the much-cited proverb, "A hen is not a bird, and a woman is not a human being," is given any cultural weight. While other proverbs acknowledge women's importance, it is undeniable that Russian popular culture embodied a strong vein of misogyny. Denigration of wives, stereotypes of old hags, and lewd innuendo about loose women were the stuff of many a comic routine in the popular entertainments of St. Petersburg and Moscow, and promoted male bonding through the stories and jokes workers regaled each other with in the taverns.[14]

To emphasize the masculinity of smoking, however, advertisements did not need to refer to women at all, but could focus instead on the physical prowess of the male. While anti-tobacco campaigners railed against the unhealthy effects of smoking, tobacco manufacturers continued to tout its benefits.[15] Cigarettes could be sources of vigor and virility, as exemplified by the wrestlers in Figure 7.3. "The idols are overthrown, the ideals smashed!! By the quality and stylishness of *Krem*. Whoever will smoke them once—will not start to smoke others!!" The triumphant hero holds the new leading brand aloft, his foot on the chest of his rival, out cold on the floor. Indeed, the victor appears to have knocked out his opponent while smoking a *Krem* cigarette in each hand. The real rivals in this advertisement were other cigarettes, yet the image drew directly upon the popular passion for wrestling and boxing in late imperial Russia, associating the fighter's muscular physique with pervasive ideals of masculinity.[16]

Figure 7.3 Advertisement for the Shaposhnikov factory. From *Russkoe slovo*, October 29, 1909.

Figure 7.4 Advertisement for A. G. Rutenberg's factory. From *Russkoe slovo*, April 29, 1914.

Advertisers also appealed to masculinity through images of exaggerated sexual prowess. Cigars, the preserve of the wealthier elite, served as effective phallic symbols in themselves, as demonstrated in an advertisement promoting the "very best" from A. G. Rutenberg's factory (Figure 7.4). The exclusion of all but the smoker's legs and the gigantic cigar protruding from behind his armchair make the sexual allusion in this advertisement striking and unmistakable. Upper-body strength was clearly not the only way of demonstrating virility.

By commodifying or marginalizing women, and by highlighting the masculinity of smoking, advertisers implicitly contradicted the contemporary perceptions of consumer culture as frivolous and female. Addressing men in general, then, was relatively simple because it allowed manufacturers both to perpetuate and emphasize existing gender stereotypes. However, when these advertisers consciously segmented their target audience by class, the approaches became decidedly more contradictory.

The expanding spectrum of consumers created as many difficulties as opportunities for tobacco advertisers. The manufacturers found themselves in the rather uncomfortable position of extending appeals to a working-class clientele made up of people who might simultaneously be their customers and employees. The tensions evident in many advertisements for cheaper brands of tobacco unwittingly reveal industrialists' class anxieties and show how they sought to encourage consumption while still controlling consumerist aspirations among the working class.

Although all classes bought cigarettes, the brands came in varying quality and price. More expensive brands generally ranged from six to twelve kopecks for a packet of ten, whereas the cheaper brands sold for half that price or less, at five or six kopecks for a packet of twenty. Nearly all cigarette brands of all factories fell within these two price ranges during the decade before World War I, making differentiation of target audience easier to discern. Even if some better-off smokers economized and bought cheap tobacco, the intended range of consumers for the lower-end cigarettes were the lower classes, as the content of the advertisements quite often made clear.

The tobacco manufacturers' appeals to working-class custom tended to fall into three main categories. The first echoed Russian liberals' attempts to draw in working-class political support by promoting universal, rather than class values, evoking the spirit of "classlessness."[17] In this approach, class distinctions disappeared, from the liberals' perspective in the world of politics and from the manufacturers' perspective in the world of cigarette sales. The second tactic exemplified the modern consumer ethic in which consumption of the right goods purportedly elevated the status of the consumer. According to this approach, the correct choice of cigarette rendered the smoker one of the elite. The third category represented the traditional paternalism of the factory owner, suggesting that the cigarettes manufactured by him would transform the smoker into an ideal worker, with resultant happiness for all.

CLASSLESSNESS

Russian liberals' notion of classlessness derived from their belief that a primary identification with class would undermine their emphasis on universal individual rights. Therefore they preferred to avoid the word "class" when writing about workers' issues, seeking to transcend such distinctions in the spirit of classlessness.[18] In a sense, the interests of industrialists (whatever their personal politics) demanded a commercial version of the liberals' agenda: universal individual rights of consumption. Perhaps it is not surprising then, that some of their advertising echoed the liberal appeal to classlessness.

The possibilities of transcending class boundaries through consumption of a single type of cigarette were touted in a 1913 advertisement for a Bogdanov Company brand, *Smirna* (from the city in Turkey).[19] To smoke *Smirna* was to become a member of the "brotherhood" of smokers, depicted by a line of identical smokers in Fez hats. The name of the brand and the Turkish headgear implied Masonic unity, a fraternity, as the advertisement stated, of "old and young, Orthodox and non, rich and poor, knowledgeable and ignorant, family men and bachelors"—differences that would fade in the pleasure of smoking this cigarette. The play on words in the slogan, "*Smirno* (peacefully, or tranquilly) *Smirna* appeared!!," suggests that the tranquility of this good smoke would erase unimportant distinctions based on education and income level, age, ethnicity, family status—even religion. The emphasis on brotherhood would have a special resonance for workers recently transplanted from their villages. Most of these workers lived and worked with fellows from their own home regions, forming a bond to mitigate the anonymity of the city and provide mutual support (as well as rivalry between regional groups). In his study of the transition undergone by peasant-workers in St. Petersburg, S. A. Smith notes that, in the absence of native family networks, brotherhood loyalty replaced the bonds of filiality that predominated

Figure 7.5 Advertisement for *Kapriz* cigarettes. From *Gazeta-kopeika*, September 18, 1910.

in the villages.[20] By invoking this term in the context of brand loyalty, then, the Bogdanov Company was expanding the concept of brotherhood beyond geographic—and class—boundaries.

The same company made this leveling even more explicit in an earlier advertisement for *Kapriz* (Caprice) cigarettes, smokers of which transcended political as well as class lines (Figure 7.5). Here is not only classlessness but also non-partisanship depicted clearly through caricatures of right- and left-wing, upper and lower-class types, all finding common ground in their insistence on smoking only *Kapriz*.[21]

The comic nature of such depictions demonstrates a conscious distancing from the advertisements' claims, suggesting that the advertisers knew, and knew their audience knew, how far from reality the community of smokers was. It was a transparent fiction, but one that in this case would include everyone in the shared humor. In contrasting the projection of classlessness for the cheaper brands with the images in advertisements for more expensive cigarettes, however, we might wonder if the advertisers' laughter did not contain a hint of nervousness. That the brotherhood of smokers was only a palliative or a joke for the poorer consumers was underlined by the frequent association of more expensive brands with a quintessentially bourgeois lifestyle. A 1910 advertisement for the Shaposhnikov factory's expensive *Krem* cigarettes, for instance, depicted a portly, self-satisfied gentleman in a fine suit and monocle deriving "nothing but pleasure" from his tobacco, as well as his luxurious surroundings.[22] In the world of consumer culture, the notion of transcending class was only relevant for those who had more material cause to wish for it.

THE VICARIOUS ELITE

In the second category of tobacco's sales pitches for the cheaper brands of cigarettes, manufacturers sought to defuse working-class identity not by erasing differences but by lifting the workers up out of their lowly poverty to a vicarious association with the elite. Most often this was done simply through selection of brand names. A number of cheap brands were given grand labels such as *Roskosh* (Luxury) or *Zolotyia* (Golden). Attaching associations of quality with lower-end products implied that smoking these cigarettes would bring the same satisfaction as luxury or gold; no doubt some who did smoke them recognized with bitter irony that inhaling this richly named, cheap tobacco would be the closest they could hope to come to experiencing luxury and wealth. The unattainability of the reality behind the names was clearer still in the case of *Tsarskiia* (Tsar's) cigarettes, for who, even among the elite, could hope to live a tsar's existence? The further the reality, the more harmless the dream.

Even beyond allusions to royalty, some manufacturers invoked an element of spiritual salvation in advertising their cheaper brands. The following is a ditty for the Dukat Company's *Tsarskiia* cigarettes:

> In life's difficult moments,
> When I burn with anguish,
> I smoke Dukat's *Tsarskiia*,
> It's as if a burden rolls off my soul,
> And grief is far away,
> And things become cheerful,
> And so, so easy.[23]

Words were not even necessary to convey the message in a poster advertising Bogdanov's *Zolotyia* brand (Figure 7.6). The packet of cigarettes, surrounded by shining light, is greeted by a peasant and a worker as if they are witnessing a revelation from the heavens or hailing the advent of a spiritual savior. The placement of the cigarettes on this poster would have been immediately significant to any Russian, as the icon corner of every peasant hut was found high in the corner to the left of the front door. In this advertisement, the Bogdanov Company transfigured their cigarettes into a religious icon, embellished in name as the icon would be in paint or trim, and complete with attendant worshippers.

Both of these first two advertising approaches—the nicotine-induced approximations of material and spiritual salvation and the classless community of smokers—represent adaptations to the Russian context of more widespread methods of appealing to consumers since the advent of modern advertising in the late nineteenth century. The basic messages of belonging and of transformation of status through consumption are still overwhelmingly with us today, even if the historical particulars are very different. In these two categories, the manufacturers were adapting to the modern marketplace by approaching their poorer customers as consumers, despite the persistent differentiation of class. The same cannot be said of the third category of advertising appeals, which was rooted in far more traditional attitudes.

THE PATERNALIST AGENDA

Didactic portrayals of ideal workers constituted the largest of the three categories targeting working-class consumers. Given that the paternalist approach was the tactic least likely to resonate with workers themselves, it may have more closely reflected the manufacturers' own attitudes.[24] Messages in this group represent heavy-handed social as well as commercial propaganda. A 1913 Shapshal advertisement, for instance, featured this little verse (a typical example):

Figure 7.6 Poster for *Zolotyia* cigarettes. From the Russian State Library Poster Collection, (1910s).

He who is resigned to his fate
He who is clever, dexterous in labor,
He who is not a mischief-maker,
That person always smokes our *Kumir*!!![25]

Kumir (Idol) cigarettes created the ideal worker, although in this example, hardly an idol of the heroic variety. That such an overtly patronizing sales pitch could be printed in *Gazeta-kopeika* (Penny Gazette), a working-class newspaper, is testament to the persistence of paternalistic views among Russian industrialists on the eve of Revolution. Apart from its folk ditty format, it is difficult to see this as an advertisement intended to attract working-class consumers; its purpose seems rather to control the factory's own workers and assuage the manufacturers' anxieties.

That the lower-end customers targeted by the manufacturers sometimes were their own workers was made explicit in a 1910 series of advertisements for the Shaposhnikov and Laferm factories. Both of these companies used verse in their advertising, usually signed by "Uncle Kornei," for Laferm, or "Uncle Mikhei," for Shaposhnikov. This personalizing device may have been the brainchild of one man: Sergei Apollonovich Korotkii, a self-styled crusader for tobacco who wrote countless advertisements in newspapers and pamphlets and was certainly the writer behind Uncle Mikhei. A nobleman and decorated veteran of the Russo-Turkish War of 1877–1878, Korotkii initially rented out his literary skills to the Laferm Company, but began working for Shaposhnikov around 1905. He was thus the avuncular voice behind Shaposhnikov's 1910 attempt to advertise to its own workers.

One advertisement in this campaign pretended to reproduce correspondence from the hall porters, doormen and watchmen of the Shaposhnikov factory to Uncle Mikhei, expressing their appreciation for the company's *Mashinka* (Little Machine) brand cigarettes.[26] These workers supposedly wrote the following verse:

In our monotonous lives,
We are all drawn to fashionable *Mashinka*,
You pay a five-kopek piece for twenty,
And you enjoy yourself like anything!!
They aren't cigarettes—they are delight,
Merci, Mikhei! Regards! Compliments!![27]

A second advertisement carried Uncle Mikhei's gracious reply to the grateful workers, but the ruse of this "correspondence" was ludicrously exposed by a mix-up in printing dates: Uncle Mikhei's reply appeared the day before the initial "letter." The proletarian guise was thinly drawn to begin with, not least by putting French words into the mouths of porters and watchmen.

In good paternalistic style, the expectation of gratitude from workers for their bosses was a common thread throughout many of the advertisements in this third category. Another was the manufacturers' concern about working-class morality, especially in the areas of alcohol consumption and sexuality. As Laura Engelstein and others have demonstrated, the educated elite's perception of innocence among the common folk also led to anxiety over their susceptibility to corruption, especially after the mass upheavals of 1905.[28] Since alcohol was seen as a major source of dissipation among the poor, tobacco manufacturers emphasized the fact that their goods produced their desired effect without inebriation. They could side with the temperance movement by preaching the virtues of cigarettes over liquor for both health and happiness. The Dukat company, for example, depicted its happily sober workers in a poem entitled "Labor and Rest":

> The whistle has blown and the factory folk
> Are already going to rest after working all day . . .
> One hurries home, one drops into the tavern,
> Yes, and there'll be friends there to drink tea with,
> They remember the village, acquaintances, family,
> And dream of time off towards Ivan's Day.
> Fellow countrymen discuss sowing and mowing . . .
> "Young lad! Give us *Tsarskiia* cigarettes!!" . . .
> In the smoke of the cigarettes from the firm of Dukat,
> The hours while away—everyone is glad of the rest.
> Look: time is flying, it's already time to go home,
> Each having taken his *Tsarskiia* with him for tomorrow.
> In the morning the whistle calls everyone early,
> The factory worker goes to work once again
> He begins to smoke, cheerful and glad,
> Invigorated by *Tsarskiia*, from the firm of Dukat.[29]

Here was the perfect worker, happy to snatch a few hours' rest with friends, drinking tea not vodka, rejuvenated by a cheap cigarette, and cheerfully reporting to work on time. He subsumed himself willingly, if wistfully, to the routines of modern factory life and was content with his lot. Simple lives required only simple pleasures. Such a worker would naturally never go on strike or make revolutionary demands on the owners. Such a worker was no threat.

Not only were cigarette-smoking workers happy at work and with friends but they also kept their marriages intact thanks to the correct choice of tobacco. An advertising verse for the Ottoman Company was purportedly written by a worker who claimed his wife loved him better now that he smoked the firm's *Berezka* (Birch tree) brand—a "wonderful creation" due to which he had stopped gambling and drinking and received a raise.[30] Another advertisement for the same brand, with a verse explicitly entitled "A Proletarian Ditty," equates the pleasure derived from wife and cigarette:

I married very young,
Took a beautiful wife
And—from Ottoman's—I smoke
"*Berezka*," and that alone.
Both are tasty, both are sweet—
Both "*Berezka*" and my wife—
And they give me strength
To clamber upwards from my day.[31]

The sexual implications of this verse are quite explicit, yet within the legitimate bounds of marriage. In those advertisements for the cheaper brands that fall into the paternalistic category, there are no hints of extramarital sexuality, although other advertisements might appeal to lower-class consumers through sexual fantasies of women beyond reach, such as some of the orientalist images discussed earlier. When it came to suggestions of real life, however, the pleasures of the working class were to be kept strictly inside the realms of moral probity.

Such strictures did not apply further up the social scale. On the contrary, when sex was used to sell the more expensive brands of cigarettes, it was nearly always extramarital, and often in an actual, rather than dreamworld setting. Shaposhnikov's Uncle Mikhei cast an upper-class smoker, the "bon-vivant Serge," directly in the "demimonde" of prostitution.[32] Serge was depicted equally enjoying his expensive cigarette and his elegant

Figure 7.7 Advertisement for *Rua*. From *Gazeta-kopeika*, June 8, 1913.

female companion. Similarly, a portly, monocled gentleman in a caricatured advertisement for *Rua*, one of Shapshal's higher-priced brands, practically seemed to drool over his cigarette at the much younger beauty under his wing (Figure 7.7).

* * *

If Foucault is right in asserting that sexuality as a social discourse was originally the creation of the bourgeoisie, then the fact that the working class was outside the bourgeois purview also adds an element of territoriality to the separation of moral categories evident in Russian tobacco advertising.[33] The manufacturers were part of a bourgeoisie that was still very much seeking its own definition in the last few years of the imperial regime, and this insecurity only fueled the need to draw social parameters. Nevertheless, the moral division was a futile one, not only because it ignored social realities (such as the fact that prostitution existed among all classes), but because cigarettes of both prices were advertised in the same newspapers. Tobacco manufacturers could hardly have supposed that working-class readers would not notice the allusions to illicit sexuality and bourgeois lifestyles in the other advertisements. Perhaps the fatuity of the attempted propaganda only emphasized the advertisers' own view of the workers as unsophisticated children, unschooled in the ways of the world—potentially dangerous yet still susceptible to the influence of straightforward moral tutelage. Yet this conclusion does not credit the manufacturers with much sophistication either.

The likelihood that the tobacco manufacturers actually believed that their moralizing messages would work is slim, but their persistence in them ultimately says more about their own difficulty in moving beyond the stereotypical relations of paternalism than about their understanding of the workers. Stereotypes only remain stereotypes as long as they trigger knee-jerk reactions. The manufacturers found it difficult to pry loose their own protective reflexes to be able to treat workers as fellow consumers in the modern marketplace. The obstacle surely lay as much in their failure to transcend their own past identities as in fear of workers' rebelliousness. As James von Geldern has pointed out, history has to allow the influence of absence of identity, as well as its presence.[34] The industrialists' fallback to the paternalist attitude reflects lack of a fully-fledged, modern identity to fit the changing society in which they now found themselves.

The dilemma of the tobacco advertisers was not simply one of how to sell their products to a particular group of customers, but of how best to reconcile their own conflicting positions as both old-style factory bosses and modern promoters of commerce. In addition, they had to reconcile their customers' dual identities as workers in need of control and as independent-minded, modern consumers. In trying to adapt, the tobacco manufacturers and their spokesmen too often worried over preserving old dividing lines in shifting sand, rather than fully acknowledging that the days of the happy laborer (if they had ever existed) were over, as indeed were the days of those who could believe in him.

NOTES

1. *Svod dannykh fabrichno-zavodskoi promyshlennosti v Rossii za 1897 god*, (St. Petersburg: Ministry of Finance, 1900), 159.
2. *Svod statisticheskikh dannykh po fabrichno-zavodskoi promyshlennosti s 1887 po 1926 god*, (Moscow: Gosudarstvennoe Izdatel'stvo, 1929), Tables 2 and 21, 5–6 and 25–6.
3. On the modernization of trade, see Marjorie Louise Hilton, "Commercial Cultures: Modernity in Russia and the Soviet Union, 1880–1930," (Ph.D. Diss., University of Illinois at Urbana-Champaign, 2003).
4. A broader examination of advertising's role in late imperial Russian consumer culture is the subject of my book: *Consuming Paradoxes: Advertising and the Creation of Modern Consumer Culture in Late Tsarist Russia*, (in progress).
5. On the rise of the mass-circulation press, see Louise McReynolds, *The News under Russia's Old Regime: The Development of a Mass-Circulation Press*, (Princeton, NJ: Princeton University Press, 1991).
6. *Peterburgskaia gazeta*, May 9, 1892.
7. *Peterburgskaia gazeta*, May 6, 1903.
8. *Russkoe slovo*, November 28, 1910.
9. Erving Goffman, *Gender Advertisements*, (New York: Harper and Row, 1979).
10. Rita Felski, *The Gender of Modernity*, (Cambridge, MA: Harvard University Press, 1995), 62.
11. *Albanskii*: *Russkoe slovo*, March 11, 1914. '*Chudo-tsvet*': *Gazeta-kopeika*, August 19, 1909. '*Duchess*': *Russkoe slovo*, November 12, 1913. Eastern associations with smoking were common in the Russian tobacco industry (for instance, the Ottoman Company was Russian owned despite its name) and orientalist images played into this perceived link. On the prevalence of orientalist attitudes in western culture, see Edward Said, *Orientalism*, (New York: Vintage Books, 1979).
12. *Gazeta-kopeika*, August 10, 1911.
13. In 1897, the population of St. Petersburg comprised 121 men for every 100 women. With the greater influx of women workers by 1910, the disparity grew smaller at 110 to 100. S. A. Smith, "Masculinity in Transition: Peasant Migrants to Late-Imperial St. Petersburg," in *Russian Masculinities in History and Culture*, ed. Barbara Evans Clements, Rebecca Friedman, and Dan Healey, (New York: Palgrave, 2002), 95.
14. Catriona Kelly, "'Better Halves'? Representations of Women in Russian Urban Popular Entertainments, 1870–1910," in *Women and Society in Russia and the Soviet Union*, ed. Linda Edmondson, (Cambridge: Cambridge University Press, 1992). See also Smith, "Masculinities in Transition," 98–9, on the treatment of women by workers.
15. See Starks, this volume.
16. On the popularity of wrestling, see Louise McReynolds, *Russia at Play: Leisure Activities at the End of the Tsarist Era*, (Ithaca, NY: Cornell University Press, 2003), 131–53. Smith discusses the centrality of physical strength for images of Russian peasant and working-class masculinity, "Masculinities in Transition."

17. *Nadklassnost'*—literally "above-classness."
18. William G. Rosenberg, "Representing Workers and the Liberal Narrative of Modernity," *Slavic Review*, 55 (1996): 249.
19. *Gazeta-kopeika*, March 14, 1913.
20. Smith, "Masculinity in Transition," 102.
21. Non-partisanship (*nadpartiinost'*) was another appeal from the liberal political arena. See Rosenberg, "Representing Workers," 249.
22. *Russkoe slovo*, February 26, 1910.
23. *Gazeta-kopeika*, October 27, 1911.
24. On the persistence of workplace paternalism, see Mark D. Steinberg, *Moral Communities: The Culture of Class Relations in the Russian Printing Industry, 1867–1907*, (Berkeley: University of California Press, 1992). It should also be noted that the ideal worker was always portrayed as male, even though women made up the majority of the workforce in the tobacco industry.
25. *Gazeta-kopeika*, June 9, 1913.
26. Although the current translation of *mashinka* is "typewriter," the literal translation "little machine" is more likely the intended one in 1910. It may refer to the increasing mechanization of tobacco production, which the industry proudly touted, and also to the implied association of lowly doormen and watchmen with the more modern (and in this context flattering) image of industrial workers. My thanks to Tricia Starks for bringing this latter possibility to my attention.
27. *Gazeta-kopeika*, April 16–17, 1910.
28. Laura Engelstein, *The Keys to Happiness: Sex and the Search for Modernity in Fin-de-Siècle Russia*, (Ithaca, NY: Cornell University Press, 1992), 6.
29. *Gazeta-kopeika*, October 31, 1911.
30. *Gazeta-kopeika*, May 10, 1911.
31. *Gazeta-kopeika*, April 21, 1911.
32. *Russkoe slovo*, April 18, 1910.
33. Michel Foucault, *The History of Sexuality*, (New York: Vintage Books, 1990 ed.), vol. 1:127.
34. James von Geldern, "Life In-Between: Migration and Popular Culture in Late Imperial Russia," *Russian Review*, 55 (1996): 382.

8 Tobacco Prohibitions as Ritual Language

Roy R. Robson

One of nineteenth century's most revered Russian Orthodox figures, St. Seraphim of Sarov, died in his cell at night during prayer in January 1833. This beloved man—who could pacify bears and bring hardened men to God—was canonized in 1905.[1] His face and icons were nearly ubiquitous in early twentieth-century Russia, often shown in his simple cassock kneeling in the woods of Sarov, his home. But, according to rumors passed around by Old Believer opponents of the Russian Orthodox Church, Seraphim was a fraud. Instead of dying standing at prayer during the middle of the night, it seemed that Seraphim had fallen asleep with a lit pipe of tobacco. When the pipe fell from his mouth, rags in the cell burst into flame and killed the old man.

Why would the rumor of tobacco use turn the reputation of a holy man into that of a sinner? How would smoking a pipe during prayer undo Seraphim's piety? And how could an Old Believer be able to use tobacco-smoking as shorthand for impropriety? Answers to all of these questions come from tobacco's perception as an idolatrous activity among much of the Russia population at the turn of the twentieth century. Tobacco use must therefore be understood within the language of ritual and symbol as it had developed in nineteenth-century Russia.

THE OLD BELIEVERS

To study the fractious nature of tobacco use, it helps to understand the differences between Old Believers (who eschewed tobacco) and the state-sponsored Russian Orthodox Church, which tacitly condoned its use. The term "Old Believer" is shorthand for an amalgamation of many small "concords" that, while separate, had a number of things in common. First, the Old Believers sought to retain liturgy, symbols, and rituals of the Russian Orthodox Church before reforms carried out in the mid-seventeenth century. Second, Old Believers tended toward communal rather than hierarchal organization, emphasizing parish decision-making over centralized authority in the church. Third, the Old Believers often distrusted state authority, given that they were actively persecuted for much of their history. Finally, Old Believers place extremely high significance on the importance of ritual and symbol. For them, salvation came through living the image and likeness of God, which could be achieved through rigorous adherence to the symbols and rituals of Orthodox Christianity, which Old Believers saw as the realization of theology.[2]

Interest in ritual and symbol did not get left at the church door. Since Old Believers sought to recreate the icon of God through rituals and symbols, it makes sense that they would imbue their lives with this concept, extending it into their everyday affairs. In this way, Old Believer rituals took on their anti-establishmentarian nature; in essence, ritual actions were a form of anti-governmental and anti-Western language. They were a way both to affirm the "correct praise" of old-style Christianity and to engage in a dialogue with Russian society on terms defined by the Old Believers themselves. In short, the Old Believers could work toward salvation through symbol-laden ritual actions. At the same time, by using these same rituals, Old Believers could thumb their noses at the dominant Russian Orthodox Church and its sponsoring government.

Old Believers made up about 10% of the imperial Russian population in the second half of the nineteenth century, though their support may have been significantly larger than that since many refused to take part in censuses. Though quite varied in ideology and geography, the refusal to use tobacco on ritual grounds was virtually universal among Old Believers before the early twentieth century.

OLD BELIEVERS ON THE ORIGIN OF TOBACCO

Tobacco and its use played an important part in Old Believer ritual language. In an attempt to order their world and maintain the iconic purity of the Old Belief, adherents to the old ways developed a large number of ritual prohibitions. Not to be confused with Mennonite and Amish abhorrence of the modern world, the Old Believers took a more nuanced view of life. Instead of barring all innovation, Old Believers sought to find their place in the world by prohibiting substances and activities that they perceived to be in opposition to Russian Orthodox tradition. In general, the Old Believers looked askance at innovations that came from the West (Europe or America), centralized power in the hands of the state-sponsored church or the state, or the undermining of rituals or symbols held dear by the faithful. Smoking fell into all three of these categories, making it among the most universally-despised activities among Old Believers across Russia in the imperial period.[3]

By the late imperial years, Old Believers had developed a large repertoire of songs, essays, tales, and poems about tobacco use. These illustrated the origin of tobacco and its dastardly effects on human beings. Though transmitted mostly orally, some of these songs and poems found their way into print through the illegal Old Believer press and reports of both Russian Orthodox missionaries and scholarly ethnographers. In 1905, the Old Believers were free to publish their own stories and essays about the horror of tobacco use.

Much of the literature described the antichristian source of the evil weed. One widely-disseminated story, "Tale about the Origin of Tobacco," linked tobacco to the apocalyptic Whore of Babylon, often interspersing biblical texts with fanciful descriptions of tobacco.[4] In spiritual songs, tobacco was linked to potatoes and coffee as foreign substances, brought from Hell via the New World with the express intention to lure humans:

> The youth grew
> Tobacco and potatoes
> And the maiden had
> Tea and coffee,
> And these hated ones [devils]
> Brought those seeds from the pit,
> And they planted them on Earth
> And told Satan about this.
> And Satan says:
> "Now the young people
> Will smoke tobacco,
> Drink tea and coffee and eat potatoes,
> They will be ours, and the older people
> Will condemn them
> And in that way please us.
> So everyone will come to us."[5]

Many elements of Old Believer folk beliefs about tobacco could be found here. First, tobacco was clearly linked to Satan's devils, who transplanted tobacco seeds on earth, picking faraway America as its earthly home. Next, showing the "youth" and the "maidens" using these foreign substances reinforced the modish nature of foreign foods, which were more attractive to foolish youngsters than their wise elders. Finally, however, even older people were brought into the sin of tobacco use, not because of their own experiments but rather through anger at the younger generation for using the substances. Condemnation of the youth by their elders, the song explained, would cause discord within families, which would make Satan happy.

Another work, highly illustrative of Old Believer views, was first published by Fedor Vasil'evich Livanov in 1871 based on fieldwork among Old Believers outside of Moscow. In this composition, called "A Satirical Poem on the Origin of Tobacco," an anonymous author created a sophisticated version of the Old Believer tales. This poem, which apparently circulated around central Russian Old Believer communities in the mid-nineteenth century, will form the central theme of this chapter. Like the spiritual song quoted above, the text began with a devil scheming to find a new way to ensnare humans:

> Beelzebub, the demonic prince with horns . . .
> Considered how to introduce an inhuman sin.
> He thought in hell for a thousand years:
> What deep ditch could he dig,
> With which sin could he bring down the whole world
> And fill up hell with sinful souls?
> . . .
> "I already created drunkenness and fighting
> But my soul was not satiated.
> I have a new wish.
> . . .
> I will bring into the world a great fashion,
> I will take away freedom of prayer.
> I want to get even with the Messiah with an idea
> That will inflict a terrible wound."[6]

Beelzebub decided to introduce a new sin—tobacco use—that had never before tempted civilization. "Read all the mythology of the gods," wrote the poet, "you will see that they did not honor tobacco." The poem then recounted the history of Greek gods, Hippocrates, and Alexander, none of whom used tobacco. Even Egypt, with its magical use of herbs, knew no tobacco:

> The Egyptians were keen for spices
> They made everything from herbs
> According to laws written in that country
> There were three hundred million herbs.
> There was born garlic, carrots, lettuce
> Parsley, onions, cabbage, and spinach
> Most herbs and parsnips,
> But no one hears that tobacco was there![7]

Seizing his opportunity, Beelzebub "Sent for tobacco, where Vespucci had gone," and his demon "flew like lightning to America. He brought a heap of roots for stinking, disgusting pipe-smoking," which he let loose on Western Christendom, including Italy and Germany."[8] Old Believers' distrust of tobacco thus fit their world view that impurity came from outside Holy Russia, as had liturgical and theological innovations. As an "American weed," though, the Russian people had to be duped into using tobacco, since it had no Russian counterpart. In Old Believer legend, the Deceiver claimed that tobacco use was actually healthful. Beelzebub instructed a demon to walk on earth with a smoking pipe in hand. Then, when a human asked what he was doing,

> He would answer "I am healing, this is an expensive medication."
> They will ask: where you got such a strange medication?
> You tell them "I went overseas to a faraway kingdom—
> I swear by the prince that rules hell,
> And whose might frightens the whole world.
> I swear! I strongly believe it,
> Smoke! You will be healthy from it;
> Tobacco can be taken in the form of smoking and sniffing in the
> nose,
> It is always helpful for everyone,
> Tobacco is a true healer for you;
> And I am your mentor and an eternal patron;
> Who sniffs even a little, even once in a hundred years,
> Will be healthy, smart and without boredom;
> And whoever is sad, it will make him happy,
> And it heals any ailment."
> This is how the prince of darkness, the ruler of all Gehenna,
> Introduced smoking to the whole universe.[9]

And so both the foreign nature of the weed and its allegedly salutary properties were able to ensnare everyone in the new fashion.

Yet, at first, Russia's holy tsar understood tobacco's curse and outlawed it from his land. Texts on the subject regularly quoted prohibitions of its use by Aleksei Mikhailovich or Mikhail Fedorovich, saying that "the blessed sovereign took all measures not to have tobacco introduced and it was especially forbidden for use by the clergy, as it was such a destructive activity."[10] Our poet agreed, saying that

> The Russian sovereign Tsar Aleksei
> Made a decree in all his land.
> He prohibited the sale of tobacco
> And whipped lawbreakers without pity.
> Whoever sniffed, their nostrils would be torn
> And they were sent to hard labor.
> So the highest minds worked
> To end the contagion of this disease at its root![11]

It was particularly important to the Old Believers that Aleksei banned tobacco *before* he fell into apostasy by embracing the ritual reforms of Patriarch Nikon. His defense of Russia was strongest when he had not yet fallen under Nikon's Westernizing influences. When, however, Peter the

Great (Aleksei's son) further opened Russia to the West, he also condoned tobacco use. For the Old Believers—who suffered under Peter's tax on beards and refused his census as enrollment in the book of Antichrist—Peter's approval of tobacco confirmed its place among corrupt foreign imports. While potatoes and vodka sometimes also fell into this category, the hatred of tobacco was far broader and deeper among Old Believers than any other import. Potatoes, after all, could be shown to have an obvious benefit to humans but tobacco caused nothing but trouble.

TOBACCO USE AS IDOL WORSHIP

In addition to their distrust of tobacco itself because of its foreign *origin* and its Petrine proponents, Old Believers almost universally despised the active *use* of the weed. The distinction here was important. The devil created tobacco to ensnare humans and Peter the Great let it conquer Russia. It was the action of individuals, however, that damned them. More specifically, Old Believers claimed that tobacco use (in any form) was actually a form of idolatry since it set up tobacco as a god, creating ritual actions that both linked the sinner to his new deity and also made antichristian mockery of Orthodox rituals.[12]

At first glance, tobacco might seem to be an unlikely form of idolatry. How could smoking or taking snuff be the equivalent of raising an idol for worship instead of God? The answer lay in the Old Believers' perception of tobacco's addictive qualities. In this linkage between addiction and idolatry, Old Believers were particularly prescient, since they perceived the effects of tobacco more clearly than most other people of the period.[13] The satirical poem claimed that Beelzebub desired souls for all eternity. To this end, when the demons were done milling the tobacco, "the devil put in hellish powder to attract everyone to it and forever would he not lose his hellish power."[14] The poem continued, saying that:

> This American poison
> Took away spiritual wisdom from the world . . .
> In it hid a magical power
> Which, like a bottomless pit in the sea, swallowed all people.
> Like an evil Chaldean sorcerer,
> Tobacco attracted people to it forever.
> It contains a magical power,
> Whoever smells it does not leave it until death.

According to Old Believer traditions, any action that defiled the body was sinful because it besmirched the temple of God. Tobacco rose to the rank of idolatry because the addict could not stop himself. In this, tobacco took the place of God for the tobacco user, replacing Christ with pagan desires:

So, judge wisely and healthily:
Is this crop really created for the nose?
Yet all these people are praising it
Everyone is giving honor to its inventor.
All over the world the tobacco sparkles as if beneficial
It places detrimental Peruns into hearts.
Proof that it's not beneficial is the fact
That through addiction everyone loves it,
This secret demonic magnet. . . .[15]

Once a tobacco-user became converted—addicted—to tobacco, he sought solace only there. Moreover, converts sought strength, friendship, and health in their new "Peruns." In this passage, the poet created some of his most biting satire, pointing out the ways tobacco addicts found everything they needed in their new God:

A pharmacy of drugs is then not needed,
When tobacco heals a person from disease.
Ah! Ah! What am I rambling about—
I am leaving the borders of the mind!
No! We need to thank nature
For giving healing tobacco to the people.
Which gives health to all those who are ill;
And is a friend for those saddened and makes one that is bored
happy.
It doesn't heal one too soon,
But soon one loses one's soul from it.

In these passages, the satirist covered ground well-known to Old Believers in the nineteenth century. In "A Letter to ones who love Christ," the Old Believer K. K. Borisov noted that tobacco use was even worse than drunkenness because "people cannot and do not want to turn away" from its use.[16] This addiction was regularly described as "suicidal" by Old Believers of the period, both because of its physical effects but also because it murdered the soul, smelling "like a rotten stinking corpse, the everyday favorite sacrifice to the demon, a sure death. . . ."[17]

Was it possible to recover a soul that had been prisoner to this addiction? The answer seemed to be yes, but only after a period of ritual purification. Wary of the tobacco user's descent into idolatry, Old Believer communities sometimes forbade their children baptism until the parent stopped smoking. Likewise, an Old Believer who had fallen prey to tobacco sometimes had to get clean before he could marry. In the Siberian village of Beziamka, for example, the community decided that a tobacco-user had to wait six months after quitting before he could be married. Throughout the empire, Old Believers were not allowed into church services if they were known users of tobacco. Once they stopped and repented, they could again come into the temple of God. This ritual prohibition differentiated Old Believers from other Christians, who let smokers into their churches. This, according to the poet, "in all the nations, everyone goes to pray, carrying tobacco with him. Those with holy titles, pastor or sacristan, they all go to the altar with tobacco."[18]

Tobacco's power kept an otherwise-faithful Christian from taking part in the duties of his or her religion—"even on a holiday, even during a fast, day and night [he] smokes tobacco and stuffs it in the nose." Likewise, according to the poem, tobacco consumes its user, rendering him less cognizant than a drunk:

> Oh! The hellish stinking tobacco! More evil than all sins,
> Tobacco is a thousand times more sinful than drunkenness.
> The drunk, when he is sober,
> Judges himself before God.
> The smoker does not realize that he has sinned
> Although before lunch he had filled his nose a hundred times.
> Tobacco-users will never realize their wrong.[19]

Tobacco addiction also had social effects. Wary of the tobacco user's descent into idolatry, Old Believer communities sometimes forbade their children baptism until the parent stopped smoking. Likewise, an Old Believer who had fallen prey to tobacco sometimes had to get clean before he could marry. In the Siberian village of Beziamka, for example, the community decided that a tobacco-user had to wait six months after quitting before he could be married. Throughout the empire, Old Believers were not allowed into church services if they were known users of tobacco. Once they stopped and repented, they could again come into the temple of God.[20] The poet agreed that tobacco and churchgoing were incompatible: "And having cleaned the tobacco out of your nose, wipe it, utter a prayer, and cross yourself."[21]

TOBACCO AS RITUAL

For the Old Believers, the rituals of pre-Nikon Orthodoxy provided both the glue and the language for their faith. If, as Robert Crummey has pointed out, the Old Belief was a "textual community," then its texts extended into the words, gestures, and movements of the church liturgy.[22] As a replacement for God, therefore, tobacco also had to have its own rituals. Importantly, these actions represented an abomination of God's purpose for the body:

> What does all this lawlessness look like?
> You gave us the nose to smell,

Not to fill it with grated tobacco.
All the people are acting unnaturally
And fill their noses with tobacco every minute.

Smoking also controverted some of the most beloved Old Believer rituals. The most important was the act of censing, which Old Believers held up as a mark of their greater piety than the dominant Russian Orthodox Church. In the Old Belief, the censer was used more frequently and more specifically than among the other Orthodox. Priests did not just swing the censer; they made a cross in front of the believers. Likewise, Old Believers held their hands up "as if in evening sacrifice," symbolically accepting the smoke as it wafted toward them then making the sign of the cross and bowing. In some communities, only those who had not recently interacted with those outside the community could accept the incense. Others, who had been sullied by worldly activity, simply bowed as the censer passed by. To the Old Believers, the Russian Orthodox Church did not take censing seriously enough. Its method of censing and its haphazard reception by believers was not so clearly defined as it was in the Old Belief. For that reason, censing and incense were particularly potent rituals; undermining them was a significant sin.

Tobacco smoke was a diabolical ritual, the inverse of incense. Incense symbolized the Holy Spirit, which came as the Paraclete—the Comforter—to Christians. Tobacco smoke, however, was the antichristian comforter, offering a drugged feeling of well-being rather than the peace of God. The poet asks, "Is one not supposed to smell incense in church? While he is used to filling the nostrils with tobacco, when the deacon censes the whole church, even he whose nostrils are filled with tobacco, how can he not understand, that he can not smell the incense?"[23]

According to the poem, this was all part of a diabolical conspiracy. Instead of gathering for prayer, these high priests of tobacco would come together to celebrate:

Look: the tobacco-users will gather in a circle,
They will call on a horn
And a hundred of them will gather.
They will fight for the tobacco.
Come into the huge palaces
Where the earthly demigods reign,
Go into their lavishly decorated offices,
Where everyone dresses in golden cloth.
You will not find incense or censer in these rooms—
Only sparkling tools for smoking tobacco.
There are multitudes of gilded pipes
And in these rooms there are only pipes and pouches.
There is no censor or incense anywhere.
The words of the Apocalypse came true:

Smokers become rich from tobacco,
And for such an evil stinking fashion
They build large factories.
But the merchant who sells incense
Becomes impoverished and suffers.[24]

In addition to its symbolism as the Holy Spirit, incense was also supposed to be beautiful, a sweet smell of sanctity. Many times during the liturgical cycle—including the morning prayers and the wedding service, Orthodox Christians invoked an "odor of spiritual fragrance." Specifically, during the Proskomedia (Offertory), the priest said, "We offer you incense O Christ our God for an odor of spiritual fragrance. Receive it upon your heavenly altar, and send down upon us in return the grace of your all-holy Spirit." Instead of the sweet smell of incense, however, tobacco-smokers always smelled foul. The poet asked his readers to "look, how the body, from the stench of tobacco stinks from the brain to the heels. The whole Earth will fill with this stinking and miserable disgustingness. Smell, it is the stench of evil: it stinks with tobacco, like a goat in autumn."[25]

Smelling like a goat and addicted to his weed, a tobacco user could not take part in the Christian ritual actions of the community. "Now, think wisely about this," wrote the poet, "can tobacco not be the devil's invention? Whoever starts smoking a pipe, can he then utter a prayer?"[26] Even more damning was the way the snuffers picked up their drug from a little box—they held together the thumb, second, and middle fingers. For the Old Believers, this was a sin piled upon sin. The most famous symbolic difference between Old Believers and their Orthodox counterparts was the manner of holding the hand when making the sign of the cross—Old Believers touched the thumb, pinkie, and ring fingers together, while others touched the thumb, second, and middle fingers. Both practices, however, interpreted the fingers touching each other as a symbol of the Holy Trinity, while the other two fingers symbolized the two natures of Christ. And so, when the user picked up snuff, he was both making the sign of the cross incorrectly (with fingers in the new fashion) and simultaneously blaspheming:

Look: tobacco is taken with three fingers
A sign that also stands for a cross.
Do they not vex the Trinity,
When every hour they befoul their fingers?
The devil does not like prayer or fasting,
Here they smoke tobacco without the sign of the cross;
The stench enters the brain, where the soul lives,
It darkens the whole mind and the soul. . . .[27]

The point here could not be lost on Old Believers who read or heard this poem. By smoking or taking snuff, tobacco users replaced the true faith with another god, the inverse of all that was holy. To that end, the false god needed his own rituals that mocked the real traditions of the Old Believers. As he spoke in this new ritual language, the tobacco addict showed himself to be both a sinner and an apostate.

CONCLUSION

Hope for a Christian tobacco addict could be found, therefore, only in the smoker's ability to rejoin the community of the faithful by rejecting tobacco-stained rituals for the cleanness of Old Believer actions. Some Cossacks, for example, regularly fell into tobacco use when they were away from home. As they approached their towns, however, the Cossacks threw aside their pipes and snuffboxes so that they might be ritually clean upon return. This illustrated the paradox of addiction, from the Old Believer point of view. Like a false idol spawned by the devil, tobacco ensnared a good Christian and led him away from God. The weed perverted faith and turned holy rituals into satanic activities. Yet, in the end, Christianity was a message of hope and triumph. Endowed by the ability to repent, even the worst smoker could find his way back to a Christian life. "Understand," commanded the poet, "given the powers of mind and word, you, as opposed to the other animals, have free will. Become afraid of tobacco and think. Quit smoking. Learn to live soberly."[28] By doing so, the smoker would simultaneously throw off his addiction and be settled back into the bosom of true religion—the Old Belief.

NOTES

1. See Gregory L. Freeze, "Subversive Piety: Religion and the Political Crisis in Late Imperial Russia," *Journal of Modern History*, 68 (1996): 308–50.
2. See Roy R. Robson, *Old Believers in Modern Russia*, (DeKalb, IL: Northern Illinois University Press, 1995), 7–10.
3. Ibid., 107–11.
4. See Roy R. Robson, "A Legend on the Appearance of Tobacco" in *The Human Tradition in Modern Russia*, ed. William B. Husband, (Wilmington, DE: Scholarly Resources, 2000), 19–30. The "Tale" has many characteristics of Old Believer literature as it developed in the eighteenth and nineteenth centuries. Like the poem discussed in this article, the "Tale" intertwined Old Believers' mistrust with foreign cultural influence with the apocalypticism developed in the early period of the movement. Likewise, the "Tale" sought to legitimize anti-tobacco ideas by linking them to Biblical text, especially in the Revelation of St. John.
5. "Otkuda chai i kofe, tabak i kartofel'," in *Stikhi dukhovnye*, ed. F. M. Selivanova, (Moscow: Sovetskaia Rossiia, 1991), 301.
6. Fedor Vasil'evich Livanov, *Raskolniki i ostrozhniki: ocherki i razskazy,* vol. 1, (St. Petersburg: Tipografiia M. Khana, 1872), 234.
7. Livanov, *Raskolniki*, 241–2.

8. Ibid., 241–2, 244.
9. Ibid., 236. In fact, by the nineteenth century, as chapters in this volume show, there was a substantial literature in Russia on the supposed health benefits of tobacco use. Old Believers not only rejected these ideas but, as the poem shows, perceived them as diabolically inspired.
10. Viktoria Vladimirovna Vlasova, "Povsednevye zaprety v komi staroobriadcheskikh obshchinakh," *Staroobriadchestvo: istoriia, kul'tura, sovremenost'*, (2002): 517.
11. Livanov, *Raskolniki*, 244.
12. This opinion is still prevalent among Old Believers. See, for example, P.L. Asanova, "Po materialam ekspeditskii MGU v Urzhumskii i Slobodskoi r-ny Kirovskoi obl.," <http://www.ruthenia.ru/folklore/folklorelaboratory/Asan.htm>. For a contemporary Old Believer leader's views, see Bishop Innokentii Nizhegorodskii, "O tabakokurenii," <http://portal-credo.ru/site/print.php?act=lib&id=1706>.
13. As Chrissidis and Levin show elsewhere in this volume, tobacco had long been considered an intoxicant. Old Believers certainly knew of this perception and may have connected tobacco use to addiction just as they would have linked alcohol consumption with *pianstvo* (heavy drinking or alcoholism).
14. Livanov, *Raskolniki*, 235. The author plays on the words "iad" (poison) and "ad" (hellish).
15. Ibid., 238. Perun was an ancient pre-Christian Slavic god.
16. Kupriian Klimentovich Borisov, "Pis'mo khristoliubivym," in *Dukhovnaia literatura staroverov vostoka rossii xviii–xx vv.*, (Novosibirsk: Sibirskii Khronograf, 1999), 326.
17. Livanov, *Raskolniki*, 238.
18. Ibid., 245
19. Ibid., 246.
20. For information on baptism and tobacco, see *Dukhovnaia literatura,* 357–58. For marriage, see *Dukhovnaia literatura,* 392. The ban on church use was widespread. For one view on the subject, Borisov, "Pis'mo," 372.
21. Livanov, *Raskolniki*, 244.
22. Robert O. Crummey, "Old Belief as Popular Religion: New Approaches," *Slavic Review*, 52 (1993): 700–12.
23. Livanov, *Raskolniki*, 242. The poem uses the older Church Slavonic word "fimian" rather than the more regularly-used "ladon" to emphasize the holiness of incense.
24. Ibid., 249.
25. Ibid.,
26. Ibid., 248.
27. Ibid.
28. Ibid.

9 *Papirosy*, Smoking, and the Anti-Cigarette Movement[1]

Tricia Starks

In a years' later memoir, N. A. Semashko, the first Commissar of Health, recalled that Lenin was the one to start the entire thing when he asked, "Why don't you start a fight against that poison tobacco? I will support you."[2] Semashko set forth with great enthusiasm—little realizing that the battle would be, as he later recalled, "one of the comic episodes of [his] life."[3] What ensued from Semashko's taking up of Lenin's lightly proffered challenge was more than his own "comic" tale. In the battle over tobacco regulation in 1920 competing visions of health, state power, and national priorities combined in a story of health advocates calling for reform while representatives of the state and industry answered even more strongly for the health of the economy in the short term over the protection of the population's health in the long term.

Even though revolutionaries undertook this challenge, and would take it to a higher level and further point than any other contemporary state, this was, in many ways, not an unprecedented move in public health either in Russia or on the world stage. Semashko's attack built upon long-standing disgust with the tobacco habit among health reformers in Russia—a disgust that had risen up in vehemence in an arc that coincided with the rise in tobacco consumption in the late nineteenth century. In addition, Soviet views reflected worldwide disgust with tobacco by health and moral reformers of the period. What distinguished Semashko's attack was that the Soviets had the means and seeming willingness to address the problem. The concrete challenges to tobacco culture that Semashko proposed in 1920 were largely the same in reasoning and intent as the positions of prerevolutionary and worldwide anti-tobacco advocates.

Though the ubiquity of tobacco in Russia today makes it easy to believe that the Russian was born with cigarette in hand, the cigarette, in the form of the Russian *papirosa,* actually came into common use only in the late nineteenth century.[4] Widespread tobacco use was a relatively new phenomenon. The Russian cigarette was, as its name implies, paper-wrapped, and in the nineteenth century a few cottage shops produced hand-rolled paper tubes which female workers packed with either strong Turkish or light Maryland tobacco and occasionally batting as a crude, filtering device.[5]

Papirosy provided a stronger jolt of nicotine, even as new curing methods resulted in milder smokes with more appealing tastes.[6] The potency made for a product poised for popularity, the portability increased the attractions for those on the go or for use at work, and the increased smoothness encouraged smoking by previously non-smoking groups.[7] The switch to machine-produced cigarettes greatly increased their production and popularity. Whereas the most skilled hand-rollers could produce about two to three thousand cigarettes a day, mechanization allowed one worker to turn out the same amount in a few hours.[8] *Papirosy* share in the market grew over time, just as the cigarette gained popularity in Europe and the United States.[9] Smoking's traditional association with the military gave it overtones of both manliness and patriotism, and new manufacturing techniques made it cheap and associated it with modernity.[10] By 1913, 46% of tobacco production went to *papirosy* and much of the loose tobacco ended in self-rolled cigarettes.[11]

Print advertising and broadsheets appeared in larger numbers as manufacturers, able to produce more, sought to build markets. In stunning, full-color posters usually at least three feet, and sometimes five or six feet tall, advertisers promoted smoking as glamorous, luxurious, attractive, and modern and played upon already prominent ideas about smoking as revolutionary, transgressive, erotic, or desirable. Tobacco advertisers made appeals that transcended class and pushed smoking as manly, energizing, and enjoyable. While more and more people smoked for their own reasons, tobacco manufacturers gave the public positive images of smoking and incentives to pick up cigarettes through appealing images and concepts.

Machine-rolled cigarettes transformed the way people used and regarded tobacco. With the advertising push, the rise in production, the increase in consumption, and a decline in pipe stores and accessories, after 1890 most discussions surrounding tobacco focused on smoking. As one observer noted, "In the last twenty years tobacco use has undergone a complete change. Not even saying that with every day the pipe is disappearing, the people are more and more accustomed to the use of ready-made factory produced *papirosy*."[12] Modern, stimulating, virile, and fast-moving, the *papirosa* was the choice of the future for some. The surge in tobacco use and ubiquity of *papirosy*—especially in urban areas—led to a greater visibility for the habit, more concern for its etiquette, and greater anger over seeming violations of propriety. But the popularity of *papirosy* was not universally acclaimed. Public health advocates opined that everyone was smoking—and everywhere. As one contemporary commented, "Nowadays smoking of cigars and *papirosy* in particular is allowed everywhere, though the well-bred and good-mannered person does not permit himself to smoke in another's house, or even in a simple stand or store without the permission of the host."[13]

Propriety was but one concern of those interested in tobacco's regulation. Enemies of tobacco—doctors, the Church, and many social reformers—had long inveighed against the weed, and new antagonists arose in the late nineteenth century as public health became a prominent concern of Russian life in the wake of the Great Reforms of Alexander II (r. 1855–1881) and intellectual and cultural movements that glorified medicine. These changes encouraged discussions of hygienic, rationalized living for all elements of society but especially the lower classes. There was little definitive proof of tobacco's danger, but movements to vilify or curtail tobacco use tapped into hopes of bourgeois, state, and religious groups to rationalize, control, and shape the behaviors, and even the politics, of the masses.

As smoking rose in popularity in the late nineteenth and early twentieth centuries, Russia witnessed an upsurge in the number and frequency of didactic pamphlets against tobacco.[14] The pamphlets were often quite short, consisting of sometimes only six to ten pages. For instance, the diminutive *On Tobacco and the Threat of Smoking* was a three-by-four-inch tome and consisted of twenty-seven pages. It enjoyed multiple printings.[15] *Tobacco and Its Dangerous Influence on Man* was only twelve pages long.[16] This size would not only have allowed for ease of travel but also made the pamphlet affordable for purchase or free distribution. The pamphlet *Smoking: An Affordable Account* was billed as a "free introduction to the journal *The People's Health*."[17] Many pamphlets appeared first in medical journals or were based on public health lectures. For example, Dr. N. P. Preis not only outlined his credentials in his pamphlet—instructor of hygiene at the Khar'kov City Trade School and Khar'kov City Fourth Class School as well as instructor of hygiene for "the course for worker's and tradesmen of Khar'kov"—he noted that he gave this information to his students in a "yearly conversation" with the graduating class.[18] Another of his pamphlets—*Tobacco and Wine–Enemies of Mankind* enjoyed five printings and had been taken from a lecture he gave to the Khar'kov City Assembly on December 15, 1891.[19]

Unlike later treatises on health, these pamphlets did not always feature a doctor's title on the front page. Several authors have no professional title and quite a few include the religious standing of the author. These differences reflected the fractures of the anticigarette movement. *Papirosy* were decried on both medical and moral grounds, and the author's training did not always reflect the stance of the pamphlet on the problem. Many religious writers focused on medical issues, while medical writers quite often railed against the moral laxity of smokers. Almost all pamphlets mixed moral, medical, and social commentary in their case against smoking.

The medical case against tobacco unfolded in similar ways in most pamphlets, starting with the dangers of the poison nicotine and warning that even a capful could be deadly. For example, *Physiological Research on the Effects of Nicotine* recounted the effects of nicotine on dogs, frogs, and rabbits.[20] When it came to the consequences of nicotine for man rather than pet, a compilation of anecdotes recounted dizziness, convulsions, physical wasting, and almost always a final outcome of death. Preis's *Tobacco and*

Wine—Enemies of Mankind and Dr. Bussiron's *On the Effects of Smoking, Snuff, and Cigar Tobacco on the Health, Morals, and Mind of Man* both relied primarily on the recitation of different, thinly-documented anecdotes to underscore the dangers of nicotine.[21] A story of a smoking contest of two brothers served as centerpiece to several pamphlets. After one had smoked seventeen cigars and the other eighteen, the latter suddenly died. For each author, this was ghastly evidence of the dangers of tobacco—especially in excess.[22] While tobacco had originally come to Europe as a medicinal plant, anti-tobacco activists no longer considered pharmacological use of the herb legitimate. They noted that chaw served no use against scurvy despite the tales of sailors and found laughable the idea that smoking might fortify the mouth against microbes or cure lockjaw. Instead of serving as a remedy for toothache, tobacco caused vomiting and dizziness warned pamphlets.[23] The belief that "smoking gladdens man and invigorates the brain" was similarly ridiculed.[24]

Although many authors noted the general use of tobacco was dangerous, they saved special ire for the problem of *papirosy*, insisting, "Smoking is the worst sort of tobacco use."[25] Smoking artificially suppressed the appetite according to Russian Archpriest Mikhailovskii.[26] Dr. A. I. Il'inskii concurred and also noted that it harmed the teeth, caused lip cancer, increased conjunctivitis, and could lead to nicotine blindness (*ambylopia nicotiana*). He continued, "One rarely meets a person of good digestion, and if you do, of course, not one of them is a smoker."[27] Worse still, in Il'inskii's opinion, was the ignorance of smokers to the dangers of their habit, "Not one of these patients thinks that tobacco might be the cause of so many awful sicknesses."[28]

Not far beneath the surface of these health concerns lurked fears for moral and physical degeneracy. As *Three Poisons: Tobacco, Alcohol (Vodka) and Syphilis* succinctly argued, "Excessive use of tobacco, alcohol and alongside these the infection with syphilis . . . [serve] on the one hand as a cause of physical and moral suffering of people and on the other as a cause for the decline of the racial stock."[29] Dr. Preis lumped tea, coffee, hashish, opium, tobacco, and alcohol together as "inescapable habits" and concluded, "In our time, in our nervous century, all of these items, sadly, are extremely wide-spread and it is easy to get used to them (coffee, tobacco, alcohol)."[30] He finished, "The connection between physical and moral degeneration of mankind from tobacco and wine is established very easily. The organism addicted to tobacco and wine sustained and begat the generation which has withered physically and morally."[31] Il'inskii worried that *papirosy* were more widespread than drinking and "the number of smokers is ten to twenty times greater than the number of people in alcoholic excess; the poison of tobacco—nicotine—is more dangerous than alcohol." He even argued that tobacco served as the root of the most pressing disease of the late nineteenth century—neurasthenia.[32] The rapid spread of smoking, he opined, "explains the great number of nerve and other illnesses where the patient and even the doctor and no one in the world can diagnose the cause of the illness. Realistically if we did not bring tobacco poisoning up, not the ill, nor their companions, nor his doctor would be able to diagnose the illness."[33]

According to Archpriest Mikhailovskii, tobacco weakened the mind, as a smoker was unable to work—or even converse—without tobacco.[34] Another pamphlet warned, "Severe psychological disturbance with hallucinations" resulted from smoking.[35] One argued further, "Smokers are typically irritable and hot-tempered, dissatisfied with their lives and their acquaintances."[36] Moving from medical to moral issues, Appolov claimed that smokers desired this weakness, because smoking served as the crutch of the unclear conscience. He wrote, "People do not intoxicate themselves for fun and not from boredom do they gravitate to stupefying drugs but so as to muddy their mind and to hide from themselves their dirtied conscience—the evidence of their foul life."[37]

Appolov recalled how the influential religious leader Metropolitan Filaret of Moscow (1782–1867) played upon fears of enslavement, the unnatural, and the foreign in his statements on tobacco as he argued:

> Is it not strange that people invented a new kind of hunger, which nature had not known and a new kind of food, which she had not thought of; as a consequence of this habit they have made themselves slaves of an unnatural whim and multiplied their needs making the unnecessary essential. It is a foreign invention that seems sensible only because it is accepted by so many.[38]

Abbot Arsenii of the Resurrection Monastery said smokers suffered a "diabolical captivity" and compared tobacco's enslavement to the captivity of Russian soldiers under the Japanese.[39]

Russian Orthodox objections paled in comparison to the long-held and deep resentment of the Old Believers to tobacco.[40] For the Old Believer, smoking endangered man from the physical to the moral to the spiritual realm. One pamphlet thundered that smoking "leaves man lower than the animals, for not one among them uses tobacco, ruining their organism, health, and morality."[41] Other religious groups expressed their anger with cigarettes. The Baptist press issued *Shall I Smoke or Not?* (1906), Ioann of Kronstadt spoke frequently on the dangers of smoking, and L. N. Tolstoy famously opposed all "stupefying" substances including tobacco.[42]

While they shared a common enemy, the Russian Orthodox did not readily team up with other religious entities and at times even seemed resentful. Ambivalence was evident among the Russian Orthodox in relation to tobacco as some priests and monks smoked, according to contemporaries.[43] Appolov argued that while Old Believers did not smoke, they should not feel superior because of this as some good people smoke and some bad people are non-smokers. This attempt to soften the moral stigma of smoking appeared especially odd as he made this case after a multi-page diatribe on how those who used alcohol or tobacco to intoxicate themselves must be covering up sin.[44]

This lack of cooperation among religious groups set the Russian anti-tobacco movement apart from other campaigns of the time. In many countries, the campaign against tobacco—again, most pointedly smoking—took off in the late nineteenth century as health, temperance, and religious groups came together. Temperance groups lumped tobacco together with "intoxicants" that wasted resources though few limited their concerns to tobacco. In Russia, the relation of temperance and anti-smoking was less developed than in the United States, Britain, and Canada. Russian Orthodox Church-initiated temperance groups had been forming since the 1860s, but Church concerns over control hindered the growth of independent movements. Many Russians felt that temperance might even be irreligious as it was related often to groups the Church found threatening.[45] According to one 1902 pamphlet, while many resisted alcohol, tobacco was everywhere, "In Russia today there is still no action in the fight with smoking. A society that would fight with smoking does not yet exist. Popular brochures on the dangers of smoking are not available, if you do not count the self-published and freely distributed."[46] The author was obviously prone to hyperbole as quite a few brochures were available, however, his stridency revealed a strong concern for the meager resources of anti-tobacco activists.

With tobacco, mainly cigarettes, seen as a threat to race, body, mind, and soul, it is not surprising that smoking by youth and women inspired moral panic and what Archpriest Mikhailovskii called a great movement to stomp out smoking by eight- to eighteen-year-olds.[47] Smoking's effect on the developing body grounded many arguments, like Il'inskii's charge that "during the time of lung growth, from age seventeen to twenty years, the smoking of tobacco must be forbidden as the greatest problem and cause of all future consumption."[48] Mikhailovskii blamed smoking for the ruination of body as well, lamenting that smoking was the reason for the dearth of good tenors.[49] Many went on to more fantastic allegations that merged health, morality, and social concern arguing that when children smoked it tore away at society's moral fiber. Smoking ruined a boy, and "from kind, open and pleasant he is made sly and impertinent."[50] Youth who smoke, "become inaccurate and prone to slovenliness" making them accustomed "to deceit and lies" even as they steal their first tobacco.[51] According to the study of one Dr. Fisk, the poor habits of child smokers affected their later life as "only twenty percent enjoyed good success and of those with poor success fifty-seven percent were smokers."[52] Russian obsession with the smoking boy mirrored international worries over youth behavior.[53]

In addition to concern over children's smoking, pamphlet writers expressed widespread anxiety over female tobacco use with additional concern over the effects of their smoking on their progeny and on society generally. While statistical evidence is unavailable, pamphlets on female smoking, speeches, special women's brands and accessories, and foreign accounts indicated that a good number of women smoked and used other forms of tobacco in Russia. Although Russian women's tobacco use distinguished the anti-tobacco movement in Russia from that in the West, it did bring the Russian campaign into alignment with those in the East and Africa, where the campaign against the smoking boy was joined by an active attack on the smoking woman.[54]

Dr. Preis situated women's fall to tobacco in the problems of the day, "In our times often women—especially Russian women with their sensitive natures—feel the separation between life and conscience so strongly that they give themselves over to some type of narcotic."[55] Preis, however, did not feel that this explanation served as an excuse and women should instead find good works to occupy their time. Authors might reason that social conditions created women smokers but that provided no excuse and smoking woman should be reviled. Preis argued that these female smokers were hardly even women:

> If you see a woman sucking on a *papirosa*, the unavoidable consequence is the awful odor from the throat, the black and sooty teeth, and the smoky fingers. A smoking woman falls unavoidably from aesthetic quality without which in my opinion, a woman cannot exist. . . . Beyond that must I remind you that the cigarette is the first step towards moral laxity?[56]

Another author argued for further physical problems that effectively "desexed" the female smoker as smoking led to irregular menstruation.[57]

The female smoker's lack of femininity was expressed in her lack of moral sensibilities as well as her physical debilitation. One author warned that "among young women smoking awakens sexual desire prematurely and easily leads to secret vices."[58] This voracious sexuality made women more like men—interested in sexual gratification and subject to lusts. Preis argued for a connection between smoking, education, and sophistication that led to remarkable effects on the nature of woman:

> Smoking women are for the most part educated and cultivated. The soul of such an educated and cultivated woman must be reasonably good—but it turns out the opposite. Education does nothing to change them and their soul takes on the desire to do evil. Thus there can be no discussion of the perfect and eternal good of the soul of woman if a woman smokes and threatens herself, her husband, her children, and others.[59]

With his diatribe, Preis made one of the other arguments often seen against women's smoking—danger to children. These women exposed not just themselves but others to the poisons of nicotine and endangered future generations. In addition to upsetting menstruation, "Smoking by pregnant women harms not just the mother but also the fetus."[60] Further still, the poison of smoking passed from the mother to the infant through the breast and such negligent, self-indulgent mothers were to be held beneath contempt. One pamphlet coldly argued that mothers who nursed their infants with nicotine-laced milk deserved no sympathy for the future of their children: "Later this self same mother in the face of their child's serious illness will cry and wail," the writer noted sarcastically. He concluded: "The tears of such a mother have little value."[61]

Women took center stage in another way in pamphlets as anti-smoking advocates noted that mostly women worked in tobacco manufacturing and these women were subject to problems of hearing, the lungs, the blood, and more frequent miscarriages and infant death.[62] Authors similarly decried the selfishness of smokers—both male and female—that led to land "wasted" or even "made tired" by tobacco farming.[63] Finally, they heaped blame on the smokers for fires arguing, "Most fires come out of poor care of flame, and with matches no one is as uncaring as smokers."[64] These charges against smokers' selfishness and the problems of tobacco manufacture echoed anti-smoking arguments made by groups around the world.

Pamphlets often pointed to cigars or pipes as less dangerous—with little more than the same type of anecdotal evidence they used to condemn cigarettes. The silence or disinterest in certain types of smoking in part reflected their invisibility. Pipes and cigars did not lend themselves so easily to casual, urban smoking. The *papirosa* smoker, however, must have been hard to avoid and public smokers forced others to confront their habit. A class connection may also be seen. In upper class homes, space allowed smokers to be relegated to special rooms. Many of those who pursued their habit in public may have done so because they did not have private spaces. This associates the habit with the lower and lower-middle classes. Public spaces—such as railroad cars, theaters, and pubs—became points of confrontation between smokers and non-smokers. Many pamphlets discussed the problems of smoking in these spaces in particular, suggesting that for some it was not just the habit but the public, intrusive nature of its pursuit that was worrisome and led to greater condemnation. Finally, in health literature generally lurks the elitist assumption that others must be told what to do and how to live.

Years of war and turmoil did not change the arguments surrounding smoking. Instead cigarettes found a more organized enemy in the leaders of the new state. V. I. Lenin abhorred smoking and perhaps more importantly, so too did N. A. Semashko, the head of the newly created People's Commissariat of Health. Despite the change to "mass politics" Semashko's initiatives revealed the same anxieties as those expressed by the bourgeois and religious opponents of tobacco in the prerevolutionary era. The upper-class movement of the prerevolutionary health authorities to control the behavior of the masses was taken up by the supposed representatives of the masses in the postrevolutionary period. Their concerns echoed the arguments of prerevolutionary anti-smoking advocates; however, Semashko and Lenin's methods revealed their different political and economic opinions about the relationship of state, citizen, and production. The methods may have differed, but the motives of health advocates and the counterclaims of advertisers as outlined in the late nineteenth century, remained consistent in tobacco discourse.

A long-time public-health advocate and Bolshevik, Semashko framed his task as Commissar of Health in both humanitarian and political terms. The responsibility of the workers' state was to care for workers, and a healthy state would evolve alongside healthy citizens.[65] Soviet prevention centered on concepts of hygienic living with a balanced day of work, leisure, and sleep, a strong adherence to the rule of the clock, and attention to the body as a "machine" that needed good care and good fuel in order to run efficiently. In a hygienic life there was no place for "bad habits." Semashko and others believed that smoking, drinking, and sexual excess were all decadent and problems of the past that came from capitalism's poor working and living conditions and that their appeal was irrational and would be destroyed easily by the new Socialist order.[66] The social basis for these problems—the hopelessness of life—would be obliterated and people would no longer need to turn to "soporifics" to deaden them to the pain of wage slavery. Hygienists had faith that if the people were just informed of the problems in their behavior, they would be lured by rational arguments to change. Optimism would characterize many of their programs and strongly influence Semashko's anti-tobacco agenda.

Not waiting even for the battle with epidemics to slake or for the future of the state to be settled, Semashko began his quest for a smoking ban in 1920 with Lenin's blessing.[67] On December 14, 1920, at the meeting of the Soviet of People's Commissars, Semashko brought up tobacco and emerged with a resolution to work towards the "lessening, and in the future, to the destruction of [tobacco] culture."[68] In pursuit of this goal, he was made the head of a special commission of agricultural, production, and distribution representatives. Over the next several weeks the commission met to discuss a draft decree on the sale, spread, and fight against tobacco. Semashko urged dramatic measures including the limitation of tobacco growing within Russia and forbidding the export of tobacco because, he argued, the Soviet republic should not furnish the external market with a dangerous product.[69] Looking for some type of middle ground, industry representatives pushed to stamp out speculation.[70]

Semashko brought a draft of a decree, "On the Fight with Smoking Tobacco," to the February 3, 1921, meeting of the "Small" Soviet of People's Commissars. While the commission had allowed for input from other agencies, the grandeur of the proposal spoke to Semashko's heavy influence. The ten-point plan was ambitious. If it had been fully instituted it would have been the first of its kind in the world. Semashko spread his attack along three fronts—production, access, and image. First, he wanted to limit the supply of tobacco. Controlling the allotment of land to tobacco tillage and banning foreign imports would control supply and decrease the amount of tobacco available while government controls over the sale of tobacco, forbidding private tobacco factories, and attacking speculators would limit supply for the entire country.[71]

In addition Semashko proposed restrictions on the sale of tobacco products. The government would take a heavy hand in distribution of tobacco, including issuing tobacco cards for those of age within the republic and barring those under the age of twenty from buying tobacco.[72] Men from age twenty to thirty-five and women of all ages would be allowed only a restricted amount of tobacco on a scale decided upon by health authorities and these limits would apply to the Red Army too.[73]

Not all of the decree focused on the economics and supply of tobacco. Semashko included a ban on smoking in public places and buildings; as well as at all meetings, conferences, and hospitals; and places where children might be present (orphanages, kindergartens, and schools). To ensure that this ban had teeth, Semashko asked for a meeting of the Commissariats of Health and Internal Affairs to decide upon fines.[74] The last point called together various agencies for the "energetic agitation against tobacco" in all union, cultural-enlightenment, and medical-sanitary organizations.[75]

Semashko's program melded with the prophylactic mission of the Commissariat of Health, but they echoed the less-scientifically-founded fears of prerevolutionary activists regarding the physical, mental, and moral effects of tobacco. For example, the restriction of women's access to tobacco hid concerns—about birth rates, infant death rates, and the strength of Russia's population in numbers as well as individually—that were fundamental to the Commissariat of Health's founding and featured heavily in prerevolutionary anti-smoking tracts. The ban on children's access to tobacco echoed the same fears for continued health of the population. Fear for the delicacy of youth must have figured heavily into Semashko's reasoning. Accompanying Semashko's draft decree in the archival file was a report on the dangers of youth smoking and the measures taken by the German government to thwart this menace between 1917 and 1920. The German measures incorporated similar moves to the Semashko plan including the restrictions on buying as well as smoking in public areas (assumedly a way to keep children from having models of smoking behavior, enduring passive smoke, and having access to cigarettes).[76]

While not immediately apparent, the attack upon smoking men aged twenty to thirty-five engaged the same issues of fertility and control that were important in the planks addressing women's and children's tobacco use. The fears of an epidemic of neurasthenia in the late nineteenth century only intensified in the contemplation of national strength in the wake of the demographic catastrophe of 1914–1920. Soviet hygienists believed that modern life, which divorced men from productive labor and nature, drained essential forces. Bad habits, which enslaved the practitioner to vice—masturbation, drink, and tobacco—all weakened the will and led to wasting away and sexual impotency.[77]

These fears over tobacco use of women, youth, and men were not restricted to Russia nor were bans against tobacco a particularly Soviet response. Russians had attempted restrictions before, and in the United States, tobacco use was banned in public places (or for women) in several states. While these bans were overturned, they showed a definite urge towards government intervention. In this regard the Soviets were reflecting the attitudes of public health advocates throughout the world. A great difference, though, was in the all-out ban on *all* tobacco use that Semashko proposed. Many health advocates distinguished between pipe smoking and cigarette smoking, finding the former less harmful and thus displaying a discomfort with the latter. While Semashko's restrictions for use focused primarily on smoking, the restrictions on production would attack all levels of tobacco consumption.

The body of the decree and its stridency came from the mind of the Commissar of Health. The "Small" Soviet of People's Commissars, which met more frequently and in smaller gatherings than the larger body, would seem a more congenial place for Semashko's proposal, and indeed according to his memoirs, the economic representatives were so "scared" that they readily signed on to his proposition.[78] The record for the meeting gives a similar account of his reception. The committee concluded by asking Semashko to edit and submit the decree to the larger group. While a smooth meeting, this suggestion revealed the fractious nature of the debate. Rather than simply adopting the decree, an option for the "Small" Soviet of People's Commissars, it was instead tendered to the full body.[79]

The further history of the decree did not go as swimmingly as its early days of investigation and drafting. According to Semashko's account, when he broached the subject at the full Soviet of People's Commissars the reception was far different. Semashko said that the economic organizations fell upon him "with bayonets." He tried to hold his ground, but finally he looked to Lenin for help. Instead of a defender, Semashko saw Lenin sitting silently with his head bowed slightly and a sly smile on his face.[80]

The July 12, 1921, resolution of the larger body pulled the decree "with discussion."[81] Semashko lost the legislative war and with no production controls or regulations he retained only plank ten—the general sanitary enlightenment mission—which was already his as the Commissar of Health.[82] Given the large mission of the Commissariat—fighting everything from typhus to bottle-feeding babies—and the horrid financial situation it would soon enter, there would be no balance between anti-smoking propaganda and the massive influx of advertisements from a reanimated tobacco industry. Semashko was closest to success in the fight against tobacco at a point when the Russian tobacco industry was in danger of expiring on its own. While *Pravda* suggested that in 1918 Moscow housed 600,000 smokers of which 360,000 smoked prepared cigarettes, the war and the Civil War had severely disrupted production and distribution of tobacco products, leaving this a slightly empty figure.[83] Tobacco plants were plagued by lack of paper, fuel, and labor in addition to having problems accessing the supply of tobacco.[84] Tobacco supplies fell precipitously with the start of World War I and still farther with the Revolution as many of the areas of prime production happened to be those which experienced a great amount of turnover and fighting.[85] By 1920, tobacco production was at under half of pre-war levels.[86] Not only was there no supply of tobacco, that which remained was extremely expensive. Prices were well above pre-war levels for all tobacco—from cheapest to most expensive—and prices did not begin to come down until the general recovery period of 1926.[87] Semashko had pushed for tobacco legislation at precisely that point when many Russians were pressured not to smoke for reasons little related to health.

After the fight in the Soviet of People's Commissars was over, according to his memoirs, Semashko went to find Lenin. This time he looked not for support, but for explanation. Why had he not come to his aid? Lenin replied, simply, "You, old man, were crushed."[88] According to a recent history, Semashko did succeed in convincing the military establishment to stop sending out tobacco to the military, but this again seemed probably a necessity due to decreased supply, and as other sources still discuss tobacco rations sent to the front, it is doubtful that this victory, if it occurred, was long lived.[89]

With no halt on production, no ration cards to control access to tobacco, Semashko turned to the last idea, prophylaxis and propaganda. Arguments familiar from the fin-de-siècle anti-smoking movement continued to rattle through the propaganda. A capful of nicotine could kill a horse, warned posters and pamphlets. Smoking subjugated the will argued others. The smoking boy still inspired horror but either the smoking women had decreased in number or this particular social anxiety had fallen away.[90] Semashko would see the loss of not just his tobacco campaign but also his commissariat. Having lost the legislative war, having lost the image war, in 1929 Semashko would lose the power battle as well, as he and many of his most visionary colleagues were purged from the health administration of the Soviet Union. Stripped of their posts, they would see the health administration taken over by bureaucrats and the change towards worker-centered care rather than universal provision more firmly entrenched. Their rhetoric in the battle against bad habits would be softened soon after they were thrown from power, and cigarettes would become so firmly entrenched in Soviet society over the course of the century, it would not be until 1970s that action would again be contemplated in the fight with tobacco. In the face of such devastating consequences, the tale of Semashko's "comic" battle against tobacco in the 1920s becomes all the more serious.

NOTES

1. Material for this article was gathered courtesy of a National Endowment for the Humanities/National Council for Eurasian and East European Research Collaborative Research Grant and with the aid of my collaborators Iu. P. Bokarev and N. I. Sokolov.

2. N. Semashko, *Nezabyvaemyi obraz*, (Moscow: Gosizdat, 1959), 11.
3. ibid.
4. Nineteenth-century Russians generally referred to a difference between the *papirosa* and the cigarette. According to Brokgauz's encyclopedic dictionary, the *papirosa* is a paper-wrapped tobacco smoke, while cigarettes are wrapped in tobacco leaf. Others distinguish the two forms according to the type of tobacco—a cigarette is paper-wrapped American tobacco and a *papirosa* contains *makhorka* (Russian, mercerized, low-grade tobacco). In the twentieth century the *papirosa* became associated with a cardboard-mouthpiece smoke used by lower-class smokers. In all cases, lower quality is associated with the *papirosa*. F. A. Brokgauz and I. A. Efron, eds., *Entsiklopedicheskii slovar XXXII*, (St. Petersburg: I. A. Efron, 1901), 421–423. No author, *Kratkii ocherk tabakokureniia v Rossii, v minuvshev 19-m stoletii: Za period vremeni s 1810 po 1906 god*, (Kiev: Petra Varskago, 1906), 6.
5. Igor' Bogdanov, *Dym otechestva, lli kratkaia istoriia tabako-kurenia,* (Moscow: Novoe Literaturnoe obozrenie, 2007), 58.
6. Jordan Goodman, *Tobacco in History: The Cultures of Dependence*, (London: Routledge, 1993), 5–6.
7. Cigarette smoke is acidic and smoother, allowing it to be inhaled into the lungs, while cigar and pipe smoke is alkaline, enabling absorption through the mouth. Jordan Goodman notes this milder smoke may have increased female and youth smoking, therefore anti-child smoking legislation began appearing at this point. "Webs of Drug Dependence: Towards a Political History of Smoking and Health," in *Ashes to Ashes: The History of Smoking and Health*, ed. S. Locket et al., (Amsterdam: Rodopi, 1998), 16.
8. In Russia, cartridge machines produced up to 80,000 paper-tubes a day, and one woman, working one tobacco-packing machine, could fill 1,800 cartridges per hour; Brokgauz and Efron, eds. *Entsiklopedicheskii slovar XXXII*, 422. The first clunky, yet productive machines emerged in the 1880s. Richard Kluger, *Ashes to Ashes: America's Hundred-Year Cigarette War, the Public Health, and the Unabashed Triumph of Philip Morris,* (New York: Vintage Books, 1997), 19–20. In the United States, even though early machines broke and jammed, Duke's skilled hand rollers could not match their output. One machine produced as many cigarettes in a day as forty-eight skilled rollers. Cassandra Tate, *Cigarette Wars: The Triumph of 'The Little White Slaver,'* (New York: Oxford University Press, 1999), 14–15. For the evolution of *papirosy* machinery, see Gorchakova, this volume.
9. *Kratkii ocherk" tabakokureniia,* 435.
10. In the Russo-Turkish War of 1876–1878 tobacco smoke was said to hover "like thunderclouds" over both camps. V. G. Kiernan, *Tobacco: A History*, (London: Hutchinson Radius, 1991), 140.
11. See Bokarev, this volume. Additionally, *papirosy* exports were increasing, mostly to Germany and Finland (about two-thirds of exports), but also to China and many other countries of Europe. Brokgauz and Efron, eds. *Entsiklopedicheskii slovar XXXII*, 433.
12. Brokgauz and Efron, eds. *Entsiklopedicheskii slovar XXXII*, 433.
13. *Kratkii ocherk tabakokureniia*, 14.
14. A sampling of the Russian State Library, Moscow showed that in the 1880s and 1890s anti-tobacco tracts came out with increasing frequency. After 1902 two to five came out nearly every year and earlier pamphlets came out in new editions. The majority of publications focused on smoking rather than other tobacco use like chaw and snuff.
15. D. P. Nikolskii, *O tabake i vrede ego kureniia*, (St. Petersburg: Ministerstva vnutrennikh del, 1894).

16. Bishop Evlogii, *Tabak i ego vrednoe vliianie na cheloveka*, (Saratov: A. F. Vinkler, 1914).
17. Bek, *Kurenie: V obshchedostupnom izlozhenii.* Bezplatnoe prilozhenie k zhurnalu "Narodnoe zdravie," (St. Petersburg: St-Peterburgskaia elektropechatnia, 1902).
18. Nik. Pav. Preis, *Tabak–Vrag chelovechestva (Avto-kompiliativnyi sbornik")*, (Khar'kov: Pechatnoe delo, 1902), 5.
19. Nik. Pav. Preis, *Tabak i vino–Vragi chelovechestva*, 5-oe izd., (Khar'kov: Pechatnoe delo, 1902), 1.
20. Aleksandr Tugendgol'd', *Fiziologicheskiia izsledovaniia o deistvii nikotina*, (Moscow: V. Grachev, 1864), 25–95.
21. Dr. Bussiron, *O vlianii tabaku kuritel'nago, niukhal'nago i tsigar, na zdorov'e, nravstvennost, i um' cheloveka*, (St. Petersburg: K. Zhernakov, 1845), 13–18; and Tugendgol'd', *Fiziologicheskiia izsledovaniia.*, 25–95.
22. Appolov, *Perestanem kurit'!* 10; also in A. Blindovskii, *Kak brosit kurit'*, (Kiev: A. O. Shterenzon, 1912), 13.
23. Appolov, *Perestanem kurit'!* 10.
24. A. I. Il'inskii (Dr. Med.), *Tri iada: Tabak, alkogol' (vodka) i sifilis*, 2-oe izd., (Moscow; Tip. Kh. Barkhudarian" 1898), 38–43.
25. Dr. Preis as quoted in A. Blindovskii, *Kak brosit kurit'*, (Kiev: A. O. Shterenzon, 1912), 12.
26. V. Mikhailovskii (Archpriest), *Tabak i vrednoe vliianie ego na cheloveka*, 5th ed., (St. Petersburg: Tipografiia E. A. Pozdniakova, 1894), 20.
27. Il'inskii, *Tri iada*, 26, 29–33.
28. Ibid., 28.
29. Ibid., 1.
30. Bek, *Kurenie*, 3.
31. Preis, *Tabak i vino*, 3.
32. Laura Goering details not just the interest in neurasthenia but a bleeding of the language of disease into cultural critiques in her "'Russian Nervousness': Neurasthenia and National Identity in Nineteenth-Century Russia," *Medical History*, 47 (January 2003), 23–46.
33. Il'inskii, *Tri iada*, 24–25.
34. Mikhailovskii, *Tabak*, 21.
35. Bek, *Kurenie*, 34.
36. Appolov, *Perestanem kurit'!* 37–8.
37. Ibid., 18.
38. *Drep. i nov. Rossiia za 1877: Zametki i Novosti*, no. 6, p. 175, quoted in Mikhailovskii, *Tabak*, 10–11.
39. Archpriest Arseniia (Nastoiatelia voskresenskago monastyria), *O poroke tabakokureniia*, (St. Petersburg: A. S. Suvorina, 1905), 3–4.
40. Roy R. Robson, "Old Believers in Imperial Russia: A Legend on the Appearance of Tobacco," in *The Human Tradition in Modern Russia*, ed. William B. Husband, (Wilmington, DE: Scholarly Resources, 2000).
41. Vl. M-ov", *Neskol'ko slov o tabake i ego upotrebelenii (otdel'nyi ottisk iz zhurnala "Staroobriadets" no. 5 za 1906 g)*, (Nizhnyi Novgorod: Tip. T-va I. M Mashistova, 1906), 1.
42. No author, *Kurit' li mne ili net'?* (Rostov-na-don: A. Pavlov, 1906); on Ioann, see V. P., *Shto takoe—dymnaia privychka? O tabakokurenii*, (St. Petersburg: G. P. Pozharov, 1914), 1–2; on Tolstoy see, Preis, *Tabak i vino*, 50.
43. Archimandrite Arsenii, *Bros'te kurit' tabak'*, (Moscow: A. I. Snegireva, 1907), 5.
44. Appolov, *Perestanem kurit'!* 24.

45. W. Arthur McKee, "Sobering Up the Soul of the People: The Politics of Popular Temperance in Late Imperial Russia," *The Russian Review*, 58 (April 1999): 224, 227–8; see also his "Taming the Green Serpent: Alcoholism, Autocracy, and Russian Society, 1881–1914," (Ph.D. Diss., University of California–Berkeley, 1997), 278–330, 383–438.
46. Bek, *Kurenie*, 40, 46.
47. Mikhailovskii, *Tabak*, 5. See also O. Dedelin, *Kak uchit'sia ot kureniia*, 2-oe ed. and trans. from German, (Moscow: Izdaniia, 1909), 5; Evlogii, *Tabak i ego vrednoe vliianie.* According to Nikol'skii 32% of students at the St. Petersburg mining institute smoked, and he cited from other studies that 54.6% of medical students and 47.2% of technical students smoked. He further distinguished that mostly little Russians and Greeks smoked while fewer Jews, Armenians, and Georgians did. Medical and merchant classes smoked more, while nobles, petty bourgeois, clergy, and peasant smoked less. D. Nikol'skii, *O kurenii tabaka sredi uchashchikhsia*, no. 42, (St. Petersburg: Russkago vracha, 1902), 3.
48. Il'inskii, *Tri iada*, 20.
49. Mikhailovskii, *Tabak*, 16–17.
50. Arsenii, *Bros'te kurit'*, 2.
51. Preis, *Tabak,* 32.
52. Bek, *Kurenie*, 34.
53. John Welshman, "Images of Youth: The Issue of Juvenile Smoking, 1880–1914," *Addiction*, 91:9 (1996): 1379–1386.
54. Manako Ogawa, "The 'White Ribbon League of Nations' Meets Japan: The Trans-Pacific Activism of the Woman's Christian Temperance Union, 1906–1930," *Diplomatic History*, 31 (January 2007): 21–50; Rumi Yasutake, "Men, Women, and Temperance in Meiji Japan: Engendering WCTU Activism from a Transnational Perspective," *The Japanese Journal of American Studies*, 17 (2006): 91–111.
55. Preis, *Tabak,* 15.
56. Ibid., 16.
57. Bek, *Kurenie*, 34.
58. A. V. *Shto govoriat' uchenye liudi o kurenii tabaka*, (St. Petersburg: Aleks-Nevsk. O-va trezvosti, 1914), 9.
59. Preis, *Tabak,* 18.
60. Bek, *Kurenie*, 34.
61. Arsenii, *Bros'te kurit' tabak'*, 3.
62. Mikhailovskii, *Tabak*, 14. Match factories were another dangerous outgrowth of smoking. Appolov, *Perestanem kurit'!* 41.
63. Appolov, *Perestanem kurit'!* 6–7, 42
64. Ibid., 43.
65. On Soviet Public Health, see N. A. Semashko, *Okhrana zdorov'e rabochikh i rabotnits krest'ian i krestianok za desiat let*, (Moscow: NKZ RSFSR), 5–8.
66. I. V. Sazhin, *Pravda o kurenii*, (Leningrad: Leningradskaia Pravda, n. d.), 18.
67. Semashko, *Nezabyvaemyi obraz*, 11.
68. Gosudarstvennyi arkhiv Rossiiskii federatsii, Moscow, (GARF), f. a-482, op. 1, d. 155, l. 444.
69. GARF, f. a-482, op. 1, d. 288, ll. 112–113.
70. GARF, f. a-482, op. 1 d. 288, l. 120.
71. GARF, f. a-482, op. 1, d. 155, l. 447, points 1–3.
72. "Tabachnye kartochki" in the 1919 *Pravda* mentioned tobacco cards to be handed out to those over age seventeen suggesting that such cards were already in use for rationing. January 16, 1919, 3.

73. GARF, f. a-482, op. 1, d. 155, l. 447, points 4–5.
74. GARF, f. a-482, op. 1, d. 155, l. 447, points 6–9.
75. These groups were Narkomzdrav, Narkompros, and Vsesobuch , see GARF f. a-482, op. 1, d. 155, l. 447 (back), point 10.
76. GARF, f. a-482, op. 1, d. 155, l. 446.
77. Sazhin, *Pravda o kurenie.*
78. T. H. Rigby, *Lenin's Government: Sovnarkom, 1917–1922*, (Cambridge: Cambridge University Press, 1979), 76–82. Semashko, *Nezabyvaemyi obraz,* 12.
79. Rossiiskii gosudarstvennyi arkhiv sotsial'no-politicheskoi istorii, Moscow, f. 19, op. 2, d. 627, l. 3.
80. Semashko, *Nezabyvaemyi obraz*, 11–12.
81. GARF, f. a-482, op. 1, d. 155, l. 711
82. Semashko, *Nezabyvaemyi obraz,* 12.
83. "Chislo kuriashchikh v Moskve," *Pravda,* November 12, 1918, 4.
84. "Zakrytie tabachnykh fabriki," *Pravda,* November 5, 1918, 4.
85. A. Kaplan warned in 1918 that tobacco production would halt in four months without heroic measures. See "Kak spaset tabachnuiu promyshlennost," *Pravda,* July 18, 1918, 4. See similar concerns in "Sostoianie tabachnoi promyshlennost," *Pravda,* August 14, 1918, 4.
86. See Bokarev, this volume.
87. Ibid.
88. Semashko, *Nezabyvaemyi obraz*, 12.
89. Bogdanov, *Dym otechestva,* 192.
90. See for example, Sigal, *Vrednaia privychka (Kuren'e tabaka)*, (Moscow: Gosmedizdat, 1929); Sazhin, *Pravda o kurenii*; Sigal, B. *I. Sud nad pionerom kurivshim i II. Sud nad neriashlivym pionerom: Dve instsenirovki*, (Moscow: Zhizn' i znanie, 1927).

10 Tobacco Production in Russia

The Transition to Communism

Iu. P. Bokarev
Edited and Translated by Tricia Starks

Although the tobacco business struggled in Russia under Peter the Great (1689–1725), by the time of Catherine II (1762–1796) it began to grow. On July 31, 1762, the empress established the free trade of tobacco, and soon thereafter the first tobacconists in St. Petersburg were opened by foreigners. They sold crumbled smoking tobacco and by 1812 the number of such production houses rose to six; however, all of these worked with imported raw materials.[1] Russia received is first large-scale, internal raw material base in 1783 with Catherine's annexation of Crimea. With the 1801 inclusion of Georgia, Caucasian tobacco production was added and soon the cultivation of tobacco spread to the Kuban region in Ukraine.

As this chapter details, from these beginnings, internal tobacco cultivation and manufacture expanded. Over the next 150 years, against a background of internal unrest, external wars, civil strife, and massive economic upheaval that challenged the abilities of first the Russian, and then Soviet economic systems, Russian manufacture underwent massive development to satisfy the demand of a rapidly increasing market interested in consuming tobacco in forms requiring greater and newer technological investment. Astonishingly, the tobacco business emerged after all these troubles with a largely increased capacity by the mid-twentieth century.

Already by the nineteenth century domestic tobacco was beginning to successfully compete with imported. Soon thereafter, homeland tobacco factories supplanted (or incorporated) foreign manufacturers, resulting in a strong tobacco industry. By 1853, Moscow had four tobacco manufactures: Bostanzhoglo with 676 workers, Musatova with 200 workers, Perlova with 100 workers, and Dunaev with 88 workers.[2]

The internal market for tobacco in this period relied largely upon snuff. Until the October Revolution, snuff was regularly sold in the stores of the capital. In the years of Alexander I (1801–1825) pipes and cigars began to crowd out the snuffboxes from the lives of city inhabitants. Traditionally, mercerized tobacco (known as *makhorka*) had dominated tobacco sales. The appearance of *papirosy*, a cardboard-wrapped Russian version of the cigarette first mentioned in a circular of the Russian Ministry of Finance from April 29, 1844, brought a revolution in domestic tobacco production.[3]

To meet increasing demand a few dozen factories produced hand-rolled *papirosy* as did countless small cottage shops.

Agricultural and industrial data indicate a growing Russian tobacco industry throughout the 1800s. Official statistics show larger and larger tobacco harvests in Russia. It is possible, however, that these numbers are less than the actual harvests. Of the entire harvest of tobacco only a part ended in the factory and the other large portion went to cottage industry and local consumption. Most tobacco was consumed in the region of cultivation and was therefore not subject to excise tax; with no tax it was not counted in official statistics.[4] By 1860 the number of tobacco enterprises in Russia increased to 551. By the end of the nineteenth century the concentration of production strengthened and, along with increased mechanization of production, contributed to changing the makeup of the industry. The number of enterprises decreased by two times and the output of tobacco products rose by ten times.

Tobacco company consolidation accompanied the rise of products that required more intensive investment for their manufacture—chief among these was the *papirosy*. In the last decade of the nineteenth century, tobacco production increased across all types of products. While production of the low-grade, mercerized tobacco—*makhorka*—rose over the period from 1887–1900 by 16.2% and smoking tobacco manufacture was up by 29.1%, *papirosy* production increased by a stunning 167%. Thus, *papirosy* rose from 10.3% to 19.1% of all manufactured tobacco by 1900.[5]

As Figure 10.1 shows, in the period from 1900 to 1908 *papirosy* production increased—specifically from cheaper tobacco. This change to lower sorts of tobacco helped intensify the turn toward *papirosy* by the industry at large. Over the course of the period, the production of cheaper *papirosy* rose from year to year at an average of 10.1%. This trend in manufactured smoking tobacco, fueled mostly by the urban population, was joined by a general rise in production of *makhorka*, mostly for the rural population. The average yearly growth in *makhorka* production for the period was 5.7%. The strengthening distribution network explains this rise in part, but clearly tobacco consumption was on the rise.[6]

In the years leading up to World War I, shown in Figure 10.2, tobacco output grew less dramatically, though previously noted tendencies did intensify. The trend towards the production of the cheapest and lowest sorts of tobacco continued, particularly from the growth in production of *papirosy*. By the eve of the war, *papirosy* constituted 46% of tobacco production. The working of *papirosy* necessitated machinery—for rolling, wrapping, and packaging, and this required capital investment that intensified previous moves towards large-scale manufactures, tobacco trusts, and increasing factory size, even as the number of factories decreased.[7] In 1914, the first large Russian tobacco monopoly arose—the St. Petersburg Merchant-Export Joint Stock Society (*Sankt-Peterburgskoe Torgovo-Eksportnoe Aktsionernoe Obshchestvo*). The organization consisted of thirteen tobacco

Year	Tobacco produced			*Papirosy* produced by million items		All tobacco and *papirosy* in million smoking units	Yearly percentage growth
	First sort	Second sort	Third sort	First sort	Second sort		
1900	1191.6	5987.6	6297.2	2994	4781	40683	2.9
1901	1268.9	6543.3	6162.9	3047	5665	42839	5.3
1902	1271.7	6395.4	5948.4	3006	5875	42252	-1.4
1903	1330.1	6747.5	6016.7	3085	6746	44250	4.7
1904	1430.5	7004.8	5954.7	3083	7732	45954	3.8
1905	1268.6	6473.7	5232.1	3090	7717	42490	-7.5
1906	1559.6	7951.7	6732.9	4018	9833	53519	25.9
1907	1334.1	6627.2	5502.0	3349	9753	45979	-14.1
1908	1352.0	6729.6	5593.8	3293	10044	46731	1.6

Figure 10.1 Tobacco and *papirosy* production, 1900–1908. Data drawn from L. B. Kafengauz, *Evoliutsiia promyshlennogo proizvodstva v Rossii (Posledniaia tret' XIX-v–30e gody XXv)*, (Moscow: Epifaniia, 1994), 106–7.

factories, including manufacturers in Petersburg, Moscow, and Rostov-na-Don, and produced 56% of the tobacco product output in Russia.

Makhorka output increased markedly over the same period rising yearly by over 5%. In contrast to the low-grade, machine-rolled *papirosy* made to satisfy the urban market, the tobacco produced as *makhorka* in this period was mostly used for self-rolled smokes and sold to rural areas.[8]

As in a number of countries, World War I led to a tobacco boom in Russia. As seen in Figures 10.3 and 10.4, tobacco output grew during the first years of the war and only in 1917 did they decline to 91.8% of pre-war production. *Makhorka* production did increase slightly compared to pre-war levels.

Year	Establishments	Workers	Wholesale Production in 1000 r.	Production of tobacco and *papirosy*			
				Smoking tobacco of all sorts	*Papirosy* of all sorts in million pieces	All smoking units in million pieces	Share of *papirosy* of the general product
1908	205	28635	81508	13675.4	13337	46731	28.5
1909	190	25657	77416	11777.4	13487	42247	31.6
1910	184	25813	76957	10143.5	14537	39278	36.2
1911	186	25560	82036	10459.8	17089	42631	40.1
1912	184	27431	88571	10092.2	19272	43917	43.8
1913	177	28256	96355	10474.9	22055	47634	46.3

Figure 10.2 Tobacco production, 1908–1913. Data drawn from Kafengauz, *Evoliutsiia promyshlennogo proizvodstva v Rossii*, 156.

Year	Smoking tobacco		*Papirosy*		All tobacco and *papirosy*		*Makhorka*	Yearly rise in *makhorka* output
	Tonnes	% of total	Mill. Pieces	% of total	Smoking units (mill.)	% growth		
1913	10475	53.7	22055	43.6	47634	8.5	78676	4.0
1914	10803	50.6	25725	49.5	52106	9.3	84654	7.6
1915	9300	42.2	31112	57.8	53821	3.2	73304	-13.4
1916	12744	51.5	29346	48.5	60465	12.3	82330	12.3
1917	8885	49.6	22009	50.4	43704	-27.7	81564	-0.9

Figure 10.3 Output of tobacco products, 1913–1917. Data drawn from Kafengauz, *Evoliutsiia promyshlennogo proizvodstva v Rossii*, 198.

Year	Smoking tobacco	*Papirosy* in million pieces	All tobacco items in million smoking units	*Makhorkha* tobacco
1913	10475	22055	47634	78676
1917	8875	22009	43704	81564
1918	6917	12703	29593	28468
1919	4798	10249	21965	18722
1920	7525	4850	23225	21384

Figure 10.4 Tobacco production, 1913–1920. Data drawn from Kafengauz, *Evoliutsiia promyshlennogo proizvodstva v Rossii*, 230.

Papirosy output as a share of overall tobacco production continued to grow during the war, largely because, as in other countries, tobacco became part of rations for soldiers and officers. Tobacco output generally grew with the war, as well, until 1917 when a precipitous drop began, because of the culmination of shortages of paper, fuel, and workers. Following the Bolshevik Revolution of 1917, tobacco factories were nationalized, but this proved no staunch to the continued decline in production. The drop in tobacco production was much less noticeable, however, than in other branches of industry. General, private industry fell in 1920 to 15.9% of pre-war levels and the production of items of immediate use fell to 10.6% of pre-war levels. Against this background, tobacco production—at 46.1% of pre-war levels in 1919—looked to be in good shape.

Tobacco manufacture supplies were generally stored for two years or even three, so it is likely this surfeit of raw material came from bumper crops of tobacco in 1917 in the Kuban region of Ukraine, Crimea, and the Caucasus, as well as the collapse of the export market.[9] But by 1920, fuel, electricity, and paper shortages led to production problems for *papirosy*. *Makhorka* supplies fell considerably due to struggles with harvests, falling to 72% of prerevolutionary levels.[10] This was a reversal from the war years, when mercerized tobacco had increased slightly. In the early years of the Soviet Union, all tobacco products had become more difficult to purchase.

With the introduction of Lenin's New Economic Policy (NEP) in 1921, the tobacco industry was better positioned for a recovery than other groups because of the relatively quick restoration of tobacco cultivation areas, the demands from industry, and the dearth of imported crops. In 1921–1922 a restructuring of tobacco production and works set the industry on a new foundation as many trusts were formed and took over most of the tobacco production.[11] By October of 1921, however, these trusts began experiencing raw materials shortages. *Makhorka* production also changed in this period. In the north, *makhorka* production was limited by the rise of new, local collective farms. The collective farms enjoyed relative freedom in their production, and many opted for agricultural products other than tobacco. Supply issues in the southern Russian territory known as the Black Earth Region, and in Ukraine's traditional tobacco-producing regions, led to the emergence of new tobacco trusts to manage production in the factories. Similarly, supply issues forced the north into a tobacco syndicate to resolve their own difficulties with *makhorka* production. In this way, the northern factories faced slight declines in their output, while in the south and Ukraine, 1921–1922 was a year of slight production increases. Overall *makhorka* output decreased from 1920–1921 to 1921–1922 by 10%.[12]

Prices for tobacco stood higher than the majority of agricultural products, surpassed only by hemp, leather, and wool. Even with strong demand and increased prices, the restoration of tobacco production did not proceed without a hitch. In 1926–1927 the sown area of tobacco fell by 16% as a result of low prices from the state. Variable price increases were instituted to try and stimulate production. One of these projects was the attempted export of *makhorka* raw material in 1926–1927. At the same time, state manufactured *makhorka* increased its market share, suggesting the continuing decline of private manufacturers.[13]

By the late 1920s, as seen in Figure 10.5, production increased for both tobacco and *makhorka* as a consequence of a strong market. Rising harvests and the quick re-establishment of the raw material base allowed tobacco production to reach pre-war level by 1925–1926. The type of tobacco produced changed decisively as crumbled tobacco replaced other tobacco in *papirosy*. Whereas in 1913, about 47% of tobacco came out as *papirosy*, following the Revolution, *papirosy* dominated the total tobacco market.

Even as pre-war prices were surpassed in 1925–1926, the number of *papirosy* produced only reached 80.6% of pre-war levels. The increase in production greatly intensified pressure on over-stressed, older tobacco factories. By 1926–1927 the large tobacco factories already worked in two shifts and the average capacity of all manufacturers reached 140%. Moreover, special factory and mechanistic processes were imported that took over work that until the war had been done by hand. The end of NEP was met with the appearance of even newer machines of larger capacity. This mounting tobacco production helped in the expansion of exports.[14]

Year	Papirosy		Tobacco		In all	Makhorka
	Million items	% k. of total	Kilos	% k. of total	Smoking units in millions	t.
1913	22054,9	46.3	10474983	53.7	47634	78676
1922/3	10790,9	83.2	888036	16.8	12959	19546
1923/4	12993,7	91	529990	9	14266	30599
1924/5	26285,0	96.5	411000	3.5	27290	46506
1925/6	37284,0	95.2	782004	4.8	39161	81458
1926/7	40736,6	94	1149000	6	43543	82486
1927/8	48989,8	94.4	1186000	5.6	51885	83815

Figure 10.5 Tobacco production before and after the Revolution. Data drawn from N. Sharov, "Tabachnaia promyshlennost': Promyshlennost' SSSR v 1926/1927 g.," *Ezhegodnik VSNKh* vyp. 7, (Moscow: Gostekhizdat, 1928), 468.

The *markhorka* industry also recovered quickly. By 1924, sowing area for *makhorka* was at pre-war levels and in the succeeding years it continued to rise. With the increase of sowing areas, first supplies and then finished output from the factories also rose. Here, again, many factories worked on two shifts and mechanization proceeded quickly, especially visible in the import of new, more able, packing machinery.[15]

Massive collectivization of agriculture in the early 1930s resulted in changes for raw materials and consequently in tobacco production. Until 1930 tobacco harvesting was almost exclusively a product of small, peasant agriculture. In 1931, the collective farm replaced the small farms with large-scale agriculture. At that same time, there was a significant rise in the sowing area of both tobacco and *makhorka* on state farms. By 1934, small-farm peasant agricultural production provided only for household, not market, needs. In other words, fifteen years after the Revolution, almost all tobacco products had become state enterprises.

Unlike with grain agriculture, there was no significant decrease in tobacco production during the critical first years of collectivization as shown in Figure 10.6. This was likely a result of the greater state prices for tobacco in comparison to prices for other field and livestock products. While butter, meat, and eggs were moved towards a card system in 1929, this did not occur with tobacco. Instead, there was a slight shift in the tobacco producing regions. The majority of tobacco production now occurred in the Kuban (40.7%) and the Caucasus republics (38.4%). *Makhorka* production shifted south as well, with the majority now in Ukraine (53.2%), while that in the Central Black Earth Region had diminished (22.6%).[16]

As with any other critical, transitional period in Soviet history, a sharp rise in demand for tobacco and *makhorka* accompanied the social dislocations of Stalin's industrial and agricultural programs. During collectivization it became a habit to smoke *makhorka* through the many meetings of the village soviets, party cells, and general meetings of the *kolkhozy*. It was permissible to smoke in trains, movie theatres,

	1928	1929	1930	1931	1932	1933	1934
Peasant agriculture							
Tobacco	44.5	44.3	26.2	23.9	16.4	8.2	0.2
Makhorka	36.0	42.3	26.3	27.7	19.2	10.0	1.8
Kolkhoz							
Tobacco	0.6	2.7	26.2	59.5	65.1	70.0	73.2
Makhorka	0.1	0.5	13.3	52.3	62.2	74.8	88.1
Sovkhoz							
Tobacco	0.1	0.1	1.2	5.4	11.2	18.5	27.4
Makhorka	0.1	0.0	1.1	13.4	20.6	26.2	29.5
In all							
Tobacco	45.2	47.1	53.6	88.8	92.7	96.7	100.8
Makhorka	36.2	42.8	40.7	93.4	102.0	110.6	119.4

Figure 10.6 Sown areas of tobacco and *makhorka* by category of management, in thousands of hectares, 1928–1934. Data from *Narodnoe khoziastvo SSSR v . . . godu* (Moscow: TsUNKhU, 1932–1935).

meeting halls, and even hospitals. *Papirosy* and *makhorka* use and production grew.[17]

Production grew despite the slow spread of sowing area and harvests, but this is explained by the destruction of domestically grown tobacco and its cottage industry. Almost all the harvest began to go to tobacco factories. For the most part, the rise in demand for tobacco significantly surpassed supply. This led to increasing the tax rate in 1931 on factory-produced tobacco by 71.5%.[18] From 1930 to 1932, *papirosy* prices in the city rose 140% and in the village by 150%. *Makhorka* prices increased in the same two-year period by 155% in the city and 250% in the village.[19] In the spring of 1932, the price for one pack of *makhorka* (50 g) reached 20 kopeck in the city and 25 kopeck in the countryside. Before 1917, similar packs cost 3 kopeck. The only low-cost alternative remained snuff tobacco, which had steadily diminished in popularity since the introduction of *papirosy*. A 50-g pack of snuff cost 8 kopeck in the city and the same in the village. In June of 1932, a fixed price was established for *makhorka* for the city and countryside at 25 kopeck for a 50-g pack.[20] For the most part this was sufficient for clearing the deficit and *makhorka* was sold in the city for the "free-market" price of 1 ruble for a 50-g pack.

By the mid-1930s, the provisions situation began to improve. In 1935, there was a lowering of the price for bread and the repealing of the card system for meat, fish, lard, and potatoes. The situation of tobacco products remained difficult. In 1935, the price for *makhorka* in the city and countryside was established at 40 kopeck per pack.[21] This became in fact a lowering of prices for city dwellers and a significant increase for the primary users of *makhorka*—peasants. With the downward trend in prices for tobacco products in the city came also a lowering of taxes.[22] In June of

1937, during the widespread campaign for the lowering of prices on consumer goods, the price of tobacco products was lowered by 10%—but only on *papirosy* of the highest sorts.[23] These were not goods of mass demand, and their users, members of the party and state elite, did not have a problem with money. The retention of the high prices for lower sorts of tobacco and *makhorka* meant that the state continued to use tobacco production for budgetary purposes.

With the coming of World War II and, specifically, the grand evacuation of industry, many tobacco factories were moved to the east and established in the region along the Volga River, the Urals, and Siberia. Similarly there was an increase in production in Central Asia. As production relocated, the central regions of the country began to experience a profound shortage of tobacco products. This shortage was felt more by the civilian population, for much of tobacco and *makhorka* production went directly towards provisioning the military. For the most part, tobacco products were not among those products rationed from July 17, 1941; however, they were included in provision packets for factory, transport, scholarly, and scientific workers.

By 1942, the price for tobacco items in the state stores in comparison to June of 1941 had doubled.[24] The price for *papirosy* in state commercial stores was higher than the provision packet price by ten times.[25] Even for that price, tobacco was not always available for purchase. Therefore there was also another type of state sales—the network of state stores.[26] In the Moscow stores, the price for one pack of cigarettes stood at 2,000 rubles. By comparison, the price for one jar of conserved vegetables in that office was 50 rubles and the standard bottle of vodka—"the half liter"—stood at 400 rubles. On the informal level of flea markets, the price for homegrown *makhorka* rose by 100 times.[27] Faced with shortfalls in raw materials, producers began to barter manufactured goods for raw tobacco. This method met with some success; however, the Sovnarkom tried to redress this practice with the hopes of restoring confidence in currency.[28] In these conditions, when *kolkhoz* workers could buy nothing with their money, the idea of the Sovnarkom seemed strange. Therefore bartering of manufactured goods in exchange for the sale of tobacco remained a practice and continued until December 15, 1947.

By the beginning of 1945, the shortages of tobacco products began to weaken, and the commercial price fell by 20%. The price for a pack of *papirosy* from state stores fell to 1,600 rubles; however, almost to the monetary reform of 1947, the tension in the tobacco market remained.[29] In 1948, a new price for tobacco raw materials and manufactured products was put forward. On average these were lower than the 1947 price by 8%. New production may, in part, explain the changes in prices. During the 1950s, the factories destroyed during the war were rebuilt with newer, more advanced technology. The tobacco industry, however, appears to have recovered faster than most sectors of the economy, suggesting the centrality of tobacco to Soviet economic concerns.[30] For the next two decades the average yearly production of tobacco factories rose from 2.9 to 7.9 billion smoking units. The tobacco problem that had begun with the Revolution finally appeared solved. The high prices of tobacco products began to lessen, dropping for the first time since 1940.

In March of 1949, a postwar campaign to lower prices resulted in the lowering of prices on tobacco products by 10%.[31] In March of 1950, prices were lowered for *papirosy*, cigarettes, tobacco, and *makhorka*; this time it was by 20%.[32] For 1951, prices for *papirosy*, cigarettes, and tobacco were lowered by 10% and for *makhorka* by 15%.[33] In the following year, prices fell again but without publicity. In 1954, prices remained stable. As product prices decreased, there was investment in the agriculture of tobacco.[34] As a result, even though prices were lower than during the war years, there was still a substantial increase from prices following several decades of change. For example, a 50-g pack of *makhorka* which in 1913 cost 3 kopeck in 1954 now sold for 55 kopeck.[35] By 1955, tobacco prices were only 112% of 1940 levels, although they had risen 200% during the war.[36]

By the late 1950s, domestic tobacco production had stabilized. Tobacco production had transitioned to a Communist-era economy, surviving the dramatic upheavals of the Revolution, collectivization, and two world wars, and had emerged with largely increased capacity. The physical challenges to production had been matched by a change in consumption habits, as the earlier tobacco goods, crumbled tobacco leaf and *makhorka*, had been mostly displaced by the newer *papirosy*. Of course, while the economy stabilized in the 1950s, it was hardly a permanent state of affairs. Tobacco consumption continued to outpace supply, requiring imports and further changes to an ever-expanding arena of the Soviet economy.[37]

NOTES

1. *Kroshenyi kuritel'nyi tabak* was suitable for smoking in pipes and cigars.
2. V. K. Itsunskii, *Sotsial'no-ekonomicheskaia istoriia Rossii, XVIII–XIX v. Izbrannye trudy*, (Moscow: Nauka, 1973), 259.
3. The term in Russian for a paper-wrapped smoke is *papirosy*, while the term *tsigaret* in Russian is more comparable to a cigarillo in English, until the twentieth century when the term *cigarette* becomes associated with a paper-wrapped smoke and the *papirosy* is exclusively a cardboard-mouthpiece cigarette.
4. *Sel'skoe khoziaistvo i liesovodstvo zhurnal Ministerstva zemledieliia i gosudarstvennykh imushchestv*, (1879), no. 6.
5. L. B. Kafengauz, *Evoliutsiia promyshlennogo proizvodstva v Rossii (Posledniaia tret' XIX- v.—30e gody XXv)*, (Moscow: Epifaniia, 1994), 106–7.
6. Ibid., 107.
7. Ibid., 157.
8. Ibid.
9. A. E. Sokolvskii, ed., *Syr'evye problemy promyshlennosti: Sbornik statei i materialov*, (Moscow: Gosudarstvennoe izdatel'stvo, 1928), 442.

10. S. B. Narkir'er, *Proizvodstvo tabachnykh i makhorochnykh fabrik RSFSR v 1920–1921 gg. Statisticheskii obzor deiatel'nosti mestnykh administrativnykh organov Narodnogo komissariata vnutrennikh del RSFSR*, (Moscow: Komissariat, 1922), 22.
11. *Narodnoe khoziaistvo Rossii za 1921/1922*, (Moscow: Izd-vo "Ekonomicheskaia zhizn," 1923), 504.
12. A. N. Malafeev, *Istoriia tsenoobrazovaniia v SSSR, 1917–1963 gg.*, (Moscow: Mysl', 1964), 392.
13. Ibid.
14. In 1927, the world's first tobacco fermentation factory was built in Krasnodar. N. Sharov, "Tabachnaia promyshlennost': Promyshlennost' SSSR v 1926/1927 g.," *Ezhegodnik VSNKh* vyp. 7, (Moscow: Gostekhizdat, 1928), 468.
15. Sokolovskii, *Syrev'evye problemy promyshlennosti,* 392.
16. Tobacco factories were fairly widely distributed, but tobacco production was centered mostly in the northern Kavkaz and Zakavkaz while *makhorka* was a product of the central, Black Earth, and Ukrainian regions. This distance made the development of tobacco and *makhorka* production relatively independent. *Narodnoe khoziastvo SSR Statisticheskii spravochnik 1932*, (Moscow: TsUNKhU, 1932), 182–5.
17. *Narodnoe khoziastvo i kul'turnoe stroitel'stvo RSFSR,* (Moscow: n.p., 1935), 33.
18. *Biulleten finansovogo i khoziaistvennogo zaknodoatel'stva*, (1931), no. 12, 7.
19. Rossiiskii Gosudartsvennyi Arkhiv Ekonomiki, Moscow, (RGAE), f. 6759, op. 1, d. 1, ll. 19–20, 147. Data for the 1932 year was taken from the official price.
20. *Biulleten finansovogo i khoziaistvennogo zaknodoatel'stva,* (1932), no. 39–40, 20.
21. RGAE, f. 5446, op. 16, d. 1711, l. 6.
22. *Sbornik zakonov i rasporiazhenii raboche-krest'ianskogo pravitel'stva SSSR*, (1936) no. 2, 21.
23. *Sbornik zakonov i rasporiazhenii raboche-krest'ianskogo pravitel'stva SSSR*, (1937), no. 28, 116.
24. RGAE, f. 4372, op. 42, d. 301, l. 158.
25. RGAE, f. 1562, op. 12, d. 3141, l. 37.
26. *Osobtorga.*
27. RGAE, f. 1562, op. 12, d. 3141, l. 55.
28. RGAE, f. 4372, op. 45, d. 808, ll. 11–14.
29. RGAE, f. 1562, op. 12, d. 3141, ll. 37, 55.
30. The Soviet economy struggled from massive shortages in the postwar era. See Elena Zubkova, *Russia After the War: Hopes, Illusions, and Disappointments, 1945–1957*, ed. and trans. Hugh Ragsdale, (Armonk, NY: M.E. Sharpe, 1998).
31. *Pravda*, March 1, 1949, no. 60.
32. *Pravda*, March 1, 1950, no. 60.
33. *Pravda*, March 1, 1951, no. 60.
34. RGAE, f. 4372, op. 48, d. 880, ll. 84–5; "Postanovleniia sovieta ministrov SSSR," August 1950, chap. 2, 836–7; "Postanovleniia sovieta ministrov SSSR," August 1955, 82–83.
35. RGAE, f. 1562, op. 327, d. 850, ll. 15–24.
36. RGAE, f. 1562, op. 12, ll. 6–7.
37. See Neuburger and Gilmore, this volume for a discussion of the later economic transitions.

11 "The lads indulged themselves, they used to smoke . . ."

Tobacco and Children's Culture in Twentieth-Century Russia[1]

Catriona Kelly

In the early months of 1905, Vologda was, like many other parts of the Russian empire, seized by unrest among the schoolchildren of the city. To the disquiet of authorities, both locally and in St. Petersburg, the children boycotted classes and held a number of political meetings at which they made a list of demands attacking the restrictions imposed on their lives by the rules in force at secondary schools since 1874. What the boys and girls of Vologda wanted, according to a secret letter by the chief of police at the Interior Ministry, included not only political changes such as "the abolition of searches" but also "the right to visit the theatre freely," "the right to wear one's own clothes outside school hours," and not least "the creation of a smoking room."[2] The situation in Vologda neatly illustrates how smoking can be seen at one and the same time as an activity signifying maturity, which children may be encouraged to emulate round about the borders of adulthood, and as a subversive practice that requires restriction and which may accordingly be espoused as a way of asserting children's difference from adults and their solidarity with their peer group.

This paradox—earlier explored by Konstantin Bogdanov in a chapter about the status of smoking in Russian culture generally—shaped a good deal of children's experience of smoking in later decades as well.[3] Particularly during the hygiene-obsessed 1920s and 1930s, much propaganda was devoted to discouraging smoking among children. Pioneers were regularly reminded that members of the organization were not supposed to smoke any more than they were supposed to drink, gamble, attend church, or rob birds' nests, to name several other activities also roundly condemned in posters and newspaper articles from the period. Typical is a poster published in Khar'kov in 1931 that shows a child of Pioneer age actively engaged in pressing home the message—she, or more likely he, is daubing the slogan "Pioneer, Do Not Smoke or Drink" on a wall (Figure 11.1). At the same time, even quite young children who wished to smoke could rely on a degree of collusion or even encouragement.

Figure 11.1 "Pioneer, Do Not Smoke or Drink," 1931. From the poster collection of the Russian National Library, St. Petersburg.

The significance of smoking did not end with its function as an age threshold. In some contexts—for example, traditional peasant culture—the meaning of smoking could be generational: smoking on the part of children and young people could signify epochal shifts and a new commitment to "modern" practices eschewed by parents and grandparents.

As one of the contributors to the Tenishev project commented in the late 1890s, "In families only men smoke, and young ones at that [. . .] children learn to smoke either away on the side somewhere, or from older members of the household, or from other adolescents." He added, "Old men and women think it is a sin, but young people don't see anything bad in smoking."[4]

In later decades, however, smoking played a role in social bonding not so much because it was novel, but because it was traditional—an established practice that had become encrusted with a range of accepted meanings. For example, a whole network of beliefs had grown up about the predictive significance of the way that ash fell, while using "to smoke" as a euphemism for fellatio proliferated in places such as young offender institutions. Potentially, children could share widespread cultural appreciation of smoking obtained in adult culture—that asking for a cigarette (or refusing one) was an aggressive act, for example.[5] The practice could have purely pragmatic functions for children as well as adults—as an appetite suppressant in conditions where food was short.[6] Most of the evidence that I have collected—based on an oral history project with informants born between the 1910s and the 1980s living in four Russian cities, Moscow, St. Petersburg, Perm', and Taganrog, and in two different rural sites, and on questionnaires circulated to informants born between the 1930s and the 1970s in Moscow, St. Petersburg, and Taganrog—does relate precisely to the role of smoking in maturation and in self-definition, though it points to different meanings as well.

By no means all smokers in Russia began smoking as children. At the same time, developing a relationship with smoking (whether positive or negative) was a near-universal constituent of childhood experience in Russia from the late nineteenth century onwards. The evidence of interviews suggests that the peak age for beginning to smoke (among those who began before adulthood) was fourteen or fifteen to eighteen, but that there was also a minority that began earlier. Even across long periods of time, the stories are remarkably consistent. Certainly, people from the Soviet era remember being exposed to health propaganda, but the creation of a new ideological context had little impact on smoking in the playground, the city courtyard, or the village street.

Smoking by children occupied a broadly stable place in social relations over the course of the twentieth century; hence, evidence from the 1920s and 1930s may safely be used alongside earlier and later material. In the post-Soviet era, however, the supposed "laxity" that was said to have developed towards smoking became part of a broad discourse of social atomization and moral decline that was generally very widespread in informants' accounts of the past. Here, though, we are dealing with the place of smoking in historical mythology, rather than with shifts in social practices as such, which were in significant respects homogeneous over the decades.

SMOKING AND GROWING UP

Children's earliest encounters with smoking did not necessarily involve tobacco. A variety of parallel practices involved non-tobacco cigarettes that might be used for oral gratification. Children do not seem to have been offered the candy and chocolate cigarettes that were given to British children in my own youth, for example. In the words of one woman born in the late 1940s, "The biggest treat was 'Assorti' chocolates, which included, among other delights, chocolate bottles—but never any cigarettes."[7] However, often, children constructed their own "fake" cigarettes out of moss and other substances that came to hand. As on informant noted, "In '43 I got expelled from the Pioneers because we, well, we'd made kind of cigarettes, *papirosy*, out of moss and we were smoking them. And we got caught."[8] Toy cigarettes, however, were for real "babies;" smoking required that ordinary cigarettes were used. It was only in desperate circumstances that older children would turn to ersatz cigarettes: "Once we were sent out of town to help bring in the harvest (picking tomatoes, as I remember). We soon ran out of cigarettes and we decided to smoke rolled-up dry leaves. But that's the only time I remember that happening."[9]

One obvious source for getting hold of real cigarettes was one's parents or other relations, if they smoked—in which case the cigarettes could be found just lying round at home. "He pilfered some [cigarettes] from my brother, I think, and gave [the other children] some," a woman recalled of her son's behavior in the early 1970s.[10] If parents did not smoke, or concealed the fact that they did from their children, things were more complicated. But sometimes children would "strike lucky" out on the street, as in the case of a boy playing football with his friends in the 1980s. When the ball struck a box, they discovered two pristine packets of twenty cigarettes, the last of a case of two hundred that had been put on the trash heap accidentally. On another, more mundane, occasion, the boy "found some 'Laika' ones and gave them to my uncle."[11]

Another way of gaining access to tobacco would potentially have been to pick up cigarette butts from the street. This strategy was associated with the behavior of street waifs, however, and hence abject. It was resorted to only *in extremis*: "We hardly ever did that, it only happened if you were a regular smoker and for some reason hadn't the chance to buy a cigarette when you wanted."[12] The commonest way of laying one's hands on tobacco was simply purchasing cigarettes. Sometimes shop assistants would sell to children (especially if they thought they were purchasing for adults).[13] If not, an intermediary could be arranged. "If you had money, then you asked older children to buy them—ones who had no trouble in buying them. If you didn't, then you bummed one off one of your friends."[14] A man brought up in a Perm' province boarding school a couple of decades later had similar memories:

Interviewer: So where did you get the cigarettes?
Subject: Well, in the usual way. . . . first I filched them from my dad, then later, once I had some money, I bought them at school.
Interviewer: So they sold them to you there directly?
Subject: No, they didn't sell them, but we found people to buy them for us.
Interviewer: So who bought them for you?
Subject: Older lads, men, someone you knew would buy them.
Interviewer: So did you have to pay them a consideration for doing that?
Subject: No, they never asked us for anything [over and above the cost of the cigarettes].
Interviewer: So they just bought them? Simple as that?
Subject: Yes of course. Sometimes we had an older visitor from someone's village, and they bought them. No, they never asked us for anything in return.[15]

Such memories are widespread: "The older kids were happy to get them for us if we gave them a cigarette or two in return," recalled a man born in 1962.[16] Barter played an especially important role in the postwar years, when it was almost the only way of obtaining tobacco. In southern parts of Russia, this might be home-grown: "We usually rolled our own, and getting hold of a real one was a real treat. You couldn't buy cigarettes for love or money, sometimes you could arrange a swap with some lucky person," recalled a man born in Taganrog in 1937.[17] A woman from this generation, also from Taganrog, remembered, "We had no money to buy cigarettes, but adults locally used to grow tobacco for the men around the place and you could swap something they wanted (a penknife, a ball, a sweet, a ride on your bicycle) for a roll-up."[18] Thus, under ordinary circumstances, children could expect a high degree of collusion from older acquaintances, who were only too ready to facilitate purchases of tobacco.[19]

All in all, practical obstacles were easy to overcome; ethical or aesthetic boundaries were often non-existent. Smoking was perceived by children themselves as something making you seem mature.

Interviewer: So why did you smoke?
Subject: Smoke? I can tell you that. To show you were grown up. That was the only reason. [. . .]
Interviewer: So if you don't smoke, you're not one of us, yes?
Subject: Not so much "not one of us," it was done to show you were grown up. An idiotic kind of being grown up, if you ask me: look at me, I'm big now, I'm already smoking.[20]

But this was by no means all. It was not so much maturity as such, a man born in 1967 remembered, "It was more an interesting adventure." "You felt curious," a woman born in 1952 observed. "And we were all suffering in different ways—some of us were in love, some of us had problems with our parents, some of us had this and that else wrong; cigarettes were a consolation. Cigarettes brought people together, they let you make contact with someone—'here, give us a cigarette,' 'let's have a cigarette.'"[21]

Smoking, then, had strong attraction for large numbers of children, and some children who did not smoke felt they did not fit in, as a woman born in 1977 remembered:

> I stood out from the general run. For instance, say everyone else in the class got bad marks, but I got very good ones. You stood out, they didn't accept you. Didn't ask you to play this and that. And I'm not sociable either. Then everyone started smoking, and a few of them tried drinking too. And I didn't do either, so I stood out again.[22]

On the other hand, those who were sociable were all the more likely to get involved in smoking, which is invariably recalled as a group activity, rather than one carried out in furtive solitude:

> *Interviewer:* So where did you smoke: in the boarding school itself or during the breaks?
>
> *Subject:* During the breaks at school, once we got a bit older. Not during all of them, of course. But sometimes during one or two. Maybe we'd nip out into the street or out beyond the back courtyard. In Shabury, during my last year, we used to go round the corner specially. The teachers knew perfectly well what we were doing, they could see us going off. But all the same we didn't smoke openly. We hid. And in Pikhtovka we hid as well.
>
> *Interviewer:* So didn't the teachers even try to catch you?
>
> *Subject:* I don't think so, really. I can't remember them trying to catch smokers.[23]

This last case illustrates the centrality of collusion by adults where children's smoking was concerned.[24] In later decades, children living in cities seldom had trouble in persuading shop assistants to sell them cigarettes or tobacco, or, should this fail, in finding an adult who was prepared to make the purchase on their behalf.[25] Teachers regularly turned a blind eye to smoking in the lavatories or quiet corners of the school playground, just as Pioneer leaders did in Pioneer camps. Some children's institutions—including penal colonies—had places where smoking was officially allowed.[26]

Adults might even encourage smoking by children, along the lines, "It's about time you learned to smoke now."[27] Boris Rodoman, born in 1931, remembered how "once when I was three, my uncle stuck a lighted *papirosa*[28] into my mouth: 'Well, smoke it, you're a big boy now.'"[29]

Yet prohibitions against smoking by adults often had a genuine inhibitory function; even where ignored they could enforce a sense of authority ("We didn't smoke openly. We hid.")[30]—though, as we shall see, they could also work to foster the practice that was the subject of disapproval.

PROHIBITIONS

If adults quietly facilitated children's smoking in everyday life by turning a blind eye, the official attitude was quite different. Smoking was definitely not approved in schools and in the Pioneer movement children were regularly reminded of this. Didactic literature represented smokers as bad guys. A story by Aleksei Tolstoy, written in the mid-1920s, contrasted Vas'ka, "a revolting young man with a snub nose, lips gone yellow with smoking, and pop eyes, and a forelock hanging down over his low brow," who "never did anything, filched money from his mother, and thought about what mischief to get up to, or how to get hold of fifty kopecks for beer and expensive Samorodok brand cigarettes," with Mitia Strel'nikov, an upright boy who spent his leisure time indoors, reading improving stories about Polar explorers.[31] Anti-smoking cartoons were widely published in *Pioneer Pravda* during the 1920s as well. Even at periods other than the full-out anti-smoking campaigns of the 1920s and the 1970s, it was standard for "moral education" in schools and in other children's institutions, such as orphanages, to include strictures about smoking. For example, a former physical education teacher from Moscow remembered that not smoking was about the only instance where physical education and the cult of *mens sana in corpore sano* had made itself felt by the late Soviet era, and former pupils have vivid recollections of intervention by some teachers of this kind:

> Generally, the teachers all thought it was their duty to [lay down the law], they all read us sermons of some kind. It was the physical culture teacher who was the most active, he used to organise "crackdowns" in his free time (and he knew very well the places smokers went and hid in). He'd take people he caught to the school director, and he'd get your form teacher in, and then your form teacher would get hold of your parents. He scared us and we hated him.[32]

A man born in 1949 likewise remembered, "The clerk of works used to chase you like mad. The toilet would be completely full of smoke. He'd arrive . . . He was this big strapping fellow. He'd chase everyone out, chase them all away."[33] Alongside teachers, the medical personnel of schools—doctors and nurses—might organize anti-smoking campaigns "with pictures of smokers' lungs, charts of mortality statistics and diseases, and so on."[34] Anti-smoking posters were displayed and medical staff and the school director might read lectures on the subject.[35]

Agitation included not only action by adults but also activities involving children themselves. For example, anti-smoking messages and shaming of deviants might take place at the occasional formal assemblies that were held in Soviet schools: "They made a spectacle out of kids from class five and six there."[36] If these reminiscences go back to the 1970s, another woman, this time educated in the late 1950s and 1960s, remembered an equally hard line, supported by a wide range of anti-smoking activities:

> We were forbidden to smoke at school, anti-smoking poems got published in the wall newspaper too. I can even remember a couplet about a heavy smoker in our class: "He's smoked so hard, he's smoked himself dry/And smoke'll soon pour from his eyes." Half the children in my eight-year school were delinquents. Most of the boys were straight off the street—and every one of them smoked (they did it in the toilets, the playground, the courtyards). Of course they all smelled of smoke. The teachers and the director could smell it too, and they'd tell them off in public. They put it down on file in the class register, they called people's parents in.[37]

It was not just teachers, orphanage supervisors, and Pioneer leaders who put pressure on children; members of their own families often conveyed their disapproval of smoking:

> They always made an example out of Kostia, a friend who was a bit older than me: he got good marks at school, did sport, read lots: his mother, who was a librarian, used to bring him books on modelling, he made models and he let me do a few of the simple ones. He never touched a cigarette in his life, even though his mum and father both smoked. And he hadn't the slightest interest in drinking spirits, even though in almost every back courtyard you could find someone who made decent home hooch.[38]

Parental guidance was often less elaborated, though: among the typical exhortations, as remembered by a man born in 1933, were "Don't stay out late. Don't smoke. Study hard. And all that."[39] Adults did not have even to be related or in some official relationship with children—it was common for passers-by to rebuke children, especially smaller ones: "Adults usually never passed up the chance of telling off children, even ones they didn't know, and often spoke harshly too them—though they might think twice about saying something to whole crowds of [underage] smokers."[40]

Adults who wished to prevent smoking could make use not just of exhortations, but of actual sanctions. With parents, at any rate those whom Soviet guidance on rational upbringing had not reached, these might extend to a thrashing.[41] Corporal punishment was officially forbidden in children's institutions, schools, and the Pioneer movement, so other measures had to be used. "They used to chuck you out if you smoked outside the camp grounds. They used to chuck you out of the Pioneer camp for that," recalled a man born in 1960.[42] A man two years younger remembered that conditions in his Perm' province boarding school were just as strict:

> *Interviewer:* So what else could you get into trouble for?
> *Subject:* Everything. Smoking, drinking. . . . Say you'd had a beer or a smoke. Things were really strict with us.
> *Interviewer:* But probably that didn't stop people drinking and smoking?
> *Subject:* It did happen, of course. Once you got to seventeen or so. But you got the same treatment: you weren't allowed any dinner.[43]

Another informant remembered frightful threats in order to curtail smoking:

> Lots of people smoked, yes. Almost everyone had tried it. Me too. Yes. But it was still . . . you were still scared. You were afraid, to begin with . . . Afraid of your parents getting cross and all that . . . And the "children's room" at the police station . . .There was no messing round with that. "Off to the PTU [vocational college] with you! The youth colony! The children's room!" Prison and all. That was the way you were taught at school.[44]

Yet anxiety about being caught tended to generate frantic efforts to conceal what you were doing, rather than a moratorium on the activity.[45] Just as adults who smoked hid their smoking from their children; children hid their smoking from their parents:

> I started smoking fairly early—in class seven, and I hid it from my parents almost till I was old enough to leave school. Back then (in the 1960s), adults were extremely disapproving about children smoking and so children did their best to avoid being caught with a cigarette. [But] I think my parents were essentially putting on an act, pretending they didn't know. There was a sort of unspoken agreement: I'd hide my smoking and they'd pretend they didn't suspect. But everything depends on how old you are. In class seven, even thinking about my parents catching me smoking was unimaginably awful; by class ten I knew nothing so frightful would happen, it was just best all round if they didn't catch me.[46]

Thus, adults at once disapproved of children's smoking and considered it inevitable that the smoking would occur: smoking was at once "normal" (the social view) and "harmful to health" (the medical view). The result was a kind of "normative doublethink" according to which rules were at once enforced and ignored. In a whimsical story, Evgeny Popov suggested the paradoxes of this situation from a child's eye point of view. The difficulty for the hero of his story lies not in the fact that he does smoke, but that he does not: arraigned before an informal council of the teachers at his school for smoking "in front of the entire school, in front of the windows of the entire school, brazenly, without even trying to hide in the gateway like the other boys do."[47] The boy has great difficulty in proving that what the teachers saw was actually white breath coming out of his mouth in the cold, not smoke. In Popov's story, it is better to smoke and not be caught than not to smoke at all. In fact, a non-smoker was "a lad who is not one of us [*paren' ne nash*], a stranger lad [*paren' chuzhoi*], a lad remote from our life [*otorvannyi ot nashei zhizni*]!"[48] In British schools, "behind the bike sheds" or "outside the lavatory" were standard places to enjoy a "secret" cigarette; in Russian schools, various corners of the playground and *inside* the lavatories played the same role.[49]

There is thus some doubt whether strictures and sanctions were actually meant to stop children from smoking, as opposed to enforcing an age-related social hierarchy where adults regulated behavior. Constant dread of punishment—"he's shaking with fear," "it was strict with us"—acknowledged the authority of those who had the capacity to exact punishment. But prohibitions did not always enforce the authority of adults. If the dreadful warnings about the effects of smoking that were meted out to children did not at first seem fulfilled, the prohibitions would themselves be discredited and quite possibly long past childhood as well:

> *Interviewer:* So what age were you when you started smoking?
> *Subject:* Around fifteen or so.
> *Interviewer:* And other people?
> *Subject:* Other people started earlier, I think. Some people were at it really early. I wasn't, because I was keen on sport. But then when I did start I didn't have any trouble with my breathing, I decided nothing had any impact. We had this teacher, she used to say, "Anyone who smokes won't grow big and tall." Well, just look at me: I'm no gimp, am I? It never did me any harm.[50]

In the contest between official values and peer pressure, the latter sometimes won out, as was graphically described in a school essay by a pupil at a school run by the First Experimental Station of the People's Commissariat of Education around 1926:

> REPORT ON OUR WINTER HOLIDAYS
>
> We were able to do some of our homework over the holidays but of course not all of it. In school we agreed we wouldn't spend too much

> time having parties in our digs, we wouldn't smoke. Wouldn't kiss. But when we got to our digs the big girls and boys made us kiss and if we wouldn't they thrashed us with their belts. The big boys taught us to smoke. And we didn't want to leave our digs early ourselves.[51]

This rather muddled account—the children claimed "we agreed we wouldn't" do forbidden things, and that they had ended up doing them under compulsion, yet also claimed that wasting time in their digs was something they did not want not to do—suggests the level of confusion experienced by younger children when they tried to negotiate mutually exclusive behaviors. The values of peers and elder children (which were often in favor of smoking) and the values of parents and teachers (mostly against, at least if it were done openly) were at odds.

As a result, it was easy for a kind of circular process to be set up where children espoused smoking not *despite* the fact that it was forbidden, but precisely *because* it was forbidden, and once they had moved beyond the pale anyway, they became attached to the practice as a sign there was no way back. The autobiography of a boy from a youth colony published in an official Ministry of Internal Affairs anthology from 1955, for example, sees smoking as an important step towards bad behavior:

> So I'd already got bigger, and got interested in shooting, I learned how to use an army rifle. An interest in literature then developed: Tolstoy, Lermontov, Nekrasov, Saltykov-Shchedrin, Gorky. I read in every spare moment I had, even during lessons. That created problems at school.
>
> Now I was in Odessa, swimming in the sea, sunbathing; I had my first close friendship with a girl. Then I was back in Moscow: theatres, concerts, the movies, and bad marks at school, skipping class
>
> . . . I began smoking.[52]

In 1976, a Soviet journalist recorded another case where a teenager had seen smoking as part of a general pattern of anti-social behavior, something unavoidable when you had "gone wrong." She related that she had met, in the yard of the Moscow Pioneer Palace, a fourteen-year-old boy who "was smoking one cigarette after another without the slightest anxiety about what adults were going to think." The boy himself had remarked "with some irony" that "I smoke because I'm 'difficult' and everyone's washed their hands of me, and you can't do anything about that, missus." Though the story was told as an exemplum in a didactic narrative about the importance of providing summer leisure facilities for teenagers (once he had been given a placement at a work camp, the boy was transformed into a useful member of society), the psychological standpoint that it recorded at the outset was more plausible than the resolution.[53]

The case of children who were in the "neglected" or, to translate the Soviet term exactly, "unsupervised" category to begin with was of course highly specific. There were cases, however, where more "normal" children also saw prohibitions on smoking as part of an entire complex of over-regulation. A striking example is the following account of the behavior of the director of studies of a Leningrad school, who appears through a mist of remembered school folklore as a positive monster:

> *Subject:* That director of studies, if you ask my opinion, she was a werewolf. Really. She had these big whiskers and everything. I can remember her taking a cigarette off this boy and 'pff' she goes right on his cheek, right there in the toilet, that's where she stubbed it out. He went round later with it, with that burn there on his cheek.
>
> *Interviewer:* You mean one of the children?
>
> *Subject:* Yes, exactly.
>
> *Interviewer:* Someone from one of the senior forms, presumably?
>
> *Subject*: Well, by then . . . by then we were in class seven. One boy already smoked. Yes. So he turned up with that [i.e., the burn], and everyone's like: "What on earth is that?" And he's like, "It was her with the whatnot, right there . . ." But he wasn't the only one who smoked. Lots of other people did too. She used to love meatballs rare, with the blood running out of them. They made them for her specially in the school canteen. "I want mine really rare."[54]

Here there is an explicit contrast between the extremity of the sanction and the fact that the activity of smoking was itself "normal" (to reinforce the point of his narrative, the informant moves from presenting this case in isolation—"One boy already smoked"—to presenting it as typical ("he wasn't the only one who smoked"). The sinister nature of the director of studies appears as all of a piece: only a "werewolf" could treat the pupils like this, and such a reaction to smoking is compatible with demanding your meatballs rare (literally "bloody"), a decidedly eccentric taste.

The glamorization of smoking was also aided by fictional examples. No doubt the Soviet and "trophy" films in which elegantly dressed foreign spies puffed away at cigarettes in holders may have played some role. Concrete examples from literature made smoking look romantic and fun. As a woman from Leningrad remembered, "Smoking wasn't associated with bad behavior for me and wasn't a sign of criminal tendencies. It was associated with 'street children' (but we didn't have a hard-and-fast [negative] view of them, not after *Konduit i Shvambraniia* [a 1930s piece republished in the 1960s]."[55] Smoking might be a "deviation" but it was not inevitable that "deviations" were seen in a negative light.

Ubiquitous in recollections and commentaries is an association between drinking and smoking. As we shall see, the fact that members of one's family (particularly one's father) "didn't drink or smoke" was often a source of pride;

the converse was of course that those who enjoyed drinking tended to enjoy smoking, and vice versa. The age of fourteen or fifteen was a standard time among city children for trying alcohol, and this was also a fairly common age for starting to smoke as well.[56] Thereafter, parties and ceremonial meals among young people would likely involve both smoking and drinking (and first sexual contact as well).[57] A complex of pleasurable deviance emerged, and one associated with its own cultural spaces—one's own home when one's parents were away, but otherwise, back staircases, the dark corners of courtyards, hidden landings, attics, and cellars in apartment blocks.[58]

Thus attempts by adults to prohibit smoking could rebound, bringing those who made them into disrepute, and by association discrediting the very idea of adult authority. But not all children were necessarily moving down a slippery slope when they began smoking, or saw themselves as exercising defiance. Some escaped coming into serious conflict with adults about their smoking, and thus never internalized the sense that smoking was subversive. Others took an ambivalent stance towards the activity. Traces of this are found in the language used to describe smoking—the verb *balovat'* (to behave in a self-indulgent way, to "mess around") is frequently used.[59] And more active feelings of disapproval are often recorded too.

REFUSING TO SMOKE

For an important contingent of children and young people, *rejection* of smoking became something that was character defining. "I was the only person in my group at university who didn't smoke, and I started to see that as a form of self-assertion," remarked one informant.[60] Self-definition can also be traced by informants to a much earlier stage of their lives. "I didn't either drink or smoke. My uncle was eight years older than me, and I never saw him come home drunk once," recorded a woman born in 1959.[61] Company at school sometimes provided encouragement to smoking, but by no means always, particularly among younger children:

> *Interviewer:* So did people smoke?
>
> *Subject:* Hey, listen, no one smoked. Well, I know some girls in the top forms did, but we didn't approve of that at all.
>
> *Interviewer:* In the top forms? And you left in class eight?
>
> *Subject:* Yes, but while you were still at school you'd see the seniors, they'd be smoking away in the toilets, and we didn't approve at all. But I do know that after I left, my former classmates were in there smoking too. And I expect the juniors didn't approve of them either.[62]

Sometimes informants record that parental disapproval played a role in their decision to avoid smoking. "I only started to smoke when I was a student, and even then I kept it from my mother. All her life I tried to hide it. She was terrified of us smoking—she thought we were bound to get tuberculosis. I was afraid of upsetting her," one woman born in the 1940s recalled.[63] Disapproval on the part of orphanage staff could work in the same way to that of parents:

> *Interviewer:* So did you have the feeling you were being brought up in an active sense?
>
> *Subject:* Of course. We didn't grow up any way we felt like. Of course they brought us up actively. They'd say the right thing. There was discipline. We didn't muck about, didn't steal things. There was no theft in the orphanage. No one called anyone else names. Well, we had nicknames, the way you do now as well. Inoffensive ones, we had those. And if you ask me, that was down to how we were taught. They used to tell you all that—stealing was bad, smoking was bad, they told you all that.[64]

Here, one sees a direct link between indoctrination and social practices. But interestingly, *encouragement* to smoke could also be a factor in rejection on the part of children, as in the case of Boris Rodoman, mentioned earlier, who was permanently deterred from smoking by his uncle's intervention when he was three: "I coughed huffily. And from then on I've never smoked."[65] The association of what was supposed to be a pleasurable and mildly subversive activity with compulsion acted as a deterrent in itself. Likewise, peer pressure could manifest itself not just through urging other children to smoke, but through policing other children's behavior:

> I managed to train my sister out of smoking rather in the same way. When she was in form two, she came home one day and said confidingly, "I've started smoking." Yes. I had some Cuban "Ligeros" cigars, they're done up in paper that tastes sweetish. Yes. They're made of rice-paper or something like that. Yes. So I said, "Well, let's have a smoke together then!" And I gave her a taste of one of those cigarettes, they don't have filter tips. My sister tried the paper, when she found out it was sweet, she went, "Mmmm, tasty!" So then I lit one for her. And she didn't inhale, she just let some smoke in her mouth and then blew it out again. It was just a bit of childish fun and so on. So I said, "That's not right!" And I showed her how to inhale. So she inhaled, and I got the most awful fright—she went bright green, greener than the walls in the entrance to our block! So I whacked her on the back, she coughed and coughed. . . . She's twenty-two now, and she still doesn't smoke and I'm pretty sure she never will.[66]

Gender played quite a significant role in decisions about smoking. In rural Russia, smoking was very much a masculine activity. In the words of one of the Tenishev project informants, "It's usually men who smoke, even down to boys of eleven or twelve, out there on the street in amongst the crowd."[67] The view of smoking as a masculine activity persisted significantly later: compare this recollection of Iaroslavl' province in the 1940s from a man who spent time there when his orphanage was evacuated from Leningrad: "They used to plant a lot of tobacco in Iaroslavl' province back then. The elderly men, they smoked tobacco. Women didn't smoke at all back then, I don't remember it."[68]

Such attitudes persisted into the late twentieth century. In the words of a woman from a village in Novgorod province, born in 1927, "I don't like girls who like vodka or girls who smoke. Now that I really don't like. Not . . . I don't want . . . but do they listen to me? No, no one listens to me. But it just disgusts me. I've never smoked or got drunk. Well, if there's a wedding or a wake, I might take a glass, but I've never enjoyed it."[69] Of course, views of this kind also conditioned the behavior of boys and girls when they were growing up. One of our village informants recalls that she and her friends even told on boys whom they knew were smoking:

> *Subject:* Oh, if we saw someone light up [. . .] if they were doing it among themselves, we'd start: we're going to go and tell on you right now.
> *Interviewer 1:* You told on them?
> *Subject:* Well of course, they were indulging themselves, weren't they?[70]

The sense that it was somehow unfeminine to smoke conditioned attitudes among urban children as well. Only one girl in her class at school smoked, recalled a woman born in 1947, "And she was a real tearaway, a tart, to put it bluntly."[71] A woman born five years later confirms this, "The boys were very disapproving of girls who smoked, it was supposed to be a sign of being a slut."[72] At the same time, the sense that smoking was not feminine did not necessarily inhibit the activity completely, more its public expression, "I began smoking back in school. But I only smoked outside in the courtyard and in the street. Yes. But as for talking about it . . . I think other people must have done it in secret too. So I've been smoking since I was fourteen."[73]

More overt and persistent than the idea that "nice girls don't smoke" was the association of smoking and manliness—in the sense of machismo. "Lots of my classmates smoked—you could see the older kids doing it. You did it even if you didn't like it. No one wanted to seem a 'mummy's boy'."[74] Another recalled:

> Children are different and they have different attitudes [to smoking] as well. The ones who smoked thought that smoking was not so much a sign of maturity in the general sense as a sign of manliness and being part of masculine society. The ones who didn't (the "botanists" [i.e.,

> the nerds]) thought that smoking was a sign that you were a real little hooligan.[75]

Thus, *not* smoking was directly associated with gentility—a factor that made girls less likely to smoke (or more likely to conceal their smoking), while the association had the opposite effect on some boys. Such appreciations were also conditioned by appreciations of social status—so the hooligan was not only a manifestation of masculinity, but also of proletarian, marginal values, the social practices of streets and courtyards.

Generational as well as gender factors drove choices. A crucial factor in not taking up smoking was often that some relative provided a negative role model, inspiring disgust because their habit was part of a general, unclean profile, as one man recalled of his grandfather:

> I had this grandfather, one of my grandfathers. . . . You know why I don't smoke? Hum, one of my grandfathers . . . he lived where we did . . . he was the one the Nazis gave a beating . . . and he was a smooker . . . and a drinker . . . and he used to swear too. . . . he liked to speak . . . his mind, so, he smoked a lot, and he coughed all night too [said with disgust], and he used to spit into this, this pot, and then I had to take the pot out in the morning. I didn't like that at all, to be honest.[76]

The informant also remembered, "And my other grandfather, he didn't smoke, he didn't drink, he was just amazingly tall, two meters tall, and strong, and healthy, he was a carpenter." Thus, smoking could be a minus in one's relatives, and non-smoking a plus.[77] But things could work the other way round. For one Leningrad woman, the negative associations of smoking were softened by the fact that "all the best and most humane teachers in the school smoked."[78] At the same time, children could come to their own decisions even where they had an affectionate relationship with a given person:

> We always told Anton at home, "You're a boy. And those are the girls. You're supposed to defend them. You're a boy, after all." All boys want to be soldiers. But I do remember that when Anton was growing up he said to me, "When I grow up I want to be like Uncle Grisha. I'm not going to drink and I'm not going to smoke". Because his dad does both.[79]

Not smoking on children's part did not have to be a matter of principle, sometimes they simply didn't like the activity in a physical sense. As one recalled, "The first time I ever smoked was with my mate Vova K., I must have been about ten. I went bright green and blue and red, I felt sick, that cigarette turned my stomach over, just a couple of drags did it."[80]

In fact, people often remember that their *first* smoke did not appeal at all, particularly if taken at a very young age. Sometimes, though, this did not stop them from having a go later on:

> *Interviewer:* So did you smoke? Did you start that early?
> *Subject:* I first tried when I was about five, but I didn't like it. I began smoking properly at eighteen.[81]

In circumstances where personal taste was a major factor in whether to start smoking or not, decisions about the activity were not necessarily permanent: as tastes changed, so might practice. This did not necessarily stop people seeing incidental decisions in quite categorical ways: the assertion of a Leningrad man born in 1933, "I never have smoked, I don't smoke now, and I never will smoke," represents a typical totalization of the association between smoking and selfhood.[82]

SLIPPING STANDARDS

Whether they themselves ever smoked as children, the vast majority of commentators were inclined, when interviewed from the vantage point of adulthood in 2002–07, to see juvenile smoking as reprehensible. They now associated smoking with a whole spectrum of moral laxity, even if they remembered taking a different attitude to the activity as children. Informants who actually did smoke as children often recalled this in a slightly embarrassed way and tended to play down the extent to which they smoked ("I just took a little puff or two on some moss," and so on). It was also common for informants to assert that no children smoked "back then."[83] As one man born in 1949 recalls, "No one drank or smoked, you simply didn't get that back then. They didn't smoke, or drink, or sniff. The only interest was hanging round in the streets or maybe climbing into someone's vegetable garden [and stealing apples, etc.]."[84]

Compare the following recollection from a brother and sister born in 1939 and 1946:

> *Interviewer:* So were there any schoolchildren who smoked?
> *[pause]*
> *Interviewer:* I mean, smoked at all? Well, probably girls didn't smoke back then, but boys. . . .
> *Subject 2:* Our girls . . . I can't remember a single girl, not even in the eleven-year school. And even there, only one boy did, and he'd only tried it. I can remember that for sure, that he was the only one. And you used to hear: "Sasha, hey, he's having a go [at smoking] behind the cubby-hole!" No. It really wasn't widespread.

Subject 1: I don't know, we didn't have anyone who smoked.[85]

The corollary of this was an assumption that standards had slipped since the collapse of Soviet power, and there was nothing now to stop children puffing away:

> *Subject:* So now, when I see all those crowds of smoking and swearing children, and the teachers just walking past and not showing they care at all—it sort of makes me feel quite ill.
>
> *Interviewer:* And now we, the parents—I have the right to send a note to the director, I think, or the form teacher that I give my permission for her to smoke, and she gets let out during the breaks.[86]

A teacher who had worked in Leningrad schools since the 1950s was particularly scathing about the changes:

> Now some schools have it all down in their rules: "A pupil of School No. 586 does not have the right to smoke in school." But he just goes out into the school porch and stands there puffing away. I think the teachers are all cowards, it's blatant hypocrisy. It says in the rules: "A pupil of School No. 18 does not have the right to smoke."[87]

An orphanage supervisor, who herself grew up in an orphanage, was also highly critical of what she saw as the decline in the manners of modern youth:

> *Subject:* Honestly, when we were in the orphanage we'd never have been rude like that. And they sometimes turn up several sheets to the wind too.
>
> *Interviewer:* So that didn't used to happen?
>
> *Subject:* What are you saying!! What are you saying! Smoking!!! Well, I just . . . I can't even get my head round the idea, honestly I can't. And now, you know, every one of them does—not just the older ones, the youngest as well.[88]

Occasionally, people recognized that attitudes might have changed. In the words of one commentator, "If someone drank and smoked in the past, they were considered the big boy of the courtyard and so on. But now they're called 'bruises,' everyone thinks they're the dregs of society."[89] A shift in attitudes to smoking went alongside a shift in attitudes to behavior in courtyards. Already by the late 1950s, it was becoming common for middle-class parents to avoid letting their children play out of doors, and the courtyard was increasingly becoming the haven for deviants. A major clean-up campaign in the early twenty-first century did little to change this culture, keeping the courtyard as problematic place for "respectable" teenagers to use, even for marginally permissible activities such as smoking.[90]

At the same time, a degree of tolerance continued to be exercised by at least some of those who actually had to deal with children in the mass day by day—as opposed to those who simply held a view about how children should behave in the abstract. One might take the down-to-earth comments of a policewoman with years of work in the "children's room" at a local station in Leningrad-St. Petersburg. She confided that she was prepared to tolerate smoking because allowing it gave her the chance to supervise the adolescents to some degree; drinking, on the other hand, was definitely not allowed:

> It's not a good idea to tell them off, no, you have to put them in the right conditions. I said yes, and then they went on gathering there [i.e., on the landing of the building where the woman lived], but they didn't make a mess any more. I took out a dish for them to smoke into [i.e., to use as an ashtray]. They're going to smoke whatever happens. So let them smoke indoors in the warm—then I can see what they're up to. Otherwise who knows? But if they drink I tell them, excuse me, out you go.[91]

And some informants were more inclined to emphasize continuities: "Nothing's changed. It was exactly like now back then," insisted one man born in 1960.[92] Such commentators perhaps had the weight of evidence on their side: most sources do indeed suggest long-term stability in the social status of smoking by children.[93]

CONCLUSION

This chapter has put forward a historical ethnography of smoking among children in Soviet Russia. Smoking had an important place as a marker of maturation, but this was by no means its only function. Smoking (or not smoking) also acted as a gesture marking one's personal identity and affiliation with some social sub-group; it attracted curiosity and projected a sense of adventure and it was pleasurable (or disgusting) in its own right. Smoking was a major site for different types of negotiation with adults, who rarely directly encouraged the practice, but might sometimes collude in it or at the least turn a blind eye to it. This was not necessarily a subversion of adults' authority. Children were usually terrified of "getting found out," while conversely, extremely authoritarian anti-smoking behavior on adults' part could be counter-productive since it made them feared and hated and also played a role in glamorizing smoking as part of a whole complex of seductively transgressive behavior.

In Russia generally, attitudes to smoking were shaped by the fact that tobacco was cheap and widely available, incidental shortages of particular brands notwithstanding, and that there were few social or moral prohibitions on its use in most public places.[94] Smoking therefore came into the category of "an activity that was perfectly licit at a specific age and in most circumstances" (one might compare driving or sex within marriage), rather than "an activity that was morally questionable at whatever age" (as in the case of masturbation or extramarital sex), or even "an activity that was only permissible within strict limits" (as with drinking). While the use of tobacco by children was carefully regulated, such regulation often extended to places where smoking might take place, and more broadly, contexts in which it might happen, rather than whether it might take place at all. Control of the activity was meant to impress adult authority on children in a general sense, rather than to discourage smoking for good and all.

This did not mean that all children smoked. Girls in particular might be inclined to find smoking distasteful in members of their own sex (including themselves) if not in men. There is a notable distinction in the recollections of informants depending on their sex and the male smoker—female non-smoker distinction is ubiquitous. Yet there were also women who smoked, and the sense that smoking was "unfeminine" could make girls furtive about smoking rather than stop them doing it altogether. All in all, though smoking was a collective activity, and although non-smoking could suggest membership of some particular set, opposition to smoking often came about for individualistic reasons—"I don't smoke because I don't want to." "I think it's disgusting." "People I like don't smoke." Rather than, "I don't smoke because I know it's unhealthy," or "No civilized person smokes." A culture where adults widely accepted the "right" of smokers to smoke more or less wherever they felt like it was both the cause of such attitudes and, one might say, also the product of these.[95]

NOTES

1. The research for this chapter was sponsored by the Leverhulme Trust under grant no. F/08736/A "Childhood in Russia, 1890–1991: A Social and Cultural History" (2003–2006). I am also grateful to the British Academy, to the University of Oxford, and to New College, Oxford, for financial resources. The thirty-six interviews cited here coded Oxf/Lev and CKQ were conducted in St. Petersburg (SPb.), Moscow (M), Perm' (P), and Taganrog (T), and villages in Leningrad (2004) and Novgorod (2005) provinces (V), and in the UK (Oxf) as part of the above project (for further information, <www.mod-langs.ox.ac.uk/russian/childhood> and <www.ehrc.ox.ac.uk/lifehistory>). My thanks go to the interviewers, Aleksandra Piir (St. Petersburg), Iuliia Rybina and Ekaterina Shumilova (Moscow), Svetlana Sirotinina (Perm'), Iurii Ryzhov and Liubov' Terekhova (Taganrog), Oksana Filicheva, Veronika Makarova, and Ekaterina Mel'nikova (village interviews), and also to the project coordinators, Al'bert Baiburin and Vitaly Bezrogov, for their help. Interviews coded CKQ were conducted by Catriona Kelly using the same questionnaire; the code "CKI" refers to informal interviews (not taped) also conducted by Catriona Kelly. A written questionnaire was also circulated by email: the twelve answers to this are cited as WQ [written questionnaire] with a respondent number. The following abbreviations are used with reference to the interviews: WB, parents working-class;

PB, parents professionals; HE, informant has higher education; VE, informant has vocational education. When provided, city and year indicate place and date of birth. Fuller biographical details are available online. The quotation in the title (‘*parni balovalis’, kurili* . . .’) is taken from Oxf/Lev P-05 PF24B, p. 18. *Balovat’sia*—“spoiling oneself” (in the sense both of giving oneself a treat, behaving self-indulgently, and of “ruining” one’s character, messing around, behaving reprehensibly)—is difficult to translate by one English word.

2. Letter from Assistant Minister of Internal Affairs (Head of Police) to the Minister of Popular Enlightenment. March 28, 1905. Tsentral’nyi gosudarstvennyi istoricheskii arkhiv Sankt-Peterburga, (hereafter TsGIA-SPb) f. 139, op. 1, d. 10235, l. 226. Publication of this text forthcoming in V. Bezrogov and C. Kelly, eds., *Gorodok v tabakerke: Detstvo v Rossii ot Nikolaia II do Boris El’tsina*, 2 vols., (Moscow: Rossiiskii gosudarstvennyi gumanitarnyi universitet, 2008).
3. Konstantin Bogdanov, “Pravo kurit’,” in his *Povsednevnost’ i mifologiia*, (St. Petersburg: Iskusstvo-SPb, 2001), 285–378, esp. 302.
4. Recorded Tver’ province. *Russkie krest’iane: Zhizn’. byt. nravy. materialy Tenishevskogo arkhiva kniazia V. N. Tenisheva*, vol. 1, (St. Petersburg: Delovaia tipografiia, 2004), 459. In a 1920s record of a children’s game, *sniffing* tobacco [= taking snuff] is presented as an old man’s occupation: NA RAO (Learned Archive of the Russian Academy of Education, Moscow), f. 1, op. 1, d. 246, l. 2; publication forthcoming in Bezrogov and Kelly, eds., *Gorodok v tabakerke.*
5. Bogdanov, “Pravo kurit’,” 300, 305, 317–8.
6. For example, CKI-SPb. 2003 (M., 1947, small town Southern Russia). Note that this individual is still smoking away, after nearly fifty years.
7. WQ 2 (F., 1947, SPb.). WQ 1 (M., 1947, small town S. Russia), 4, 5, 6, 7, 8, and 10 confirm that no such cigarettes were on sale; but a younger informant recalled gum cigarettes as imported and very hard to get hold of (WQ 3. 1967, brought up in Leningrad). WQ 9 (F., 1965, T) and 11 (M., 1975, T).
8. M., Leningrad, 1933, Bashkir, WB, HE, Oxf/Lev SPb-03 PF8A, p. 14–15. See ibid., PF9A, c. 61. A village informant recalls moss cigarettes, (M., 1927, village, Novgorod province, mother swineherd, father *kolkhoz* [collective farm] chairman; five classes primary education. Oxf/Lev V-05 PF18A, p. 27).
9. WQ 1, M., 1947. small town, Southern Russia. On substitute cigarettes, one village informant remembered smoking empty twists of paper sitting out in the earth trench near his village: M., 1925, village, Novgorod province, father *kolkhoz* worker [?], mother housewife (could not read or write), attended factory school; served in army from age 16, Oxf/Lev V-05 PF7A, pp. 5–6.
10. F., 1927, village, Novgorod province, father carpenter, mother *kolkhoz* worker; moved to settlement, Leningrad province, as young woman (date unknown), attended but did not complete seven-year school. Oxf/Lev V-04 PF3A, p. 30. See the recollection from another rural informant (male informant, 1928, village, Tver province, father mechanic, mother factory worker (later housewife), moved to settlement, Leningrad province after war [date not known], graduated from seven-year school, Oxf/Lev V-04 PF12A, p. 10) of how his middle and youngest brothers “used to thieve tobacco from my grandfather.”
11. M., Leningrad, 1975, IB, HE. Oxf/AHRC-SPb-07 PF 8 IN, p. 10.
12. WQ 11 (M., 1975, T). Of all respondents to my questionnaire, only one other (M., 1947, Krasnodar region) remembered gathering *okurki* (“cigarette butts”). “We didn’t collect them from rubbish bins and rubbish tips—that was considered for “filth” only—but you might pick up a cigarette or *papirosa* that hadn’t been smoked right to the end off the street.” He, however, describes himself as a *dvorovyi mal’chik* (“courtyard boy”).

13. WQ 4 (F., 1952, Moscow); WQ 8 (F., 1955, Taganrog); WQ 9 (F., 1965, Taganrog).
14. To bum a cigarette was to *streliat* literally "to shoot" off. WQ 1 (M., 1947, small town Southern Russia).
15. M., 1962, village, Perm' province: mother milkmaid, father tractor-driver. Secondary education, works as loader. Oxf/Lev P-05 PF26B, pp. 13–14.
16. WQ 10 (M., 1962, Taganrog).
17. WQ 6 (M., 1937, Taganrog).
18. WQ 7 (F., 1939, Taganrog).
19. See e.g. the account of a male informant using the black market (Tatar Republic, 1949; in 1951 family moved to Perm' [Molotov], WB, VE), Oxf/Lev P-05 PF20A, p. 11).
20. F., 1958, Perm', WB, VE, Oxf/Lev P-05 PF24B, p. 18.
21. WQ 3 (M., 1967 Leningrad); WQ 4 (F., 1952, Moscow).
22. F., 1977, Perm', IB, HE (works in arts education). Oxf/Lev P-05 PF15A, p. 2.
23. M., 1962, village, Perm' province, mother milkmaid, father tractor-driver. Secondary education, workers as loader. Oxf/Lev P-05 PF26B, pp. 13–14.
24. Recorded Kostroma province, *Russkie krest'iane*, 248.
25. CKI-SPb. 2003 (M., 1947, Southern Russia).
26. F., worked in youth colony 1984–94, Oxf/Lev P-05 PF1A, p. 6.
27. See West, this volume.
28. A *papirosa* was the cardboard-tipped "Russian cigarette" usually considered the choice of a workman or "tough guy."
29. Boris Rodoman, *Tetrad' po grafomanii byvshego uchenika 1–10 klassov shesti raznykh shkol Moskvy, Omska i Kolosovki Rodomana Borisa. Avtobiograficheskie zapiski*, (1949). Author's archive. Typescript p. 13. Publication forthcoming Bezrogov and Kelly, eds., *Gorodok v tabakerke*, vol. 1. See a child's essay collected by the First Experimental Station of Narkompros in which an adult encourages a child to think of smoking as "mature" while rebuking him for other misdemeanours (NA RAO, f. 1, op. 1, d. 244, l. 3 rev. [no date, ca. 1923]; publication forthcoming in Bezrogov and Kelly, eds., *Gorodok v tabakerke*, vol. 1). All this is not specifically Russian—one has to think one's way back to the era before the epidemiological studies by Richard Doll and others definitively demonstrated the link between smoking and lung cancer. I myself recall being encouraged to smoke by the so-called "mother's help" when I was perhaps eleven-years-old, and my sister nine. As we sat on a miniature railway train making its progress through the marshes of Dungeness one interminably wet summer's day, she got out a cigarette and made my sister and me take several puffs; when we objected, she said scornfully, "Come on! It's high time you both learned to smoke."
30. In the villages of Kostroma province in the late nineteenth century, where and when members of the household smoked or not "depends on the boss of the family: other smokers smoke if and where he smokes," *Russkie krest'iane,* 248.
31. A. N. Tolstoi, "Rasskaz o kapitane Gatterase, o Mite Strel'nikove, o khuligane Vas'ke Taburetkine i zlom kote Khame," in his *Polnoe sobranie sochinenii*, vol. 12, (Moscow: OGIZ, 1948), 52–8 (quotes 52). The story is dated 1925 in a reprint of 1935, but the earliest publication found by the editors of PSS was 1929 (ibid., 347).
32. WQ 1 (M., 1947, small town, Southern Russia). For the reminiscence by a PE teacher, see Oxf/Lev M-03 PF9A, p. 37 (M., began work 1960, career spent in Moscow).
33. M., Tatar Republic, 1949; in 1951, family moved to Perm' [Molotov]; WB, VE, Oxf/Lev P-05 PF20A, p. 11.
34. WQ 9 (F.,1965, Taganrog).

35. See e.g. WQ 6 (M., 1937, Taganrog), WQ 10 (M., 1962, Taganrog), WQ 11 M., 1975, Taganrog. All respondents, independent of generation, remembered anti-smoking initiatives of one kind or another.
36. F., 1959, settlement, Perm' province, mother accountancy clerk, father crane driver; HE. Oxf/Lev P-05 PF8B, p. 17.
37. WQ 2 (F., 1947, Leningrad).
38. M., 1946, small town, Krasnodar region, WB, HE, Oxf/Lev T-05 PF24A, p. 10.
39. M., Leningrad, 1933, Bashkir, WB, HE, Oxf/Lev SPb-03 PF9A, p. 43.
40. WQ 9 (F.,1965, Taganrog). See WQ 11 (M., 1975, Taganrog).
41. As in the case of the brothers of one of our village informants (M., 1928, village, Tver province, WB, graduated from seven-year school, Oxf/Lev V-04 PF12A, p. 10).
42. M., Leningrad 1960, WB, VE. Oxf/Lev SPb-03 PF24B, 23.
43. M., Perm' 1976, educated in specialist school for educationally backward children; VE. P-05 PF14A, p. 7.
44. M., Leningrad 1960, WB, VE, Oxf/Lev SPb-03 PF24B, p. 18.
45. See e.g. Oxf/Lev T-04 PF11A, p. 22 (F., 1949, small town, Tatarstan province, WB, HE) recalling how pupils at the technical school where she taught in the 1970s would hide from the master craftsmen in the workshop "shaking with fear," but still went on smoking.
46. WQ 1 (M., 1947, Southern Russia).
47. Valery Popov, "Bozh'ia pomoshch'," *Rasskazy Leningradskikh/Peterburgskikh pisatelei*, (St. Petersburg: Duma, 2007), 66.
48. Ibid.
49. My thanks to Ian Thompson for reminding me of school conventions in Britain. On lavatories, corners of the playground, etc., see the interviews quoted above.
50. M., Tatar Republic, 1949; in 1951 family moved to Perm' [Molotov]; WB, VE, Oxf/Lev P-05 PF20A, p. 11.
51. NA RAO, f. 1, op. 1, d. 245, l. 17. Undated; other material in the file dates from 1926. Publication forthcoming in Bezrogov and Kelly, eds., *Gorodok v tabakerke*, vol. 1.
52. A. Ponizovskii, "Ia vernus!" (1955), *V dobryi put': Sbornik proizvedenii literaturnogo tvorchestva vospitannikov detskikh kolonii,* (Moscow: Ministerstvo Vnutrennikh Del, 1958), p. 82.
53. L. Arkad'eva, "Chem zaniat seichas podrostok?," *Leningradskaia pravda* July 15, 1976, p. 2.
54. M., Leningrad 1960, WB, VE, Oxf/Lev SPb-03 PF 24A, p. 14.
55. WQ 2 (F.,1947, Leningrad).
56. See e.g. CKI-SPb-2003 (M., 1947, small town, Southern Russia).
57. As pointed out to me by Evgeny Dobrenko.
58. On the significance of these spaces generally for childhood and adolescence, see Alexandra Piir, "What is a Courtyard For? Generations and the Use of Space in Backyard Leningrad," forthcoming in *Forum for Anthropology and Culture*, 4 (2007).
59. Contrast this fairly mild term of condemnation with the overtly disapproving *pakostit'* (to do nasty things), used about girls' gossip: F., Moscow, 1944, WB, HE, Oxf/Lev M-03 PF6A, p. 16.
60. M., Moscow, late 1950s. CKI-Oxford, 2005.
61. F., 1959, settlement, Perm' province, mother accountancy clerk, father crane driver; HE. Oxf/Lev P-05 PF8B, p. 17.
62. F., 1977, Perm', WB, VE, Oxf/Lev P-05 PF10B, p. 14. See Oxf/Lev P-05 PF5B, p. 16 (M., b. 1973, Perm', WB, mother and father both recent migrants from the countryside, VE).

63. WQ 2 (F., 1947, Leningrad).
64. F., 1938, settlement in Perm' province; from age 9–15 was in children's institutions. VE. Oxf/Lev P-05 PF29B, p. 14.
65. Rodoman, "Tetrad' po grafomanii," p. 13.
66. Oxf/Lev SPb-03 PF27B, c. 47. M., Leningrad Province 1960, lived in Leningrad from 1961, PB, HE.
67. Recorded Kostroma province, *Russkie krest'iane*, 342.
68. Oxf/Lev SPb-03 PF9B, p. 61.
69. F., 1927, village, Novgorod province; father roofer, mother housewife, VE. Oxf/Lev V-05 PF2A, p. 32. See F., 1933, village, Novgorod province, mother *kolkhoz* worker [?], father carpenter, secondary ed. Oxf/Lev V-05 PF11A, p. 16. In an interview with another village informant (F., 1933, village, Novgorod province, father and mother *kolkhoz* workers, attended four-class primary school but education interrupted by illness and closure of school; began work at 13, Oxf/Lev V-05 PF18B, p. 21), the fact that one of the teachers smoked needs special explanation—*vidimo, uchenaia* ("obviously, she was a learned woman").
70. F., 1930, village, Novgorod province, parents *kolkhoz* workers [?], divorced when informant was a child, she was brought up by mother and stepfather; secondary vocational education. Oxf/Lev V-05 PF13B, p. 6.
71. WQ 2 (F., 1947, Leningrad); WQ 4 (F., 1952, Moscow).
72. M., Tatar Republic, 1949; in 1951, family moved to Perm' [Molotov]; WB, HE, Oxf/Lev P-05 PF20A, p. 11.
73. F., 1952, Elektrostal', WB, HE, Oxf/Lev M-03 PF16B, p. 18.
74. WQ 10 (M., 1962, Taganrog).
75. WQ 1 (M., 1947, small town, Southern Russia).
76. M., 1931, Moscow, PB, HE, Oxf/Lev M-04 PF26A, p. 7.
77. See the recollection, F., 1936, Moscow, WB, HE, Oxf/Lev M-03 PF19A, p. 4; or F., 1929, village, Sverdlovsk province, father agronomist, mother housewife, lived in settlement, Leningrad province from 1973, graduated from seven-year school, Oxf/Lev V-04 PF7A, 3; 20.
78. WQ 2 (F., 1947, Leningrad).
79. F., 1960, small town, Perm' province, WB, VE,. Oxf/Lev P-05 PF12B, p. 14.
80. M., 1965, Taganrog, WB, VE, Oxf/Lev T-05 PF27A, p. 12.
81. M., 1950, Taganrog, WB, HE, Oxf/Lev T-04 PF18A, p. 26.
82. M., Leningrad, 1933, Bashkir, WB, HE, Oxf/Lev SPb-03 PF8A, p. 14.
83. On how people did smoke "back then," see e.g. the testimony of F., 1941, Moscow, WB, HE: Oxf/Lev M-03 P4A, p. 20.
84. M., 1949, Perm', WB, VE, Oxf/Lev P-05 PF6B, p. 14.
85. : M. 1, Leningrad 1939, : F. 2, Leningrad, 1946; brother and sister; WB, HE, Oxf/Lev SPb-03 PF37B, p. 59. See Oxf/Lev T-04 PF13A, p. 28. M., 1947, Lugansk province, grew up mainly in Krasnodar region, WB, HE.
86. M., Leningrad Province, 1972, brought up Leningrad, WB, VE, Oxf/Lev SPb-03 PF29A, p. 33.
87. F., began work 1954, career spent in Leningrad, history teacher, class supervisor, Pioneer leader. Oxf/Lev SPb-03 PF30B, p. 31.
88. F., 1971, in orphanage in Perm' province from age three, remained there till age 16. Trained as teacher, orphanage worker from 1991. Oxf/Lev P-05 PF9A, pp. 6–7.
89. M., Leningrad 1960, WB, VE, Oxf/Lev SPb-03 PF24B, p. 18
90. On shifting attitudes towards the courtyard, see esp. Piir, "What is a Courtyard For?" on the 1950s and 1960s; Mariia Osorina, *Sekretnyi mir detei (v prostranstve mira vzroslykh)*, (St. Petersburg: Piter, 1999), on the 1970s, 1980s, and 1990s; and Ol'ga Kol'tseva, "Udarim po raionu blagoustroistvom,"

Peterburgskii dnevnik, August 27, 2007, 11, on the situation in the early twenty-first century.

91. Oxf/Lev SPb-06 PF79B. pp. 16–17.
92. M., Leningrad 1960, WB, VE, Oxf/Lev SPb-03 PF24B, p. 18.
93. As one of our respondents points out, it did get easier for children to purchase tobacco once privatization had set in—sellers who were employed by cooperatives or who were selling packets of cigarettes on the street were unlikely to bother about the strict letter of the law (WQ 11, M., 1975, Taganrog).
94. Only one of the twenty-five teachers interviewed for our Leverhulme project mentioned that the school she worked in forbade smoking by the teachers—and this among a group generally working in elite schools during the post-Soviet period. She also mentioned that setting up this prohibition caused a good deal of distress at first. (F., began work 1966, career spent in Moscow, maths teacher, also worked in educational administration, Oxf/Lev M-03 PF8B, pp. 40–41).
95. According to figures from 2004, 8%–12% of schoolchildren in classes 7–8 were regular smokers, 24% among school-leavers, and 75% of students at PTU (vocational colleges) and universities smoked. See "Kak otuchit' detei kurit'?" posted March 5, 2004, <http://www.nedug.ru/news/6593.html>, accessed May 16, 2008.

12 "Tobacco is Poison!"

Soviet-Era Anti-Smoking Posters

Karen F. A. Fox

The Third All-Russia Congress of Soviet Workers met in Petrograd (later Leningrad) in January 1918. A formal photograph of the event shows about two hundred attendees, most standing on the main floor of the meeting hall, others behind the two-tiered podium on the speakers' platform. One might expect to see, at the front of the hall, a huge banner proclaiming "Workers of the World, Unite!" Instead, the one banner draped across the front of the podium presents the admonition "*Prosiat ne kurit'*"—"Please don't smoke."[1]

Smoking or non-smoking was not the central concern of the new regime in 1918 when Lenin appointed physician Nikolai Semashko as his first People's Commissar of Health. But Semashko held strong opinions about the harms of smoking and was eager to take action against it. He laid out a comprehensive program to restrict production of, and access to, tobacco products, including banning smoking in many public places and issuing ration cards to limit tobacco consumption. The other component of his planned approach was propaganda against smoking. Semashko's plans were dashed when Lenin and other leaders did not give approval for his comprehensive anti-smoking program.[2] Semashko was only able to move ahead in the one area he controlled: health education activities, including anti-smoking posters.

THE APPEARANCE OF HEALTH POSTERS

In the second half of 1918 posters suddenly appeared everywhere in the Soviet Union, as publisher after publisher started to print posters, mostly on orders of state agencies: "Every Soviet agency responsible for indoctrination, such as local soviets, commissariats, and mass organizations, commissioned artists, and hundreds of new posters appeared every month."[3] Western visitors remarked on the profusion of posters. A German economist visiting Moscow in 1920 wrote that "you find posters on all the walls, in thousands of Moscow shops, on telegraph poles, in pubs, in factories, everywhere you find posters."[4]

Many of these posters aimed to marshal support for the Bolshevik side, warning people to fight opponents of the new regime. But soon posters promoted the creation of a new socialist society, urging the populace to embrace new values, ways of thinking, and practices.[5] Posters exhorted people to forsake "bourgeois" attitudes and other outdated ways of thinking and behaving, and to adopt "modern," socialist ones. For example, in a before-and-after poster of 1920 the text reads, "This husband used to pull his wife around by the hair; now he reads to her aloud."[6] Posters touted other positive changes brought about by the Bolshevik regime, such as a poster stating that all children could now attend school, not just children of wealthy families.

By 1921 the Bolshevik regime had solidified its control throughout the country, and could turn more of its attention to social needs, including health: "The question of health protection of the country's citizens arose as one of the most serious internal political issues."[7] But the Soviet Union was short of money, doctors, medicines, and medical facilities. Therefore the first approach to meeting health needs relied primarily on prevention, not treatment. In March 1921 at the first All-Russia Conference on Health Protection, the value of the "visual teaching method" was especially emphasized, as the use of vivid imagery would provide the best conditions for the population to master "the knowledge of how to protect the national health."[8] Vivid, simple, and direct posters could be understood even by illiterates and could be viewed many times. The conference concluded that posters were the optimum means of providing health information and mobilizing action.

The Soviet state had ideological, political, and practical motivations for addressing the health of the population. The 1918 Constitution stated the objective of the "abolition of the exploitation of men by men, the entire abolition of the division of the people into classes, the suppression of exploiters, the establishment of a socialist society, and the victory of socialism in all lands."[9] One part of the regime's mandate was public health.

To speed recovery from Civil War destruction and a shattered economy, and to demonstrate the merits of Communism, the Soviet leadership was committed to health "for political stability, productive industry, and military manpower."[10] Essential to this recovery was maximizing worker productivity. All able-bodied Soviet citizens were required to hold jobs and by 1929 most employment was in state enterprises. To perform efficiently in the workplace, workers needed to be alert and healthy. Communicable diseases, alcoholism, smoking-related conditions, and other ills weakened the worker's labor contribution and, in the big picture, undermined the state. This view of the importance of health drove the state's health promotion efforts and the expansion of medical services.

POSTERS AS PROPAGANDA OR SOCIAL ADVERTISING

The Soviet Union was not the only country to use posters to promote health and other causes. Posters had been used in Europe and the United States to promote commercial products, entertainment (including films), political candidates, and war mobilization.

The Soviet use of posters to address health issues was similar to what later became known as "social advertising" in the United States, but this similarity was not apparent in the respective countries. Social advertising emerged from commercial advertising.[11] Many people were convinced that commercial advertising wielded a powerful influence on people's attitudes and behaviors, including their decisions about what products to buy, and also what behaviors to adopt, including smoking. Social advertising aimed to take the lessons of commercial advertising and other forms of commercial promotion, and to apply these lessons to promote health.

In contrast, the Communists would never have employed commercial terms such as "advertising" or "marketing".[12] Early on the Soviet regime launched a special department to carry out *agitprop*, meaning a combination of *agitation* or incitement plus *propaganda*, designed to influence mass beliefs and actions. In the West *agitprop* carries the connotation of "political propaganda, especially favoring communism and disseminated through literature, drama, art, or music."[13] In the Soviet Union the term *propaganda* did not have a negative connotation, but rather meant "the dissemination or preaching of an idea or doctrine, along with the recruiting of supporters for the idea disseminated."[14]

In the United States and Great Britain, wartime needs encouraged the adoption of advertising know-how. Both countries sought to promote volunteering for military service, and to encourage support for the war effort by conserving and recycling at home.[15] These appeals were conveyed through posters, billboards, and advertisements in newspapers, magazines, and radio to reach a mass audience. After World War II, with the advent of television, such advertising often took the form of televised "spot" announcements. The theme came from a non-profit organization or government agency, the creative work and production were typically done by a participating advertising agency on a pro bono basis, and the resulting advertisement was broadcast at no charge. Themes included avoiding littering, conserving energy, quitting smoking, using seat belts in automobiles, and many others.

In the United States these social messages, presented on commercial media, appeared alongside paid advertising for cigarettes, alcoholic beverages, products with lots of wasteful packaging, and high-powered, gas-guzzling cars. In the Soviet Union, state monopoly of all media could have created a media environment for health messages that was, at least in principle, uncluttered by competing and conflicting messages. The Soviet state could have chosen to forbid advertising of so-called "vice products" in the interest of promoting health. Instead the Soviet state used poster campaigns to point out the deleterious personal, societal, and economic costs of alcoholism and tobacco use, while at the same time the state was promoting vodka, wine, beer, and tobacco products from state factories, and was heavily dependent on tax revenues from the sale of these products.

Posters were valuable vehicles for health promotion efforts for several reasons. A special attribute of posters was their combination of images and text, which could be crafted in many styles. They were cheap to make, and could be created, printed, and distributed rapidly, to respond to the situation at hand.[16] The uneducated could quickly grasp their meaning from the vivid images. Many identical copies could be speedily made, and posters could be easily transported and widely distributed. Once the poster was affixed to a wall in a suitable location, it could be viewed by many people many times, reinforcing the message:

> Posters have been a powerful force in shaping public opinion because propagandists have long known that visual impressions are extremely strong. People may forget a newspaper article but most remember a picture. A pamphlet or a newspaper can be thrown away, unread; the radio or television turned off; films or political meetings not attended. But everyone at some time or other notices messages when walking or driving, or sees posters on bulletin boards in offices, hospitals, clinics or pharmacies. The main objective of posters, as with other communications media is to influence attitudes, to sell a product or service or to change behavior patterns. Public health posters are clearly in the third category, their purpose being to alter the consciousness of the public to bring about an improvement in health practices.[17]

Health posters adorned first-aid posts, clinics, hospitals, clubrooms, and schools in the Soviet Union. The posters also functioned as decoration in new clinics and hospitals built from the 1920s on as part of the system of universal health care, and these health posters attracted even greater attention once bans on most commercial advertising were enforced. A British physician and an American charity administrator visited medical facilities throughout the Soviet Union in 1932. At a stop at a Moscow marriage bureau they noted that "on the walls of the pleasant waiting room were posters and placards giving advice on the care of babies and promoting general hygiene."[18] On a collective farm near Tiflis (Tbilisi, in Georgia) they visited the daycare center, the clinic, and "various clubrooms, decorated with the usual health posters and large pictures of Lenin and Stalin."[19]

THE DEVELOPMENT OF HEALTH POSTERS

Many posters were issued by the Institute for Health Education, established in Moscow in 1928, reportedly the first such institute in the world.[20] A literal translation of the institute's Russian name is "sanitary enlightenment" rather than "health education", underscoring the institute's lofty purpose and socialist motivation. D. N. Loransky, while director of the

Institute, wrote in 1978 that the health promotion work of the various branches of the Soviet public health services "could develop successfully only on a strong base of Marxist-Leninist methodology, constantly reinforced by the creative experience of mass Party-political agitation and propaganda."[21] To promote this "sanitary enlightenment," the institute was staffed with professional health educators and conducted research and carried out a wide range of health promotion activities, including training, research, preparation of audiovisual materials, and publishing, including the preparation of posters.[22] Russian-language publications often refer to these as "sanitary posters"—*sanitarnye plakaty*—rather than as "health posters," reflecting the Soviet Union's early emphasis on sanitation and hygiene.

Each poster lists the names of several people involved in its development and creation—the editor, advisors, and artist—as well as the name and location of the institute where the poster was created—typically but not always Moscow or Leningrad. Each poster also carries the censorship registration number, the number of copies published, and the date. The Soviet Union was a multilingual, multicultural nation. Thus some general health posters were published in several languages and with different images, for posting in non-Russian-speaking republics of the Soviet Union, but no anti-smoking posters in multiple languages were found in archival collections.[23] Health authorities in various republics produced posters, as did the *Krasnyi-Krest* (Red Cross).

Ruben Suryaninov, a noted poster artist at the institute from 1956 through the 1980s, explained that a scientific council would determine the topics and themes, an artistic editor (*redaktor*) would assign the topic to a particular artist whose style was considered a good match, and the artist would then work with a *metodist*, a health education professional, to discuss the assignment and what approach to use.[24] The aim was to produce a poster that would convey the message in a clear, correct manner. The artistic quality of the health posters greatly improved when two art critics became artistic editors at the institute in the early 1960s. The new editors wanted posters to be better thought out and more visually appealing, to enhance their attractiveness and thus their effectiveness as health communications.

Most poster artists were not full-time employees, but rather were paid only for specific posters that were selected for publication. Before the publication decision was made, posters were reviewed internally, and were often pre-tested. Finally, health posters were scrutinized by Glavlit censors and, if approved, each was given a Glavlit registration number. When a poster was rejected, Glavlit provided no explanation.[25]

Thus we know that, for most of the Soviet period, health posters were neither ad hoc productions nor the fancies of individual artists, but productions of collectives of health education professionals and artists, often subjected to audience pretesting and always reviewed by the censors, who had the final say. Therefore anti-smoking posters can be examined as reflections of official policies and professional decisions, making these posters all the more valuable as artifacts worthy of close examination.

WAVES OF ANTI-SMOKING POSTERS

Two significant waves of anti-smoking posters appeared, the first in the late 1920s–early 1930s and the second from 1967 through the 1970s, with just a trickle from 1935 to 1967.[26]

In the 1920s the rate of smoking was growing in the Soviet Union. During this decade some efforts were undertaken to intensify educational and propaganda efforts against smoking.[27] Research on smoking prevalence, reported by the Ministry of Health (Minzdrav), showed that the rate of smoking among the Moscow Komsomol (Young Communist League) was 61%, and among high school students, from 20% to 35%. In 1927 68% of men and 45% of women in the Soviet Union were smokers.[28]

The earliest Soviet-era anti-smoking poster found in the archives (Figure 12.1) dates from 1920 and features six distinct frames, each presenting one danger of smoking. The first frame shows three men loitering on a sidewalk, all smoking. The older man looks ill and appears to be coughing. On the wall behind them is a poster that says, "Don't smoke, tobacco is poison." One of the two younger men is peeping toward an open window where a naked woman is visible. The frame is titled, "How people get started smoking," and the clear message is that youthful smoking leads to other evils as well as a sickly old age. In the second frame, a black-robed "Grim Reaper" holds a scythe and a huge bottle labeled "Nicotine" and warns "Tobacco contains nicotine, a poison." The middle two frames present the effects of tobacco smoke and nicotine on animals: "Tobacco smoke can kill a frog" and "One drop of nicotine can kill a horse." The bottom rank shows the healthy lungs of a nonsmoker and the shriveled, blackened lungs of a smoker, and a picture of a smoker "after twenty years," very ill, holding a cane, seated on a bench, his pale, wrinkled face aged from smoking.

The harmful effects of smoking were already well known in the early twentieth century, and tobacco and smoking had their vocal opponents well before the 1917 Revolution.[29] The 1920 poster (Figure 12.1) presents compelling arguments against smoking, with the lesson summarized in the text at the bottom of the poster: "Comrades, if you want to be healthy, quit smoking, this will save your life and your money which you waste on tobacco." The unique claim in this poster appears in the final sentence: "You will liberate for more useful labor thousands of workers who now labor unproductively in tobacco factories." This particular argument probably had little or no effect on changing smokers' habits.

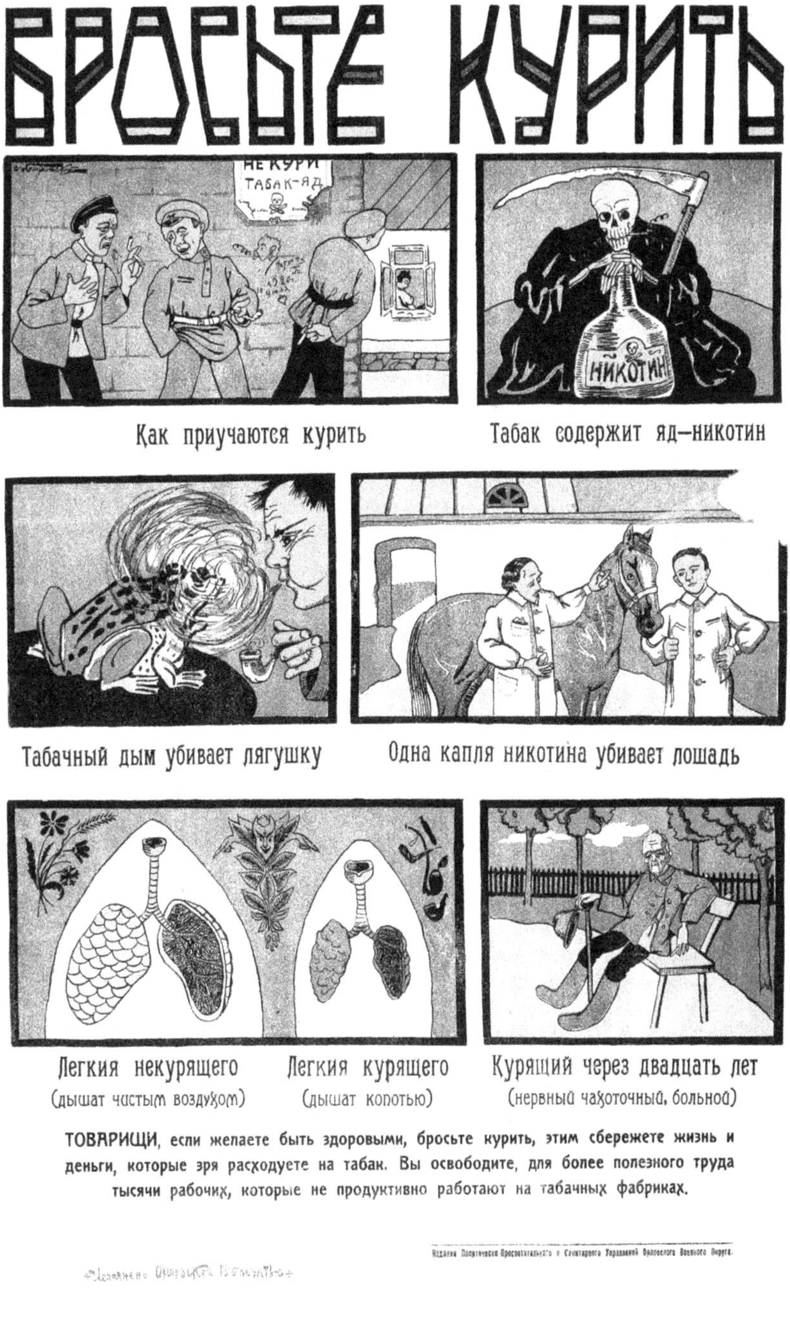

Figure 12.1 "Stop smoking!" (1920). From the collection of the Russian State Library, Moscow; reproduced with permission.

THE FIRST WAVE OF ANTI-SMOKING POSTERS: 1930

In 1930 the Institute for Health Education of the Ministry of Health Protection issued a series of posters taking aim at smoking. A recurring theme is poison—tobacco is poison, nicotine is poison, cigarettes contain various chemicals that are poisonous—and the exhortation to quit smoking. One poster informs the viewer that a drop of nicotine can kill a rabbit, and that in thirty years of smoking a smoker consumes tobacco containing 800 grams of poisonous nicotine. Another poster depicts a stack of rubles with a burning cigarette lighting the topmost bill, with the headline that smoking tobacco is expensive and harmful—to one's health and financial well-being. The same poster presents detailed statistics on the quantity and value of the tobacco output of Soviet factories in 1927–1928. A small box notes that in the textile industry, smoking takes up 14% of worker time, an obvious drain on worker productivity.

One poster actually provided guidance on quitting, depicting a young man and the title "Anyone can stop smoking." The text states that "If it is difficult to do it on your own, organize a group with others who want to quit, or go to the Narkodispensary" where hypnosis is available. Such clinics specialized in the treatment of alcoholics and drug addicts, and going there for help to quit smoking was probably an unattractive proposition.

Figure 12.2 Anti-smoking poster with quotation from the writings of Lenin, advising taking a walk outdoors instead of lighting up a cigarette; and a quotation from Nikolai Semashko, People's Commissar of Health, warning of the dangers of second-hand smoke. From the Hoover Archives, Stanford, CA.

Lenin, who died in 1924, was held up as an authority on all topics throughout the Soviet era. The Institute for Health Education managed to locate perhaps the only mention Lenin ever made of smoking in his writings, a tangential reference at that. Figure 12.2 shows a profile of Lenin, a reformed smoker, with the words: "Trust me, your work will be more productive if you walk in the forest for an hour or two, rather than sit in a stuffy room, rubbing your forehead and smoking *papirosa* after *papirosa*." In the same poster, the viewer is reminded by Nikolai Semashko, the People's Commissar of Health, that smokers not only affect their own health, but also the health of those around them.

In the iconography of health posters, children wearing their red Young Pioneer scarves are spokespersons for correct behavior, and they chide adults for failing to live up to expectations. Children push adults to discard "old" habits and ways of thinking, and to adopt healthier, safer, and more politically correct ones in their place. Two 1930 posters feature children in such roles. One poster on poisonous tobacco urges that children be protected from smoking. The wholesome, smiling Young Pioneer states that he absolutely does not smoke, while two "bad boys" are shown lighting up surreptitiously. One quarter of the poster presents a histogram of study results, comparing children who smoke and those who do not smoke. The statistics indicate that nonsmoking children are less nervous and have better memories, and experience fewer health problems than children who smoke. The message of the poster is that parents and other adults are responsible for steering their children away from the harms of smoking, and that parents may themselves be smokers presenting a bad example.

Figure 12.3 Poster, "Our Ultimatum to Adults!" (1930). From the Hoover Archives, Stanford, CA.

The other poster, titled "Our Ultimatum to Adults" (Figure 12.3), features a group of Young Pioneers with serious expressions presenting their demands regarding smoking:

Adults!

1. Do not poison the air that we breathe with cigarette smoke at home, in the club, at the institution.
2. Do not be a bad example to us by smoking cigarettes.
3. Quit smoking yourself before telling us about the harms of smoking.

If you don't fulfill the above requirements you lose your right to demand our respect.

In a separate box at the lower right is a guide to Pioneer conduct:

A Pioneer doesn't smoke and doesn't drink
A Pioneer will leave a gathering where others are smoking if they refuse to stop smoking.

An impressively detailed poster (Figure 12.4), also from 1930, clearly spelled out the physical damage caused by smoking. Titled "Smoking affects the normal functioning of the body," it depicts a wisp of smoke from

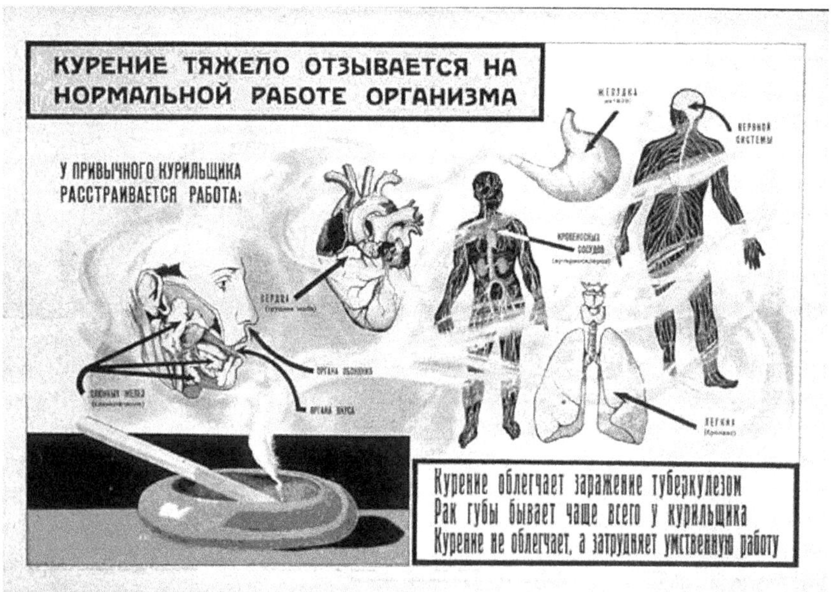

Figure 12.4 Poster, "Smoking seriously affects the normal functioning of the organs of the body" (1930). From the Hoover Archives, Stanford, CA.

a cigarette at bottom left which enters the man's mouth, and then shows the health problems created by the smoke as it moves through the body. The box at lower right states:

> Smoking contributes to infection with tuberculosis
> Lip cancer mostly affects smokers
> Smoking doesn't help, but rather interferes with mental work

This explicit mention of the relationship between smoking and cancer predates such revelations in most countries by three decades, and clearly makes the point that smoking is harmful to health.

THE TRICKLE: 1935—1966

From 1935 through 1966 few anti-smoking posters were published.[30] During the years of the Great Patriotic War, 1939–1945, smoking provided some stress relief to military personnel and civilians alike, and the state either ignored smoking as a health issue or decided to place priorities elsewhere. The only wartime posters found in the archives are directed at children. A 1944 poster shows a Young Pioneer, looking directly toward the viewer and saying, "Don't smoke" and giving a long explanation of why smoking is bad, especially for young people. Another poster of this period repeats the mantra "Tobacco is poison, stop smoking!" and recounts the power of nicotine to kill rabbits and horses, an account that was engraved forever on the memories of Russians, whether they smoked or not.

A 1962 poster by noted health-poster artist Ruben Suryaninov presages the direction of next wave of posters, evoking the lethal effects of smoking. The text warns that smoking will "burn up"—and thus waste—your health, as a skeletal hand daintily lights a cigarette in the mouth of a smoker.

THE SECOND WAVE OF ANTI-SMOKING POSTERS: 1967–1980

A second wave of anti-smoking posters began to appear in 1967 and lasted a little more than a decade. Five principal themes dominated: a fear appeal to current smokers, warning that smoking leads to death; an aspirational appeal to youth, to avoid (or quit) smoking so they can be strong and athletic; an appeal to parents to provide a good example to their children, to discourage them from smoking; an appeal to parents and others to consider the physically harmful effects of smoking, including second-hand smoke, on others, including fetuses and children; and a variety of appeals that link smoking and heart disease.

Fear appeals: Smoking = death. The posters issued in 1967 really "took the gloves off." Rather than admonishing the viewer to quit smoking and appealing to the words of Lenin, doctors, Young Pioneers, or ordinary workers, the posters directly presented the viewer with strong imagery to evoke fear of smoking-caused death. A cigarette is depicted as the barrel of a revolver, pointed at a heart, which cries out, "Spare me!" A *Belomorkanal* cigarette pack has taken on a crab-like form, and moves toward a smoking man—a clear threat of smoking-related cancer. An image of blackened lungs on a black background shows a burning cigarette in place of the windpipe. A "road" formed of cigarettes laid side-by-side recedes from the viewer to the not-to-distant "end of the road" marked by the huge, red-lettered word *RAK Legkogo*: lung cancer. Lungs with aureoles depicted as burning cigarettes accompany the message "Smoker—Think! 96%–98% of lung cancer cases are smokers."

Several posters explicitly evoked death itself, albeit with a touch of wit. One poster simply depicts a grave with a traditional Russian Orthodox cross composed of three burning cigarettes, inscribed with the name of the deceased. The "name"—Kurilkin Kuril Kurilich—is written in the manner traditional for grave markers—with the family name, then first name and patronymic (from the father's first name), and dates of birth and (early) death. But here the deceased's name is not the common man's name, "Kiril," but rather "Kuril." This word in Russian definitely evokes smoking as the cause of death, for the word "kuril" means "he smoked." The name of the deceased is an explanation and indictment of the behavior that killed this smoker.

A dramatic poster from 1968 shows a funeral wreath (Figure 12.5). Here the traditional funeral wreath is formed not of flowers, but of packets of very well-known brands of tobacco products, including *papirosy*, cigarettes, and *makhorka* (cheap tobacco), all manufactured by state factories. The black funeral ribbon is inscribed with the word "kurilshchiku," which has a double meaning in this case: the word "kurilshchiku" translates "to the smoker" and the word "kurilka" also refers to a wreath, such as a funeral wreath.

Aspirational appeals to teenagers. Posters directed to young people contrast the health and vigor of the nonsmoker with the debilitating effects of smoking. Figure 12.6 from 1967 contrasts the two conditions in a two-frame presentation, under the title that asks, "Which do you want to be?": on the left, a scrawny boy, smoking and holding up a pack of *Sever* ("North") cigarettes, or, on the left, a more mature young man, his muscled arm holding up a barbell—and with no cigarette in sight. Another 1967 poster shows a young man—looking "cool" and wearing yellow socks and pointy-toed shoes, markers of the "jazz" youth abhorred by the authorities. The young man is blowing smoke rings around a death's head, with text "Smoking harms health." A 1969 poster shows a young man proudly looking at himself in a mirror as he lights a cigarette. Above and behind him in black outline is the spectre of a stooped, unhealthy older man smoking, a harbinger of the young man's future, with the text "Just one puff starts a habit."

Figure 12.5 Poster, "To the smoker" (1968). From the collection of the Russian State Library, Moscow; reproduced with permission.

Two related posters from 1970 point out to children and youth that smokers cannot be good athletes. One poster shows a runner's leg, to which an oversized pack of *Belomorkanal* cigarettes is shackled by a heavy chain, with the statement that "he will never be an athlete." The other depicts an adult athlete, wagging his finger at a smoking child and lecturing, "Athletes don't smoke!"

Appeals to parents to avoid being a bad example to children. The third main theme of this period is the effect of adults as models for their children.

Figure 12.6 Poster, "Which do you want to be?" (1967). From the collection of the Russian State Library, Moscow; reproduced with permission.

A poster first issued in 1968 and reissued in 1978 shows a mother's profile. Inside the mother's profile is her young son, also smoking. The message asks, "Mama, pay attention: Do you smoke? Then how will you tell your children that smoking is harmful?" A 1977 poster shows a man and a woman—parents—smoking, and their small child also smoking, presumably in imitation of his parents. A clever poster shows a kangaroo smoking—and her joey is taking a cigarette from her pouch! Another, from 1978, shows an adult hand holding a lighted cigarette, and a child's hand holding a rolled-up piece of paper in imitation, with the text "Remember: Children look to us as role models."

Appeal to parents to protect their children's health. A fourth theme is the effects of smoking and second-hand smoke on others in the family, starting with effects on infants and fetuses. A 1978 poster depicts a father looking down at his baby, in fact smoking near the baby's face. The text reads, "Daddy and I are smoking." Another poster from the 1970s asks, "Do you want a girl or a boy? Don't smoke, expectant mother!" and employs a picture of cigarette butts stubbed out in a broken egg shell to signify the damage smoking can cause to the fetus. A third poster, published by the Soviet Red Cross, shows an expectant mother smoking. The smoke from her cigarette forms an image of an infant on crutches. Two posters, from 1977 and 1978, present more general warnings: "Smoking is pollution. You do harm not only to yourself, but also to those around you;" and "Remember! Nicotine also harms those around you."

Appeals linking smoking and heart disease. A fifth theme, appearing in 1974, is the explicit linking of smoking to heart disease. Three versions of a poster on this theme were published. One shows an "equation"

Figure 12.7 "Tobacco is poison!" (1970s). From the collection of the Russian State Library, Moscow; reproduced with permission.

of a smiling cartoon heart, "plus" a pack of *Belomorkanal* cigarettes, and these "equal" a sick heart, a cartoon heart on crutches. Another version of this poster shows only a vodka bottle as the center element, while a third version shows a vodka bottle and a lit cigarette. In each of the three versions this "equation" adds up to illness for the heart on the right.

Another poster on the same theme shows a realistic heart being consumed by stylized "flames," with the simple words "Alcohol Smoking." In another poster an enlarged heart, smoking, plopped in front of a television set, is accompanied by the warning "Have mercy on your heart."

This analysis of anti-smoking poster themes highlights the wide range of appeals and the variety of messages and images that were employed to carry the message that smoking was harmful. The most enduring message, illustrated in the earliest poster (Figure 12.1) and used throughout the Soviet period, was the statement that tobacco was poison. Figure 12.7 shows a version of this message in the 1970s, showing the burned ash of a cigarette that has morphed into the head of a snake—the symbol for poison—with glowing red eyes.

WERE SOVIET ANTI-SMOKING POSTERS EFFECTIVE?

At the Institute for Health Education in Moscow, individual posters were subjected to a series of internal reviews. Most posters were pre-tested by being shown to members of the public, to see if viewers understood the poster's message.[31] But we have no information on measurement of the impact of Soviet-era anti-smoking campaigns on rates of smoking, which of course was the aim of anti-smoking posters.

Measuring the impact of any mass communication campaign is difficult, but smoking statistics indicate that Soviet-era anti-tobacco posters and other programs had little or no effect on Soviet citizens' rate of smoking. The second "wave" of posters started in 1967, yet cigarette consumption rose significantly during the late 1960s. During the 1970s, the most hard-hitting anti-smoking posters appeared, employing intense fear appeals and links to cancer and other fatal diseases. A "full-out" national anti-smoking campaign was launched in 1977. Yet cigarette consumption remained high and quite stable throughout the 1970s.[32] The decline in tobacco consumption in the late 1980s was due to shortages of tobacco products, not due to a decline in demand.[33]

The lack of results is of particular interest because public health workers and health communicators in other countries presumed that health promotion campaigns in the Soviet Union would be particularly effective. They believed this for three reasons: First, every citizen was guaranteed free education so that quite rapidly the Soviet Union had a very high literacy rate, and universal free health care, so that citizens could read and understand health information, and had access to needed diagnosis, advice, and treatment. Second, except for the brief New Economic Policy period, the state controlled and censored all media and could, in principle, assure that information content was screened to present only consistent, approved messages. Third, health communicators could use all means of communication at no cost and could coordinate radio and television broadcasts, newspapers, magazines, posters, and school and workplace programs to provide integrated communications in support of health promotion programs. But despite these presumed advantages, Soviet anti-smoking efforts had little or no impact.

Soviet anti-smoking efforts were not more successful for several reasons. While the Soviet state had the power to "just say no" to tobacco, there were conflicting official priorities between production and advertising of cigarettes and other tobacco products by state factories on the one hand, and anti-tobacco campaigns and posters by state health authorities on the other. Since the Soviet state controlled all aspects of industrial production, and all imports, it would have been possible to impose a wide variety of restrictions on tobacco importation and manufacture of tobacco products, just as Semashko had proposed in the first years of the Soviet Union. Instead, in the 1970s the Soviet Union was going in the opposite direction, trying to modernize the Soviet tobacco industry by purchasing machinery from the West to modernize leaf processing, cigarette making, and packaging.[34] Soviet tobacco factories continued to advertise their wares.

Another possible explanation is that Soviet health educators were not in fact sophisticated about how to influence attitudes and behaviors. During the Cold War period, many US social scientists became quite interested in the opinions of Soviet leaders, the attitudes and beliefs of Soviet citizens, and the effects of official Soviet propaganda efforts in shaping public opinion.[35] To Western observers, propaganda—mobilizing the masses through newspapers, posters, radio, parades, films, and speeches—appeared to be a social change technology in which the Soviet state excelled. In reviewing the Soviet literature on public opinion and the practical journals and handbooks for propagandists and agitators, sociologist Alex Inkeles was surprised to learn how unsophisticated a foundation underlay Soviet propaganda efforts, and specifically how little attention was given to problems of method: "The importance of content is stressed infinitely more than questions of how, by what devices and mechanisms, one can influence attitudes and change opinions."[36]

Russia's health-related problems have mounted after 1991, including declining lifespan and increasing incidence of tuberculosis and HIV/AIDS, leading to suggestions that the traditional Soviet information-based approaches were seriously inadequate. In the late 1990s Karl Dehne, a German scientist in the United Nations AIDS Office in Geneva, was responsible for coordinating HIV-prevention efforts across the entire former Soviet Union. Dehne was stunned to learn that his Russian counterparts did not have any knowledge of behavior change approaches beyond issuing health information:

> They don't know anything [in former Soviet countries] about outreach, behavioral change, counseling. They say, "Information! Information!"

> When I say, "Information isn't enough to change behavior," they say back, "Well what else is?" Imagine—they have no methodology at all for outreach.[37]

ANTI-SMOKING POSTERS IN CONTEMPORARY RUSSIA

In 1991 the State Committee of Labor and Social Questions set out a renewed health education mandate: "To carry out among the population educational activities regarding a healthy life style, family planning, and exercise of sanitary and hygienic norms, and the prevention of fire, accidents, and the violation of the law."[38] Instead these activities came to a standstill when the Soviet Union dissolved in late 1991. The Institute for Health Education and its program of health posters came to an end, and health poster artists found other work.[39]

In recent years some Russian government agencies have turned to what they call *sotsialnyi reklama*, "social advertising"—using posters and billboards to convey health-related and social messages. A 2000 Moscow law ordered that 5% of Moscow's 40,000 advertising spots be reserved for such social advertising; recently that figure was raised to 15% in some parts of the city.[40] Poster topics are provided by government ministries to serve government priorities, such as posters urging Russian couples to have more children to counter Russia's population decline.

Metroreklama ("Metro Advertising") is a small agency that does creative development of advertising for Moscow's gigantic Metro system, a system that transports nine million passengers daily.[41] The agency got its start when the founders won a prize in a 1995 festival of "social ads." The Metroreklama staff operates with a modest budget, choosing topics themselves and producing two series of ads each year. Metroreklama started producing posters in 1995 when subway advertising space was going begging for lack of commercial advertisers. As of 2008, social advertising posters are used to fill unsold space in Moscow Metro stations. There is little or no pre-testing of posters, and no assessment of the impact of the posters. Each Metroreklama poster stands alone, and is not part of a sequence of posters, nor part of a coordinated campaign.

The rapid expansion of sophisticated commercial advertising for cigarettes, especially saturation campaigns in Moscow and St. Petersburg, makes it extremely difficult for anti-smoking social advertising to compete. In fact, the only anti-smoking poster seen on public display in Moscow in 2008 was a Metroreklama poster, first published in 2006, showing an attractive young blonde woman with a blasé look, exhaling cigarette smoke. She is clad in a spaghetti-strap dress completely covered with cigarettes. The text says, "*Ne Modna*"—"Not Fashionable." But smoking *is* in fact very fashionable among young women and men in contemporary Russia, as can be seen outside university buildings (including medical institutes), restaurants, and night clubs. In one Metro station the young woman smoking in the "not fashionable" poster looks across the escalator at a poster advertising "Kiss" cigarettes, targeted to young women.

NOTES

1. Piotr Otsup, "Piotr Otsup. The Space of Revolution: Russia: 1917–1941," photographic exhibition, pARTner project Gallery, Moscow, November 8–December 2, 2007.
2. Tricia Starks, "Red Star/Black Lungs: Anti-Tobacco Campaigns in Twentieth-Century Russia," *Journal of the Social History of Alcohol and Drugs*, 21:1 (Fall 2006): 50–68.
3. Peter Kenez, *The Birth of the Propaganda State: Soviet Methods of Mass Mobilization, 1917–1929*, (Cambridge: Cambridge University Press, 1985), 112.
4. The German economist was Alfons Goldschmidt, cited in Stephen White, *The Russian Poster: From Revolution to Perestroika*, (Glasgow: Collins Gallery, 1989), 108.
5. David L. Hoffman, *Stalinist Values: The Cultural Norms of Soviet Modernity, 1917–1941*, (Ithaca, NY: Cornell University Press, 2003).
6. White, *The Russian Poster,* 108.
7. E. V. Sherstneva and M. V. Poddubny, "Meditsinsky plakat kak sredstvo sanitarnogo prosveshcheniya v 20e godu," *Problemy sotsial'noi gigieny i istorii meditsiny*, issue 3, (May–June 2001): 61.
8. Ibid.
9. Constitution of the Russian Soviet Federated Socialist Republic, 1918, Chapter 2, Article 1. From the translation at <http://www.ucc.ie/acad/appsoc/tmp_store/mia/Library/history/ussr/government/constitution/1918/article1.htm>, accessed on September 2, 2008.
10. Tricia Starks, *The Body Soviet: Propaganda, Hygiene, and the Revolutionary State*, (Madison: University of Wisconsin Press, 2008), 3.
11. Karen F. A. Fox and Philip Kotler, "The Marketing of Social Causes: The First Ten Years," *Journal of Marketing*, 44 (Fall 1980): 24–33. Further explanation of social advertising is provided in Karen F. A. Fox, "Za Zdorovye: Soviet Health Posters as Social Advertising," *Journal of Macromarketing*, forthcoming 2009.
12. Karen F. A. Fox et al., "The Soviet Evolution of Marketing Thought, 1961–1991: From Marx to Marketing," *Marketing Theory*, 5:3 (2005): 283–307.
13. *The American Heritage Dictionary of the English Language,* 4th ed. (Boston: Houghton Mifflin, 2006). Definition of *agitprop* at <http://dictionary.reference.com/browse/agitprop>, accessed May 17, 2008.
14. Alex Inkeles, *Public Opinion in Soviet Russia: A Study in Mass Persuasion*, (Cambridge, MA: Harvard University Press, 1967), 40.
15. Terrence H. Witkowski, "World War II Poster Campaigns: Preaching Frugality to American Consumers," *Journal of Advertising*, 32 (2003): 69–82.
16. Kenez, *The Birth of the Propaganda State*, 112.
17. W. H. Helfand, "To Your Health: An Exhibition of Posters for Contemporary Public Health Issues," National Library of Medicine, National Institutes of Health, Rockville, MD, <http://www.nlm.nih.gov/exhibition/visualculture/vchome.html>, accessed on March 7, 2007.

18. A. Newsholme and J. A. Kingsbury, *Red Medicine: Socialized Health in Soviet Russia*, (Garden City, NY: Doubleday, Doran & Company, 1933), <http://www.marxists.org./archive/newsholme/1933/red-medicine/index.htm>, accessed on November 11, 2007.
19. Ibid.
20. D. N. Loransky, "Profilaktika" ("Prophylaxis"), *Zhurnal zdorov'e* (*Health Journal*), 10 (1978), <http://lechebnik.info/452/19.htm>, accessed on August 8, 2008.
21. Ibid.
22. George Rosen, *A History of Public Health*, (Baltimore: Johns Hopkins University Press, 1993), 379.
23. One of the few identified exceptions was a series of posters on the importance of household cleanliness, with the same text but different housing type (flat, hut, yurt), furnishings, and dress depicted.
24. The details of poster development and review were provided by Ruben Suryaninov in an interview in Moscow on October 29, 2007.
25. One of Ruben Suryaninov's posters on the dangers of drinking *samogon* (a potent, sometimes harmful, home-distilled alcohol) was rejected by Glavlit, with no explanation or suggestion of changes that would have made it acceptable.
26. This on-again, off-again pattern characterized Soviet-era anti-smoking efforts, as described in Starks, *The Body Soviet.*
27. L. P. Fedorenko, *Kurenie v Rossii*, (Slavanksk-na-Kubani: Russian Academy of Education, Southern Department, 2002), 6.
28. Reported in Fedorenko, *Kurenie v Rossii*, 6.
29. See Starks, this volume.
30. This statement is based on examination of the contents of three of the largest collections of Soviet posters, as well as poster collections accessed online.
31. Suryaninov, interview in Moscow, October 29, 2007. More information on how posters were pre-tested is provided in Fox, "Za Zdorovye."
32. See Figure 15.4 in this volume.
33. Ibid.
34. Richard Cooper, "Smoking in the Soviet Union," *British Medical Journal,* 285 (August 21, 1982): 549.
35. Inkeles, *Public Opinion in Soviet Russia*, 24–5.
36. Ibid.
37. Karl Dehne, cited in Laurie Garrett, *Betrayal of Trust: The Collapse of Global Public Health*, (New York: Hyperion, 2000), 233.
38. This quotation from the State Committee of Labor and Social Questions appears in Salvatore Imbrogno, "Emergence of the Profession of Social Work in the Russian Republic," in *Education for Social Work in Eastern Europe: Changing Horizons*, ed. Robert Constable and Vera Mehta, (Chicago: Lyceum Books), 91–103.
39. Suryaninov, interview in Moscow, October 29, 2007.
40. Alastair Gee, "Making the Metro Smile," *The Moscow Times*, October 12, 2007.
41. The information on Metroreklama came from Gee, "Making the Metro Smile," and from a telephone interview with Evgenii Koval of Metroreklama, August 8, 2008.

13 The Iava Tobacco Factory from the 1960s to the early 1990s

An Interview with the Former Director, Leonid Iakovlevich Sinel'nikov[1]

Elizaveta Gorchakova
Edited and Translated by Tricia Starks

LEONID IAKOVLEVICH, TELL US ABOUT YOUR BACKGROUND AND HOW YOU CAME TO THE IAVA TOBACCO FACTORY?

I was born in Moscow in 1939, just before the beginning of World War II, and I lived my entire life in Moscow. I was an only child. My parents were, by profession, veterinarians. Frankly, I wanted to be a chemist. I wanted to go to Moscow's Mendeleev Institute of Chemical Technology, but I did not make it in. With the same scores, I went to the Moscow Institute of Food Technology and placed in the mechanical department. I finished the institute as a mechanical engineer of food industry technology. I was given two career options: enter the All-Union Research Institute for Experimental Food Processing Machinery or the Iava factory. I thought hard and consulted with people I knew from the food industry and outside of it to decide which would be better. My neighbor told me, "Iava is a very interesting factory. It is a state within a state with a very interesting group of people."

I decided to go to work at the factory. This was an opportunity to start at the productive foundations of the industry. Manufacturing provides the basis for self-reliance and a way to prove yourself. Everything else is in the sphere of service, not production. The factory was state property—as was the entire industry. There was a Soviet Ministry of Food Industry and then a similar ministry for each republic. In each of these ministries there was a committee which managed tobacco industry (Glavtabak in the Ministry of Food Industry of the USSR and Rosglavtabak in the similar ministry of the Russian Federation). There were tobacco factories in each republic, but in Russia there were few. The ministry ran the factories through the committees, gave the factories the plans for production, the price indices, and managed the number of personnel. A factory could submit their own proposals, but we had to work with ministry dictates for production, financial performance, number of employees, and average salary. The ministry received orders from Gosplan [the State Planning Committee of the USSR Council of Ministers], which determined its figures on the basis of the country's consumer demand. After these factors were determined, they budgeted everything—tobacco, paper, and metal for spare parts. It was a strictly planned economy.

I began at Iava as a shift master. It was a big job. When I arrived, there were about sixty-eight people working there in two shifts. I worked in shifts too—one week during the day and the next during the evening. Until I was brought into the factory, I had not had a lot of contact with regular people—with workers. I was impressed by these very talented people and excellent specialists. The men who came in during the war had no special education, but they were the backbone of the factory. By the time I came to the factory they were professionals of the highest class. These people were interesting to talk to. They had a unique outlook on life. Many, of course, drank. They mostly drank after work, though occasionally at work there was drinking. They grew up in the factory, married there. When I arrived many were nearly seventy-years-old. They took me on as a friend, and I tried to help them.

For example, when I came in, I learned that the shop workers were not provided with work clothes. They came to work in their old, street clothes. I was surprised and asked, "Who is in charge of this?" They answered that it was up to the Deputy Director—Garnik Kegamovich Azizian. I made an appointment with his office. When I met him, he was encouraging. We sat on a sofa and he asked me questions. I told him that the shop workers were not provided with work clothing, and that workers of the mechanical shop constantly worked with metal chips and coolant. He said he'd fix things, and, indeed, he got them specialized clothing. It was my first victory. The workers barely believed it when I said, "Here are your work clothes." There were many such interesting moments.

Our mechanical shop made spare parts not just for the Iava factory but for other tobacco enterprises. For a year I worked as the shift master and then they named me the senior master. In 1963 the chief of the mechanical shop left to become chief of the technical department and I became the chief of the mechanical shop. I was only twenty-four-years-old. After that I became the chief engineer. It was a very desirable position, but there was not another suitable candidate at Iava at this time. Many people were already too old. The chief mechanic had worked there for years and hadn't an education. The head of the technical department was also too old. For four months the factory worked without a chief engineer and in that period the duties were performed by the chief mechanic. The director called me and said, "Leonid, I have thought and thought. You are young and energetic. I would like you to become the chief engineer." To become the chief engineer was a big step. I said that I had to think about, and discuss, this serious decision with others.

Finally, I decided that never again in life would I receive such an attractive proposal, and I agreed to become chief engineer. It was a great opportunity to prove myself. This was a turning point in my life and the rapid take-off of my career. As chief engineer I was first deputy director. Nowadays the chief engineer is more a technical post, but during the Soviet era, the chief engineer was in charge of everything. The director fulfilled ceremonial functions, but the chief engineer did it all and reported to the director. It was responsible work. I worked as chief engineer for nearly sixteen years and in 1982, I was named director.

WHAT WAS THE RELATIONSHIP OF THE EMPLOYEES TO THE FACTORY?

When I came to the Iava factory it employed about 1,500 people—mainly in the production of *papirosy*. This may be unique to the tobacco industry, but people worked at the factory for thirty to forty years—sometimes even fifty. No one left, they worked into old age. The tobacco industry was very stable, profitable, and had other incentives. Usually, people were not hired from the street. When there was a vacancy at the factory, news of it went through the collective, and workers brought in their relatives, neighbors, and friends. Everyone was connected with each other one way or another. It was kind of like a family.

People thought it was prestigious work. Now, not everyone wants to be associated with tobacco because it is considered controversial. But then, tobacco was a strategic commodity. In the 1960s–1970s, the idea of smoking being hazardous was not even discussed. In the Soviet Union it didn't come up until after 1985. During the war and after the war, all to a man smoked. We fulfilled the demands of the smoking population in a market with permanent tobacco product deficits. The industry as a whole could not meet the demand for tobacco products of the period. We did not have the equipment or the raw materials.

WHO WORKED IN THE FACTORY? IN WHAT CONDITIONS?

Because it was mainly manual labor, most of the workers were women. The ratio was roughly 70% female to 30% male. That ratio changed as the factory developed. As more modern cigarette machines came in, the tobacco shop was reconstructed and the amount of hand work was lessened. In the period of reconstruction the ratio of men and women was about 50–50. Now men make up about 60% or more of workers.

In leadership there were not just men. The Communist Party directives were that women needed to advance and the party organizations watched this and the relationship between men and women in leadership. The party secretaries could say, "We see that you have few women in leadership positions. You do not work sufficiently with women. You need to promote more women to top positions." The same applied to admission to the party. To bring one engineer into the party we were required to take in three workers. In general, the workers did not want this. In the first place, they had to pay party dues. People did not want to take on extra responsibility. Once, an engineer went to the party secretary saying he wanted to join. The secretary answered, "I cannot accept you. I need to take in three workers. If you can find some and persuade them, then you can enter the party. Otherwise, you'll have to wait."

WHAT WAS THE WORK LIKE IN THE 1950S AND 1960S?

Working conditions were difficult. Tobacco production was considered hazardous. All the machines were designed with reciprocating momentum rather than modern, rotary mechanisms. Therefore the shops were extremely noisy—from 96–97 decibels. When I, as chief engineer, saw the shop, I was immediately deafened. The noise was very detrimental to a person's health: vessels, hearing, and blood pressure. The machines were open, without aspirators, and therefore the air contained a great deal of dust. For instance, the current norm is 3 mg of tobacco dust per cubic meter. At a contemporary factory the level of dust is about 1–1.5 mg. But at that time, it was 8–10 mg and in some areas up to 20 mg. This caused certain diseases—such as emphysema. The work destroyed people's health. People worked in such difficult conditions when their health was not protected.

There were respirators and ear plugs but no one used them. They were inconvenient. It was a time that there were few things that were made truly convenient for people. The equipment was open and so occasionally fingers got caught in the mechanisms. This did not happen often but it did happen. At that time, labor conditions were difficult everywhere. There were not enough resources. Factories were old. Work sites were old and cramped with low ceilings and poor ventilation. Dust was at five and six times the level of today. Noise was at an extremely high level. It drained people of their vital juices.

It is sad for me to recall that generation of people—hardy workers who lived and worked in difficult conditions—a really hard life. These workers lived in barracks, without kitchens, without heat, without hot water. They went to the *bania* once a week and even for this they had to stand in line for two to three hours on the street. Now people do not even remember it, but it was just a nightmare.

At the factory, there was an engineer in charge of labor protection . . . and labor protection was discussed at party meetings. Hazardous conditions were considered normal, but all the same there were demands of the engineers and the chief engineer to improve conditions. They could not change anything drastically, but they had to do something. Pregnant women were invariably switched to light work. In that regard, the regulation was very strict. They normally did not work in the shops and they did, they were assigned less hazardous and dangerous workstations. Not on the line, but perhaps in the storeroom.

There were benefits, but they were not distributed to all, just to those who worked constantly with tobacco. For instance, mechanics did not get benefits. They were not considered to be on the line 100% of the time. Metal workers were also not given special benefits. Tobacco people went on retirement five years early—women at fifty years and men at fifty-five. That had a big impact, because at that time a pension allowed you to live comfortably. While the general vacation was two weeks, tobacco workers were allowed a full month. Plus, they were given free milk and vouchers for food. Their pay was higher. There was a special tariff grid for enterprises with hazardous conditions—somewhere around 15% higher than the average.

People appreciated that there were benefits. Women liked that they could retire five years earlier. Some received a pension and continued to work. It was a stable job. People appreciated the free products (*raskurka*). Every worker could take home, free, thirty *papirosy* a day. They could smoke these themselves, give them to family, or sell to their neighbors for a discount. When the factory moved over to cigarette production, the workers were given thirty cigarettes. These cigarettes had been rejected for sale with minor defects, but they were quite fine for consumption.

HOW WAS THE IAVA FACTORY ORGANIZED?

People were paid by the piece. Pay went to the entire brigade. A brigade consisted of five machine operators and a mechanic, and in the brigade everyone received the same pay based upon the productivity of the line, the quality of product, and loss of materials. Workers could also get premiums, but poor quality or high losses could result in lowered premiums.

There were seventeen *papirosy* lines. Each line had ten units producing *papirosy* and one packaging unit. Each unit consisted of machines that produced tubes from *papirosy* paper, that is, a *papirosa* without tobacco. The *papirosy* paper was curled into a cylinder of about 70 mm in length (that is the length of the full *papirosa*) and a diameter of 7–8 mm. These tubes were made mechanically and completely without glue. This method was created in Russia, indeed, *papirosy* are a completely Russian invention. Later, at the beginning of the 1970s, the German firm Hauni tried to develop a modern production line for *papirosy* given the high level of consumption of *papirosy* in Russia. They worked on different methods for producing *papirosy*—such as the methods used to produce cigarettes—but they were unable to think up a better method for *papirosy*. In the end, they returned to that technology with a more modern execution.

The tube was connected to a mouthpiece and then a machine stuffed the tubes with tobacco. Each *papirosa* then went to the common carrier and was transported to the packing machines. One line produced in one eight-hour shift about 1.3–1.4 million *papirosy*. There were seventeen such lines in production and work was carried over three shifts. The *papirosy* shop produced a large amount. The cigarette shop worked with machines that were brought from Germany as reparations after World War II. In about 1947, Iava had around eight such machines, but they worked only for one shift because cigarettes were not in much demand at the time.

One mechanic and five machine operators worked on each *papirosy* line. Machine operators prepared the tube paper and filter papers and changed bobbins. During the work, there could be breakdowns at which point the equipment was stopped, cleaned, fixed, and restarted. The tubes needed to be watched. Cleanliness had to be monitored because the tobacco spilled. The machine operators were overworked and were unable to step away from their machines for long.

WHAT KIND OF PROBLEMS DID PRODUCTION FACE?

The most difficult question of the factory was supplying spare parts. I was faced with this problem as head of the mechanical shop. The shop did not have the ability to produce enough spare parts and the parts we did produce quickly wore out because we were given steel of lower quality. Therefore, there was often equipment failure. For example, there might be a piece on a machine that needed to work for a month and it would break after two weeks. I tried to organize work so as to address these shortcomings. I began an initiative, and I think I was nominated for the post of chief engineer because of that. I tried to give these problems a public airing and diagnose their source because otherwise shops often wrote off their defects as the mechanical shop's failure to deliver parts on time. I had to be ready to answer such charges forcefully.

There were other problems, too, such as theft. Shipments were sealed at the factory, but there were drivers and loaders who could open a shipment without disturbing the seals and remove twenty to forty packs without detection. If, when they made it to the sales site, they opened them and found they were missing packs, a call was sent to the factory and our specialists went out to prove we were not at fault using all sorts of different evidence. Otherwise, blame went to the factory. In general the question of theft was very serious and it occurred in the factory among the workers and also in the warehouses of finished products. There were groups involved and the temptation was great as pay was not that high and people wanted to live better. We had trusted informants who advised us. It was difficult to fight a conspiracy among a group of people, for instance, in the warehouse. We identified certain groups and tried to separate the members. The most important thing was to prevent theft by stopping groups from coming together and by using good accounting and control procedures. The thieves traded their goods or sold them to kiosks. The kiosks took them as it was cheaper. For example, a pack went for forty kopecks, but they bought them for twenty kopecks or even ten kopecks. Factory workers had arrangements with kiosk people with agreements and protection money. It was the main headache of the leadership.

HOW DID THE FACTORY CHANGE IN THE 1960S AND 1970S?

In 1965, we began producing filtered cigarettes to fit with international practice. To do this we had to buy large quantities of equipment from the British firm Molins. Molins was the leader in tobacco equipment. The firm supplied the Soviet Union with fifty-five high-performance Mark-8 cigarette machines (at that time these were the most modern machines and could produce 2,000 cigarettes a minute), along with machines to produce hard packs from both the Molins firm and the German firm Schmermund. Altogether, the equipment cost 2.5 million dollars. Now that sounds funny, but at that time it was a very large sum. The bulk of this equipment (seventeen of fifty-five lines) went to Iava because Iava was the head factory in the sector. Part of the contract was that specialists from the firm helped with the set-up, debugging, and trial period. During the testing period, the machines were put through all their paces and our mechanics studied the works. This was a serious debugging process.

Iava began with one line as a demonstration. The first cigarettes produced on that line came out not for widespread sales but special cafeterias for regional party groups and Soviet authorities. We could not immediately start a full seventeen lines. The shops were old, crowded, and unsuited to modern production. Building facilities in Moscow was very difficult. You had to have a special permit from the Council of Ministers of the USSR. Moscow was a closed city. It was impossible to simply come to Moscow and take up residence. It was similarly difficult to build production facilities. To get around this, the factory leadership built a warehouse with the intent of re-purposing it later into factory space. Which they did successfully. I was chief engineer at the time and all this lay on my shoulders. A new building was not fully operational until 1972. Until then the new machines were installed in the old production space; it was extremely crowded. The new equipment was based on rotating action and was therefore less noisy. Also, the equipment was enclosed and therefore there was not any open tobacco. It was equipped with general and localized aspirators and therefore there was less dust. The labor conditions dramatically improved especially after we moved the new machines to the new site. There the ceilings were higher and the ventilation was better. Of course, today the level of labor is even better, but at that time it was a huge step forward.

The next biggest problem was that we did not have operating experience. To use the equipment and produce high-quality cigarettes required acetate filters and cigarette paper that the USSR did not produce. The tobacco was also of a completely different quality. Every machine was serviced by a mechanic and a machine operator. The packing machine was serviced at first by two mechanics and three operators but later was served by one mechanic and three operators. We had to quickly hire young people and train them to work on these seventeen lines. A mechanic on a cigarette machine can work effectively up to a certain age. The machines were high speed. A person over fifty simply could not keep up. They did not have the dexterity or the speed of reaction. Iava actually had a very good system of training. At the factory there was a training center. Right in the middle of the yard at Iava stood a separate, two-story house. People, including ordinary workers, studied there. The student immediately stood at a machine next to an experienced mechanic who taught him and during the time of training they were already on salary. After the students completed training and took an exam, the mentor was given a bonus. In addition to work in the shop there was also theoretical work. At a minimum, training was six months and sometimes seven or eight. Training also allowed people to continue their education, improve their professional standing, and move to higher pay grades.

There was also a branch of the Food Industry Technical School at the factory. There they had lessons and the program of the Technical School. Many factory workers were able to complete the school right at the factory and received their diploma (technician-mechanic, technologist). The bulk of our engineering-technicians were mechanics who had completed the Technical School. I came to the factory after the institute. At that time at the factory there were, maybe, a few people with a higher education. The remainder learned on the job and moved up to be engineers. Maybe they were not very cultured, but they knew their work well. They understood the machines and their specifics. Some people came after the war and at the factory they got a profession and learned to be mechanics. Then they went to learn the job from the production or technical institute. Gradually, they advanced to senior positions. These were people who pulled themselves up through the ranks. The factory gave people the opportunity to study and encouraged those who were good at their work and ready to assume responsibility.

At the same time, during the Brezhnev era certain things were devalued. Already, the discipline of earlier times was lost and people began to be less concerned about their work. Under Stalin, it had been difficult to find a job, but under Brezhnev there was a labor shortage. Everywhere there were signs "Workers needed." For example, the leadership might try to fire a worker who showed up to work drunk, but he just said, "Eh, I work poorly? Well, if you don't like me, I'll go work for another factory." There were people who constantly moved from one job to the next. You could dismiss someone for absences or drinking, but you also had to think, "who will take his place." The next one might be worse. We fired people only as the last resort as there was a constant labor shortage.

WHAT KIND OF SERVICES DID THE FACTORY PROVIDE TO EMPLOYEES?

At the factory there was a cafeteria that one could eat at comfortably. There was hot food during the day and evening and even dietetic food. The meals were very cheap. In addition, the factory had a medical post where doctors checked on workers. Employees could get vouchers for summer recreation or treatments—sometimes free or at a discount with help from the state. The factory had a really good library and it also got newspapers. There were two kindergartens. We guaranteed children, and even the grandchildren, of our employees placement in the kindergarten. There was also a Pioneer camp—fundamentally for the employees' children. All this was very cheap for employees. This was our social responsibility—we upheld an entire group of organizations for our workers. There was also a cultural program with tickets to the theater and concerts. It helped develop the people.

Entities, including factories, were encouraged to build housing for their staffs. Of course, that was allowed for only the successful organizations. Much depended on the director and his connections. Once the building was completed the management had to give a part of the building to the local government for the district and the rest was distributed among the staff. The decision on who exactly would get an apartment was not made just by the director but together with the union and of course the party organization. For people at the time there were not many opportunities to get an apartment. The factory made it possible.

WHAT DISTINGUISHED IAVA FACTORY CIGARETTES?

Our tobacco came mostly from Bulgaria. We also bought tobacco from Turkey, Greece, and India. These were high-quality tobaccos, and our blends were oriental. We had specialists in the factory. For instance we had in service a chief tobacco master. There were others involved including specialists in leaf quality and others who each day created a tobacco blend and developed future products. Specialists called *kupazhisti* monitored the blending process. There was a chemical laboratory, which undertook research and helped develop new products. In the Soviet period, people liked a strong cigarette more. In the first place, there was no question of the danger of smoking for health. These questions appeared only after 1985. There were no regulations for tar or nicotine content and products were not even tested for such. Tar content was somewhere around 17–18 mg (below 20 mg), and there was up to 2 mg of nicotine. Some had more than two, but in principle it was not controlled. There was never talk about it being dangerous. When people spoke of quality they meant primarily the smoking satisfaction or the need to produce a cigarette with a filter because that was seen as a good area for development. It was not tied to health.

Near the end of the 1970s, the beginning of the 1980s, we began to produce light cigarettes. We worked up cigarettes in a really beautiful pack and called them "Lights" (*Legkie*), but, when we prepared to start up production, somebody upstairs said, "What kind of name is that 'Lights'? [*Editor's note*: *Legkie* is also the Russian word for lungs—*E. G.*]. Is that some kind of hint that these cigarettes hurt your lungs?" These cigarettes were abandoned. Then we worked up another cigarette with a lower concentration of nicotine—there were two brands, "Evening" (a beautiful light blue pack with candles) and "Rus" (in a rather garish pack). There was no technology at that time for the production of light cigarettes like they use now. It was just according to the sort of tobacco used. We did not sell these cigarettes in high numbers, but Iava was the first factory in the Soviet Union to produce light cigarettes. It was written on the pack "with lower nicotine content." We also developed menthol cigarettes and cigarettes with other additives. People mainly smoked the traditional cigarettes all the same, and light cigarettes were produced in small quantities.

Label designs were put together in the Ministry of the Food Industry in the Product Design Department. It was quite a professional group, and they did the designs for all the tobacco factories and for all food production. Certain artists worked on the tobacco theme. At Iava we had our own specialist—Liudmila Pavlovna Vasil'eva. She worked in contact with the ministry artists. She had excellent taste. Our factory produced *papirosy* of the highest sorts, for example, "Bogatyr," "Gertsegovina Flor," and "Sovetskii Soiuz." They were packaged in beautiful boxes with flip covers, foil inserts and twenty-five pieces to a box. The boxes were sealed with a beautiful stamp. There were also gift sets. These boxes were done by hand in the box shop and then the *papirosy* were packed in them manually. Iava produced arresting designs with many innovations and released various types of new products started at Iava. For example, we produced gift sets with the motif of Russian fairy tales. In each set there would be ten to twelve packs and all of it was printed in Finland. In the USSR there was no printing enterprise of that level.

People bought anything new with great enthusiasm. Now the market is open and there are international brands, but at the time everything was quite poor. Prices were connected to the class of *papirosy* or cigarettes. It was difficult to create a price for every separate type of production. In general the price was not too high. That was state policy. Prices were adapted to people's incomes. That is why everything we produced was bought up. There was always a deficit. As there was not a large selection of products, everything was bought up.

New production was done not in order to increase sales. It was not a response to the market. It was part of the planned economy and important to development. It was considered positive if we put out new types of products, introduced new technological processes, and improved the organization of the workplace. There were plans for new technology, new types of products, and if we fulfilled the plan targets, the Ministry allowed us to give the employees rewards.

WHEN DID THE WARNINGS ABOUT SMOKING APPEAR?

These started in 1978, again under Western influence. In Europe they also had the warning. It troubled the leadership that the entire civilized world had a warning about smoking, and we did not have it anywhere. It happened to be during a period when Moscow had a deficit of "Iava" brand cigarettes. Stores had lines of people trying to get "Iava." It was proposed to put an inscription on the "Iava" soft packs. People believed that this would not affect the sales of the brand (though this was feared), and thus in 1978 Iava was instructed to make a small batch with a warning "The Ministry of Health warns that smoking is hazardous to your health."

We experimented with the sale of cigarettes with the warning label in a shop on the outskirts of Moscow. I do not remember the exact district. We watched how people reacted. I was chief engineer of the factory at the time, and we went as a threesome—me, the chief of the Tobacco Committee of the Russian Food Ministry, Vadim Aleksandrovich Grigor'ev, and the Instructor of the Central Committee of the Communist Party responsible for the tobacco industry, Anatolii Mikhailovich Usachev. We got to the store at the lunch break, and by two o'clock there was a large line for Iava. The sellers were told to show every customer the warning. We stood and watched. One man walked up and he was told, "Do you see the warning about the danger of smoking? What do you think?" He answered, "This is nonsense. Give them to me more quickly and I'm out of here." Another walked up and he was also asked, "Do you see the warning? What do you think?" "I think it will raise the prices for cigarettes." Everyone snatched them up and said, "We will sort out later if these are dangerous or not." Thus the warning was tested, and after that it was decided that all packs would have the warning label. It was done not immediately but gradually over several years.

DID THE FACTORY KEEP ANY CONSUMPTION STATISTICS?

Such statistics were not particularly prevalent in the USSR. Statistics are more closely linked to marketing, and therefore I cannot exactly say. I do not think that now there are any fewer or more smokers than during the Soviet period, but the types of smokers have changed. The structure of consumption was also different. Cigarettes with filters only accounted for about 20% of consumption. The rest was in *papirosy* and cigarettes without filters. Today, cigarettes with filters represent about 90% of consumption and *papirosy* are virtually nonexistent. I do not have exact data, but I think that when cigarettes with filters and in beautiful packaging came onto the market more women began smoking.

WHAT BRANDS WERE MOST IMPORTANT IN THOSE YEARS?

It differed over time. In the period up to the war, during it, and after, the most popular were "Belomorkanal" *papirosy*. Others were popular, too, like "Sever" and "Priboi." Among more affluent people the *papirosy* "Kazbek" were popular. During the war all the generals smoked only "Kazbek." I was told that when the Iava factory returned from evacuation in 1944 orderlies from marshals and generals came to the factory to get "Kazbek." After the war . . . cigarettes slowly grew to popularity. People were used to *papirosy*.

In the 1960s, the brand "Iava" became popular. The first "Iava" cigarettes were produced in 1966 and mass production began in 1967—immediately in both soft and hard packs. The labels were printed in Finland and the design was made there. "Iava" became very popular. In general, those who could get them smoked them. If we look at the structure of tobacco production, approximately 180–200 billion sticks were produced, and that was not enough. Some 65 billion cigarettes were purchased each year from Bulgaria (under the Council for Economic Mutual Aid [SEV] market agreement). Cigarettes were brought in from other countries as well, such as Indian cigarettes, but these were occasional purchases. Bulgarian cigarettes were imported constantly. There were cigarettes from Ukraine, too. Ukraine produced more cigarettes than it consumed and supplied some to Russia. In this way, a balance was reached in Russia for consumption even though there was a steady deficit. In Moscow they generally smoked cigarettes made by Iava and Dukat. Bulgarian cigarettes were about 10%–15% of Moscow consumption. In Leningrad, about 80% smoked Bulgarian cigarettes as local brands were not popular. The production from Leningrad ended up going to Arkhangel'sk or Murmansk regions. Moscow produced cigarettes mainly for itself and the most popular by far was "Iava."

HOW DO YOU EXPLAIN THIS POPULARITY?

I think the quality of "Iava" was indeed higher. At Iava we had really excellent personnel, and at that time quality was dependent upon personnel as much of the operation was hand work—manually mixing the ingredients. Also, Iava introduced modern, technological tobacco preparation earlier than others. The first workshop for preparation of tobacco, imported from Bulgaria, was installed at Iava and automatic mixing of blends was started. In 1974 we began assembling the equipment, and in 1975–1976 it was up and running. It was a real breakthrough and no other factory had it.

Iava really made the highest quality products in terms of excellent taste and appearance. The packaging of other factories' products—the ribbons were askew, cellophane crumpled, and under it there were tobacco crumbs. It was sloppy and unpleasant looking. Iava packaging was very different. It looked imported. It was a completely different look and that was easy to explain because Iava bought the very best materials. We worked with the best foreign suppliers. Because Iava had advantages over other factories in terms of guaranteeing materials and equipment, our packs were presentable. In Moscow it was impossible to sell poor packs with the leadership all here. If, God forbid, some chief found a bad pack or other problem there was immediately an outcry. He called the ministry, and got the director called "on the carpet." People came to Moscow to buy Iava products from areas where they were not available. "Iava" was used in the special cafeterias for regional party committees, but it was not available for open sale in these regions. In the outlying areas they sold local or Bulgarian and Ukrainian cigarettes. We made a maximum of ten billion "Iava" cigarettes a year and sixty-five billion Bulgarian cigarettes were imported.

WERE "IAVA" CIGARETTES MADE ONLY IN THE IAVA FACTORY?

Yes. For a time Dukat was allowed to produce "Iava" cigarettes—during the Mostabak period. This was a period when the two Moscow tobacco factories—Iava and Dukat—were operating within one produciton unit. At that time, there was a huge deficit of "Iava," but people all the same searched for "'Iava' from Iava," that is, those made at the Iava factory. We even patented the brand name "Iava." Other brands were developed for the industry as a whole and produced at various factories.

WERE SOME CIGARETTES PRODUCED BY SPECIAL ORDER?

Yes, everything for the government and high leadership was done by special order and that has its own history. For example, Brezhnev liked "Novost" cigarettes made by Dukat. "Novost" cigarettes were a soft pack, 70-mm length (not 85 mm) with a paper filter, not the acetate filter of a good cigarette. Their appearance was awful. Dukat did not have equipment to make better cigarettes, but when Brezhnev smoked "Novost," these cigarettes became very popular among the top leadership. Then, someone raised the question of how the Secretary-General could smoke cigarettes that did not meet modern standards. But Dukat did not have the technology to do longer cigarettes. Therefore they took the decision to have Dukat supply Iava with a finished, sliced tobacco blend as well as paper, packaging, etc. and have Iava prepare and package the cigarettes. At this point, they became different cigarettes entirely—long with a hard pack and an acetate filter. These cigarettes were not for sale but only available by special order. It said on the pack that the cigarettes were fabricated at Dukat. After that they decided to buy Dukat a modern production line to put out the "Novost" cigarettes but before it was even installed, Brezhnev said in an interview that his doctors had ordered him to quit smoking.

WERE THERE OTHER TOBACCO PRODUCTS RELATED TO WELL-KNOWN CELEBRITIES?

It is widely known that Stalin smoked a pipe, but he packed it with Iava made tobacco for *papirosy* of the highest sort—"Gertsegovina Flor." He personally broke *papirosy* to get tobacco out and stuff his pipe. When Brezhnev went abroad and met with foreign leaders he proudly gave them pipes which had been made at Iava. There was a smoking accessories shop at the factory that made not just pipes, but also the tobacco to go in them. For instance, Brezhnev met with Georges Pompidou and brought with him a gift box filled with candy, vodka, and many things selected by the ministry. In the collection was our smoking tobacco and a pipe from our greatest master. On the pipe between the mouthpiece and the bowl there was a golden ring. We were immediately reimbursed. After that Brezhnev personally sent a letter of gratitude to the factory and especially the masters who created the pipe. We created such gifts for Fidel Castro and Chancellor of Germany Helmut Schmidt.

WHEN DID FOREIGN BRANDS FIRST BEGIN TO APPEAR ON THE MARKET?

In 1975 Iava, with the licensing of Philip Morris, produced the cigarette "Soiuz-Apollo" to commemorate the joint space mission of Soviet and American cosmonauts. These were very high-quality cigarettes. In 1977 a new agreement was signed with Philip Morris for the production of Marlboro cigarettes. The production would happen at several factories, but the main one would be Iava. We produced about one billion cigarettes annually. The United States sent us special plastic bags of the blend and also all the needed materials. All we did was produce the cigarettes. . . . Philip Morris sent supervisors to check the equipment, prepare specialists, and to monitor quality control. This project was carried out over about five years. After this the program was shut down because of difficult economic times.

The first major purchase of international brands was in 1980 when Moscow hosted the Olympics. The government negotiated an agreement with Finland to produce large quantities of cigarettes for Moscow. If I am not mistaken it was on the order of ten billion sticks. These cigarettes were intended for the Olympic guests, but many countries boycotted the Olympics over the Soviet invasion of Afghanistan. Thus, the leading world brands appeared for sale to our smokers. At first, no one bought them as they were expensive—1.5 rubles—but then our smokers appreciated the taste of imported cigarettes and they were quickly sold.

There was no smuggling since the free exchange of hard currency was banned. In principle there could be small, clandestine workshops producing fake products, mainly low-quality, consumer goods. But cigarette production is a complex process requiring special equipment and getting raw materials was impossible. There were situations related to illicit production in the Caucasian republics (Georgia, Abkhazia, Armenia, and particularly Georgia). These areas were isolated from the center and the center did give them a certain amount of freedom. They would work to fulfill the plan and their quota to the state early—even working nights—and then the last two to three days of the month they worked for themselves. They did this in collusion with local authorities; they then shared the profits. The director got a truck full of cigarettes, for example; the chief engineer a little less. Everyone involved got a share. What was the problem? Well, they got the planned amount of materials—tobacco, paper, stickers, etc. Representatives of these factories came to Russian factories and made deals with warehouse employees to steal the raw materials. They did not come to Iava, but they did do it to other factories where there was a surplus. Of course, these were not fakes but made by state tobacco factories under the same brand names. It was not counterfeit; it was simply undocumented. The trading network also participated in the conspiracy at all levels.

HOW WAS THE ECONOMIC SITUATION OF THE COUNTRY REFLECTED IN THE TOBACCO INDUSTRY?

The tobacco industry was powered by foreign equipment. Only *papirosy* were produced on equipment that was from the Soviet period. Already when I was in the industry, the cigarettes were being made on imported equipment. In such circumstances the currency condition of the country is of great significance, and the hard currency market was dependent upon the price of oil. Therefore, good and bad periods in the market were dependent upon the price of oil and the economic situation in the country. The tobacco industry was a kind of indicator. Few industries were so dependent upon imports—especially during a time when the priority was to wartime industry.

Around 1967–1968, the price of oil rose. I remember that I was called to the ministry and told to apply for equipment since there would be extra large funds for such purchases. I remember how we turned in the order and they bought us modern, rotary equipment—at that point the situation in the country with hard currency was good. Iava rose to the highest level. In the late 1970s the price of oil fell and a deficit in tobacco occurred because there was no currency for its purchase. As a consequence a tobacco crisis arose. It was not as bad as the crisis of 1991, but it was sufficiently serious. The tobacco crisis was a striking manifestation of what happened in the industry. People could not get along without tobacco. They would soldier on without sugar or potatoes, but they could not do without cigarettes.

The Politburo turned its attention to the explosive situation. We read a letter that had come to the government. People wrote, "I understand when there is no cooking oil, but when there is not smoking material. My husband is a miner and comes home tired and sends me out to get him cigarettes and they are nowhere to be found." Moscow was still somehow provided for, but on the periphery nothing was available to smoke. Cigarettes are a product to which a person becomes accustomed.

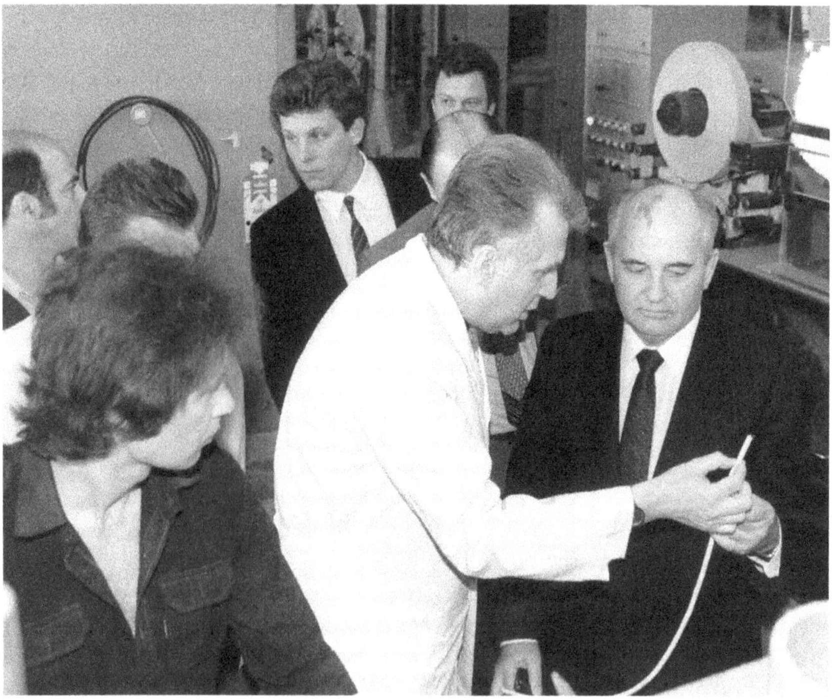

Figure 13.1 Leonid Sinel'nikov explains the technology of filter cigarette production at the Iava factory to Mikhail Gorbachev (1990). Reproduced with permission.

WITH PERESTROIKA, HOW DID THE SITUATION IN THE COUNTRY AFFECT THE TOBACCO INDUSTRY AND IAVA SPECIFICALLY?

The first years of perestroika primarily affected the political system, but this took place against the backdrop of a worsening economic situation in the country. We stopped buying new equipment. Over the course of seven or eight years we did not buy any new equipment. Purchases of tobacco were limited. The 1980s were characterized by a great strain on the work of industry in terms of raw materials and supplies. Little territory in the USSR was devoted to tobacco growth. Basically tobacco was purchased abroad in India, Greece, Turkey, and Bulgaria. In the 1980s the flow of tobacco from overseas declined sharply because of the deteriorating economic situation. It came to the issue of whether the industry could continue without tobacco, and at that point attention went towards the development of tobacco cultivation. A special decree came from the Central Committee and the Council of Ministers to address the problem, and they decided to boost the development of tobacco cultivation in Moldova and Kyrgyzstan. This question was given so much attention because the leadership was worried about a tobacco crisis. Attempts were made to develop local production of components that previously had been imported. For example, Armenia built a factory to produce acetate filters. It should be noted that the quality of the cigarettes during this period was in decline. The primary task was to assure quantity, and quality took a back seat. Different ideas were put forward such as doing a cigarette with a longer filter and thereby reducing the amount of tobacco needed.

During perestroika there was another very serious problem associated with reforming the political system. The Soviet Union had a directed economy. It was not built on a market but on an administrative mechanism upheld by party discipline. The measures which Gorbachev put forward for the reform of the political system dismantled the communist party involvement in the economy. Administrative methods for the economy ceased to exist, and they were not replaced with new mechanisms. In addition prices were still low. This did not promote development. Supply lines broke down. For instance, we stopped receiving *papirosy* paper. I called the supplier, but he said that he could not do anything because he was not getting any cellulose. The wood pulp product was not being supplied because logging had stopped, and so on. They proposed that we barter with cigarettes or use hard currency. We called the Chief Supply Department—Glavsnab—and notified them of the raw materials problem, and we got the response that no one could help us because there was no leverage to change the situation.

It can be said that from 1987 until the collapse of the USSR, industry was left to itself, and the situation was simply catastrophic. There were practically no resources in the country. We sat as if on a powder keg. There were constant threats to production. Iava was the main enterprise in the

Soviet Union for producing filtered cigarettes, and we produced about 25%. Without us, Moscow would have been without cigarettes. At that point, Mosagroprom was established in Moscow and Iurii Luzhkov (current mayor of Moscow) was named its head. He was the first deputy chairman of the Moscow Soviet and a very energetic person. I went to him with many issues. Luzhkov understood that it was impossible to stop the production at Iava and helped us sort out problems at the highest level. Iava did not stop production, though we always hung by a hair.

To revive the economy, Gorbachev set up cooperatives, issuing a special decree to establish them. The goal was to allow people to earn more and thereby lessen the discontent in the country. The following scheme was implemented, for example. There is a state-owned enterprise that produces a product. The company employs people who receive a salary. The director would make a decision to found a cooperative along with the employees. The first and second shifts were a state enterprise and at night these people worked as members of the cooperative, renting the enterprise and taking care of the raw material supply. They did the exact same production as the state enterprise, but received much higher pay for it. This corrupted people; they no longer wanted to work for the state enterprise. Then in around 1988–1989 the Law on State-Owned Enterprises was instituted. The goal was to democratize enterprise. It introduced election for company directors. No state organ could fire a director without the consent of the workers. The factories were still considered state property, but the state no longer managed them and the de facto master of the enterprise became the director. The director acted practically alone and no one had control over him. In such a situation, many directors abused their power, violated laws, and worked for their own benefit.

In 1990 there was a harsh tobacco crisis, a reflection of the crisis in the country as a whole. There was a currency crisis. Money lost its value and the ruble ceased to be a desirable currency. People and businesses began to barter, and one of the most attractive goods for barter was cigarettes. They became a type of currency and were used to pay for work and services. This sparked a run on cigarettes and an avalanche in demand. We tried to maintain production, but we could not meet demand. We worked at night; we lived at the factory. But everything we produced was instantly bought up. Then, ration tickets were issued for cigarettes, and set amounts given to both smokers and non-smokers. Everyone took the tickets with enthusiasm, even those people who had never smoked. In the provinces they began selling cigarettes individually and began to sell cut tobacco for self-rolled cigarettes. In Moscow, they swarmed kiosks. Every evening, I went home, turned on the television and listened to the news on the tobacco crisis. I was not able to sleep because I felt responsible.

In August of 1990, at the height of the crisis, Gorbachev was on vacation. I do not know who organized it, but smokers planned to march on Red Square and cut it off on the day that Gorbachev returned. They wanted to show their anger over the cigarette shortage. Sergei Stankevich, an important actor in the perestroika period and representative of the democratic wave, went there urgently. He was at that time the chairman of the Moscow Soviet and worked alongside Gavril Popov. He went to the march, negotiated with the demonstrators, and persuaded them to disperse—but only on one condition. They picked from their group delegates who would go with Stankevich to the Iava factory. They did not even warn me, the director of the factory, in advance. I was sitting in my office and the security guard came to me to say that Sergei Stankevich had arrived with some other people. I brought them into my office. At the time there were many rumors; people said that the factory was not working. Stankevich wanted to show that the factory was producing. We went into the shop—it was about 6:00 or 7:00 pm. People saw that all lines were working and saw the products going along the conveyor belt. Later, Stankevich demanded . . . trucks with cigarettes be sent where there were large groups of people perturbed by the shortages.

Interestingly, I read about this episode with the smokers' riots later in an article from the economist Shmelev. He wrote of how he attended a meeting with the recently-returned Gorbachev. They discussed further reforms and then Stankevich called Gorbachev. After speaking with him, Gorbachev returned to the meeting and said, "Comrades, here we are discussing how to reform the country, and Stankevich calls me to say that the smokers have closed down Red Square over the cigarette shortage." Gorbachev told Stankevich, "Look, you're the Moscow authority. You deal with it." I recall that Gavril Popov, then head of Moscow Soviet, held a meeting. He was a very good economist. Popov took a risk and established a commercial price on cigarettes. Kosmos had been sixty kopeck and now stood at three rubles. As soon as he did it, cigarettes appeared in the kiosks. The run began to cool. Popov was sent to court for this by the price committee—the torments of the Soviet system.

HOW DID THINGS CHANGE AFTER 1991?

In January of 1992, market prices were introduced. Manufacturers could set prices for themselves; it was a lifesaver. Everything was transformed in front of our eyes. Companies were prepared to supply materials at market prices. The supply chain reemerged. It was a massive change. I remember the first meeting where we discussed what prices to set. The price at the time was only about sixty kopecks a pack, and we set the price at three to four rubles per pack. We still did not know how the market would respond, our consumers, or what prices our competitors would set.

That was when the market began to include international companies. In the Soviet period, in 1990–1991, Philip Morris sent in cigarettes on credit for the sum of three to four billion dollars. At that point groups emerged that supplied imported cigarettes. The State Sports Committee—Goskomsport—and the Church had the right to import cigarettes duty free. A lot of money was made at that time! The state monopoly on foreign trade was abolished and every company could buy equipment, raw materials, and supplies directly from abroad. Hard currency could be received by converting rubles at the commercial banks. It was a real revolution and a revision of the very foundations of the economy. Of course, there were great difficulties such as the colossal inflation of 200% per year and the very high cost for currency. The biggest problem we had was to learn to work with a market where a great variety of international brands appeared, and we had to compete with them.

When market prices and mechanisms were introduced it was a shock. People were not ready for it emotionally, psychologically, nor materially. The next step was the privatization of industrial enterprises, because the state structures in the new environment were no longer leading industry. Privatization was led by Anatolii Chubais. Iava was transformed into OAO Iava-Tabak as a result of the privatization. In accordance with the law, 51% of shares were transferred to the workers and 49% to the state. We chose one of several different schemes for privatization. Of the 49% of government shares, 29% were set up for open voucher or cash auction, and 15% of the shares were reserved for the top bidder of the investment competition.

Why did we choose this scheme? In the Russian open market there appeared a large selection of international brands. There was huge diversity in the stores; I think even more than now. Now on the market there are only the brands that were able to stand up to competition; at the time, there was no such narrowing of selection, just a huge influx of products from different countries. Under these circumstances, we understood that we could not survive on our own. We needed to find an investor from among the international companies, and this would give us an opportunity to use their experience and technology, as well as investments necessary for the further development of production and the replacement of obsolete equipment.

At the time our factory equipment was very worn and outdated. Since there was no hard currency, we had not purchased new equipment since the late 1970s. We needed a complete reconstruction, but also we needed to relaunch our brand, because compared to the international brands, our products looked second-class. They were not able to withstand the competition. We were only able to compete in terms of price and that was not productive. Therefore we chose a variant where we needed to look for investors. The top bid was to receive 15% of our shares. It was a very difficult period for us. All of it was totally new, and we were negotiating with international companies.

Iava had a good reputation in the international tobacco community. It was the only former Soviet tobacco factory that had its own brand—"Iava." It was a brand widely known in Russia and since we had patented it, we were its owners. This was important in drawing interest from international companies. We had serious contacts with various companies, but primarily from Philip Morris because we had worked with them on the "Soiuz-Apollo" and Marlboro brands. We also had contacts with the Reynolds Company. As a result of all these negotiations, I decided, as the director, to work with British American Tobacco. In the first place, this company pursued a policy of active support for local brands in the different markets where they were involved. Other companies promoted their brands first. I met with the company president, Sir Patrick Sheehy, and he made a strong impression on me as a person. He was a very interesting and clever man, capable of showing great flexibility. Actually, I really liked that the leadership of British American Tobacco was made up of very intelligent people with broad horizons.

I must mention that British American Tobacco somewhat held back from entering the Russian market, which at that time was considered very promising. Philip Morris, Reynolds, and other companies were actively working in the market, but British American Tobacco had not yet entered the Russian market and the negotiations with Iava, if successful, would allow them to catch up quickly. Our main condition to British American Tobacco was that they develop the "Iava" brand. There was serious work to be done and the discussions lasted about two years. On our side, there was a very strong team of negotiators. The result was a developed business plan with British American Tobacco committed to investing seventy million dollars in the factory over the next two years. In 1994, the British American Tobacco business plan was deemed most successful and they won the bid. By that time the other shares had been auctioned off. In early November the first meeting of shareholders was held, and it approved the investment plan of British American Tobacco.

It was very important that the workers' collective supported us. We explained privatization to them, why it was needed, what were shares and vouchers, as well as detailing what advantages we would get out of an alliance with a major international company. I am proud to say that Iava's privatization was very fair. We apportioned 51% of the shares to the workers according to their earnings, which reflected the impact of the person on the collective as well as their length and quality of service. We followed our guidelines carefully. The leadership of Iava had no advantage, unlike what happened at other enterprises where the leadership seized major stakes. The factory workers were satisfied with the results of privatization and supported our decisions.

There were some difficulties. At that time there were many schemes for hostile takeovers by those with a great deal of capital. Iava would have been a great prize—the leader of the industry with its own brand name. There were attempts to seize management by a third party. During the voucher auction, 29% of shares had been sold. About 12%–15% of these shares were purchased by the American fund New Age. After the auction they came to me and offered to cooperate in buying back shares from the employees and managing the factory. I explained that we had negotiated with British American Tobacco because they would truly develop Iava and invest in it. New Age wanted control over the factory just to sell it. I said no. They then entered into a contract with the financial company Olma and started to buy shares from workers. Their agents went around the factory and gave the workers leaflets that said they could go to such and such address and sell. The shares were given as one ruble, but the leaflets promised 300 rubles per share. The situation was very grave. We managed to persuade British American Tobacco to invite the workers to sell their shares to them at 400 rubles not 300 rubles. There was no other choice. We talked with people and explained why it was necessary. British American Tobacco had to have assurance that they would get a return on their seventy-million-dollar investment in the factory. Workers who sold their shares received a big pay out. Many were able to improve their housing conditions. Some even bought a car. It was excellent compensation.

Every worker had to sell 100% of their shares before the shareholders meeting where they approved the British American Tobacco investment program. After that, those who wanted to buy them back could get back 50% at the same price. Many took advantage of that. Each decided for themselves whether to buy back shares or not. The scheme was well thought out and people understood and supported it. So when I think about privatization, I see that we did it honestly, openly, in the interests of the enterprise, and the collective. Our people kept their jobs, and by selling their shares, they earned good money. We attracted a company that transformed our manufacturing and has invested 120 million dollars in the enterprise up to now on reconstruction of the factory. "Iava" brand was retooled and a successful "Iava Gold" was launched. Now "Iava," and our whole family of brands, has a very good market share. If we look at all "Iava" cigarettes, it is the largest domestic brand family in the Russian tobacco market.

I am proud that our factory survived the most difficult times and never stopped production. Such enterprises can be counted on just your fingers. I am also proud that in those days when many companies did not pay their employees for months, we never held on to people's salaries for even one day.

NOTES

1. Gorchakova conducted a series of interviews with Leonid Sinel'nikov in Moscow in spring and summer of 2008. Sinel'nikov approved her transcription of the interviews, for the publication in translation of these interviews on August 12, 2008. Starks translated, condensed, and edited the interviews for this volume with considerable help and advice from Gorchakova.

14 Smokes for Big Brother

Bulgaria, the USSR, and the Politics of Tobacco in the Cold War

Mary Neuburger

In the summer of 1973, Dimitur Iadkov, the director of the Bulgarian state tobacco monopoly, Bulgartabak, visited the New York City headquarters of Philip Morris at the end of his tour of tobacco facilities in the American South. After the whirlwind of sites and smells of American tobacco, Iadkov had the pleasure of coffee, smokes, and a chat with Hugh Cullman, then CEO of Philip Morris. In Cullman's office Iadkov realized the real reason that the Bulgarian tobacco delegation had been wined and dined across the South:

> A few things were clarified in the office of Philip Morris during our last meeting in New York. . . . I looked at the map behind the president's desk and BULGARTABAK was written across it from East Germany, over the Czechs, to the huge area of the USSR all the way to Vladivostok. . . . I told him I felt like I was in the Pentagon and he said—"You are not mistaken, Mr. Iadkov, that this is the 'pentagon' of Philip Morris. We look at the world this way." The president stood and pointed at the map. "You see the spheres of interest. Look here is BAT's [British American Tobacco] market, here is Reynolds [RJ Reynolds], this is Reemtsma [a German firm]. And these are the markets of Philip Morris. I would say that we are almost everywhere with the exception of this huge territory that is held by Bulgartabak. I have to admit, Mr Yadkov that I really envy you. I always dream of those markets. I say this with sincere envy, because for our company the market rules.[1]

In the course of his American tour, Iadkov had been exposed to a great deal, from new tobacco harvesting and processing technologies, to ways of business and the capitalist notion of markets. All of this would have a profound influence on the future of Bulgarian tobacco. At the same time, Iadkov began to fully appreciate the benefits of the Bulgarian position within Comecon and the fact that its "captive" market had propelled it to a place of prestige in the jet-setting, international circles of global tobacco. The jewel in the crown of the Comecon market for cigarettes, of course, was the Soviet Union.

By 1972, the USSR imported more cigarettes than any other country and also produced more than anyone in the world, yet they still could by no means fulfill the demands of their immense and increasingly-smoking population. Bulgaria, by contrast, was the biggest *exporter* of cigarettes in the world (and in some years second only to the United States) from 1966–1988.[2] Bulgaria fulfilled the demands of its own increasingly heavily smoking population in these years, and managed to export roughly 80% of overall production. About 90% of exported cigarettes went to their closest trading partner and political ally, the Soviet Union, a fact that did not go unnoticed in the capitalist world. As reported in the international journal *Tobacco*, "Bulgarian cigarettes have accounted for most of the growth in Russian cigarette consumption in the last twenty years."[3]

The map of global tobacco interests followed the contours of the Cold War. As Iadkov, Bulgartabak's most successful director points out in his voluminous memoirs published in 2003, "Tobacco and politics were always connected."[4] In the Bulgarian case, both the protection of the Iron Curtain and its later perforations put Bulgaria in the position of global leader in cigarette exports. The Sino-Soviet split of 1960 cut off the USSR from its other major outside supplier and opened the door for Bulgaria to become the primary cigarette producer of the Eastern Bloc. Détente gave Bulgarian tobacco access to technology, resources, and business models to expand its reach outside the Bloc while maintaining its position within. Soviet demand, in fact, necessitated the Bulgarian adoption of Western technologies to fill ever growing yearly quotas. In turn contacts with the West brought about changes in smoking preferences within the Bloc, a development with far-reaching consequences for the shape and future of the tobacco industry. Only with the fall of Communism did these consequences become clear, and the intimate love triangle of Bulgarian, Soviet, and American tobacco collapse onto the "dust heap" of history.

TOBACCO LOYALTIES

As World War II came to a close, Bulgarian tobacco interests were in serious need of reordering. After all, during the war 80% of Bulgarian tobacco had gone to her closest ally, Nazi Germany.[5] Not only were German soldiers stationed in Bulgaria and the nearby Balkan provinces provisioned with Bulgarian cigarettes, but the bulk of Bulgarian raw tobacco and cigarette shipments went to the Third Reich, other Axis states, and the quisling governments of "New Europe." With the occupation of the Soviet Army, Bulgaria's newly-established Communist-dominated regime, the Fatherland Front, changed sides in the war to the Allied side, and abruptly redirected shipments of tobacco. Not only were the occupying Soviet soldiers provisioned with cigarettes, but also massive shipments of raw tobacco and cigarettes were redirected to Moscow. The new Russian partner filled an immediate void left by the collapsing German state. In early 1945, the USSR bought 24,000 tons of tobacco that would have otherwise languished in Bulgarian warehouses in the midst of political and administrative chaos. Apparently, however, a good deal of tobacco that went in the northeasterly direction, some of which was never paid for or collected on, was perhaps considered part of the Soviet "war restitution," looting of German and other Axis properties across Eastern Europe. At the same time, the Fatherland Front began the mass confiscation of tobacco and tobacco properties that they defined as "Fascist" manifestations of "illegal profits made from war speculation."[6] As the government tobacco monopoly began to gradually form, foreign tobacco interests were meagerly "compensated" and local tobacconists were put on trial as "Fascists." Only tobacco growers and workers were embraced, wooed, and rewarded as "heroes" in the struggle against fascism and as the imagined core of working-class struggle from the interwar years. As Iadkov, ever the convinced communist, later reported, finally "people became masters of one of our greatest riches"—tobacco.[7]

But the Iron Curtain lowered slowly, and in the meantime American tobacco interests penetrated Europe. Cheap—and high-nicotine—American cigarettes flooded the European market as never before and many of these made their way into aid packages to Bulgaria and elsewhere in the Bloc.[8] Bulgarian tobacco began to quickly regroup and, in addition to making an export deal with the Soviet Union in 1948 for 80,000 tons, some 15,000 tons were sold to France and other West European states.[9] Although many factories had been initially closed for "streamlining and improving the system," by 1948 the Bulgarian tobacco monopoly (later named Bulgartabak) had its first national conference. Among other things a new system of "stimulus" for growers was put in place that promised a certain number of rations for every *dekar* (about one-quarter acre) planted—74 kg of flour, 20 kg fodder, 1 kg soap, 1 liter of olio, 2 meters cloth, 1 pair of shoes, etc.[10]

But while the tobacco industry was just beginning to recover from massive "re-organization," tobacco trade dealings were implicated in Bloc politics and communist political consolidation. In the purge trails that swept Eastern Europe, trade policy became a central issue as it seemed to point to Western orientation and hence "espionage." In Bulgaria, Traicho Kostov, former President of the Economic-Financial Committee of the Council of Ministers, took center stage in the December 1949 show trials. Along with treason, Titoism, Trotskyism, and Anglo-American espionage, he was accused of committing acts aimed at the "disorganization of the national economy" and the supply system of the country. Trade relations, in fact, were central to his "Anti-Soviet" activities, which included attempts to sell tobacco to France and withhold information on tobacco prices from the Soviet Union.[11] Although not among the primary list of "traitors," Angel Timov the head of the Buglarian tobacco monopoly served as a "witness" to the trade-related crimes of his peers and finally fell victim of the purge trials. Imprisoned in 1949, after his release and rehabilitation in 1956, he became director of Bulgartabak once again.[12] Undoubtedly, the making of a Communist and Soviet-loyal tobacco industry was costly, and the change of personnel and the loss of trade with the West threw the industry into disorder.

After Timov's rehabilitation in 1956 Bulgartabak began to recover and it took off with a significant increase in demand particularly after the 1960 Sino-Soviet split resulted in increased Soviet demand. Timov streamlined Bulgartabak by merging production and trade departments; increasingly exports became the focus of Bulgartabak activities. As Iadkov reports, people began to recognize that "tobacco was the gold of Bulgaria."[13] Not only was the Bulgarian Communist Party increasingly aware of the potential of tobacco and cigarette exports but also Bulgaria's export numbers grew at an enviously fast rate, while world tobacco watched. As reported by the American Tobacco Institute's *Tobacco News* in 1960, "Bulgaria replaced mainland China as Russia's chief source of tobacco and cigarettes."[14] According to Iadkov, exports of tobacco and cigarettes from Bulgaria to the Soviet Union increased from 700 tons in 1955 to 5,000 tons in 1960.[15] Philip Morris, like other Western tobacco companies, was keenly aware of the huge and exponentially growing market behind the Iron Curtain, particularly in the Soviet Union, which was listed in a 1953 report as a "closed but potential market."[16] Postwar recovery and a number of other economic and social developments—including the return of soldiers who were provisioned and began smoking at the front—built smoking societies on both sides of the Cold War. As a 1954 article in *The New Yorker* noted, for the first time there were ashtrays placed around the table at the UN Security Council in "recognition that the common man's right to a good cigarette transcends ideological difference."[17] In the 1950s this seeming "convergence" in tobacco appetites was not accompanied by agreement over tobacco types or aesthetics. Such differences, solidified by the ideological divide, became apparent only once fissures in the Iron Curtain emerged and widened in the post-Stalinist period.

TOBACCO TASTES

By the 1960s explosive growth in tobacco production and export in Bulgaria was driven by the rising Soviet, as well as Bulgarian and Bloc, demand for cigarettes. Ever-rising expectations of production in Bulgaria's annual and Five-Year plans inspired Bulgartabak directors to seek out any means to fulfill and over-fulfill quotas. The Bulgarian tobacco industry charted tobacco production, and especially the ever-growing manufacture of cigarettes, with pride as a clear marker of "socialist achievement."[18] As Comecon began to demand that Bulgaria specialize in cigarette production for the Bloc, cigarettes became what Iadkov called the "locomotive of the Bulgarian economy."[19] The leafy yellow plant literally came to be widely called "Bulgarian gold," as it essentially became the currency with which

Bulgaria obtained machinery and other means of industrialization from within and (increasingly) outside the Bloc. The slow opening of the Iron Curtain to trade with the West in the 1960s offered new possibilities for Bulgartabak to exploit the experience and technologies of the West, while holding on to its coveted Soviet market.

For Western companies, the pursuit of the Soviet market began in earnest under the Lyndon B. Johnson Administration, which pursued trade relations with the Eastern Bloc as a way of ameliorating—or perhaps fighting—the Cold War. In 1964 Justus Heymans, representative of Philip Morris International, went on a fact-finding mission to Moscow. Although they allowed a tour of the Dukat cigarette factory, which Heymans deemed "not up to date," the Soviets gave the American the cold shoulder in the Soviet capital. This is not altogether surprising considering that along with cigarette samples and the Philip Morris annual report, Heymans brought a particularly unwelcome message. "American blend" cigarettes, he claimed, were increasingly in demand across the globe and the wave of the future. For their part the Soviets dismissed what the Bulgarians later referred to as "trade tricks of the capitalists."[20] The Soviets responded "that their taste was mainly Oriental."[21] In 1964 it became clear to Heymans that in terms of cigarette aesthetics there was an Iron Curtain of taste that divided East from West.

By this time the "American blend," composed primarily of Virginia and Burley broad-leaf tobaccos with a smaller amount of the narrow-leafed Oriental type, dominated Western cigarette production. Introduced in 1913 with the famous "Coming of the Camel" campaign, this type of blend had a predominance of broad-leaf type tobaccos, grown in America and around the world, which had come to dominate the market by the postwar period.[22]American-blend cigarettes required a small percentage—usually 10%–15%—of Oriental type tobaccos grown in more selective, often mountainous, regions of the globe including Bulgaria, Yugoslavia, Greece, Turkey, Italy, and parts of the Soviet Union. Oriental tobaccos had a much stronger natural flavor than broad-leafed tobaccos and contained less nicotine. The broad-leafed varieties had a lighter *flavor* and desirable burning properties, and they were also easier to "aromatize" and "saucify"—to infuse with aroma and flavor. Although limited Virginia tobacco had been grown in Bulgaria since 1927 and Burley would be introduced in 1967, high-quality Oriental tobaccos dominated, and in the 1960s Oriental cigarettes were the most widely available to smokers in Bulgaria, the USSR, and elsewhere in the Bloc. Although this type of tobacco was in no way inferior to "Western" tobacco types—in fact, it was historically deemed superior and was still highly coveted by the West to use in its famous blends—its packaging gave the impression of inferiority. Cigarette papers, packaging, and wrappers were of lower quality and filters were of a lower quality material and scarcely available. In spite of such deficiencies, Oriental cigarettes still reigned in the East by the 1960s. Whether this was a result of "taste" or simply availability is unknown. But change was in the air.

By the mid-1960s in spite of right-wing opposition, the Johnson administration actively encouraged American firms to establish trade with the Eastern Bloc.[23] The tobacco industry immediately began stepping up its efforts to penetrate Bloc markets in whatever way possible. Although direct and mass penetration with American cigarettes was not achieved, aesthetic penetration of American blends, filters, and styles of packing proceeded apace in the 1960s and especially the 1970s. After receiving the cold shoulder in Moscow in 1964, Philip Morris began to pursue market penetration at the source of the Oriental tobaccos that the Soviets claimed to prefer. Beginning in 1964, Philip Morris began to canvass various officials in Bulgaria with "samples" of cigarettes, including the American ambassador and embassy staff in Sofia, directors and vice-directors of Bulgartabak and Korekom (the institution in charge of hard currency stores), and other export officials.[24] As trade contacts slowly began to develop, "scientific" and technological exchanges began to occur in the tobacco world.

In September of 1956 Bulgaria hosted its first ever "Tobacco Symposium" in Plovdiv, one of the primary sites of cigarette production in Bulgaria. Representatives from across the Bloc attended, including the Soviet Union, along with representatives from the United Sates, a number of Western European countries, Turkey, Greece, Yugoslavia, Egypt, and Israel among others.[25] In the same year Bulgaria joined the international tobacco organization Koresta and by the 1970s would play a leading role, even hosting the first-ever Coresta conference behind the Iron Curtain in Varna in 1978.[26] As Iadkov later reported, among tobacconists there was a certain camaraderie of the traditional "guild type," though certainly Cold War ties and tensions still seethed under the surface of their relationships. Conceived of as "scientific" exchange, these meetings served as sites for technology transfer, trade relations, and aesthetic influence. For American tobacco, their distinct type of cigarettes—filtered blends—which they could present as "Western" and modern were their primary selling point to an already saturated Eastern Bloc market. But their technology and the promise of dramatic mechanization of the tobacco industry was their greatest weapon in pursuing Eastern Bloc partners.

According to internal reports, Philip Morris monitored changes in production and consumption behind the Iron Curtain and in the mid-1960s keenly felt the need to expand their markets east. The famous American study released in 1964 that definitively linked smoking to cancer had not yet had a serious effect on the still-growing rates of smoking worldwide. But as Philip Morris figures for 1965 reveal, rates of growth in the United States had already slowed to 5.6%, while in the Eastern Bloc smoking was up 7.5%.[27] In the meantime Eastern Bloc countries had begun to import American (and also German) cigarettes in limited quantities, primarily for sale in major hotels and hard-currency stores. Still a certain segment of the local population sought out the rare and desirable "forbidden fruit" of Western cigarettes. The efforts to spread American taste had begun, and this assault would go beyond limited marketing and distribution. At the Plovdiv symposium of 1965, for example, virtually all of the papers presented were on boring technical subjects, such as Dr. Ternovsky of the USSR's paper on "Resistance of Tobacco to Thrips."[28] The sole American presenter, Fred Triest, whom one would expect to share some type of advances in tobacco growing or processing, instead gave a paper entitled the "Function of Tobacco Flavor." His paper gave a detailed description of the complex chemical process of creating a consistent and pleasingly flavorful cigarette using a blend of tobaccos and aromatic additives—everything from vanilla, licorice, and cocoa, to rose, jasmine, and wood resins. In positively seductive terms, Triest described how the "taste and aroma of tobacco" is heightened also by synthetic mixtures that can achieve "honey and fruit notes," "Jasmine top notes," "spicy effects," and "flowery sweetness."[29] The Bloc tobacconists could not help but be tantalized by the aesthetic possibilities of American "blend" technologies, which along with filter technologies, began to slowly penetrate local tobacco production practices. After a trip to Bulgaria in 1967, the Philip Morris director of research and development, Helmut Wakeham, reported to headquarters that Marlboro and now its competition Kent (a product of BAT) were available in all major hotels for hard currency and even some for local currency. There seemed to be a market, he reported, "among the better classes everywhere" for American type cigarettes.[30]

Indeed, by 1965 Bulgartabak documents reveal that their trading partners from across the Bloc, including the all important Soviet Union, demanded filters, American-type "king size" (85 mm), and American-blend cigarettes.[31] The need to meet such demands was coupled by the Bulgarian state's dire need for hard currency. Ever-rising cigarette production and export quotas aimed to meet such needs. While the Soviets increasingly gave the Bulgarians a green light for industry development and "cigarette specialization" within Comecon, Bulgartabak also looked west for technology and markets. Western technology became increasingly critical to mechanized, modern, tobacco processing and cigarette production, and capitalist markets were needed to accumulate more hard currency to purchase such technology and other needed goods. Also, Bulgartabak explicitly began to recognize that the know-how to make "American blend" was needed both for increasing internal demand and "so we can enter THEIR [Western] markets with the appropriate cigarettes."[32]

Negotiations between Bulgaria and Philip Morris begin as early as 1966, but would last for almost a decade. In spite of Bulgarian needs for American technology, suspicions abounded. Early on, Philip Morris proposed to move ahead with a full-blown joint-venture based in Bulgaria, with Philip Morris owning a 51% controlling share. Bulgartabak managers deemed this proposal "unacceptable," rightly fearful that "this is their effort to control the socialist market."[33] In a meeting of Bulgartabak to discuss these negotiations, higher-ups expressed well-grounded fears that

American-blend cigarettes would supplant Oriental cigarettes in the socialist market.[34] Some questioned the notion that Bulgaria should start production of American-style cigarettes at all, which would ultimately be harmful to the market for Oriental cigarettes in the Bloc and even perhaps beyond. And while one tobacco official claimed that in Bulgaria the market for American-type cigarettes was "limited to only Sofia youth," there was a wider recognition of "the luxury and fashionable nature of American cigarettes" in a global context, including inside the Bloc.[35] In spite of fears about American intentions, the Bulgarian need for knowledge about "fashionable" American blends, and especially technology and hard currency, was clear. As one Bulgartabak official noted with obvious pragmatism, "If we become partners with the devil. So be it. The form is not important, but the outcome." With this in mind, Bulgartabak began a relationship with Philip Morris that started with "technical help and the exchange of specialists" and culminated in an eventual licensing agreement signed in 1975.[36]

In the intervening decade, Bulgaria moved forward with the transfer of Western technologies to the tobacco industry and an attendant revolution in cigarette aesthetics. In 1966 they signed a licensing agreement with Eastman Kodak for filters and the machinery to produce and attach them to cigarettes.[37] The production of filters was on the rise as was the use of blends, soft-cover hard packs, and outer cellophane wrappers. Some cigarette technology was procured within the Bloc. For example Skoda (the Czech company) provided cigarette machines to Bulgaria in 1968 in exchange for cigarettes.[38] But in order to obtain the other needed state-of-the-art technologies, Bulgaria increased exports of raw tobacco to Western markets—particularly West Germany, France, and Japan. The USSR, however, was still getting 75% of all Bulgarian tobacco export and 90% of cigarette exports (the other 10% stayed within the Bloc). But the nature of these Bloc cigarette exports was changing. By 1975, 82% of Bulgarian cigarettes had filters (as opposed to 20% in 1967), 62% were king size (only 11% in 1967), and 30% were "American blend" types (a mere 8% in 1967) but mostly with Bulgarian names, packing, and materials. A small percentage of these were beginning to be actual Western-licensed brands.

Contemporary Bulgarian studies, conducted primarily at the Tobacco Institute in Plovdiv, concluded that even Bulgarian smokers seemed to prefer the flavor and mildness of blends, and so considerable resources were put into attempts to re-orient the industry towards "modern aesthetics."[39] The institute expended great effort in conducting taste tests, experimenting with blends, aromatization, and sauces to copy American blends, and also to create "Bulgarian compositions"—hybridized blends with higher content of Oriental tobacco.[40] The 1975 licensing agreements with Philip Morris and RJ Reynolds meant that Bulgarian factories produced actual Marlboro and Winston with machines imported from the two companies. Philip Morris concluded licensing agreements with Poland in 1973 and the USSR directly in the same year. Western technicians trained Bulgarian specialists to use and maintain the machines while in exchange Bulgarian producers paid a royalty—per piece—and provided shipments of un-processed Bulgarian Oriental tobacco. While neither of the companies would export directly large amounts of cigarettes to the Bloc they did mange to penetrate the Iron Curtain with their branding, and their aesthetics in this period—Marlboro, Winston, and also Kent (BAT) became desirable status symbols even though most were produced in the region, unbeknownst to their buyers.

The irony of this "aesthetic" turn is that the newly produced American blends were by nature higher in nicotine and tar. To be fair, the increased use of filters had some ameliorative effect, but regardless the switch to American blends meant a switch to a more addictive and carcinogen-laden cigarette. At a time when a revolution in production in the United States had brought about a rapid turn to "lights" and other lower-tar and -nicotine varieties, Americans were exporting—or as some would accuse "dumping"—higher tar cigarettes on world markets. In the Eastern Bloc such "dumping" was severely limited, but technology transfer favored "recipes" that were of the American "classic" high-tar and nicotine varieties. There is no way that Bulgartabak was unaware of the implications of this change. They had been studying nicotine content and tar in tobaccos themselves in this period and produced numerous, widely read (in the West as well) studies on the low-nicotine properties of Oriental tobaccos. In fact, they claimed that whereas "western tobaccos" were highly carcinogen-laden, Bulgarian tobacco actually contained anti-carcinogens that countered the carcinogens in tobacco as well as those present in air-pollution.[41]

Such claims remained in the Bulgarian tobacco industry literature until about the mid-1970s and then fell mysteriously silent. At that point Bulgarian officials launched increasingly vociferous anti-smoking campaigns in conformity with campaigns in the Soviet Union and throughout the Bloc. Bulgartabak not only played no role in such campaigns but even continued to increase production and "quality" in line with state production plans. Significantly, some anti-tobacco sources even directly implicated "trade interests," which encouraged the "production and sale of tobacco" in the failure of their efforts.[42] The contradiction inherent within Communist interests and practices on the tobacco question became clear. Now, amidst increasingly pro-active anti-smoking campaigns in Bulgaria and the Eastern Bloc, the industry quietly continued to produce and "improve" at its breakneck pace while various health officials and politicians make at least some attempts to squelch the smoking habit—which had by then reached "epidemic" proportions.[43] Indeed, in the same year that Marlboro and Winston were released on the local market, the State Council of Bulgaria issued its anti-smoking decree with the aim of "curbing and gradually doing away with this western Imperialist evil."[44] Not surprisingly, health issues were central to the growing anti-smoking literature, but behavioral and moral questions were equally fundamental. While smokers as a whole were censured, those who smoked luxurious, newly "imported cigarettes"—most likely Marlboro and Winstons produced (mostly) in local factories—were particularly disparaged for their decadence and "thingomania."[45]

Licensing was extremely profitable for Bulgartabak and the state; they charged almost twice as much for these cigarettes, which they sold at home and throughout the Bloc. At the same time, the population's desire and consumption of Bulgarian-produced American brands was held against them and deemed a sign of "irrational consumption" that did not bode well for the advancement of socialist society. But the anti-smoking literature and substance of the campaigns, which continued throughout the Communist period, contradicted the claims and goals of the tobacco industry itself. Much like in the American context, a clear fissure existed between officials and advocacy groups with concerns about public health and individuals and organizations with economic interests (or stakes). In the Bulgarian case, though, unlike the American one, without real confrontation the consumption of tobacco rose unabated.

TOBACCO MARKETS

In spite of the anti-tobacco directives within Bulgaria and the Bloc, production and exports continued their meteoric rise up until 1988. From 1972 to 1991, Dimitur Iadkov served as the enterprising and dynamic director of Bulgartabak; he became world renowned for his business prowess. In his 400-plus-page memoir published in 2003, *Bulgartabak: Memories,* he relates in colorful details the story of his "tobacco years" and the "Bulgarian phenomenon in the tobacco world." He talks of "our heady rise" in a period when he had "free reign in accessing the experience, technology, and technical know-how of the American tobacco companies."[46] In these colorful and enlightening pages, Iadkov describes his travels around the world searching for technology and developing trade relations, collecting his various awards, and becoming the toast and envy of tobacco barons around the globe. Eventually he witnessed the fall of Communism—a system he once believed in—and the tragic (to him) dismantling of the Bulgartabak that he had built into an empire.

When Iadkov at age forty-two was promoted from his position as head of regional tobacco production in Blagoevgrad to the head of Bulgartabak in mid-1972, the industry was in a moment of temporary crisis. Behind on shipments to the USSR, it seemed likely that Bulgartabak would not fulfill the plan for that year. In spite of technological improvements, the ever-increasing demands of "the plan" remained beyond the resources of Bulgartabak in 1972. Iadkov was ordered by his superiors to "fulfill the plan at any cost . . . especially shipments to the USSR."[47] In his second week at the job, he got a call from the Soviet embassy inviting him to a meeting with the Soviet trade representative, Grichin, his first audience with a foreign representative. Grichin, as Iadkov describes him, was a "military" type who "put forward his questions somehow as ultimatums." Grichin's primary "ultimatum" in 1972 concerned the delivery of 1000 tons of cigarettes. Iadkov, aware of the importance of the Bulgaro-Soviet political relationship, promised that the delivery would be Bulgartabak's "highest priority."[48] With a flurry of meetings, pep-talks across the country and added incentives for production, Iadkov somehow managed to "over-fulfill the plan" for 1972 and make all needed deliveries for that year, a feat that he received an award for in Moscow later in 1973; it would be his first of many. Although the impetus for this was local, Iadkov soon turned to other means to fulfill the ever-expanding expectations laid out by Bulgaria's central planning commission.

In fact, he soon realized that—ironically—the only way to fulfill the unrealistic production plans expected of "socialist achievement" and the growing demand of their Soviet Big Brother was massive cooperation and technology transfer from the West. But unlike many of his predecessors, Iadkov seemed to have few if any reservations about cooperation with the West. Fortuitously, President Nixon initiated an ever more aggressive policy of trade and contact with the Eastern Bloc beginning in 1972. In fact, before Iadkov had time to initiate expansion of trade with the West, the West came knocking. In October of 1973, Bulgartabak got a call from the Yugoslav-Macedonian tobacco monopoly to the west. Apparently representatives from RJ Reynolds and their close American partner Sokotab (specializing in purchasing raw Oriental tobaccos for American firms) requested a trip to Bulgaria to establish trade relations while in Skopje. For their part, the Bulgarians were quite excited by the prospect and as one official joked, "If Mohammed can't come to the mountain, the mountain will have to come to Mohammed." The next day Bulgartabak representatives met the Macedonians and their American guests at the Bulgaro-Macedonian border where Jack Wonder, the representative of RJ Reynolds and five others were ushered across in two "luxury cars." Escorted to Dupnitsa, they visited a tobacco field and factory and then engaged in what Iadkov explains as the "special ritual of bringing out the tobacco." As Iadkov later remarked, "No other commodity has such a specific and emotional ritual for sales."[49] Over coffee they looked at samples and, as Iadkov proudly describes, Wonder "got tears in his eyes" when he put his nose in a ball of Dzhebel Basma (a local Oriental variety). "Stroking the leaf with his hand he [Wonder] said, 'Oh, my old friend, after thirty years apart we have lived to see each other again.'" As it turns out, Wonder had been a pre–World War II representative of RJ Reynolds in Kavala (then part of Greek Macedonia) and had been a buyer of Bulgarian tobaccos for the company's blends.[50] With the arrival of Wonder and his delegation, the Iron Curtain had been opened, never to be sealed again.

Soon enough, Iadkov himself would "go to Mohammed." His first brush with "Western" technology was not in the United States, however, but in Japan on an eye-opening trip in early 1973. Iadkov saw for himself that in spite of official Bulgartabak pronouncements, Bulgarian industry lagged significantly "behind" the West in terms of processing and cigarette production technologies. With this in mind, Iadkov was shocked by the reactions of a Soviet delegation from Glavtabak to Bulgaria in February of 1973, which marveled that Bulgaria had "moved significantly further ahead in industrial processing, in science and especially in cigarette production." Iadkov assumed this was just insincere flattery, until he visited the Dukat and Iava factories in Moscow that June. Shocked by the low level of Soviet technology, the fact that much work was still done by hand, and the lack of cleanliness and order, he claimed he gave director of Glavtabak, Kholostov, his honest assessment of the Soviet situation. He said Kholostov glumly agreed, lamenting the fact that upgrades were not expected any time soon. This, Kholostov explained, was because Soviet priorities were strategic and that "it is accepted that Bulgaria specializes within Comecon in this direction."[51] For Iadkov such Soviet pronouncements were nothing short of a green light to move ahead.

With Jack Wonder and RJ Reynolds' invitation, Iadkov and his Bulgarian tobacco colleagues did a grand tour of American tobacco interests later that year. Starting with the obligatory meeting with political figures in Washington, DC, Iadkov then flew on an RJ Reynolds jet to Winston-Salem, where he met the company president William Hobbs and was hugely impressed by the RJ Reynolds operation. This was by far, he wistfully recounted, the most mechanized and modern institution he had ever visited. Towards the end of his trip he met with Hugh Cullman of Philip Morris in New York. As recounted above, Cullmann enlightened him regarding issues of the market and American interest in Bulgartabak and the Soviet market.[52] Energized by their experience in the United States, Iadkov and his people reported back to the authorities at home that "the study and introduction of American experience into all the stages of our tobacco production will allow us to move ahead, to build a modern, productive, and competitive tobacco economy."[53] This visit laid the groundwork for the licensing agreement signed with RJ Reynolds in 1973 and the release in early 1974 of Bulgarian-produced Winstons in the Bloc market. By August of 1975, an agreement was finally made with Philip Morris, and Marlboros were rolling off production lines, and numerous joint brands were also developed. In exchange for Bulgarians tobaccos and licensing royalties the American companies provided machines and training for the increased cultivation of Burley and Virginia tobaccos; the sorting, curing, and fermenting of tobacco; and the production and packaging of cigarettes.[54] Not only did Bulgaria obtain machines but also they purchased the "license" and training to build machines themselves for export within the Bloc and elsewhere in the "developing world."[55] In spite of the very real and perhaps well-founded suspicions about "foreign experience and especially capitalism" among many Communist functionaries, Iadkov moved forward with his agenda of rapid technology transfer and modernization.[56] Iadkov, of course, remained in close contact with the Soviets on these matters and on his next visit to Moscow in 1974 they gave him another "green light" for working with the Americans as long as the Bulgarians stayed within the parameters of Comecon and, above all, met their obligations for deliveries to the Soviet Union.[57]

By 1976 Iadkov presided over Bulgartabak's increase in hard-currency profits of 158%, from 252 million to 400 million dollars.[58] With these achievements under his belt, Iadkov began to re-orient the work of Bulgartabak away from simply fulfilling the plan, which was not a problem anymore with the new technologies in place. Now the focus was above all on "quality," which in this period meant the explicit emulation of the American-blend model of cigarettes. Philip Morris, in fact, liked to call itself the "ambassador of quality" during this period. But increasingly, this quest for quality was part of Iadkov's larger vision of Bulgarian exports outside the Bloc. In the late 1970s the exports of Bulgarian raw tobacco to the West grew exponentially while Bulgarian cigarettes remained within Bloc parameters, but it became increasingly clear to Iadkov and others in Bulgartabak that exporting *cigarettes*, not tobacco, could make much larger profits. In the course of the 1970s, Bulgaria continued its meteoric rise to fame within the global tobacco industry. Anti-smoking campaigns in the West—or the "constantly strengthening propaganda against smoking"—were certainly a concern in Bulgartabak administrative circles, but Bloc campaigns seemed to have little effect on cigarette consumption.[59] Bulgaria was on the cover of *Tobacco International* in 1977 and Iadkov was awarded a trophy for industry achievement in the Koresta meeting in Rio de Janeiro, Brazil, in the same year. In the years to come, Iadkov proved himself to be a master of maneuvering within the tobacco world. Under his leadership Bulgaria began a whole new phase of export and production practices that reached to the far ends of the globe.

Iadkov was briefly promoted to higher echelons of government in 1977–1978 but then retuned to his former post amidst another small crisis. Though Bulgaria had the technology in place to produce enough cigarettes to fulfill her plan for 1978, the tobacco harvest had been bad and deliveries to the Soviet Union were already late. Out of desperation Iadkov did some quick dealing on the regional market and purchased enough Turkish and Macedonian tobacco to fill the orders for that year.[60] Although many in Bulgartabak and the ministries higher up were skeptical about this approach, in the decades that followed, Bulgaria would become a major *importer* of tobacco (in particular broad-leafed tobacco, but also occasionally Oriental varieties) for processing in their cigarette factories. In general, raw Oriental tobacco would still be exported, but with the new focus on blends, the tobacco deficit was mainly in broad-leafed tobaccos. At the same time, for the first time, Bulgaria became an exporter of cigarettes to the capitalist world. These two trends took off with explosive power in the course of the 1980s. But Bulgaria's export wings were first spread beyond the Bloc following the Iranian Revolution of 1979. In that year, under Ayatollah

Khomeini, Iran broke off relations with the United States, which had been their major supplier of cigarettes (namely RJ Reynolds–Winston) up to that time. Iran, in fact, was the largest importer of cigarettes in the "capitalist world," and was now somewhat in between worlds; Bulgaria was an ideal trading partner.[61] During trade negotiations, Bulgarians were informed that the Iranians were used to American-type blends like Winston. For Bulgaria, this was by then an easy recipe to follow and before long they produced cigarettes closely akin to Winston but in elegant red packing with "Islamic symbols" on it, named "Azadi"—the Persian word for "freedom." Later the packs were re-designed in the requested, "more appropriate" green, but as Iadkov brags, the Iranians "grabbed our cigarettes like warm bread."[62] Flexible to such demands, the Bulgarians became the biggest supplier of cigarettes to Iran for the next decade and the hard-currency profits were astronomical.

This was apparently, somehow, not foreseen by Bulgarian central planners, who in their 1981–1985 Five-Year plan projected no growth—for the first time—in tobacco production and exports. With a view to "developing other industries," like chemicals and machine making, Bulgartabak was allowed no resources for further investment and development. The move was also justified in light of anti-smoking campaigns in Bulgaria and elsewhere; Iadkov was stunned by their pessimism and assertion that "tobacco had no future." Iadkov, however, enterprising as he was, decided to ignore the plan and move forward in the most aggressive marketing and development plan that Bulgartabak had pursued to date. Because of Bulgaria's so-called "New Economic Mechanism" inaugurated in 1979, enterprises were allowed a certain amount of initiative in planning and production—as long as quotas were met. Iadkov took this and ran with it, all around the world. Like American corporations in this period, Bulgartabak begin to look to the developing world for markets. After conducting a prognosis on the growth of smoking rates from 1980–1981, they concluded that in the West smoking was up only 1.3%, in the Bloc, 2.3%–2.5%, but in the Near East and Africa it was up 3.5%–4.8%! As Iadkov put it, with these numbers in mind there is "no reason for pessimism" as long as new markets could be found.[63]

Iadkov began to travel the world with his delegations, seeking new contacts and customers in the Near East and developing world. Political instability and de-colonization, which battered Western economic interests in Africa, Southeast Asia, the Middle East, and Latin America was a boon for Bulgartabak. The Iranian contract alone warranted a new factory in Blagoevgrad, the administrative center of the tobacco-rich region of Bulgarian (Pirin) Macedonia. Iadkov, actually met with the Bulgarian leader, Todor Zhivkov, personally to ask for permission to build the factory. And although Zhivkov readily agreed, he rather sarcastically retorted, "But won't they say we are supporting smoking?"[64] With ever more new technology pouring in, Iadkov began to travel the world *exporting* cigarettes and tobacco technologies—under license by Bulgaria—in exchange for the needed raw tobacco to meet their huge and growing demand. Among other places, Iraq, Tunisia, Morocco, Afghanistan, Vietnam, Cambodia, Zimbabwe, Somalia, the Philippines, Nicaragua, and Cuba became involved in trade with Bulgaria, many of them as suppliers of raw tobacco to Bulgaria in exchange for technology, training, or cigarettes.[65] Iadkov, who continued his contacts in the West, now was wined and dined in the "developing world." In Nicaragua, for example, Iadkov was shown around the tobacco estate of the former dictator Anastasio Somoza, where he noted the irony in the fact that they signed an official protocol "under the roof of Somoza's secret lover, connected with a secret tunnel to his residence."[66] From going on safari in Zimbabwe, to lounging on Cuban beaches at the Tropicana hotel—now a resort for Soviet Cosmonauts—Bulgaria became a proxy for Soviet influence abroad. It is noteworthy perhaps that Bulgaria also exported weapons and some foodstuffs in "aid" to many of these new trading partners as part of the project of "spreading global communism."[67] Bulgartabak became in essence, a neo-colonialist multinational corporation, quickly and successfully reversing its own role as importer of technology and exporter of raw tobacco. Now it imported raw tobacco and hard currency and exported machines (including weapons) and cigarettes, fanning out to global proportions while holding onto its Bloc partners.

In spite of these successes, the 1980s were not without challenges. After the Chernobyl disaster in neighboring Ukraine, many of Bulgaria's partners expressed reluctance at buying "radioactive cigarettes." Bulgartabak was relieved, of course, when first Philip Morris, then Poland, and the USSR resumed orders.[68] Comecon remained Bulgaria's most loyal market in this period, but even there, temporary dips in orders from everyone including the USSR required Bulgartabak to be proactive in terms of organizing taste tests, exhibitions, window displays, and trade missions in order to keep their "traditional" markets.[69] They developed new brands—many of them American blends—with higher quality packaging, cellophane wrappers, etc. They battled not only the real and potential penetration of Western brands, but also anti-smoking tendencies. In "marketing" strategies for the Bloc, Bulgartabak sought "effective forms and methods of advertisement of our cigarettes in socialist countries with the goal of popularizing these products in spite of the existing bans in advertisements of tobacco products."[70] But significantly, according to Bulgartabak marketing strategists, the Soviet Union, along with Romania and Mongolia—but unlike East Germany, Czechoslovakia, Hungary, and Poland—still preferred Oriental cigarettes in 1985.[71] On the one hand, Western aesthetic hegemony could only get so far behind the Iron Curtain. On the other hand, Bulgaria could still sell Oriental cigarettes significantly cheaper—so perhaps economic, not aesthetic choices were being made.

The Bulgartabak story, of course, ends in "tragedy" with the fall of Communism in Eastern Europe and the Soviet Union in 1989–1991 and the eventual privatization and dismantling of the Bulgartabak state monopoly. This was, admittedly, a disaster for the Bulgarian tobacco industry, which was foreshadowed by the events of 1989. That summer, Todor Zhivkov made his famous announcement on the television that the borders with Turkey were open. All "Bulgarian-Muslims" who believed themselves Turks—in spite of the well-known assimilation campaigns of 1984–1985—were encouraged to leave Bulgaria immediately. Three-hundred thousand Turks—who lived primarily in rural tobacco-growing regions—headed for Bulgaria's borders in waves leaving fields fallow and, later, tobacco un-harvested for that season.[72] In spite of Iadkov's desperate measures to save the situation, for the first time ever Bulgaria could not make promised deliveries to its trade partners, including the all-important Soviet Union. Iadkov was extremely distraught by this turn of events, recalling his own promise to himself in 1973 that "as long as I am in the Union [Comecon], I will not fail to supply the Soviet market."[73] Iadkov went to Moscow himself to personally apologize for the situation. On his return he reported back home that Moscow was full of long lines for goods and that when he saw "the lines for cigarettes" he felt like he was personally responsible. As Communism collapsed across the Bloc, Iadkov watched with horror as American and other Western cigarettes inundated the markets of the East and Western tobacco companies became major investors and buyers of former state-owned tobacco enterprises. The "golden years" had come to an abrupt and untimely end.

CONCLUSION

In the course of the Cold War, Bulgarian tobacco used the complex political landscape of loyalty, taste, and market to its own advantage. Bulgartabak flourished with the advantage of the Soviet market, while Soviet demands for cigarettes drove its mechanization and modernization. In the course of the period, Bulgartabak manipulated Western expectations in many ways, importing Western technology and know-how without opening the doors wide to direct penetration of Eastern Bloc markets. While working with borrowed technology and cigarette aesthetics from the West, Bulgartabak used these technologies to maintain its Eastern Bloc markets and to take over former markets abroad, like Iran. Bulgartabak appropriated and replicated American neo-imperialist techniques of global trade in the Middle East and the developing world. Ultimately American "indirect" penetration of the Eastern Bloc market awarded long-term success to American companies. Western brands—Marlboro, Winston, Kent—became known and desired behind the Iron Curtain—if for no other reason than their Western cachet and air of luxury. More importantly, Western cigarette aesthetics, which privileged American blends and hence predominantly broad-leafed tobacco varieties (Virginia and Burley), had a permanent impact on the status and demand for Oriental tobaccos—a necessary but only 10%–15% component of blends. As in politics, in the annals of the Cold War, the West had won.

NOTES

1. Dimitur Iadkov, *Bulgartabak: Spomeni*, (Sofia: Izdateslvo "Sibia" 34, 2003), 35.
2. *Bŭlgarski Tiutiun*, 2 (1966): 1; see also *Tobacco Reporter*, (March 1974): 17.
3. *Tobacco*, July 23, 1971, 23–26.
4. Ibid., 167.
5. Iadkov, *Bulgartabak*, 170–1. According to Iadkov, Nazi Germany made their last purchase of 22,000 tons of tobacco in the spring of 1944.
6. Ibid., 23.
7. Ibid., 89.
8. P. Penchev and St. Banov, *Tiutiun i Tsigari*, (Sofia: Izdatelstvo Ban, 1961), 138.
9. Iadkov, *Bulgartabak*, 91.
10. Ibid., 91.
11. Anton Koev, ed., *The Trail of Traicho Kostov and his Group*, (Sofia: Press Department, 1949), 233.
12. Iadkov, *Bulgartabak*, 95.
13. Ibid., 95.
14. *Tobacco News*, September 1960 (Tobacco Institute), 4.
15. Iadkov, *Bulgartabak* , 96.
16. Philip Morris collection. *Dawson, G.C. [No title]. 09 Dec 1953. Bates: 1001908576–1001908579*, <http://tobaccodocuments.org/pm/1001908576–8579.html>, 4.
17. *The New Yorker*, September 1954, 264.
18. *Bŭlgarski Tiutiun*, 2 (1966), 1.
19. Iadkov, *Bulgartabak*, 8.
20. Central State Archive in Sofia or Tsentralen Dŭrzhaven Arkhiv (hereafter TsDA), F-347, O-14, E-3, L-3: 1966.
21. Philip Morris collection. Heymans, J. "Report Visit to Moscow–Justus Heymans 640626—640706". 26 Jun 1964. Bates: 2012582923–2012582927, <http://tobaccodocuments.org/pm/2012582923–2927.html>, 2.
22. Allan Brandt, *The Cigarette Century: The Rise, Fall and Deadly Persistence of the Product that Defined America*, (New York: Basic Books, 2007), 54–5.
23. *Washington Evening Star*, Washington, DC, October 12, 1965.
24. Philip Morris collection, Heymans, J. "Letter No. 9 Rumania and Bulgaria". 28 Jul 1964. Bates: 2012582864–2012582865, <http://tobaccodocuments.org/pm/2012582864–2865.html>, 3.
25. Twenty-seven countries were in attendance, including the USSR, East and West Germany, United Kingdom, United States, France, Yugoslavia, Italy, Belgium, Holland, Poland, Czechoslovakia, Austria, Hungary, Rumania, Greece, Portugal, Switzerland, China, Vietnam, Cuba, Lebanon, Egypt, Korea, Turkey, Israel, and Somalia. *The First Tobacco Symposium, Plovdiv Bulgaria,* (Plovdiv: Conference Publication, 1965), 10.
26. Koresta, which stands for Cooperation Centre for Scientific Research Relative to Tobacco, is an international association founded in 1956 to promote

international cooperation in scientific research relative to tobacco production. Its members meet annually for exchanges of industry related information.
27. Philip Morris collection. *Foreign Agricultural Service; USDA, U.S. Dept. of Agriculture. "Foreign Agriculture Circular Tobacco". 19661000/P. Bates: 2024998585–2024998592.* <http://tobaccodocuments.org/pm/2024998585-8592.html>, 1–4.
28. *The First Tobacco Symposium*, 8.
29. Ibid., 67–70.
30. Philip Morris collection. *Wakeham, H. [No title]. 1967 (est.). Bates: 1000322484–1000322486,* <http://tobaccodocuments.org/pm/1000322484-2486.html>, 1–2.
31. TsDA, F-347, O-14, E-2, L-213: 1965.
32. TsDA, F-347, O-14, E-3, L-183: 1966.
33. TsDA, F-347, O-14, E-3, L-3: 1966.
34. TsDA, F-347, O-14, E-3, L-4: 1966.
35. Ibid.
36. TsDA, F-347, O-14, E-3, L-5: 1966.
37. TsDA, F-347, O-14, E-3, L-16: 1966. Eastman Kodak was apparently paid one cent for every 6,000 cigarettes.
38. TsDA, F-347, O-14, E-130, L-33: 1968.
39. TsDA, F-347, O-14, E-131, L-103: 1968–9.
40. TsDA, F-347, O-14, E-133, L-2: 1968.
41. Philip Morris collection. *Investigaciones Del Humo Del Tabaco; Tobacco Smoking Research; Beffinger, I.J. [No title]. 21 Sep 1967. Bates: 2025041470–2025041473.* <http://tobaccodocuments.org/pm/2025041470–1473.html>, 3.
42. Ibid., 45.
43. See Nauchnoizsledovatelska Laboratoriia za Mladezhdta Kŭm HIIM Pri TsK na DKMS, *Problemi na Tiutiunopushteneto i Alkokholnata Upotreba Sred Mladezhta*, (Plovdiv: BAN, 1983), 59 and 83.
44. *Tobacco Reporter*, April 1976, 80.
45. Atanas Liutov, Boris Atanasov, Violeta Samardzhieva, and Katia Stoianova, *Upravlenie na Narodnoto Potreblenie,* (Sofiia: Izdatelstvo na Bŭlgarskata Akademiia na Naukite—Ikonomicheski Institut, 1984), 116.
46. Iadkov, *Bulgartabak*, 8.
47. Ibid., 11.
48. Ibid., 13.
49. Ibid., 188.
50. Ibid., 21.
51. Ibid., 30–1.
52. Ibid., 31–2.
53. Ibid., 36.
54. Ibid.
55. Philip Morris collection. *Cullman, H. [No title]. 07 May 1974. Bates: 1000272443–1000272445,* <http://tobaccodocuments.org/pm/1000272443-2445.html>, 1–3.
56. Iadkov, *Bulgartabak,* 43 and 58.
57. Ibid., 57.
58. Ibid., 58.
59. TsDA, F-347, O-16, E-6, L-89: 1977.
60. Iadkov, *Bulgartabak*, 115–6.
61. Ibid., 138.
62. Ibid., 163.
63. Ibid., 143.
64. Ibid., 220.

65. Ibid., 188–190.
66. Ibid., 216.
67. Secret BCP Politburo Resolution for Military Aid Supply to Certain National-Liberation Movements and Communist Parties, 7/16/1976. TsDA (F-1-B, O-64, A-478). Cold War International History Project (CWIHP), www.CWIHP.org, by permission of the Woodrow Wilson International Center for Scholars.
68. Ibid., 311–2.
69. Ibid., 192–3.
70. TsDA, F-347, O-20, A-75, L-7: 1984.
71. TsDA, F-347, O-20, A-85, L-3: 1985.
72. Iadkov, *Bulgartabak*, 353.
73. Ibid., 370–1

15 Tobacco and Transition
The Advent of the Transnational Tobacco Companies

Anna Gilmore

The Soviet Union collapsed in 1991, precipitating immense political, economic and social changes—a transition to democracy (albeit imperfect), a sudden transfer from a command to a market economy, and the destruction of the Soviet socialist infrastructure on which the population had relied. The enormous and largely negative immediate effect of these developments on health has now been well documented, but relatively little thought has yet been given to their long-term impact on health.[1] Of particular concern in this regard are the overwhelming changes to the region's tobacco industry, most notably, the rapid and unregulated entry of the multi-national and transnational tobacco companies (TTCs) and the privatization of the state-owned tobacco monopolies, in many cases under immense pressure from the international financial community.[2] Not only is the detrimental effect on health from tobacco enormous, killing one in every two of its long-term users, but the former Soviet Union (FSU) had the highest rate of premature mortality of any part of the European region even before the political transition.[3]

Although the TTCs have been establishing global production facilities assiduously over decades, nowhere has the transformation of the tobacco market been so rapid or profound. As the FSU embraced market economics, so the doors to this previously closed market opened to the TTCs. The former Soviet Union was the third largest cigarette market in the world after China and the United States and the TTCs had been greedily eyeing it for some time.[4] Its potential importance, alongside other closed markets (and he must have been including the Chinese market in these figures), was aptly summarized by Mike Pavitt, Rothman's international spokesman in the early 1990s, when he said, "Until recently, perhaps 40% of the world's smokers were locked behind ideological walls. We've been itching to get at them . . . that's where our growth will come from."[5] Patrick Sheehy, then chairman of British American Tobacco (BAT), the world's second largest tobacco company, reflected this attitude when he stated in October 1990 "[T]he dramatic increase in the proportion of the world's cigarette market now open to free enterprise [make these] the most exciting times I have seen in the tobacco industry in the last 40 years."[6]

By the late 1980s the Soviet tobacco industry was in disarray. Approximately half of the USSR's cigarette factories were closed and cigarettes were in very short supply. Smokers in Moscow, Leningrad, Kiev, and other Soviet cities queued through the night but still came away empty handed, finally staging protests that became known as the "tobacco riots" or "rebellion." Gorbachev pleaded with the West for help and Philip Morris and RJ Reynolds came to the rescue, keen to get a foothold in this market. Between 1990 and 1991 alone, thirty-four billion cigarettes were airlifted to the FSU, the single largest export order in the history of the tobacco giants.[7] In the first six months of 1991, reports indicated that cigarette exports to the FSU from the United States alone increased more than 7,200%.[8] These imports were accompanied by a massive marketing presence, and it was this rapid introduction of cigarette marketing, a previously unknown phenomenon, which most profoundly signalled the changes to the region's tobacco market. By this stage the Soviet industry had been dismantled into fifteen national industries, and having secured the import of their brands, the TTCs then moved to acquire these failing state-owned industries. Thereafter, as local production was scaled up, imports gradually fell. There was little government opposition to the TTCs, who were welcomed as creators of economic well-being while public health concerns were shunted aside.[9]

This chapter explores the impacts of this profound transformation of the region's tobacco industry. It does so largely from a public health perspective, exploring impacts on cigarette consumption, smoking prevalence, and tobacco control and the role the TTCs played in influencing or benefiting from these changes. It draws on a growing body of work that has used routine data, surveys of smoking habits, and the tobacco industry's own documents to assess the impacts of events. These documents were released as a result of litigation in the United States and provide a unique insight to the inner workings of the TTCs.[10]

In addition to the public health impact, the chapter will also briefly review the economic impacts of this transformation. This is important because when communism collapsed, privatization was a key element of the radical economic reforms recommended and carried out under the auspices of the International Monetary Fund (IMF). The IMF, however, failed to differentiate the privatization of an industry whose product is uniquely damaging to health from that of any other industry. Indeed the IMF supported, in some cases even pressed for, tobacco industry privatization in the FSU, despite having no knowledge of and seemingly having given no consideration to its potential impacts.[11] Thus arguments that privatization would help address macroeconomic problems and promote efficiency and growth were held to apply to tobacco industry privatization despite the fact that tobacco use has been shown to be damaging to economies and that such changes would increase competition, in turn leading to reduced costs and increased marketing, both likely to stimulate sales of a product that kills.[12] The IMF's apparent justification for privatizing state-owned tobacco industries is that it frees governments to pursue more effective tobacco control policies than they would otherwise have done when directly engaged in selling tobacco (correspondence with Peter Heller of the IMF, October 2005). This chapter will therefore also seek to examine if the evidence supports the IMF's stand.[13]

AN OVERVIEW OF EVENTS

In their 1848 *Communist Manifesto,* Marx and Engels wrote that when domestic capitalism ceased to progress or experienced a crisis, industrialists would respond "by the conquest of new markets, and by the more thorough exploitation of the old ones."[14] This, unexpectedly, was to prove an apt description of the TTCs rapid entry to the FSU almost a century and a half later. This exact sentiment was captured by Tony Johnson, a BAT board member and then regional lead for Russia and Central Asia, who writing in an in-house publication, the *BAT Bulletin*, described the opportunities in the FSU as "almost limitless," explaining that:

> The emerging markets of Central Asia and the former Soviet Union in particular have immense potential and are of crucial significance to BAT. As the long established markets of north America and Europe mature and contract—and they will continue to do so over the next five to ten years—it is vital that we find new markets to grow and expand our business . . . the real opportunities for growth lie in the former Soviet Union and this is where we will be focusing much of our attention over the next few years.[15]

The TTCs recognized the opening of the FSU as a massive opportunity. A number of features made these markets attractive—the undersupply of cigarettes, the vast population, and (particularly in Central Asia) its young age structure and high rates of population growth, high male smoking rates, and the potential to increase smoking among women; although few women then smoked and those that did were more likely to smoke international brands.[16]

When the Soviet Union collapsed, each of the newly-independent states inherited its own government-owned tobacco industry. But the centrally-funded subsidies for growers and producers had ended and the centralized tobacco import and distribution system had broken down, leaving individual factories to fend for themselves. The chaotic state of the industry and the marked cigarette shortages seen at the time, combined with the rejection of Marxist-Leninist ideology and the lurch towards market reform, provided an obvious opportunity for the TTCs, one which they were quick to exploit.

The first key step was to establish imports, which was done through whatever means possible. Given the region's dire economic position, the TTCs used a number of systems to ensure cigarette imports were paid for, including counter-trade, the use of money from aid packages, and smuggling. There is extensive evidence from the industry's own documents that the TTCs actively used smuggling as a key market-entry tactic and that in the early to mid-1990s the majority of cigarette imports to the FSU were smuggled.[17] Smuggling provides a number of advantages to the TTCs. It ensures a ready supply of cheap cigarettes, thereby encouraging consumption and creating a demand for the (often highly desirable) smuggled product before the market is officially opened or a domestic manufacturing presence established. This undermines local firms which can then be more easily and cheaply acquired, and makes it easier to argue the need for local manufacture on the basis that the demand for quality products led to the illegal supply and reduces government revenues. This exact argument was used in Belarus when BAT attempted to persuade the government to privatize its state monopoly.[18]

In the Soviet era, the Western concept of branding was virtually unknown. Almost all cigarette brands were state-owned and each factory produced a variety of brands. The TTCs by contrast rapidly gained ownership of existing brands, introduced their own international brands, and developed new brands for these markets including those specifically targeting women. Japan Tobacco International, for example, introduced eight new brands in 1999 alone.[19] In the suddenly and increasingly competitive market, simply ensuring brands were present in the marketplace was insufficient for the TTCs. They required marketing back up. Concerned at the potential advent of advertising restrictions, the TTCs moved quickly to exploit the media opportunities, then available incredibly cheaply, with massive advertising and sponsorship. Within a short period of time tobacco advertising became ubiquitous, often flaunting existing tobacco control legislation. The industry journals themselves described the streets of Moscow as "a battle ground in a cigarette war of words."[20] Authors report that by the mid-1990s 40% of all foreign advertising in Russia was for tobacco, that 50% of all billboards in Moscow and 75% of plastic bags in Russia overall carried tobacco advertising and that foreign cigarette brands became the leading advertisers on Russian television and radio. Others outline how such advertising particularly targeted children and young people, using television adverts screened in the evening.[21]

There were grave concerns that in a region virtually unexposed to Western-type advertising, the population may be more sensitive to the novelty and glamour of tobacco advertising. As Vitaliy Movchanyuk, director of the Ukrainian Health Ministry's public education institute said, "The Soviet Union never had such advertising. People are used to it in the West. They have learnt to sift through it for truth and lies. . . .

But our consumers are psychologically vulnerable to being manipulated by slick advertising."[22]

The industry appeared to be aware of this; industry journal reports note that smokers "are vulnerable to cigarette advertising," even reporting that, as a result of successful advertising campaigns by the main tobacco players, "Russians see smoking as the distinction between human beings and animals."[23] Regional experts have suggested that faced with such "sophisticated and ruthless promotion" it became increasingly difficult to control the use of tobacco.[24]

Having established a brand presence, the TTCs then set about establishing a manufacturing base, competing to acquire the region's finest and most strategically positioned factories. Prioritization was based on the potential cigarette market size, geographic position, and political and economic circumstances, although the latter were rarely seen as adverse enough to preclude an investment. Competition to acquire assets was intense and the TTCs rapidly set about selling both the benefits of privatization and themselves as prospective buyers to the various governments of the region.[25]

Major investments soon emerged and only four of the fifteen countries in the region still remain without TTC investment. Turkmenistan had no tobacco manufacturing facilities available for purchase, the political situation discouraged investment in Tajikistan, and Moldova and Belarus rejected the TTC's persistent advances. In Moldova this occurred despite the IMF making its loan conditional on industry privatization and led ultimately to the collapse of the centre right government and the ascendance of the Communist party.[26]

MACROECONOMIC IMPACTS OF TTC ENTRY AND TOBACCO INDUSTRY PRIVATIZATION

Contribution to Foreign Direct Investment and Government Revenue

A detailed analysis of TTC investments in the region shows that between 1992 and 2000 they invested over $2.7 billion in ten of the region's fifteen countries, where their contribution to total foreign direct investment varied widely from 1% (Latvia, Azerbaijan) to over 30% in Uzbekistan, where BAT became the country's largest foreign investor. The earliest investments were seen in Russia, Ukraine, and Latvia (1992 onwards); Estonia, Lithuania, and Kazakhstan (1993 onwards); and Uzbekistan (1994). Later investments (from 1997 onwards) occurred in Armenia, Azerbaijan, and Kyrgyzstan. In 2001 BAT invested in Georgia, establishing a licensed production operation, leaving only four countries without direct TTC investment as detailed above.[27]

Although these sums may seem impressive, evidence suggests that they are considerably lower than might have been expected. Internal tobacco industry documents indicate that the TTCs purposely and actively sought to contain the prices they paid by avoiding competitive tenders. The fact that BAT's offer in the tender in Kazakhstan was approximately a third of Philip Morris' successful bid indicates the scale by which foreign direct investment revenues may have been limited through such action. Some regional tobacco control experts allege that, even where tenders occurred, the prices paid for assets in the region were far lower than expected citing a 1995 Deloitte and Touche report in support of this allegation. This report predicted that tobacco investments in Ukraine would, by 1999, reach over $520 million, over three times the amount actually reached.[28]

Further evidence indicates that as part of the deals established, the TTCs further reduced government revenues by negotiating a wide variety of highly favorable tax holidays (these have been documented for example in Ukraine, Uzbekistan, and Kyrgyzstan), by avoiding import and excise duties through smuggling, and by actively lobbying to ensure excise rates were reduced.[29]

Competition

Although those promoting privatization predicted the emergence of competitive markets, the market structures that arose varied from highly competitive cigarette markets in Russia and Ukraine, the two most populous states, where all the major TTCs staked a claim, to private monopolies in others. The TTCs were keen to establish manufacturing monopolies wherever possible and successfully did so in the three Baltic states, Uzbekistan, and Kyrygyzstan, where by 2000 the TTC in question had established a market share of between 47% and 84%. In Kazakhstan, although other TTCs invested, Philip Morris enjoys a de facto monopoly with a market share of 75%.[30] Of these countries, Uzbekistan is the only one that has been investigated in more detail, and analysis of internal industry documents reveals that BAT established a manufacturing monopoly and protected itself from any internal competition by absorbing potential internal competitors, securing exclusive rights to manufacture tobacco products and process leaf, and acquiring a veto over the registration of cigarette brands. It then precluded any external competition from imports by redesigning the tobacco taxation system, erecting barriers to market entry, and establishing exclusive deals with local distributors and advertising agencies.[31] Such activities contravene not only the companies' own business conduct standards but also Organization of Economic Cooperation and Development standards on competition, raising concerns about the conduct of the TTCs in the region and suggesting that transnational corporations may have contributed to the failure of privatization in the region, a fact largely overlooked by the work of international financial organizations on this topic.[32]

Employment

Private companies generally run more efficiently than state-owned monopolies, often introducing updated technology that increases labor productivity and may thus lead to employment losses. Data from Ukraine show that total employment in the tobacco industry fell between 1995 and 2000, particularly in the factories with private investors. This decline in employment occurred despite marked increases in output. Industry document research supports these findings by indicating that, not only did TTCs perceive job losses as likely, but the possibility of losses was so sensitive that it was deliberately hidden from a government when investment was being negotiated.[33]

Evidence from Ukraine indicates that in addition to the job losses, working conditions declined measurably post-privatization. In one factory, for example, the kindergarten for employees' children was closed, the construction of employee apartments was stopped, and hours were increased without extra pay. Conditions were so bad that workers went on strike; 300 people finally lost their jobs and the factory was then closed just before the profit tax holiday ended.[34] Similar social impacts were a problem across all sectors in transition countries as private firms divested state-enterprise social assets without other social safety nets being in place. Perhaps a particularly dreadful example is seen amongst tobacco farmers in Uzbekistan, whose appalling plight has been documented by the British Helsinki Human Rights Group in 2002. They argue that BAT "appears to be exploiting local Uzbek farmers in what amounts to de facto slave labour," and due to BAT's status as the primary purchaser of tobacco leaf, farmers "are at the mercy of BAT when it comes to the price."[35]

Impact on Cigarette Production and Tobacco Trade

Privatization totally changed the patterns of cigarette production and trade. Cigarette production capacity across the factories receiving private investments tripled from 146 billion cigarettes per annum pre-investment to 416 billion post-investment. Increases varied by country, with increases as great as tenfold seen in Kyrgyzstan. As most factories were operating well below capacity pre-investment, absolute increases in production are likely to be higher than the capacity figures suggest.[36]

In line with the increase in capacity, analysis of routine data shows that cigarette production increased exponentially across the region, reaching far higher levels than ever previously recorded. Moreover, comparison between the seven countries that received investments prior to 1997

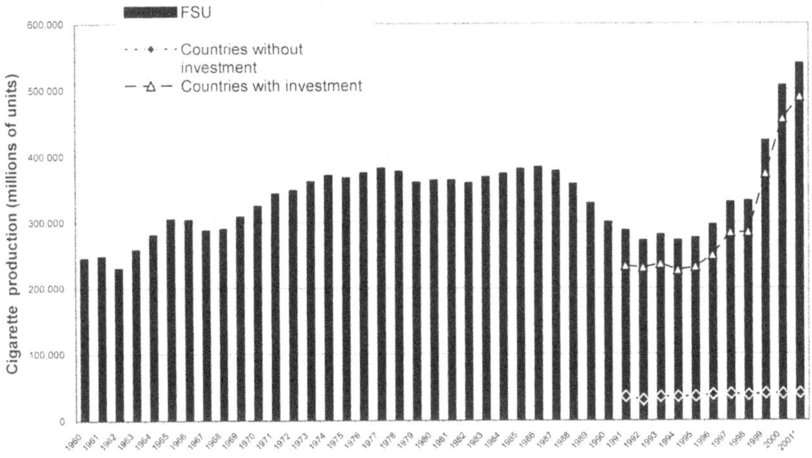

Figure 15.1 Cigarette production in the USSR/FSU, 1960–2001. Source: USDA data taken from Gilmore and McKee, "Exploring the Impact of Foreign Direct Investment," 13–21. Note: 2001 data are estimates.

(Estonia, Kazakhstan, Latvia, Lithuania, Russia, Ukraine, Uzbekistan) and the five countries that had received no investment by 2000 (Belarus, Georgia, Moldova, Tajikistan, Turkmenistan) showed that this increase was seen almost exclusively in the countries receiving TTC investments (Figure 15.1). Production increased by 96% in the seven countries receiving investment compared with just 11% in those without investment.[37] Within-country analyses shows that the increase in output was seen exclusively in the privatized factories.

Despite this massive increase in production, little improvement in the region's trade figures has been seen because the vast increases in cigarette production have been channelled almost entirely into local consumption, leaving no surplus for export. Indeed, although the initial increase in cigarette imports seen in the early 1990s had reversed by the turn of the century, and exports increased through the 1990s, imports still substantially outweigh exports across the region (Figure 15.2). At a national level, the pattern varies only slightly, with very few countries showing a trade surplus, and even in those countries export levels remain tiny compared with the level of cigarette production.[38]

The rapid increase in cigarette production and the shift in output from local to international-blend cigarettes introduced by the TTCs have had major implications for the region's leaf trade. Leaf imports have increased exponentially, the increase seen exclusively in countries receiving TTC investments (Figure 15.3). As a result the regional trade deficit in tobacco leaf increased ten-fold from 1992 to 1999, with leaf production still lower than ever recorded in Soviet times. These changes pour ridicule on the

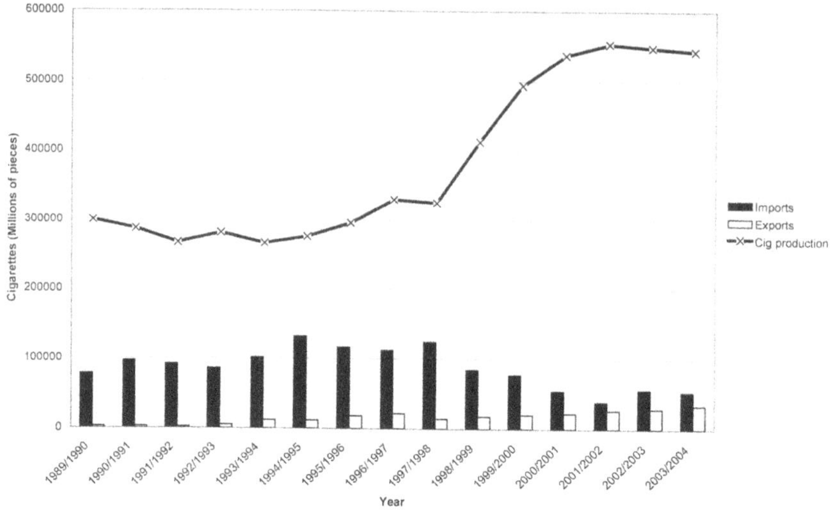

Figure 15.2 Cigarette production and trade balance, FSU 1989/1990–2003/2004. Source: USDA Foreign Agricultural Service data, http://www.fas.usda.gov/psd/psdreport.asp, accessed July 3, 2006.

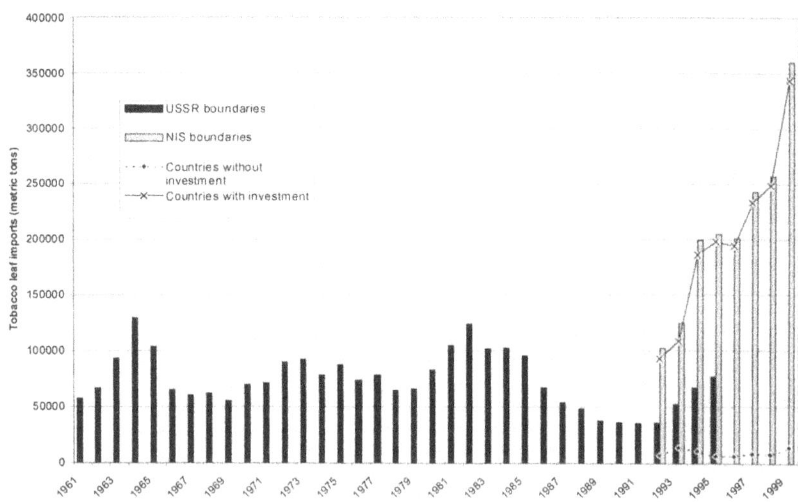

Figure 15.3 Tobacco leaf imports, USSR/FSU 1960–1999, in metric tons. Source: UN FAO agricultural food and trade database, taken from Gilmore and McKee, "Exploring the Impact of Foreign Direct Investment."

TTCs attempts to argue that improvements in tobacco leaf agriculture and leaf import substitution would be key benefits of privatization, tactics that were used to persuade governments in the region to accept TTC investment.[39]

Data from Ukraine show that over the period 1996–2000 import spending on tobacco products (cigarettes, leaf, and other tobacco products combined) exceeded export earnings by US $525 million, $100 million more than the tobacco excise revenue for the same period. Although the balance has improved from 1999, there is still a considerable trade deficit to overcome.[40]

PUBLIC HEALTH IMPACTS OF TTC ENTRY AND TOBACCO INDUSTRY PRIVATIZATION

Cigarette marketing and price are key determinants of consumption, and understanding the impact of transition on marketing and price are therefore key to explaining its potential impacts on consumption and smoking prevalence and thus public health. Each is considered in turn below.

Marketing

The advent of the TTCs with their new Western brands and marketing back-up led to the rapid and massive increase in marketing described earlier. Analysis of the industry's own documents reveals the strategy and targets behind this marketing push. In the documents examined it is clear that the TTCs aimed to drive up consumption. In Uzbekistan, for example, BAT projected a 45% increase in consumption in just six years between 1993 and 1999, while in Moldova (where BAT ultimately failed to invest) a more modest 34% increase from 5.6 to 7.5 billion cigarettes between 1994 and 2003 was planned. Reports from Uzbekistan also suggest BAT was successful in its aims, with consumption apparently increasing by 7%–8% annually and sales by 50.5% between 1990 and 1996. Such increases were to be achieved through both push (increased supply and improved distribution) and pull (marketing and brand awareness) strategies, as well as economic and, in some instances, population growth.[41] In terms of distribution and marketing, a number of targets are repeatedly referred to—young people, urban residents, opinion leaders, and women. In Russia, for example, marketing was to be focused initially on Moscow and then expanded to other key cities and the regions, as distribution systems, initially concentrated on Moscow and St. Petersburg, were expanded.[42] A similar plan was seen in Moldova with distribution and marketing to target "YAUS"—an industry acronym for young adult urban smokers.[43] As noted above, women were of particular interest across the whole region owing to their low rates of smoking and their preference for international filter brands. In both Uzbekistan and Moldova, the documents refer clearly to increasing the "incidence" of smoking among women, in one instance suggesting that "females can be drawn into the market via menthol offers or lighter brands."[44] It is clear that plans to stimulate consumption were predicated on having an unrestricted advertising environment, and that efforts were therefore made both to exploit the media opportunities available in the early 1990s, to avoid the imposition of restrictions, and to aggressively campaign against the advent of such restrictions.[45]

The status afforded to Western products in general was noted by the TTCs. BAT for example noted that "most young Russians aspire to Western international F.M.C.G. [fast moving consumer goods] brands and will forego 'necessities' in order to afford them," and that "western cigarettes are seen as relatively inexpensive status symbols. Anyone who smokes foreign cigarettes distinguishes himself from the egalitarian doctrine of socialism and thus demonstrates more individuality or personal freedom on a small scale."[46]

Observers of the advertising that emerged note that it seized on the population's desire to "Westernize" with cigarettes promoted as an indispensable part of the "Western lifestyle," and that concerted efforts were made to appeal to women, young people, and opinion leaders. The scale of the increase in advertising is apparent through marketing data, which indicate that in the four countries in the region where data were available the TTCs soon ranked among the top three advertisers, and continued to do so through the 1990s in advertising categories that remained unrestricted.[47] For example with the advent of television advertising bans in Russia, industry spending shifted to other media, and tobacco became the product most heavily advertised outdoors, with the three major TTCs ranking as first, second, and third heaviest advertisers in this category. The speed and extent to which these changes occurred are also illustrated in Uzbekistan, where in 1993 BAT described the advertising environment as "unique in the world in terms of its singularly unexploited advertising and promotional environment"—only one electronic billboard was seen in the whole country.[48] Less than one year later the Ministry of Health noted that large-scale advertising was already undermining health promotion efforts.

Cigarette Prices

The little formal analysis of price trends in the region suggests that cigarettes have tended to become more affordable. In Russia the growth rate of cigarette prices between 2000 and 2006 was 5.8%, which compares with 13.9% for bread, 17.8% for meat and poultry, and 22.1% for public transport. Moreover, according to Rosstat, from 1999 to 2005 inflation in Russia grew by 227.6%, while cigarette prices grew by only 140%.[49] In Ukraine analysis of real prices (adjusted for inflation) from 1996 onwards shows no change for two years followed by a rise in 1998 and a fall from 1999 onwards. Between 2000 and 2006, the average price of cigarettes fell by 30% in real terms and even nominal prices of filterless cigarettes fell over this period.[50]

Tobacco Control Policies

Numerous descriptive reports across the region outline how TTC entry led to the gradual erosion of tobacco control measures and to a highly effective lobbying against the introduction of new control measures. In Ukraine, for example, the industry responded to efforts to implement advertising restrictions with a report from the so-called "Association of Independent Advisors," for which Philip Morris later admitted responsibility, arguing that Ukraine would lose US $400 million as a result of an advertising ban. This led rapidly to a presidential veto.[51] Other than the three Baltic states, tobacco control policies in the region are weak. It has been suggested that the effectiveness of the tobacco control policies that emerged in each of the fifteen countries in the region corresponds broadly to the nature of the political and economic transition in each and the size of the industry investment. Thus, more effective measures tend to be seen in the more democratic states with smaller or no industry investments, notably the Baltic states and in Moldova, which retained its state-owned tobacco monopoly. The least effective measures are seen in highly centralized one-party states with high levels of industry investment (Uzbekistan, Kyrgyzstan, and Kazakhstan) or those with limited governmental capacity (Tajikistan and much of the Caucasus). Turkmenistan is unusual in having no TTC investment and because the autocratic then President Saparmurat Niyazov, after being advised to give up smoking after heart surgery, decreed smoking a vice and banned it in public, so advertising and smoking restrictions there are more advanced than in much of the region.[52]

Such findings are supported by detailed document research, which shows how the industry worked assiduously to undermine tobacco control. The most detailed work on policy influence covers Uzbekistan. In Uzbekistan, BAT, having already succeeded in reversing a local advertising ban in the capital, Tashkent, overturned Health Decree 30, a highly effective piece of legislation which, *inter alia*, banned cigarette advertising and smoking in public places. It had the decree replaced with another, designed by BAT to be ineffective, and in which the advertising ban was specifically replaced with a voluntary code, itself based on a code already implemented in Russia. To achieve this, BAT used its high-level political contacts, threats to abandon its investment, and misleading advice—refuting tobacco's negative health impact and the impact of advertising on cigarette consumption. Yet publicly it had the audacity to present its actions in developing the voluntary code as "an example of the company's responsible attitude to its advertising practices," concealing the fact that the code had only been necessary because BAT had overturned far more effective legislation.[53]

BAT also thoroughly redesigned the tobacco taxation system in Uzbekistan to advance its commercial objectives, bolster its monopoly position, and reduce competition. It secured a significant 50% reduction in excise on cigarettes, the design of an excise system to benefit its brands and disadvantage those of its competitors, and the introduction of a tax stamp system from which it hoped to be exempt, almost certainly to facilitate its established practice of cigarette smuggling until its local production output had increased.

Although BAT's uniquely high contribution to foreign direct investment in Uzbekistan could be used to argue that the Uzbek experience may be unique, the documents suggest this is most unlikely to be the case. For example, similar, ineffective voluntary codes on advertising were implemented in Russia and Ukraine by the TTCs acting collaboratively and were planned by BAT for Moldova and Kyrgyzstan when it was considering investing in those countries.[54] BAT documents also outline how from the outset the company established a team to provide excise advice to governments. Although this was promoted as a service to prospective business partners, it is clear that the advice was to be proffered largely for BAT's benefit. The documents also outline that wherever BAT sought to invest, it aimed to influence tax policy, with documented attempts made in Ukraine, Belarus, and Kyrgyzstan. Other evidence suggests that the other TTCs expected similar concessions when investing. Moreover, four other tobacco transnationals are sponsors of the International Tax and Investment Center.[55] This claims to be an independent non-profit research and education foundation that has "developed trusted advisory relationships with key, senior-level policymakers" in the FSU, which provide ITIC and its sponsors "a seat at the policymaking table."[56] Yet three of the reports listed on the ITIC website concern cigarette taxation and all present a uniquely one-sided viewpoint while simultaneously claiming to be independent.

Impact on Cigarette Consumption

In 2000 Chaloupka and Nair remarked that there was no empirical evidence of the impact of tobacco industry privatization on cigarette consumption.[57] Two studies published since that date provide reasonably convincing evidence that privatization increases consumption. In the FSU as a whole, cigarette consumption increased rapidly from a low in the early 1990s (just prior to privatization) to reach levels higher than ever previously recorded (Figure 15.4).[58] The differential between countries with and without investment was again notable—an increase in per capita consumption of 56% was seen in the seven countries receiving early investments over the period 1991–2001, while a fall of 1% was seen in the five countries that remained without investment during this period. Given that cigarettes are normal goods whose consumption rises with income, an increase of this size at a time of major economic recession is remarkable. A key issue in analyzing data of this sort is the problem of smuggling, a major problem in the region at the time. This was overcome to a large extent by looking at the region as a whole rather than countries in isolation (most smuggling was likely to be within the region). Thus, although some of the differences between these two groups of countries could be accounted for by smuggling, it is unlikely that a difference this large could be solely attributed to smuggling.[59]

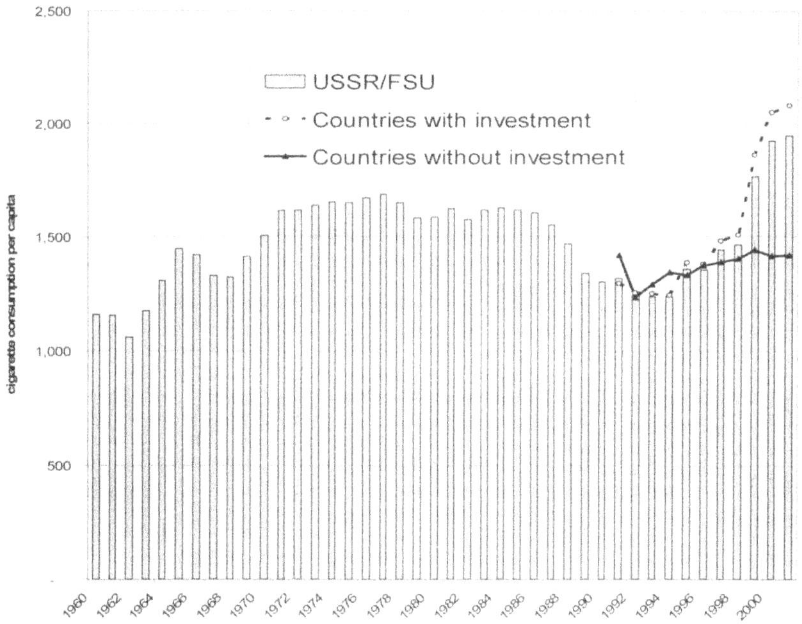

Figure 15.4 Cigarette consumption per capita in the USSR/FSU, all ages, 1960–2001. Source: Cigarette consumption, USDA data. Population data, UN data to 1989 taken from UN demographic yearbooks. WHO data from 1990 taken from WHO HFA database. Adapted from Gilmore and McKee, "Exploring the Impact of Foreign Direct Investment." Notes: 2001 data are estimates. Countries without investment include: Belarus, Georgia, Moldova, Tajikistan, Turkmenistan. Countries with investment include: Estonia, Kazakhstan, Latvia, Lithuania, Russia, Ukraine, Uzbekistan.

This evidence is also supported by an unpublished report, which examines whether the entry of private cigarette producers to Turkey and Ukraine increased cigarette consumption. The findings are remarkably similar, identifying marked increases in consumption in both countries. For Ukraine, this is not surprising as the report uses the same data to examine consumption, albeit at the national level. Nevertheless it clearly shows a rapid increase in consumption from 1993 onwards due to the substantial rise in production, which the report identifies as occurring exclusively in the privately-owned factories. In Turkey the changes to the market were slightly different. Although the state-owned tobacco monopoly, Tekel, was not privatized, in 1992 the market was opened to competition (again under IMF pressure) with other companies allowed both to import and produce locally. The TTCs were of course swift to take advantage, and analyses show that cigarette consumption rose dramatically after 1992 with the majority of the increase accounted for by the expanded production of the new private producers. Since the mid-1990s Turkey has experienced economic crises, and high inflation has eroded real incomes and purchasing power, making such an increase all the more remarkable.[60]

Impact on Smoking Prevalence

The most compelling evidence of an upwards impact on prevalence comes from a recent analysis of an established longitudinal study in Russia, the Russian Longitudinal Monitoring Survey (RLMS), a large survey with samples of at least 7,800 each year. This shows that over the ten-year period between 1992 (the year of the first TTC investments in Russia) and 2003, female smoking prevalence more than doubled from 7% to 15% with increases seen in all but the oldest age groups. Alarmingly, in men, amongst whom smoking rates were already amongst the highest in the world, statistically significant growth was also seen, from 57% to 63%.[61]

A previous study in Russia that assessed trends using repeat national interview surveys failed to reach such clear-cut conclusions due to the small sample sizes used. But a similar study in Ukraine identified marked increases in prevalence between 2001 and 2005 (from 12% to 20% in women and 55% to 67% in men). Although the Ukrainian surveys were not identical, they were similar enough that such marked increases were very unlikely to have occurred by chance. Such findings are further supported by comparisons with historical data, which suggest growth in smoking over time amongst women in Russia, Ukraine, and Belarus, the only countries where sufficient historical data are available.[62]

The three Baltic states are the only others that collect data regularly, although again formal analyses of trends are rare. One study formally assessed trends between 1994 and 1998 in Estonia and Lithuania and identified a significant rise in female smoking in Lithuania and an increase in men that was not significant once confounders were adjusted for.[63] No significant changes were detected in Estonia.

Further evidence that TTC action has directly influenced female smoking habits comes from the Living Conditions, Lifestyle, and Health study conducted in 2001 in eight countries in the FSU, namely, Armenia, Belarus, Georgia, Kazakhstan, Kyrgyzstan, Moldova, Russia, and Ukraine (Figures 15.5 and 15.6).[64] Two groupings of countries emerged from the between-country comparisons of female smoking habits—Belarus, Kazakhstan, Russia, and Ukraine on one hand, and Armenia, Georgia, Kyrgyzstan, and Moldova on the other. Women in the former group had higher smoking rates (9.3%–15.5% compared to 2.4%–6.3%), lower ages of smoking uptake (geometric mean age of smoking under twenty years compared with over twenty years) and far higher (at least twenty-five-fold) rates of smoking in the youngest compared with older generations ($p<0.0001$), a pattern not seen in the other four countries (Figures 15.5 and 15.6).[65] Russia, Ukraine, and Kazakhstan were the countries where the major TTCs invested earliest. The similar patterns seen in Belarus can be explained by the fact that the TTCs treat Belarus as an extension of the Russian market. Forty percent of cigarettes sold in Belarus are smuggled and the importance the TTCs attach to this illegal market is illustrated in the fact that, despite having little official market share, British American Tobacco (BAT) and Philip Morris have the highest outdoor advertising expenditure and the ninth- and tenth-highest television advertising expenditures of all companies operating in Belarus. Such expenditures could only be justified if they were supporting the smuggled brands. The other four countries surveyed

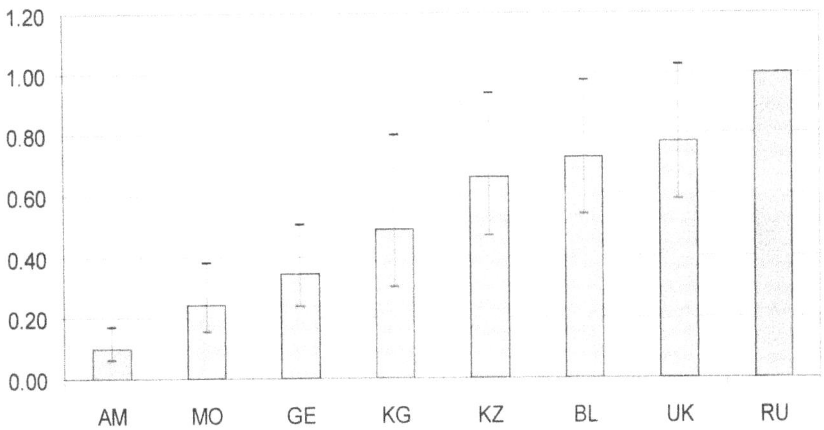

Figure 15.5 Odds (and 99% confidence interval) of smoking in women, adjusted for age, area of residence, marital status, religion, education, economic situation, and level of social support.

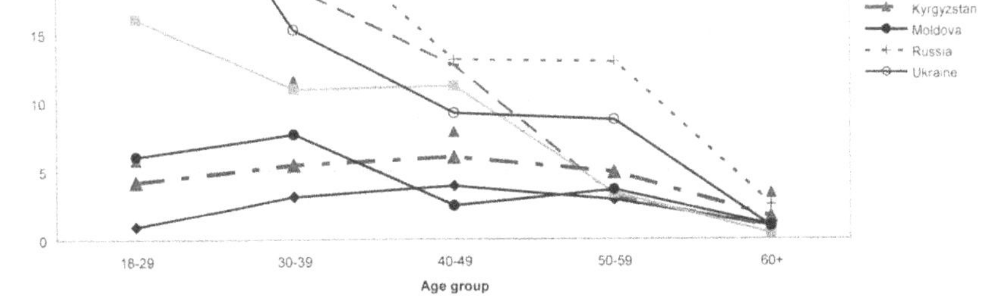

Figure 15.6 Current female smoking prevalence, by age group.

differ in that privatization and TTC investment has either not occurred (Moldova) or occurred later—from 1997 onwards, and other than Georgia (where BAT invested) did not involve the then largest TTCs.[66]

Analysis of the determinants of smoking also provides revealing insights about the impact of tobacco industry tactics, again indicating that female smoking patterns directly reflect the marketing activities of the TTCs. In women, numerous surveys in post-Soviet transition countries identify urban residence as the most important determinant of smoking.[67] Gradients as high as thirteen-fold have been observed between women living in major cities and those living in rural areas. The recent RLMS analysis showed this urban/rural gradient clearly. Interestingly, it also highlighted that, although through the 1990s and particularly the late 1990s, the increase in prevalence was greater in the major cities, by 2002 rates in the major cities appeared to have stabilized. By contrast the rate of increase in rural areas was initially slower but since 2002 has grown more rapidly. As a result, the overall increase in smoking prevalence between 1994 and 2000 was greater in rural areas, where a 320% rise was seen compared with a 54% increase in urban areas and a 36% increase in Moscow and St. Petersburg. These findings are entirely consistent with the targeted marketing and distribution strategies detailed in the industry documents and outlined above. In other words the earliest increases were seen in women in urban areas and then rates in rural areas began to grow as distribution expanded outside the urban centers. Further evidence that privatization has led to a fall in the age of uptake comes from the RLMS analysis, which shows that women in younger birth cohorts have lower ages of smoking uptake.[68]

CONCLUSIONS

This chapter outlines the monumental changes that occurred to the FSU's tobacco industry with transition. These have had an appalling impact on tobacco control and public health: cigarette consumption has spiralled and evidence from Russia and Ukraine suggests smoking prevalence rates are also increasing. Above all the impact has been felt in women, who had previously very low rates of smoking. Female smoking rates have increased significantly, particularly amongst young women living in cities, exactly those whom the TTCs have actively targeted. But smoking rates in men, already amongst the highest in the world, have also risen.

The work presented provides evidence, just as economic theory would predict, that investment liberalization and tobacco industry privatization pose major threats to public health: they tend to increase cigarette consumption and raise smoking prevalence particularly in selected population subgroups. This appears to occur as a direct result of TTC actions—massive increases in marketing, including marketing targeted specifically at groups with previously low rates of smoking, plus improvements in distribution and price reductions. The increases in female smoking, youth smoking, and the fall in age of initiation all signal the additional demand for tobacco that has been created amongst new smokers and are indicative of TCCs' success in targeting previously untapped segments of the market. Furthermore, the evidence outlines how investment liberalization and tobacco industry privatization led to serious challenges to the implementation of effective tobacco control policies, thereby worsening and prolonging the negative impacts on public health.

It also highlights that the supposed benefits of privatization (other than the increased choice and availability of cigarettes)—foreign investment flows—have been lower than expected. The TTCs reduced potential government revenues in a number of ways—by avoiding competitive tendering, negotiating a wide variety of tax holidays and investment incentives, smuggling cigarettes, and reducing cigarette excise rates. Furthermore, given growing evidence that tobacco control is good for a country's economy, the increase in consumption with the higher future burden of ill health it entails, is likely to have additional negative economic consequences. This negative societal impact will be compounded by the generally worse conditions provided to employees in the private versus state-owned industries.[69]

The findings therefore challenge the two arguments the IMF propounds for tobacco industry privatization—that it will improve efficiency and help address macroeconomic problems and that, by ridding the government of the conflict of interest inherent in both selling tobacco and controlling its use, it offers opportunities to improve tobacco control.

The failure to take active policy measures to contain the impacts can be explained in a number of ways. Market entry coincided with huge political and economic upheavals, with legislative activity focused on basic state building, and the need to develop constitutions and implement economic reform. There were no effective tobacco control policies in place to act as a buffer against the industry, and the development of new legislation was understandably given a low priority amidst other pressing demands. The entry of the TTCs, with their millions of investment dollars, was a further disincentive to effective tobacco control. Moreover, civil society was not well developed and proponents of tobacco control had little voice. As the industry journal *World Tobacco for Russia and Eastern Europe* stated with delight, "Anti-tobacco activists are almost unknown in Russia so the Russian people and government have not been bombarded with anti-tobacco propaganda."[70] As a result, TTCs met with little if any resistance. The ability to take over existing monopolies in all but the largest countries, together with their major contribution to foreign direct investment, has given the tobacco companies a unique degree of political influence. In well-functioning democracies, such influence may be effectively counteracted, as illustrated by the experience of the Baltic states. But elsewhere in the FSU, particularly in the Central Asian republics, industry and government collusion has left the industry in an extremely powerful position. Moreover, politicians, doctors, and public health activists had no experience in dealing with and countering the lobbying influence of such powerful industries.

The health impact of the increase in smoking rates will be massive. Tobacco kills one in every two of its long-term users, and Russia, like much of the region, is already facing a major demographic crisis. Yet, policy responses in most of the region are extremely slow. The best hope for change remains the World Health Organization's Framework Convention on Tobacco Control, the world's first international public health treaty. Although ten countries in the region have signed and ratified the treaty, five others have not—Moldova has signed but not yet ratified, while Russia, Tajikistan, Turkmenistan, and Uzbekistan have neither signed nor ratified. Progress in tobacco control policy is urgently needed if the activities of the transnational tobacco companies and the appalling public health impacts of their products are to be curtailed.

NOTES

1. D. Leon et al., "Huge Variation in Russian Mortality Rates, 1984–1994: Artefact, Alcohol, or What?" *Lancet*, 350 (1997): 383–8; V. Shkolnikov et al., "Changes in Life Expectancy in Russia in the 1990s," *Lancet*, 357 (2001): 917–21.
2. Various terms and definitions have been used for international corporations including tobacco manufacturers. Generally, a multi-national business is one conducting international business and operating in several countries but with little coordination of activities across boundaries. A transnational business is a business conducting its activities *across* national boundaries with varying degrees of coordination and integration. In recent years most international tobacco manufacturers have undergone significant change through mergers and acquisitions and global expansion. As a result, some small, largely nationally focused companies have transformed into major multi-nationals while others have moved from multi- to transnational status. For simplicity therefore, all major privately owned international tobacco manufacturers are referred to in this chapter as transnational tobacco companies (TTCs). R. Weissman and A. White, *Needless Harm, International Monetary Fund Support for Tobacco Privatisation and for Tobacco Tax and Tariff Reduction and the Cost to Public Health*, (Washington, DC: Essential Action, 2002), <http://www.essentialaction.org/needlessharm.pdf>, accessed July 11, 2008.
3. M. McKee, "The Health Effects of the Collapse of the Soviet Union," in *Poverty, Inequality and Health: An International Perspective,* ed. D. Leon and G. Walt, (New York: Oxford University Press, 2001): 17–36.
4. European Bureau for Action on Smoking Prevention, *Test the East: The Tobacco Industry and Eastern Europe*, (Brussels: BASP, 1991); Action of Smoking and Health, *Tobacco Explained: The Truth about The Tobacco Industry in It's Own Words*, (London: ASH, 1998).
5. M. Macalister, "Making a Packet—The New Tobacco Gold-rush," *The Observer Magazine*, November 8, 1992, 22–30; cited in *Action on Smoking and Health*, "Tobacco Explained: Emerging Markets," <http://old.ash.org.uk/html/conduct/html/tobexpld7.html#References>, accessed July 9, 2008.

6. D. Campbell, "BAT Industries Plc in the 1980s and 1990s," in *Global and Transnational Business: Strategy and Management*, ed. G. Stonehouse et al., (Chichester: Wiley, 2000), 418–30, quote 425.
7. G. B. Tkachenko and A. Prokhorov, *Tobacco and Health in the Russian Federation*, (Copenhagen: WHO Regional Office for Europe). EUR/ICP/LVNG 030101, 1997; J. Rupert and G. Frankel, "In Ex-Soviet Markets, US Brands Took on Role of Capitalist Liberator," *Washington Post*, November 19, 1996, A01.
8. Anon., "The Pushers Are Coming! The Pushers Are Coming! . . . To Russia," *Tobacco Control*, 1 (1992): 9.
9. T. Piha, "Tobacco Control Activities of the World Health Organization in Europe," in *Interventions for Smokers: An International Perspective*, ed. R. Richmond, (Baltimore: Williams and Wilkins, 1994): 232–347.
10. J. Collin et al., "Unlocking the Corporate Documents of British American Tobacco: An Invaluable Global Resource Needs Radically Improved Access," *Lancet*, 363 (2004): 1746–7.
11. Weissman and White, *Needless Harm*; and International Monetary Fund et al., *A Study of the Soviet Economy*, vols. 1 and 2, (Washington, DC: IMF, 1991).
12. Telephone interview with IMF staff member, October 2005. See also, World Bank, *Curbing the Epidemic: Governments and the Economics of Tobacco Control* (Washington, DC: World Bank, 1999).
13. F. J. Chaloupka and R. Nair, "Alcohol Supply—Domestic and International Perspectives: International Issues in the Supply of Tobacco, Recent Changes and Implications for Alcohol," *Addiction*, 95: 4 (2000): S477–89.
14. K. Marx and F. Engels, *Communist Manifesto* (London: Lawrence and Wishard, 1983), <www.anu.edu.au/polsci/marx/classics/manifesto.html>, from "Bourgeios and Proletarians," accessed September 3, 2008.
15. British American Tobacco, *BAT Bulletin* (November 1994). Guildford Depository. BAT. Bates No: 500316187–8.
16. A. Gilmore and M. McKee, "Moving East—How the Transnational Tobacco Companies Gained Entry to the Emerging Markets of the Former Soviet Union, Part I: Establishing Cigarette Imports," *Tobacco Control*, 13 (2004): 143–50.
17. Ibid.; A. Gilmore, J. Collin, and J. Townsend, "Transnational Tobacco Company Influence on Taxation Policy during Privatization: The Case of BAT in Uzbekistan," *American Journal of Public Health*, 97 (2007): 2001–9
18. G. Connolly, "Worldwide Expansion of Transnational Tobacco Industry," *Journal the National Cancer Institute Monographs*, 12 (1992): 29–35; P. L. Shepherd, "Transnational Corporations and the International Cigarette Industry," in *Profits, Progress and Poverty: Case Studies of International Industries in Latin America*, ed. R. S. Newfarmer, (South Bend, IN: University of Notre Dame Press, 1985), 63–112; Gilmore and McKee, "Moving East, Part II," 151–60.
19. M. Mitreva, "Russia's Revival," *Tobacco Reporter*, (July 2000): 48–51.
20. D. Dragounski, "Well—This Is the Russian Market," *World Tobacco for Russia and Eastern Europe*, 2 (August 1998): 32–46; Gilmore and McKee, "Moving East, Part I," 143–50; Konstantin Krasovsky, "Abusive International Marketing and Promotion tactics by Philip Morris and RJR Nabisco in Ukraine," in *Global Aggression: The Case for World Standards and Bold U.S. Action Challenging Philip Morris and RJR Nabisco*, (New York NY: Apex Press, 1998)," 76–83; and A. V. Prokhorov, "Getting on Smokin' Route 66: Tobacco promotion via Russian mass media," *Tobacco Control*, 6 (1997):145–6.
21. Rupert and Frankel, "Ex-Soviet Markets," A01; Dragounski, "Russian Market," 32–46; G. B. Tkachenko and A. Prokhorov, *Tobacco and Health in the Russian Federation*, (Copenhagen: WHO Regional Office, 1997). EUR/ICP/LVNG 030101
22. Rupert and Frankel, "Ex-Soviet Markets," A01.

23. Dragounski, "Well—This Is the Russian Market," 32
24. W. Zatonski, "An Overview of the Challenges in Tobacco Problems in Central and Eastern Europe," in *Tobacco and Health*, ed. K. Slama, (New York: Plenum, 1995), 281–3.
25. Gilmore and McKee, "Moving East, Part II," 151–60.
26. Weissman and White; A. Gilmore and M. McKee, "Tobacco and Transition: An Overview of Industry Investments, Impact and Influence in the Former Soviet Union," *Tobacco Control,* 13 (2004): 136–42; A. Gilmore et al., "Pushing Up Smoking Incidence: Plans for a Privatised Tobacco Industry in Moldova," *Lancet*, 365 (2005): 1354–59.
27. Gilmore and McKee, "Tobacco and Transition," 136–42.
28. Gilmore and McKee, "Moving East, Part I," 151–60. ibid., "Tobacco and Transition," 136–42; Gilmore, McKee, and Collin, "The Invisible Hand: How British American Tobacco precluded competition in Uzbekistan," *Tobacco Control* 16 (2007): 239-47," K. Krasovsky T. Andreeva, D. Krisanov, M. Mashliakivsky, G. Rud, 239–47; *Economics of Tobacco Control in Ukraine from the Public Health Perspective*, (Kiev: Polygraph Center TAT, 2002); and Deloitte and Touche as cited in same.
29. Gilmore, McKee, and Collin, "The Invisible Hand," 239–47; Gilmore and McKee, "Moving East, Part II," 151–60; Krasovsky et. al., *Economics of Tobacco Control*; A. A. Yurekli and J. De Beyer, "Did the Entry of Private Cigarette Producers in Turkey and Ukraine Increase Cigarette Consumption?" Unpublished report, cited with author's permission.
30. Gilmore and McKee, "Moving East, Part II," 151–60; ibid., "Tobacco and Transition," 136–42.
31. Gilmore, McKee, and Collin, "The Invisible Hand," 239–47.
32. Gilmore, Collin, and Townsend, "Transnational Tobacco Company Influence on Taxation Policy during Privatization: British American Tobacco and Uzbekistan," *American Journal of Public Health* 97 (2007):1–9."
33. Gilmore et al., "Pushing Up Smoking Incidence," 1354–9.
34. Krasovsky et al., *Economics of Tobacco Control*; Yurekli and De Beyer, "Did the Entry."
35. British Helsinki Human Rights Group, "BAT in Uzbekistan (2002)," <http://www.bhhrg.org/CountryReport.asp?CountryID=23&ReportID=5&ChapterID=31&next=next&keyword>, accessed July 25, 2005.
36. A. Gilmore and M. McKee, "Exploring the Impact of Foreign Direct Investment on Tobacco Consumption in the Former Soviet Union," *Tobacco Control*, 14 (2005): 13–21; ibid., "Tobacco and Transition," 136–42.
37. Ibid. This excludes three countries where investment occurred after 1997 (Armenia, Azerbaijan, and Kyrgyzstan)—considered too soon to have had an observable impact.
38. Ibid.; A. Gilmore, "Smoking and Tobacco Control: Economic Issues in Context," presented at the All Russian Forum on Health or Tobacco, Moscow, Russia, May 28–31, 2007.
39. Gilmore and McKee, "Exploring the Impact of Foreign Direct Investment," 13–21; ibid., "Moving East, Part II," 151–60.
40. Krasovsky et al., *Economics of Tobacco Control in Ukraine.*
41. Gilmore and McKee, "Moving East, Part I," 143–50; Gilmore et al., "Pushing Up Smoking Incidence," 1354–9; A. Gilmore, J. Collin, and M. McKee, "British American Tobacco's Erosion of Health Legislation in Uzbekistan," *British Medical Journal*, 332 (2006): 355–358.
42. Gilmore and McKee, "Moving East, Part I," 143–50; F. Perlman et al., "Trends in the Prevalence of Smoking in Russia during the Transition to a Market Economy," *Tobacco Control*, 16 (2007): 299–305.
43. Gilmore, McKee, and Collin, "The Invisible Hand," 239–47

44. Gilmore, Collin, and McKee, "British American Tobacco's Erosion of Health Legislation," 355–8; Gilmore and McKee, "Moving East, Part I," 143–50.
45. Gilmore and McKee, "Moving East, Part I," 143–50; Gilmore et al., "Pushing up Smoking Incidence," 1354–9; Gilmore, Collin, and McKee, "British American Tobacco's Erosion of Health Legislation," 355–8.
46. Gilmore and McKee, "Moving East, Part I," 145.
47. Gilmore and McKee, "Tobacco and Transition," 136–42; European Bureau for Action on Smoking Prevention, *Test the East;* R. Hurt, "Smoking in Russia: What Do Stalin and Western Tobacco Companies Have in Common?" *Mayo Clinic Proceedings*, 70 (1995): 1007–11; Zenith Media, *Central and Eastern Europe Market and Mediafact*, (London: Zenith Optimedia, 2000); Zenith Media, *Central and Eastern Europe Market and Mediafact*, (London: Zenith Optimedia, 2003).
48. Gilmore, Collin, and McKee, "British American Tobacco's Erosion of Health Legislation," 355–8.
49. N. Gerasimenko, "Smoking: A Socio-economic Problem in the Russian Federation," paper presented at the All-Russian Forum on Health or Tobacco, Moscow, Russia, May 28–31, 2007.
50. Krasovsky et al., *Economics of Tobacco Control in Ukraine*; T. I. Andreeva and K. Krasovsky, "Changes in Smoking Prevalence in Ukraine, 2000–2005: A Comparison with Changes in Russia," *Tobacco Control*, 16 (2007): 202–6.
51. Krasovsky, "Abusive International Marketing," 76–83; Gilmore and McKee, "Tobacco and Transition," 136–42.
52. Gilmore and McKee, "Tobacco and Transition," 136–42.
53. Gilmore, Collin, and McKee," British American Tobacco's Erosion of Health Legislation," 355–8.
54. Gilmore, Collin, and Townsend, "Transnational Tobacco Company," 1–9; Gilmore et al., "Pushing Up Smoking Incidence," 1354–9; Gilmore, Collin, and McKee, "British American Tobacco's Erosion of Health Legislation," 355–8.
55. ITIC, <http://www.iticnet.org/>.
56. Gilmore, Collin, and Townsend, "Transnational Tobacco Company;" International Tax and Investment Centre, <http://www.iticnet.org/about/Default.htm>, accessed July 9, 2008.
57. F. J. Chaloupka and R. Nair, "Alcohol Supply, Domestic and International Perspectives: International Issues in the Supply of Tobacco, Recent Changes and Implications for Alcohol," *Addiction*, 95 (2000): supplement 4, S477–89.
58. Yurekli and De Beyer, "Did the Entry"; Gilmore and McKee, "Exploring the Impact of Foreign Direct Investment," 13–21.
59. Ibid.
60. Yurekli and De Beyer, "Did the Entry."
61. Perlman et al. "Trends in the Prevalence of Smoking."
62. Bobak et al., "Changes in Smoking Prevalence in Russia, 1996–2004," *Tobacco Control*, 15 (2006): 131–5; Andreeva and Krasovsky, "Changes in Smoking Prevalence," 202–6; A. Gilmore, Chapter 1 in my "Tobacco and Transition: Understanding the Impact of Transition on Tobacco Use and Control in the Former Soviet Union (Ph.D. Diss.: London School of Hygiene and Tropical Medicine, 2005).
63. P. Puska et al., "Health Behaviour in Estonia, Finland and Lithuania 1994–1999," *European Journal of Public Health*, 13 (2003): 11–7.
64. A. Gilmore et al. "Prevalence of Smoking in Eight Countries of the Former Soviet Union: Results from the Living Conditions, Lifestyles and Health Study," *American Journal of Public Health*, 94 (2004): 2177–84; J. Pomerleau et al., "Determinants of Smoking in Eight Countries of the Former

Soviet Union: Results from the Living Conditions, Lifestyles, and Health Study," *Addiction*, 99 (2004): 1577–85.

65. Figure 5 shows the "odds" of smoking in women—this takes Russia as a baseline (hence Russia is assigned a value of 1.00 in the analysis) and compares the odds, or likelihood, of smoking in the other countries with this baseline. The odds of smoking in the other countries are shown by the shaded bars and the confidence interval (a measure of the degree of uncertainty around the estimate) by the black lines. The advantage of this analysis is that it takes account of other differences between women in these countries (such as their age, whether they live in rural or urban areas, their degree of education, their religion, etc.) that could account for their different smoking rates. Thus the figure shows that female smoking rates were highest in Russia and lowest in Armenia and that there appear to be real differences in smoking rates between women in these countries that are not accounted for by differences in age structure, area of residence, religion, etc. Gilmore et al., "Prevalence of Smoking in Eight Countries," 2177–84.
66. Zenith Media, *Central and Eastern Europe Market and Mediafact*; Gilmore et al., "Prevalence of Smoking in Eight Countries," 2177–84; ERC Group, *World Cigarettes 2001*, vol. 1, (Newmarket: ERC Group, 2001).
67. Gilmore et al., "Prevalence of Smoking in Eight Countries," 2177–84; M. McKee, et al., "Patterns of Smoking in Russia," *Tobacco Control*, 7 (1998): 22–6; A. Gilmore A et al., "Smoking in Ukraine: Epidemiology and Determinants," *Preventive Medicine*, 33 (2001): 453–61; A. Gilmore, M. McKee, and R. Rose, "Smoking in Belarus: Evidence from a Household Survey," *European Journal of Epidemiology*, 17 (2001): 245–53; I. Pudule et al., "Patterns of Smoking in the Baltic Republics," *Journal of Epidemiology and Community Health*, 53 (1999): 277–82.
68. Perlman et al., "Trends in the Prevalence of Smoking in Russia."
69. Leon et al., "Huge Variation in Russian Mortality Rates," 383–8; European Bureau for Action on Smoking Prevention, "Test the East."
70. Dragounski, "Russian Market," 32.

16 Up in Smoke?

The Politics and Health Impact of Tobacco in Today's Russia

Judyth L. Twigg

TOBACCO CONSUMPTION IN RUSSIA: PATTERNS AND CONSEQUENCES

More people smoke in Russia than just about anywhere else in the world (Figure 16.1). A recent World Health Organization report indicated that 70.1% of Russian men and 26.2% of women are regular smokers. Other reliable recent estimates place male smoking prevalence between 60% and 65%, and female prevalence between 13% and 30%.[1]

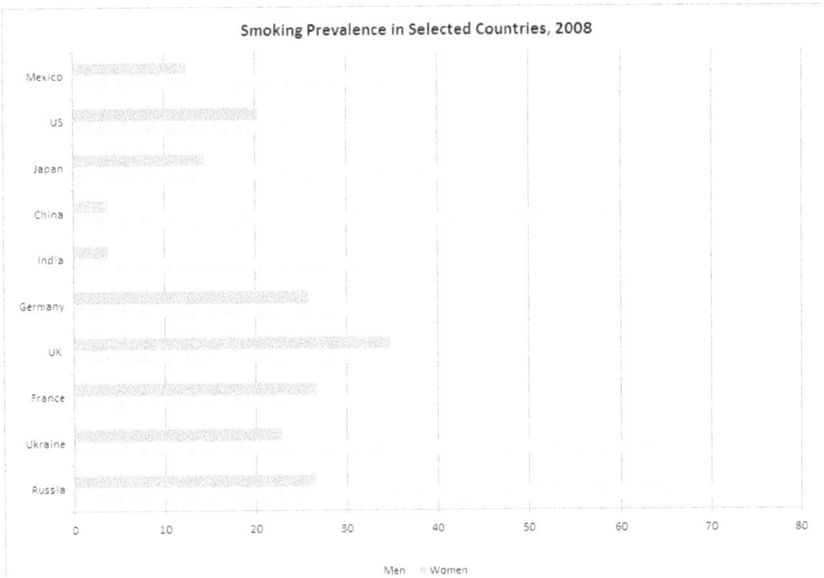

Figure 16.1 Smoking prevalence in selected countries, 2008. Source: World Health Organization, *Report on the Global Tobacco Epidemic, 2008*, (Geneva: World Health Organization, 2008).

The percentage of Russians who smoke has been steadily growing over the last fifteen years, with the rate of growth among women significantly higher than that among men.[2] Breaking down female smokers into ten-year age cohorts reveals a much higher recent increase in the rate of smoking among 25–34-year-olds than in other groups (Figure 16.2); as will be discussed later, this pattern is most likely attributable to the tobacco industry's deliberate targeting of young women with its advertising messages. Even this rate of prevalence, as well as the growth rate, might be understated, as studies have shown that Russian women tend to under-report their smoking behaviors, and virtually all of the reported statistics rely on self-identification as a smoker.[3]

Perhaps most worrisome are recent upward trends in rates of adolescent smoking. A World Bank study found in 2004 that 9% of boys and 6% of girls in the 11–15 age range were daily smokers, and that 27.4% of boys and 18.5% of girls at age 15 smoked regularly. More recent reports, however, include a 2005 Russian Ministry of Health study finding that 40% of girls and 46% of boys in the senior classes of secondary schools were smokers, and an early 2007 statement by Gennady Onischenko, Russia's chief public health official, that 60% of boys and 40% of girls smoke by the time they reach the eleventh grade.[4]

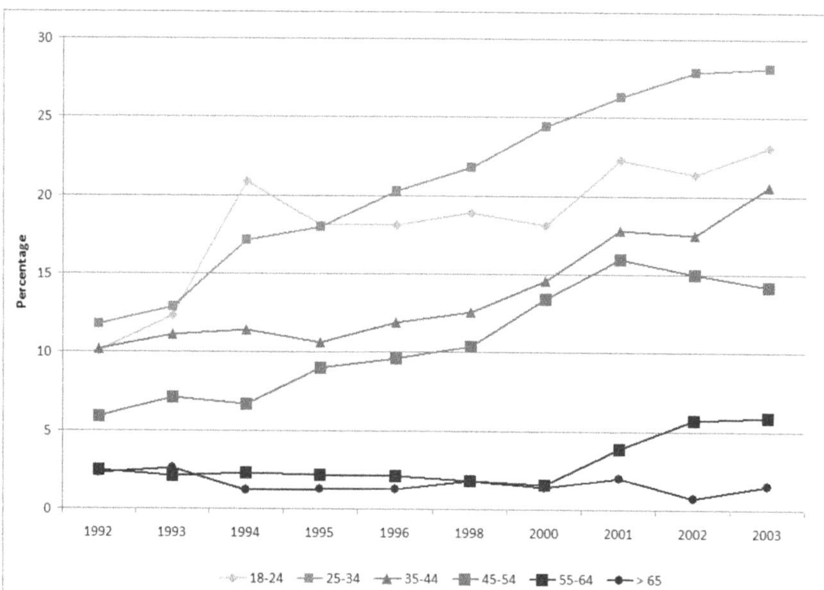

Figure 16.2 Smoking prevalence among Russian women, by age cohort, 1992–2003. Source: Data adapted from Francesca Perlman, Martin Bobak, Anna Gilmore, and Martin McKee, "Trends in the Prevalence of Smoking in Russia during the Transition to a Market Economy," *Tobacco Control* 16 (2007): 301.

A variety of studies have attempted to find convincing determinants or correlates of smoking in Russia. The most recent and comprehensive analysis concluded that, among a wide swath of variables (marital status, income, occupation, self-rated psychological distress, and others), only education tracked with smoking behavior: the less educated a Russian man, the more likely he is to smoke. This relationship does not hold for women.[5] Another study examined urban/rural differentials, finding little difference between city- and country-dwellers among men, but dramatically higher rates of smoking among urban than among rural women.[6] Other than this gender-related observation, tobacco use seems to be equally prevalent across class, income, geographic, and other boundaries. The influence of parents on their children, however, is unmistakable: 80% of children whose parents both smoke become smokers themselves; the rate is 50% in families where only one parent smokes, and 20% where parents do not smoke at all.[7]

According to the World Health Organization, Russians smoke almost a half-million tons of tobacco annually, placing Russia fourth in the world in overall consumption (Figure 16.3). Factoring in Russia's relatively low population, its per capita consumption is higher than anywhere else in the world. Although exact figures are difficult to ascertain, it is estimated that about 2,500 cigarettes per person are consumed annually in Russia; when this statistic is corrected for non-smokers, it comes to 4,300–4,500 cigarettes per person per year, or 240–250 packs per capita. At least $15 billion is spent annually on tobacco, with black market or counterfeit sales accounting for 25%–40% of the total market. Among the richest income quintile, tobacco accounts for about 1.4% of household monthly spending, rising to 2.75% for the poorest quintile. These spending patterns might seem curiously low until one takes into account the fact that cigarettes are notoriously inexpensive in Russia: the ruble equivalent of around fifty cents a pack, compared with $6–7 a pack in Western Europe and the United States.[8]

Smoking is responsible for 220,000–300,000 premature deaths annually in Russia. The World Bank's groundbreaking *Dying Too Young* report, which highlighted the prevalence and consequences of non-communicable disease and injury, calls smoking the "single most preventable cause of disease and death in Russia;" a May 2007 Russian government study found that 42% of premature death in the country among men ages 35–39 is connected with smoking.[9] There is no doubt that tobacco is one of the major forces in, if not the primary cause of, the premature male mortality that is the hallmark of Russia's current demographic crisis. Studies on fetal and infant health, however, are less conclusive. A 2002 study of 1,400 pregnant women in Russia found that maternal smoking was not a determinant of poor infant outcome (defined as pre-term delivery, low birth weight, perinatal death, or low first-minute Apgar score). Instead, as is generally the case in studies worldwide, the only significant

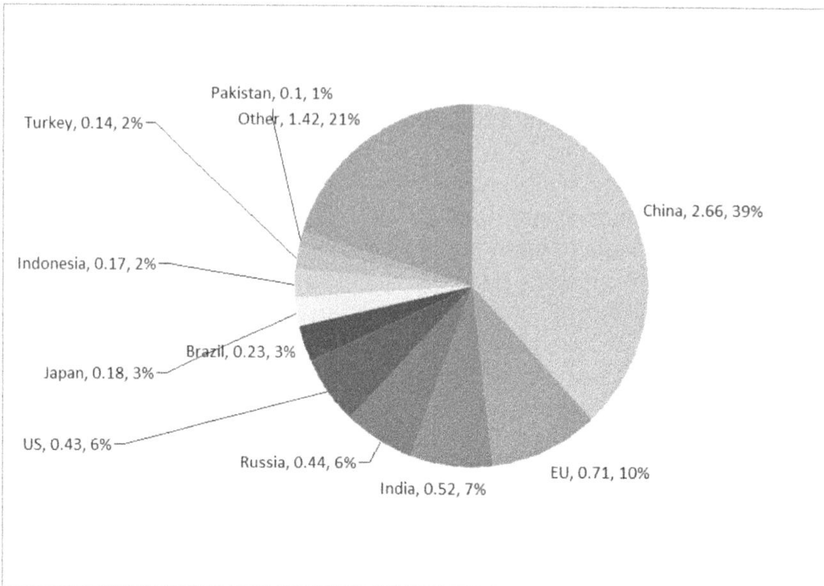

Figure 16.3 Global tobacco consumption, 2005, in millions of tons, by country. Source: http://www.who.org.

predictor of infant outcome was the mother's level of education. Other similar studies have produced mixed results: some have found that maternal smoking is not related to infant or childhood prevalence of respiratory infections or allergy diseases, but one observed that newborns of smoking mothers in Russia are on average 126 grams lighter than those of non-smokers.[10]

TOBACCO CONTROL IN RUSSIA: PAST FAILURES, RECENT PROGRESS

Restrictions on smoking are not new in Russia, having been instituted to varied success and failure since tobacco's introduction to the country.[11] During the late Soviet period, as international information on the dangers of tobacco mounted and in an environment where advertising was nonexistent in any case, the government officially banned tobacco advertising in 1980, and sales of cigarettes to children under the age of 16 were prohibited in 1981.[12] Soviet law forbade smoking in many public places (restaurants and public transportation, for example), and the government conducted extensive anti-smoking campaigns and required health warnings on cigarette packages.[13]

Confusion over the status of Soviet-era legislation during the early post-Soviet transition period dangled an irresistible bonanza of opportunity before the international tobacco industry. A significant surge in advertising and promotion was considered essential to the establishment of brand identity; by the mid-1990s, it was estimated that around half of all billboards in Moscow, and three-quarters of the ubiquitous plastic shopping bags, carried tobacco ads. Tobacco transnationals ranked among the top three advertisers in the country.[14] In response to this explosion of marketing and sales, the Russian Duma approved yet another ban on advertising in 1993, but the Association of Russian Advertisers, supported by the tobacco industry lobby and the press ministry—both concerned about loss of revenue—effectively blocked implementation. Their task was an easy one, given the law's scant enforcement mechanisms. New federal legislation prohibiting tobacco (and alcohol) advertising on television between 7:00 a.m. and 10:00 p.m. went into effect on January 1, 1996. Sponsored by the State Anti-Monopoly Committee, it also stipulated that advertisements and domestically produced cigarette packs should carry a health warning; imported cigarettes were exempt. Once again, compliance and enforcement were anemic, as they were based on the industry's voluntary code of conduct.

Yet another round of lawmaking in 2001 was intended by its drafters to limit smoking to the same extent as the European Union and Canada, with some provisions even more severe. Its first reading forbade the sale of tobacco products to people under 18, banned TV and radio ads altogether, required health warnings on all cigarette packs, prohibited the sale of cigarettes in packs of less than twenty and from vending machines, and made smoking illegal in health, cultural, governmental, and educational facilities, except for designated smoking areas. All airline flights under three hours' duration were to be non-smoking. Maximum tar and nicotine levels were specified for the first time: 12 mg of tar and 1.1 mg of nicotine per cigarette (the European Union limits tar to 10 mg). Smoking was not to be depicted on television or in films.

As the law was debated in its initial stages in mid-2001, the lack of protest from the tobacco industry led to speculation that it would be significantly watered down. Those predictions were accurate. Industry influence diluted or deleted most of its provisions. A reporter for the *St. Petersburg Times* called the changes between the first and second draft law "a textbook demonstration of the lobbyist's art."[15] Below are the changes that emerged.

Because of the toothlessness of this legislation, the only existing tobacco-related penalties were in the Administrative Code: a fine of 10% of the minimum wage for smoking on city transportation, and a larger fine for vaguely defined "illegal trade in tobacco." In addition to the obvious omissions of restrictions in the 2001 law's final version, the amendments opened more subtle loopholes. Who, for example, would determine what

First reading	*Second reading*
The manufacture and sale of tobacco products containing more than 12 mg of tar and 1.1 mg of nicotine per cigarette are forbidden.	The manufacture and sale of • filter cigarettes containing more than 14 mg tar and 1.2 mg nicotine • filterless cigarettes (*papirosy*) containing more than 16 mg of tar and 1.3 mg nicotine are forbidden.
Text on hazards of smoking must cover not less than 25% of the large side of the package.	The large side of the pack must bear a main and additional warning on the hazards of smoking. Each warning must take up not less than 4% of the area of the side.
The sale of tobacco products is forbidden in health care organizations, cultural centers, and sports centers, as well as within 100 meters of such organizations	The sale of tobacco products is forbidden in health care organizations, cultural centers, and sports centers.
The sale of cigarettes to minors shall entail a fine of three to twenty-five monthly minimum wages, and in the event of a repeat violation shall result in a termination of the license.	Omitted.
Limiting the advertising of tobacco products: • Complete ban on advertising of tobacco products • Banning of sponsorship of all types of events • Punishment of violations	Tobacco and tobacco product advertising shall be realized in accordance with the Legislation of the Russian Federation on Advertising.
Smoking in the workplace, in forms of transport, sports facilities, cultural, healthcare, and educational institutions, the premises of state departments, and trading premises shall be banned.	Smoking is banned on city and suburban transport, on airborne forms of transport, in closed sports facilities, cultural, healthcare, and educational institutions, and premises occupied by state bodies of authority, with the exception of smoking in specially designated areas.
Individuals smoking in areas where smoking is banned shall be subject to a fine of ten minimum monthly wages.	Omitted.
Employers may set lower levels of bonuses and premiums for workers using tobacco products.	Omitted.
It is forbidden to show well-known public figures smoking in the media, films, and spectacles.	It shall be forbidden to show smoking in new films if such activity is not deemed to be an integral element of the artistic design, as well as showing the smoking of tobacco by well-known public figures in the media.
The government shall annually approve the program for limiting tobacco usage and shall set aside appropriate funds for the implementation of such from the budget.	The Russian Federation government shall develop measures to limit tobacco usage and shall ensure their implementation.
The retail price of tobacco products shall be not less than 200% of its production cost including excise. The excise rate shall be not less than 80% of its release price.	Omitted.
Tax benefits for the manufacturers and sellers of tobacco products shall be forbidden.	Omitted.

constitutes an "integral element of the artistic design" of a film or TV show? A director or producer could continue to have performers light up, virtually without restriction. Even the remaining reductions in the levels of tar and nicotine benefit the international tobacco companies, whose Russian competitors produce cheaper, stronger cigarettes. Furthermore, this federal law replaced a patchwork of regional smoking laws, some of which—such as Dagestan's forbidding of cigarette sales during Ramadan, or the Moscow city fine of ten minimum wages for smoking in an elementary school—were stronger than the federal code but could be now challenged under the Kremlin's drive to achieve regional conformity. At the end of the day, the most useful observed provisions of the bill were the ban on the sale of single cigarettes and vending machine sales (which can result in decreased use by minors), and stepped-up enforcement of the insistence on health warning labels. Smoking in public places remains the norm, and the streets of major cities are still plastered with cigarette ads.

More recent events look more promising, on the surface. One very encouraging development is Russia's joining of the World Health Organization Framework Convention on Tobacco Control (FCTC), the world's first public health treaty and one of the most widely supported agreements in the history of the United Nations. Since coming into effect on February 27, 2005, 157 countries have ratified it, with Russia the most recent on June 3, 2008. Most European countries, China, and India are members; the United States has signed but not ratified the treaty. The Convention enacts comprehensive bans on tobacco advertising, promotion, and sponsorship. It obligates the placement of rotating health warnings on tobacco packaging that cover at least 30% (but ideally 50% or more) of the principal display areas. It bans the use of misleading and deceptive terms such as "light" and "mild" cigarettes. It protects citizens from exposure to tobacco smoke in workplaces, public transport, and indoor public places. It combats smuggling, including a requirement for final destination markings on cigarette packs, and it increases tobacco taxes in most countries.[16]

Russian government officials are now drafting a national strategy against smoking that would comply with FCTC requirements; this would include a complete ban on tobacco advertising within five years.[17] Already there has been concrete movement forward on cigarette pack warnings; in early 2008 the Duma passed legislation requiring that each pack carry two large-print warnings, with the main one, on the front of the pack, saying "Smoking Kills" in a font-size that occupies no less than 20% of the front surface. Nearly half of the back side of the pack must contain a list of twelve extra warnings, including that smoking causes premature death, lung cancer, heart attacks, infertility, and other conditions.[18] The forthcoming overall national strategy could, according to leading figures in the Duma, introduce a provision in the national Code on Administrative Offenses that would assign legal responsibility to ensure that production and turnover of tobacco products would meet state standards and sanitary rules, and also to guarantee that cigarettes were not marketed and sold to children and teenagers.[19] Tobacco control—specific policy and legislation would undoubtedly align well with Russia's recently-passed three-year demographic policy plan, intended over 2008–2010 primarily to reduce mortality from controllable causes; about 230 billion rubles are allocated in the 2008 federal budget to implement this plan.[20]

In keeping with recent federal-level trends, the city of Moscow is currently engaged in a fierce debate over the protection of non-smokers from second-hand smoke. Its Duma is considering legislation that would require all public places, including restaurants and cafes, to provide a separate hall and ventilation for smokers. Smoking areas would be limited to half the area of restaurants, and one-quarter of the space in other places; if a facility is not large enough to accommodate two physically separate areas, then the draft legislation would require it to become completely non-smoking.[21] The fine for violating the new rules has not yet been set, but officials have cited a figure in the neighborhood of 10,000 rubles. A limited number of facilities in Moscow already offer non-smoking sections, but decisions to move in that direction are dictated primarily by the nature of the product being sold. The popular Coffee Bean chain of coffeehouses, for example, has banned smoking because it wants its locations to smell like coffee rather than cigarettes. Most restaurant owners fiercely oppose the legislation due to the expense of renovations, and also because of the potential financial losses, as frustrated customers, accustomed to having a cigarette with their drinks or after their meals, eat at home or in other private facilities.

Probably the primary force behind Russia's evolution in tobacco control policy is Dr. Nikolai Gerasimenko, the deputy head of the Duma's public health committee. A medical doctor and former smoker, Gerasimenko has been active for several years in international forums dedicated to tobacco control, and he was instrumental in the formation of the Russian Anti-Tobacco League.[22] Andrei Demin, president of the Russian Public Health Association, has also emerged as a major intellectual anti-tobacco voice both domestically and internationally, publishing some of the best scholarly and advocacy work to combat tobacco use and sales. Gerasimenko and Demin, along with other committed scholars, policy makers, and activists, have formed the heart of a nascent but growing anti-tobacco lobby. There is some evidence that public opinion in Russia, despite the high prevalence of smoking, supports this young lobby's efforts. A February 2007 nationwide poll, for example, found that half of all Russians favor a complete ban on smoking in all public places, and a 2007 survey of Aeroflot passengers showed that 66% would support a complete ban on all smoking in aircraft.[23]

Yet anti-smoking forces in Russia, despite recent progress, face an uphill battle before Russia can boast serious and lasting protections for non-smokers and effective assistance and encouragement for smokers to quit. The government itself confronts an array of conflicting motivations: while it certainly now recognizes the negative public health consequences of tobacco use, it also enjoys the revenue from tobacco sales and fears civil discontent from smokers. In 2007, excise taxes on tobacco products amounted to 35.6 billion rubles, or 2% of the federal budget. Compared to revenues from oil and natural gas, this figure may seem insignificant, but at the regional level the money from tobacco can be indispensable: the company Donskoi Tabak, for example, pays 20% of all corporate taxes in the Rostov regional budget.[24] Additionally, the government is also concerned about loss of revenue due to illegal sales. The counterfeit market is notoriously difficult to police, largely because of the nature of the processing and production infrastructure. When the international tobacco companies moved into the country in the 1990s, they largely built their own new facilities. Soviet-era factories were abandoned and are now commonly used by black marketeers. The Internal Affairs Ministry's Chief Directorate for Fighting Economic and Tax Violations (GUBEP) uncovered a facility in 2006 in the Riazan region with a projected annual production capacity of 20–25 million cigarettes. This was the largest ever discovered in Russia, said to be one of thousands currently operating. Counterfeit operations are likely to grow as the government increases taxes on legal brands; consumers will overlook the obvious signals that their purchases are fakes in order to escape prohibitively high price tags.[25]

THE TOBACCO INDUSTRY WON'T QUIT

Although the anti-tobacco movement has just won a major victory in the Duma with the signing of the FCTC, the battle is far from over. The tobacco industry, anxious over increasingly severe restrictions on smoking and declining smoking prevalence in the United States and Western Europe, has long set its sights on Russia as one of its most potentially lucrative international markets.[26] The industry journal *World Tobacco for Russia and Eastern Europe* framed the situation in 1998, long before the likes of Gerasimenko and Demin had found the spotlight: "Anti-tobacco activists are almost unknown in Russia, so the Russian people and government have not been bombarded with anti-tobacco propaganda." Post-Soviet Russian consumers have therefore been seen as low-hanging fruit, a consumer market ripe for picking. Tobacco production in Russia has doubled over the last decade, from 206 billion cigarettes in 1996 to 413 billion in 2006, and 85% of the market share is held by dominant international corporations that rushed to take advantage of the relatively untapped consumer base in the immediate post-Soviet period. As indicated earlier, despite high rates of smoking, there has been a strong corporate perception of room for market growth, particularly among young people and especially young urban women.

The Western tobacco companies have pursued a careful and deliberate strategy for penetrating the Russian market. In the late 1980s through early 1990s, they focused on establishment of brand identity, hoping to sway consumers permanently to their particular individual brands. Opportunity certainly beckoned. In 1990, when economic turmoil resulted in a domestic tobacco production collapse, three Western companies—RJ Reynolds, Philip Morris, and British American Tobacco—rushed to contribute an "emergency supply" of 38 billion cigarettes. This infusion amounted to a seventy-two-fold increase in cigarette imports in the first six months of 1991. During the chaotic mid-1990s, when Russian consumers were giddy over the opportunity to purchase anything associated with the West, the international industry went out of its way to market its products as distinctly American, attracting consumers pursuing the panache of all things Western. After the August 1998 financial crisis, the balance tipped in the opposite direction, a trend that has only strengthened during the heady Putin years: as Russia has stabilized and even emerged as an economic power, Russian consumers have come to prefer "*nashi*" (our) products, and so international tobacco companies frequently try to mask their true identities through brand names and marketing campaigns that are identifiably Russian. Over the last few years, that strategy of pursuing an aggressively Russian identity has been coupled with efforts to get consumers to "uptrade"—switch their old brands for more upscale and expensive brands—and to market more extensively to women and youth. Premium and medium market segments have indeed grown in recent years, accounting for a significant share of the recent overall 3–4% growth (by volume) in tobacco sales each year. There are exceptions, of course, to this pattern: a Russian tobacco consortium has recently launched, for example, a harsh *Prima-Nostalgia* brand, in packs that depict images of Lenin, Stalin, and Brezhnev. The brand attempts to cash in on increasingly positive memories of the Soviet era, when *Prima* brand cigarettes were notoriously the choice of collective farm and factory workers, soldiers, and students, as well as intelligentsia who had spent time in labor camps and developed a taste for bitterly strong tobacco.[27]

The tobacco industry has also adopted increasingly aggressive tactics in Russia that mirror others around the world to counter negative public opinion. Allegedly sincere youth smoking–prevention campaigns, sponsorship of arts events and sports competitions, "academic" conferences on adolescent smoking and behavior, and sponsorship of youth smoking surveys are all intended to demonstrate the industry's intent to market its products only to adults. In reality, particularly in a relatively new market like Russia, these efforts, in addition to their public relations benefit, constitute an important data collection strategy, as the tobacco companies use the interaction with youth to understand better that important market segment—and to sell cigarettes to them more effectively.

Just a few glances at recent Russian advertising campaigns clarify the extent to which tobacco is being aggressively and deliberately marketed to young people.[28] The British firm Innovation Tobacco Company, with a Russian partner, markets "Kiss" cigarettes through a "Kiss-Club" web site <www.

kiss-club.ru> featuring pink Barbie-doll-type characters and a forum section with advice on how to manage relationships with teachers, parents, and boyfriends—clearly an attempt to market to teenage girls. That same British company, in tandem with Donskoi Tabak, similarly targets teenage boys with its "Carbon" brand, featuring display ads prominent in metro stations and elsewhere showing handsome, athletic young men on skateboards and the slogan "Play on the Edge." Winston's "Wings" brand was launched in 2006 with a cartoon-style marketing campaign that the Japan Tobacco International (JTI) press release trumpeted as specifically aimed at the 18–24-year-old market segment; the advertising strategy, however, included a special insert to a popular entertainment magazine that showed characters carrying book bags and contained advice features like "how to spend your summer break from school"—again, ads that clearly speak to adolescents and teenagers.

Individual tobacco companies have also sponsored ad campaigns ostensibly directed at improving public health, but in reality intended only to bolster the market share of their specific products. Again paralleling tactics used elsewhere in the world, JTI, for example, distributed in late 2006 a flier with the following message: "There is no such thing as safe cigarettes. It's not worth switching to cigarettes of a different type, flavor, or strength, thinking that it will lower the risk to your health." The flier goes on to argue that cigarettes with a lower tar or nicotine content are not really "safer" because smokers will just inhale more often or deeper in order to get the desired effect. On the surface, this may appear to be a laudable effort by the tobacco industry to protect the health of its customers. More plausibly, however, it was a reaction to recent market trends: "light" cigarettes, with lower tar or nicotine content, had gone from 27% of the market in 2002 to 56% in 2006, making a serious dent in the sales of JTI's main non-light brands, Winston and Camel. The ad campaign was a transparent attempt to convince smokers that there were no health benefits to switching away from the JTI's main products.

CAN RUSSIANS KICK THE HABIT?

Despite industry bombardment with alluring pro-smoking messages, most Russians say they would rather not be smokers. A 2006 survey by the Russian Academy of Science's Cancer Research Center indicated that 60% of Russian smokers would like to quit; a similar study in Karelia found that 76% of men and 71% of women who currently smoke would like to stop. In the WHO/Europe's 1996 "Quit and Win" campaign, an annual event that encourages smokers to quit through a variety of strategies, Russians enjoyed higher levels of success (defined as abstention for at least four weeks) than any other European country.

Virtually no government resources, however, are allocated to assist smokers who want to "kick the habit." While the tobacco industry invests over $2 billion each year in Russia, the Russian government spends around $20 million annually on anti-smoking messages.[29] While this figure may increase significantly with Russia's signing of the FCTC, the Russian government has little experience with social marketing campaigns, and so it is unclear that new resources allocated toward behavior change communication will be spent effectively, at least in the short term.[30] Over the last decade, many Russian business people have developed considerable modern advertising and communications skills, but talented professionals in this area are much more likely to seek well-compensated employment in the private sector than to work for government wages crafting anti-smoking messages for the Ministry of Health. So far, there have been no public health campaigns or events in Russia on a par with the 1964 Surgeon General's report on smoking in the United States, no catalysts that would shift behaviors as well as public opinion significantly against smoking.

Perhaps aspiring quitters could therefore turn to their physicians. In Russia, however, it is very common for doctors to consider alcohol a more serious problem than smoking (and drug abuse, in turn, a more serious problem than alcohol). As a result, smoking cessation is not high on most physicians' lists of health education priorities. The rate of smoking among physicians is as high as that of the general population, and Russian doctors are notoriously undereducated about the health impact of smoking. Of about 300 health professionals participating in late 2002 training sessions at the Russian Cancer Research Center, 66% of the male doctors, 21% of the female doctors, and 34% of the nurses were current or former smokers; of those, only 42% of the current smokers expressed a desire to quit. And this sample should be considered skewed, since these respondents were health workers who were sufficiently interested in cancer-related behaviors and pathologies to have attended this seminar. Furthermore, fewer than 10% of this group of Russian physicians were aware of more than three of tobacco's adverse health effects, while 30% could name only two to three diseases associated with smoking, and 18% could come up with only one. According to other physician surveys, only 58% of doctors who have never smoked, and 38% of doctors who do smoke, advise their patients to quit. Even these low figures are called into question by surveys of Moscow clinic patients, fewer than 10% of whom say they are questioned by their doctors about smoking. Most physicians say that they lack the skills to counsel cessation, and they think that such advice would be ineffective in any case.[31]

Could price increases be the answer? Many countries have tried to control tobacco consumption by raising taxes on and therefore the prices of tobacco products. The World Health Organization has estimated that, worldwide, a 10% increase in the price of tobacco cuts the general number of smokers by 4%–8%.[32] Cigarettes in Russia are relatively inexpensive, however, and studies have indicated that price elasticity of demand is low; the tobacco industry has concluded that there is plenty of room for price hikes without jeopardizing profits.[33] These studies are currently being put to the test, as prices are indeed rising. At the end of 2007, a change in the way the excise tax was calculated caused an increase in the tax on most brands, resulting in a significant bump in the retail price. So far, however, smoking behaviors seem to be relatively unchanged.

Most promising as a tobacco control measure may be the ban on tobacco advertising required by accession to the FCTC. When similar advertising bans were introduced in Norway, Canada, and France, the prevalence of smoking was reduced by 9%, 4%, and 7%, respectively.[34] A twenty-two-country study by the World Bank, however, found that limited or partial advertising bans were significantly less effective then comprehensive bans on advertising and promotion. It will be difficult to craft tobacco control legislation in Russia, as it has been elsewhere, that avoids significant loopholes, particularly in the face of aggressive and increasingly desperate industry lobbying. Tobacco companies continue to advertise in Russia through a variety of legal channels—print and indoor ads, promotional activities such as distributing free cigarettes in bars and other locations—and they also continue, despite legal restrictions, to advertise on billboards and posters in metro stations and other outdoor locations. In addition to the tobacco companies, the increasingly mature advertising industry also has a stake in the outcome of upcoming legislative battles; over the first ten months of 2007, tobacco advertising accounted for 1.4% of all ad sales in print media, worth almost $17 million.[35]

Corporate reaction to Russia's signing of the FCTC has been extremely subdued, with advertising and tobacco executives calling advertising restrictions and bans "normal and appropriate," "necessary and right." With millions of dollars at stake, it seems certain that these industries are confident that they will somehow be able to craft strategies to sustain revenue flows from the advertising and sale of tobacco products; their relatively recent experience in watering down the 2001 legislation probably makes them optimistic on this score. It appears that the industry strategy will be to support partial bans on advertising while holding firm against a complete advertising ban. Politics at the very highest levels appears to be on industry's side; Prime Minister Vladimir Putin declared early in his presidency, in 2001, that a complete ban on tobacco ads is counter to the Russian constitution.[36]

But Putin has also made explicit anti-tobacco statements, including these remarks on World No Tobacco Day on May 31, 2007: "The damage caused by smoking is obvious, affecting not only smokers, but also the people around them and, most seriously, the young generation. We can only successfully address this serious issue if the state, civic organizations, and the business community join forces. There is a need for more legislative measures as well as more intensive prevention and education work." As the Kremlin's words continue to define the magnitude and direction of political will, it would seem that there is greater potential than ever before to combat this ongoing health threat. Yet as Western sentiment continues to coalesce against them, the international tobacco companies view Russia, together with China, as their most accessible and essential markets for growth. According to Dr. Gerasimenko, they have invested around $2 billion over the last few years in the courtship of the Russian smoker, and they will not sacrifice the current pro-smoking legislative, industrial, and marketing environment without a fight. Women and youth are their major targets. Comparative research indicates that Russia may face an uphill battle. In a study of tobacco control policy in the former Soviet states, Anna Gilmore and Martin McKee have shown that the most effective measures have evolved in the more democratic countries with smaller or no major foreign tobacco industry investments (i.e., the Baltics), whereas the least effective control measures characterize the more highly centralized states with high levels of outside industry investment, like Russia.[37] The success of future tobacco control legislation and policy—and the outcome of the ongoing battle between the tobacco industry and public health—will in part determine Russia's chances to overcome its ongoing health and demographic crisis.

NOTES

1. World Health Organization, *Report on the Global Tobacco Epidemic, 2008*, (Geneva: World Health Organization, 2008); Tom Parfitt, "Campaigners Fight To Bring Down Russia's Tobacco Toll," *The Lancet*, 368 (August 19, 2006): 633–4, citing Russian Ministry of Health and Social Protection data; Francesca Perlman and Martin Bobak, "Socioeconomic and Behavioral Determinants of Mortality in Posttransition Russia: A Prospective Population Study," *Annals of Epidemiology*, 18:2 (February 2008): 92–100; M. Bobak, A. Gilmore, et al., "Changes in Smoking Prevalence in Russia, 1996–2004," *Tobacco Control*, 15 (2006): 131–5; "Russian Smokers Getting Younger—Federal Service," ITAR-TASS, June 1, 2008.
2. Francesca Perlman, et al., "Trends in the Prevalence of Smoking in Russia during the Transition to a Market Economy," *Tobacco Control*, 16 (2007): 299–305, citing data from the Russian Longitudinal Monitoring Survey.
3. T. Laatikainen, et al., "Comparing Smoking and Smoking Cessation Process in the Republic of Karelia, Russia and North Karelia, Finland," *Journal of Epidemiology and Community Health*, 35 (1999): 528–34.
4. "Teen Smoking Soars," *Moscow Times*, (February 7, 2007): 4; Steve Sussman, et al., "Speculation about Options for Teen Tobacco Use Cessation in the Russian Federation," *Tobacco Induced Diseases*, 3:3 (2007): 1–15; Hana Ross, *Russia (Moscow) 1999 Global Youth Tobacco Survey: Economic Aspects*, HNP Discussion Paper, Economics of Tobacco Control, paper no. 23, (Washington, DC: World Bank, September 2004).
5. William C. Cockerham, "Health Lifestyles and the Absence of the Russian Middle Class," *Sociology of Health and Illness*, 29:3 (2007): 457–73.
6. Martin McKee, et al., "Patterns of Smoking in Russia," *Tobacco Control*, 7 (1998): 22–6.
7. ITAR-TASS, June 1, 2008.
8. Campaign for Tobacco-Free Kids web site, <tobaccofreecenter.org>; Christopher Kenneth, "Smoking Russians To Premature Deaths," *The Russia*

Journal, no. 576, July 4, 2005; Svetlana Osadchuk, “Cheap Cigarettes Criticized at Forum,” *Moscow Times*, (May 29, 2007): 2.

9. Parfitt, 2006; Ross, 2004; <www.who.org>; Martin Bobak, et al., “Determinant of Adult Mortality in Russia: Estimates from Sibling Data,” *Epidemiology*, 14:5 (September 2003): 603–11; Patricio Marquez, “Dying Too Young: Addressing Premature Mortality and Ill Health Due To Noncommunicable Diseases and Injuries in the Russian Federation,” *Europe and Central Asia Region*, Human Development Department (Washington, DC: World Bank, 2006).
10. Andrej Grjibovski, et al., “Socio-Demographic Determinants of Poor Infant Outcome in North-West Russia,” *Paediatric and Perinatal Epidemiology*, 16 (2002): 255–62; Timo T. Hugg, Maritta S. Jaakkola, Risto O. Ruotsalainen, Vadim J. Pushkarev, and Jouni J. K. Jaakkola, “Parental Smoking Behaviour and Effects of Tobacco Smoke on Children’s Health in Finland and Russia,” *European Journal of Public Health*, 18:1 (2007): 55–62; Jouni J. K. Jaakkola, Anna A. Kosheleva, Boris A. Katsnelson, Sergey V. Kuzmin, Larissa I. Privalova, and John D. Spengler, “Prenatal and Postnatal Tobacco Smoke Exposure and Respiratory Health in Russian Children,” *Respiratory Research*, 7:1 (2006): 48; Andrej Grjibovski, et al., “Housing Conditions, Perceived Stress, Smoking, and Alcohol: Determinants of Fetal Growth in Northwest Russia,” *Acta Obstetricia et Gynecologica Scandinavica*, 83:12 (2004): 1159–66.
11. See Starks and Fox, this volume.
12. Much of the following section draws from Judyth L. Twigg, “A Habit That’s Hard To Kick: The Evolution of Tobacco Control Policy in Russia,” *Russian Analytical Digest*, no. 35, (February 19, 2008): 2–6.
13. For a first-hand account of this process, see Gorchakova, this volume.
14. See Neuburger and Gilmore, this volume.
15. Roman Kutuzov, “Lobbyists Take Fire Out of Bill On Tobacco,” *Moscow Times*, (June 8, 2001).
16. <www.who.int/tobacco/framework/en>.
17. Rebeccah Billing, “Russia Moves Toward Full Ban on Tobacco Ads,” *Moscow News*, January 17, 2008.
18. ITAR-TASS, May 31, 2008.
19. ITAR-TASS, April 10, 2008.
20. ITAR-TASS, February 18, 2008.
21. Svetlana Osadchuk, “Limits on Lighting Up,” *Moscow Times*, (May 7, 2008): 13–4.
22. See <www.antitabak.ru>.
23. Nabi Abdullaev and Nikolaus von Twickel, “Duma Takes Steps to Restrict Smoking,” *Moscow Times*, (May 28, 2007): 1; Oksana Yablokova, “Smoking Getting a Bad Reputation,” *Moscow Times*, (February 11, 2003): 1.
24. Alina Travina, “Money Vanishes in Smoke,” *Moscow News*, (November 22, 2007).
25. Kenneth, “Smoking Russians.”
26. See Neuburger and Gilmore, this volume.
27. Michele A. Berdy, “Icon: Prima Cigarettes,” *Moscow Times*, (May 15, 2007): 16.
28. Most of these examples are drawn from the extraordinary website <www.globalshame.org>.
29. Sussman, et al., “Speculation about Options.”
30. See Fox, this volume.
31. Robert A. Schnoll et al., “Smoking Cessation Counseling by Russian Oncologists: Opportunities for Intervention in the Russian Federation,”

International Journal of Behavioral Medicine, 13:1 (2006): 8–15; Parfitt, 2006; and Vladimir Levshin, "Smoking-Cessation Program Motivates Russian Physicians To Assist Their Patients—And Themselves," Center for Communications, Health and the Environment, December 12, 2007, <www.ceche.org/communications/Russian-cancer-cen.html>.

32. ITAR-TASS, June 1, 2008.
33. Peter M. Lance, et al., "Is Cigarette Smoking in Poorer Nations Highly Sensitive To Price? Evidence from Russia and China," *Journal of Health Economics*, 23 (2004): 173–89.
34. Billing, "Russia Moves."
35. Ibid.
36. Vlad Grinkevich, "Russia Butting Out," *RIA Novosti*, April 16, 2008.
37. A. B. Gilmore and M. McKee, "Tobacco and Transition: An Overview of Industry Investments, Impact, and Influence in the Former Soviet Union," *Tobacco Control*, 13 (2004): 136–42.

Contributors

Iu. P. Bokarev is Chief of the Laboratory of the Mathematical Methods in History at the Institute of Russian History of the Russian Academy of Sciences.

Nikolaos A. Chrissidis is an Associate Professor of History at Southern Connecticut State University. He has authored articles on the cultural and religious history of Russia and on Greek–Russian contacts. His current project is a monograph on education in seventeenth-century Russia.

Karen F. A. Fox is an Associate Professor of Marketing at Santa Clara University. She has written extensively on Soviet-era marketing history and on social marketing, particularly applied to health promotion. Her book *Sotsialnye Marketing* (*Social Marketing*), with Ebner, Dukarev, and Holmes, was the first book in Russian on social marketing.

Anna Gilmore is a Clinical Reader in Public Health at University of Bath and a Senior Lecturer at the European Centre on Health of Societies in Transition at the London School of Hygiene and Tropical Medicine. She is also the recipient of a prestigious Health Foundation Clinician Scientist award.

Elizaveta Gorchakova received her master's degree in Russian History from Ohio State University in 1995 and currently is an independent scholar in Moscow.

Catriona Kelly is a Professor of Russian in the University of Oxford and a Fellow of New College. She is the author of many books and articles, most recently *Children's World: Growing Up in Russia, 1890–1991* (2007) and *Comrade Pavlik: The Rise and Fall of a Soviet Boy Hero* (2005). She is now working on a study of cultural memory in post-1961 Leningrad/St. Petersburg.

Konstantine Klioutchkine is an Associate Professor of Russian at Pomona College. He has published articles on nineteenth-century Russian literature and cultural history as well as on various aspects of the media.

Eve Levin is a Professor of History at the University of Kansas and Editor of *The Russian Review*. She is the author of numerous publications including *Sex and Society in the World of the Orthodox Slavs, 900–1700*, (1989). Her recent work is focused on popular spirituality and the medicinal practices of the early-modern era.

Erika Monahan is an Assistant Professor of Russian History at the University of New Mexico in Albuquerque. She earned her Ph.D. at Stanford University with a dissertation entitled, "Trade and Empire: Merchant Networks, Frontier Commerce and the State in Western Siberia, 1644–1728."

Mary Neuburger is an Associate Professor of History at University of Texas at Austin. She is the author of *The Orient Within: Muslim Minorities and the Negotiation of Nationhood in Modern Bulgaria* (2004). Her second book project is a history of tobacco production, commerce, and consumption in modern Bulgaria.

Roy R. Robson is a Professor of History at the University of the Sciences in Philadelphia. He has published extensively on the history of Russian Orthodoxy and Old Believers. His publications include *Solovki: The Story of Russia Told Through Its Most Remarkable Islands*, (2004), and *Old Believers in Modern Russia*, (1995).

Matthew P. Romaniello is Assistant Professor of History at University of Hawai'i at Manoa. He has published several articles on the history of the Russian Empire and is currently completing a monograph on the Khanate of Kazan' after the Muscovite conquest.

Tricia Starks is Associate Professor of History at University of Arkansas. She is the author of *The Body Soviet: Propaganda, Hygiene, and the Revolutionary State* (2008). She is currently completing a monograph on the cultural history of cigarettes in the Soviet Union.

Judyth L. Twigg is an Associate Professor of the L. Douglas Wilder School of Government and Public Affairs of Virginia Commonwealth University. She is the author and editor of numerous works on health issues in the former Soviet Union, including most recently a two-volume edited collection, *HIV/AIDS in Russia and Eurasia* (2006).

Sally West is a Professor of History at Truman State University. She is currently completing a manuscript entitled *Consuming Paradoxes: Advertising and the Creation of Modern Consumer Culture in Late Tsarist Russia.*

Index

U

V

W

For Product Safety Concerns and Information please contact our EU
representative GPSR@taylorandfrancis.com
Taylor & Francis Verlag GmbH, Kaufingerstraße 24, 80331 München, Germany

www.ingramcontent.com/pod-product-compliance
Ingram Content Group UK Ltd.
Pitfield, Milton Keynes, MK11 3LW, UK
UKHW022003180926
475701UK00003B/172
9780415895972